The Structure of German

The Structure of German

Second Edition

ANTHONY FOX

This book has been printed digitally and produced in a standard specification in order to ensure its continuing availability

OXFORD
UNIVERSITY PRESS

Great Clarendon Street, Oxford OX2 6DP

Oxford University Press is a department of the University of Oxford.
It furthers the University's objective of excellence in research, scholarship,
and education by publishing worldwide in

Oxford New York

Auckland Cape Town Dar es Salaam Hong Kong Karachi
Kuala Lumpur Madrid Melbourne Mexico City Nairobi
New Delhi Shanghai Taipei Toronto
With offices in
Argentina Austria Brazil Chile Czech Republic France Greece
Guatemala Hungary Italy Japan South Korea Poland Portugal
Singapore Switzerland Thailand Turkey Ukraine Vietnam

Oxford is a registered trade mark of Oxford University Press
in the UK and in certain other countries

Published in the United States
by Oxford University Press Inc., New York

ISBN 978-0-19-927399-7

Contents

Preface to the Second Edition

The first edition of this book was published in 1990, as an attempt to meet a need that existed at that time for a discussion of the structure of modern German in 'linguistic' terms for an English-speaking readership. Since this had not been tried before, some reviewers, although positive in their praise for the attempt and appreciative of the book's contents, were a little sceptical about the likely success of the venture, since it did not seem possible that a book which combined a description of the language with an introduction to linguistics could find a market. Happily, the success of the book—which has gone through many printings since its initial publication, has been used in English-speaking countries throughout the world, and has been translated into Japanese—has proved the pessimists wrong, and testifies to the increasing interest in the linguistic study of present-day German. A number of other books have also been published since 1990 which have pursued similar aims in different ways, and the trend has extended to languages other than German.

The book was never intended to be up-to-date, in the sense of presenting the latest theories in such fields as phonology and syntax. As pointed out in the original preface, the rapid development of these areas inevitably makes discussion of current theories somewhat ephemeral. In any case, the focus of the book was on German itself and the theoretical apparatus was considered to be subordinate to the description rather than the reverse. As some books show, it is regrettably all too easy to lapse into regarding the language as a mere exemplification of a particular theoretical position. Furthermore, experience of teaching the subject over many years has confirmed my opinion that without prior linguistic training students are unable to follow, or even to see the point of, elaborate theoretical discussions which seem to have little relevance to their needs or interests. These considerations are as valid now as when the book was first published, and they continue to underlie this revised edition.

Nevertheless, some parts of the original book may be thought to be in need of an update. In this revision, sections have been added which take account of more recent developments, especially in phonology and syntax, and the bibliography has been updated and expanded. Numerous additions, corrections, and improvements have been made in all chapters and a number of sections have been restructured, sometimes quite radically. The transcription system for the vowels has been changed to one that is more widely used. To make the book more useful as a class text, I have also added exercises and discussion questions at the end of each chapter. In view of the development of the field of German sociolinguistics, and the publication of a number of excellent books in this area, the original discussion, which in any case lay somewhat outside the scope of the book's theme and title, has become redundant and has therefore been omitted, though there is an expanded section on this topic in the introduction.

I cannot conclude without thanking a number of users of the book for their helpful comments, and expressing my gratitude to John Davey of Oxford University Press for his patience and encouragement during the preparation of this revised edition.

York   A.F.
October 2004

Preface to the First Edition

Over the last few decades a linguistics component has increasingly found its way into modern-language degrees, and courses in the linguistics of various languages are now quite widely available. In the case of German, however, teachers of such courses, and their students, have found themselves severely handicapped by a lack of suitable books. They have generally had to piece together the necessary information from works on general linguistics or English and the standard reference grammars of German, sources which are often seriously at variance with one another in their approach to the subject.

In writing the present book I have tried to fill this gap. It is not intended to compete with reference grammars or manuals of the language, but rather to provide a different and complementary perspective. I have attempted to give an introduction to the description of German in 'linguistic' terms, i.e. according to the precepts and practices of modern linguistics, which sees the language not as a body of facts to be learnt, or rules to be mastered, but as a subject of investigation in its own right. Thus, rather than presenting the 'facts' of the language, I have tried to draw the reader's attention to the problems and principles that underlie these facts, and in terms of which they are to be evaluated.

It has naturally not been possible, within the limits of a single book, to cover all the areas of the language which would merit consideration in these terms, nor to invoke all the relevant linguistic concepts and theories. The aim has rather been to foster a linguistically informed approach to the study of German, to indicate the sort of questions that are raised by such a study, and the kinds of criteria that are relevant to answering them. I have also not attempted to present a single, unified theoretical approach; different aspects of the language can often be revealingly illuminated by different theoretical frameworks, and a plurality of approaches is more useful for the purposes of this book than the constraints of a single theory. As a result, I hope that the reader will not only be given a rather broader view of the phenomena to be described, but will also be placed in the position of being able to consider the relative merits of the different theories themselves, as applied to these phenomena.

The book is not, however, concerned with linguistic theory as such, but considers it only in so far as it is able to cast light on the structure of German. I have deliberately eschewed the more recent, and more tentative, versions of such rapidly changing areas as syntactic and phonological theory, as experience indicates that they are likely to have undergone considerable revision before this book even reaches its readers. I have attempted rather to provide a solid foundation in the subject and to encourage readers to ask questions about the language for themselves. In pursuit of this latter end I have not always confined myself to 'safe' and orthodox views; if readers find some of my more speculative suggestions unacceptable, and are thereby stimulated to find solutions of their own, then the book's purpose will have been admirably served.

I have had the good fortune to benefit from the sound advice of a number of people, whose assistance is gratefully acknowledged. My colleagues Patrick Leach, David Barber, and Marion Shirt have read portions of the book and offered valuable comments; Chris Wells, John Roberts, and Martin Durrell all provided a wealth of detailed and at times critical suggestions which have saved me from many errors and infelicities. I wish I could blame these people for the defects which doubtless remain, but the responsibility for these, alas, rests with me alone. Last, but far from least, I should like to thank Virginia Llewellyn Smith of Oxford University Press, who believed in the book when others might have doubted, and provided much-needed encouragement.

Leeds   A.F.
October 1988

1

Introduction

German is spoken as a first language by approximately 100 million people in Germany, Austria, Switzerland, and elsewhere, and as a second language by many others in Central and Eastern Europe. It is also learnt as a foreign language by people all over the world. There are many books which purport to describe the language, ranging from compendious grammars intended for native speakers to elementary textbooks for foreign learners, and from dictionaries of current usage to philological studies of earlier stages of the language.

The present book is none of these, however. Though written primarily for foreign learners of German, it is not a language textbook, and makes no attempt to improve the reader's practical mastery of the language in any direct way. And, though it presents a description of German, it is not a grammar of the language in the usual sense, and does not contain comprehensive lists of forms. Nor does it have anything to say about the historical development of German.

What this book offers is an introduction to the description of the structure of present-day German in linguistic terms, i.e. according to the principles and practices of modern linguistics. Exactly what this entails, and how such a description differs from those undertaken from other points of view, will become clear from the remaining chapters of the book, but the main theme can be briefly stated as follows: German is here taken to be not a body of facts to be presented or learnt but rather the subject of scientific investigation. From this point of view, the 'facts' of the language cannot be merely assumed, but must be established and their status determined. In many cases the known characteristics of German will serve merely as the starting point, rather than as the goal, of our enquiry.

In order to clarify and to justify the approach adopted here, it will be helpful to consider in the remainder of this chapter some of the basic principles of linguistic theory. The various theoretical notions will be presented not as an end in themselves but in order to provide an appropriate conceptual and terminological framework within which our examination of the structure of German can be conducted.

Language and Lingustics

All human societies make use of language, and all normal human beings have access to one or more languages. Without language such societies could hardly exist, nor could human beings exist within them. It is no exaggeration, therefore, to say that of all human institutions language is one of the most important, and that of all human characteristics the faculty of learning and using language is one of the most fundamental.

It may be argued that other species besides our own exist in complex social groups, and that central to all such groups is the ability to communicate. Individual members of these species evidently possess communicative ability which in some respects may resemble our own. Nevertheless, though some of these animal communication systems are clearly quite elaborate, they do not approach in complexity or flexibility any known human language. So great is the gap between animal and human communication systems that we are justified in regarding it as one of *kind* rather than merely of *degree.* Language, therefore, in the sense in which we normally understand this term, is unique to human beings, and such is its importance for human society and for the individuals within it that we can see it not just as an incidental attribute but more in the nature of a defining characteristic, part of what makes us human.[1]

A further characteristic of human beings is that they constantly seek to understand themselves and their environment. It is hardly surprising, there-fore, that language too should have been and should continue to be a subject of enquiry, and reflections on language have a long and honourable history in our culture and civilization. Concepts analogous to our 'sentence', 'word', 'noun', and so on were discussed even in ancient times, though modern linguistic study has naturally found it necessary to refine, develop, and supplement them.[2]

Oddly enough, it is only in relatively recent times that an independent 'science of language' has developed. This may be largely due to the intimate

---

[1] There have been a number of attempts to teach chimpanzees to communicate with human beings through signs, and the successes in this field have been impressive. But the kind of communication achieved still remains rather primitive by human standards, and thus does not force us to modify our conclusions regarding the limitations of animal communication systems.

[2] The highest level of linguistic description among old civilizations was achieved by the Indian grammarians, who produced remarkably detailed and sophisticated descriptions of Sanskrit.

connection between language and other human characteristics, which has made it difficult to separate language from thought and culture. It is to the nineteenth century that we owe the establishment of language study as a discipline in its own right, though the orientation of this discipline was rather different from that of its present-day successor. Nineteenth-century linguistics, like other nineteenth-century disciplines—parallels are found in other disciplines, e.g. biology, with Darwin's theory of evolution—was conceived in essentially historical terms. That is, the aim of the subject was to trace the history of languages and to determine the principles which underlie their development. The justification for this can in part be sought in the goals of scientific enquiry: a science is meant to be not merely *descriptive* but also *explanatory*, setting up rules and principles which account for the observable phenomena. For nineteenth-century linguists the only valid explanations for linguistic phenomena were deemed to be historical: languages are as they are because of their history.[3]

Notable success was achieved in the pursuit of these aims, and much of what is known about the history of individual languages derives from nineteenth-century scholarship. But modern linguistics no longer accepts the restrictions inherent within this approach. While acknowledging that the historical study of languages is legitimate and valuable, and indeed that many features of language can only be explained historically, most modern linguists hold the view that a historical approach also fails to account for many other characteristics. Indeed, history is seen as largely irrelevant to how languages work, how they are constructed, and how they are used.

A seminal figure in the development of this view was the Swiss linguist Ferdinand de Saussure.[4] He clarified many concepts which characterize modern linguistic theory, particularly by drawing a number of important distinctions, which we shall introduce where appropriate as we proceed. One such distinction that we have already considered is that between the DIACHRONIC (historical) and the SYNCHRONIC (non-historical) aspects of language. While nineteenth-century linguistics was essentially a diachronic discipline, Saussure gave priority to the synchronic study of language: a language is seen as

---

[3] This view was clearly stated by the late 19th-century German linguist Hermann Paul, who wrote (1975 [1880]: 20): 'Was man für eine nichtgeschichtliche und doch wissenschaftliche Betrachtung der Sprache erklärt, ist im Grunde nichts als eine unvollkommen geschichtliche ... Sobald man über das bloße Konstatieren von Einzelheiten hinausgeht, sobald man versucht den Zusammenhang zu erfassen, die Erscheinungen zu begreifen, so betritt man auch den geschichtlichen Boden.'

[4] Saussure gave lectures on linguistics in Geneva before the First World War. After his death in 1913 his students compiled a book, the *Cours de linguistique générale*, based on their lecture notes, and it is this book for which Saussure is principally famous.

something existing at a particular time, which can be described independently of its history or its antecedents.

Of crucial importance for this conception is the notion that underlying and determining a language is a *system*, and that such a system exists for every language at every phase in its history. A scientific approach to language, therefore, which aims to explain the language, must seek to uncover and describe the system which underlies it.

A number of analogies can be given to clarify and justify this point. One can perhaps compare a language to a machine consisting of various parts—cogs, axles, belts, gears, etc. Machines change with technological developments, and the various components may thus be different at different times. But studying these changes will not necessarily explain how the machine works; to do this we must see how the various parts fit together and what the role of each part is in the whole machine. In short, we must examine the 'system' of the machine at a specific time. A similar point can be made with a biological analogy: the nature of an organism such as the human body cannot be explained purely in terms of the evolution of its parts; we must see how the different organs of the body relate to one another, and what their place is in the structure and activity of the organism as a whole.

Of course a language is neither a machine nor an organism but a social and psychological phenomenon, and its system is not an arrangement of physical objects such as cogs and gears, or bodily organs. The language system cannot, therefore, be analysed in quite the manner in which a mechanic might dismantle a machine or a biologist might dissect an organism. Language certainly has its physical side: in its spoken form it involves the production and perception of sounds, and in its written form the writing and reading of letters or other characters. But neither the sounds nor the letters constitute the language itself; the language lies in the *values* given to the sounds or letters in the linguistic consciousness of the speaker/writer and hearer/reader. And, as Saussure emphasized, these values derive from the various relationships that are established between the components of the system. Thus, a language is a system of relationships, and hence a rather abstract entity which cannot be identified with its physical manifestation. To use another of Saussure's distinctions: language is FORM and not SUBSTANCE.

The most significant point here is that a language is seen as a self-contained formal system, where each part derives its significance from its relationship to the other parts and to the whole; hence, all the parts are mutually defining. From this it follows that each language must be described in its own terms and not in terms of an earlier stage of its history or in terms of categories derived from another language. For example, each language has its own grammatical system, which may include a set of tenses of the verb, and this system will not necessarily be the same for different languages or for the same language at different times. Thus, the significance of, say, the 'past tense' will depend on what other tenses are available in the system, and it will not necessarily be equivalent to the past tense in another language or at another stage of the language's history. This is one of the chief reasons why translation is so difficult, indeed often impossible: a form in one language will often have a different role and significance from the 'equivalent' form in another.

This general approach to language that developed in the first half of the twentieth century has been given the name STRUCTURALISM. In fact, languages are not the only phenomena for which we might recognize an underlying system of this rather abstract, formal kind, consisting of mutually defining entities in a closed system of relationships. Other human institutions—societies as a whole, systems of religious beliefs, cultural and aesthetic systems, etc.—share this characteristic with language to varying extents. Thus 'structuralism', though primarily and pre-eminently a linguistic 'model', has had wider applications, and has been of interest to sociologists, anthropologists, and even literary critics. During the twentieth century, it became a fashionable trend in aesthetic theory, and was developed well beyond its linguistic origins. We cannot, of course, explore these wider applications in the present book.

Apart from the characteristics that have just been discussed, there are a number of other features which distinguish modern linguistics from traditional language study and from other, 'non-linguistic' approaches to language. One such characteristic is that linguistics is *descriptive* rather than *prescriptive*, i.e. it purports to describe what language is really like rather than to prescribe what it should be like. This is perhaps an obvious point, but it is worth making, since there is a strong prescriptive element in many people's attitude to language, and a concern with 'correct' usage (revealed, for example, in the letters on linguistic matters written to the press). Such considerations are generally of little interest to linguists, except in so far as they reveal speakers' attitudes to their language.

A further, and related, characteristic of modern linguistics is its greater interest in spoken rather than written language. To some extent this is a reaction against earlier prescriptive attitudes, according to which the 'correct' forms of the language were enshrined in its literary texts, of which the spoken forms were seen as a poor and incorrect imitation. Indeed, linguists have sometimes overreacted to the traditional preoccupation with written language, and have seen speech as the *only* legitimate source of data. In so far as linguistics tries to describe actual usage it clearly cannot confine itself to the more artificial forms found in written texts, and spoken language is a more natural source of authentic data. But written language is also language, and therefore also legitimate as data, though the data it provides will be of a different and complementary kind from what is provided by spoken language, given the rather different roles and functions of writing and speech. Thus, although the focus tends to be on spoken usage, both written and spoken language can serve as appropriate data for linguistic analysis.

Linguistic Theories

The general approach to linguistic description just outlined is characteristic of most of modern linguistics, but this does not mean that there is unanimity among linguists as to how this description should be carried out, or on the theoretical basis to be adopted. In the first place, the structuralist principles that we have considered provide only a general orientation rather than a precisely formulated theory, and a number of different schools evolved which interpreted these principles in different ways. In the second place, other theoretical frameworks developed in the second half of the twentieth century which were critical of the tenets of structuralist linguistics and departed from them in a number of important respects.

In the present book the focus of our attention is the German language rather than linguistic theory as such, so the presentation and explanation of these differing theoretical positions are a secondary issue. But since our aim is to describe German in terms of currently accepted linguistic theory, it is inevitable that we shall be to some extent drawn into controversies relating to the theories themselves. Different theories make different claims about the nature of the phenomena to be described, and any attempt to examine these phenomena must evaluate these claims and hence the theoretical positions themselves. It will therefore be helpful to characterize briefly some of the different theoretical orientations that have been influential in current linguistics. Such a characterization will necessarily be in very general terms, since the details of the different theories require exemplification from specific areas of language which will not be considered in detail until later chapters.

All academic disciplines—and not just the natural sciences—strive to be scientific in the sense that they try to be objective in their approach and consistent in their methods. In the study of language this is particularly difficult to achieve, as language inevitably involves a human element, and the assessment of linguistic relationships and values is bound to be in part subjective. American structuralist linguists found a solution to this problem in the psychological theory known as behaviourism, which tried to account for human behaviour without postulating unobservable mental entities. Seen from the perspective of this theory, language is observable behaviour, and scientific objectivity demands that we analyse it without recourse to assumed underlying mental constructs.[5] One unfortunate effect of this is that meaning, the expression of which could perhaps be claimed to be the main purpose of language, becomes virtually inadmissible as evidence, since it can only be adequately accounted for in conceptual terms. But a strength of this approach is that it forces the linguist to adopt rigorous and explicit procedures in the analysis of the data. Since an appeal to meaning is excluded in the assessment of the value of linguistic forms, such procedures centre on the search for patterns in the forms, and hence the distribution of forms in words and sentences becomes a crucial factor.

Elsewhere, however, structuralist linguistics took on a different character. One implication of Saussure's conception of linguistic values is that they are based on *functionally significant relationships* and indeed that the forms themselves are dependent on the functions that they have to fulfil. One approach to the description of the linguistic system, therefore, is through these functions, and this was the orientation of the most influential European group of structuralist linguists, the Prague School.[6] The principle underlying Prague School theory is that language is not just a pattern to be described, but that the forms are there for a purpose, and that this purpose determines the forms themselves. Hence, an investigation of the functions and of the means by which they are conveyed is the chief goal of linguistic enquiry.

Again this approach has both advantages and disadvantages. On the positive side, the effect is to identify what is actually significant in the forms of the language; the negative effect is that we cannot attain complete objectivity, since differences of function are matters of subjective mental assessment. Such mental constructs are also less amenable to analysis by means of rigorous procedures. This contrast between the theoretical positions of two leading structuralist schools shows how different views of the object under investigation can arise even with the same general approach. Fortunately, the practical consequences of these differences are often less significant than the different theoretical interpretations might suggest. The same goal may be reached from different points of departure and by different routes, and similar kinds of

---

[5] The most influential American structuralist linguist was Leonard Bloomfield (1887–1949). His most important book is *Language* (1933/1935).

[6] The Prague School was based on the Linguistic Circle of Prague, which was formed in the 1920s and continued until the outbreak of the Second World War. Its most influential members were Nikolai Trubetzkoy (1890–1938) and Roman Jakobson (1896–1982).

descriptive categories may result from rather different theoretical orientations and with different procedures.

These are by no means the only schools of structuralist linguistics, and a variety of other theories evolved which placed the emphasis elsewhere.[7] But mention must also be made of approaches which differ rather more radically from any of these. One theory that became especially influential in the second half of the twentieth century is GENERATIVE GRAMMAR, associated with the American linguist Noam Chomsky, beginning with his book *Syntactic Structures* in 1957. In pursuing the goals of rigour and explicitness, Chomsky attempted to give a precise characterization of linguistic structures in terms of mathematical statements which enumerate (or 'generate') all the possible sentences of a language. This ambitious aim led Chomsky to a rather different mode of linguistic description from that found within structuralist models, some of whose consequences will be explored in later chapters. In particular, he demonstrated that the sentences of a language cannot be enumerated simply by establishing an inventory of observable patterns; what is required is a set of rules and principles in terms of which such patterns may be specified. A generative grammar will therefore take on a rather different complexion from a grammar constructed according to orthodox structuralist principles.[8]

But Chomsky's influence has extended beyond the mode of linguistic description. Saussure's conception of the linguistic system was that of a social institution, shared by a community of speakers. In another of his dichotomies, he distinguished between LANGUE, the system shared by the community, and PAROLE, the individual acts of speech carried out by individual members of this community. But Chomsky's notion of a generative grammar, consisting of rules and principles in terms of which sentence structures may be described, is rather more compatible with an individual speaker's command of his or her language than with a social institution. Instead of attempting to describe *langue* in Saussure's social sense, therefore, Chomsky takes the linguistic COMPETENCE of the individual speaker—the speaker's largely unconscious knowledge of his or her language—as opposed to the PERFORMANCE of actual utterances as the object to be described. Indeed, a generative grammar might

---

[7] Other schools worthy of mention are the Copenhagen School of Louis Hjelmslev and the London School of J. R. Firth. Significantly, there was no important German school, probably because the pre-eminence of German historical linguistic scholarship made it difficult for alternative approaches to gain a foothold.

[8] Generative grammar developed rapidly in the 1960s, and fragmented into a number of different theories. It has also been a strong influence on other theoretical approaches. The most recent version is the theory of Principles and Parameters, which uses the grammatical approach known as Government and Binding theory (see Chomsky 1981). See also the Further Reading to Ch. 5.

even be taken to be an analogue of what is in the individual speaker's mind, and Chomsky himself has claimed that his theory is more than just a way of describing linguistic structures: it offers a means of investigating the human mind itself. Whether this claim is actually justified is a matter of considerable controversy. Nevertheless, the study of the mental aspects of language, and particularly of the process of language-learning by children, has developed rapidly in recent years, under the name of PSYCHOLINGUISTICS.

One characteristic of all the theoretical positions considered so far is that they see language as an essentially formal and abstract system which underlies actual usage. The usage itself assumes a secondary role, serving at best as the initial data for our investigation, but often unsatisfactory even in this capacity, because of the inconsistencies and variation which tend to characterize natural speech. Saussure achieves the desired level of abstraction by concentrating on the social 'langue' as opposed to the individual 'parole', Chomsky by examining the speaker's 'competence' rather than his or her 'performance'. There are clearly dangers in this; though some measure of idealization and abstraction is necessary in all description, many linguists have felt that the exclusion of all variation, whether that between different speakers or that between different acts of speech performed by the same speaker, is unwarranted, especially as much of it may have important social consequences. There has therefore grown up, alongside the investigation of such abstract linguistic systems, a branch of linguistics which is concerned with the social significance of language and its use: SOCIOLINGUISTICS.

There are many other strands to contemporary language study besides those mentioned here, but this brief survey of a number of the more important ones serves to illustrate the kinds of theoretical controversies which characterize the subject. It also identifies a problem for our current aim of describing German in 'linguistic' terms: since a number of different approaches are available, which one should we adopt? As we have already noted, different theoretical positions do not necessarily lead to radically different analyses; in fact, the same problems tend to recur within different theoretical frameworks, and the same kinds of solutions are likely to be proposed, though perhaps cast in a different terminological mould. Since the aim of this book is to investigate problems in the structure of German and not to pursue linguistic theory for its own sake, different theoretical interpretations as such are of little consequence. In some cases, however, different theories create different perspectives, and what is problematical in one framework may not be so in another. Here, a plurality of theoretical positions is valuable, since approaching a problem from the viewpoint of different theories may lead to a greater understanding of its nature. In this book, therefore, no particular theoretical position will be adopted or advocated. This will allow a variety of different interpretations to throw light on the problems under discussion. There are, of course, risks in this policy, partly because the presentation of a number of competing proposals can be confusing and give the impression of arbitrariness, and partly because the resulting theoretical framework lacks coherence and unity. But since the aim of this book is to initiate the reader into the complexities of German as an object of enquiry rather than to provide facile solutions to the problems encountered, this risk is worth taking.

The Structure of Language

Language is, as we have already noted, *systematic*: underlying the observable acts of speech there is a linguistic system. We must now consider what this entails, and what kind of system is involved. One point perhaps hardly needs to be made: language is extremely complex, and its structure is intricate. One of the difficulties in analysing it is, in fact, that there is not just one layer of structure, but several, each interacting with the others, and a first step of understanding the nature of the linguistic system is to identify and isolate these different layers, or LEVELS, of structure and to see how they are related to one another, always bearing in mind, of course, that in reality they occur together, so that separating them is an artificial and unnatural procedure.

To see what is meant by 'level of structure', consider the following example:

Es schneit.

Assuming that we were to hear this sentence spoken, we would observe first of all that it consists of noise. If we happened not to know German, we could hardly progress further than this, and would be unable to make any sense of it at all, except possibly for picking out a few familiar sounds. But, as we have seen, it is not the substance of speech that is significant, but rather its form: German speakers are able to make sense of this sentence when they hear it because they are able to perceive this form. They know (not necessarily consciously) what sound-units occur in their language and what sort of relationships exist between them, and they are thus able to analyse this sentence into a succession of units in a way that those ignorant of German could not do, i.e.:

e—s—sch—n—ei—t

The first level of linguistic structure that we can recognize, therefore, is that of pronunciation, and this is known as PHONOLOGY (the level concerned with the sounds themselves, with the substance of pronunciation, is PHONETICS). The complexities of German phonological structure will be considered in Chapter 2.

But the phonological level clearly does not exhaust the analysis of this sentence; pronunciation is of no value without something to pronounce. Another kind of structure that we find here involves recognizing not just units of sounds but also units of grammar, such as words and sentences. In the unlikely event that we could be familiar with German pronunciation but know nothing more about the language, we would still be unable to make sense of the above example, since we would not know what the words are or how they relate to one another in grammatical structures. Again German speakers' knowledge of the form of the language allows them to identify the words and their grammatical significance:

es—schneit

The second level of linguistic structure is thus that of GRAMMAR. It is sufficiently complex for us to consider it under two main headings: MORPH-OLOGY, which deals with the grammatical structure of words, and SYNTAX, which considers the grammatical structure of sentences. German morphology will be examined in Chapter 3, syntax in Chapter 5.

But we have still not finished with the linguistic characteristics of our sentence. Even if we have a perfect command of German grammar, so that we can identify *schneit* as the 'third-person singular, present indicative active of the verb *schneien*', this will not permit us to understand the sentence unless we also know what the verb *schneien* means. Sentences also have a SEMANTIC structure, concerned with meanings and their relationships. Meaning is not just a property of individual words, however, as whole phrases and sentences also have meaning. The meaning of words is generally covered by the term LEXICAL SEMANTICS; it will be considered in Chapter 6.

It is also possible to see sentences from other points of view. For example, the literal meaning of *es schneit* may not be the meaning that the speaker is seeking to convey by uttering it. The speaker may actually mean 'Close the window!', or 'I've no intention of taking the dog for a walk', or the like. The level at which such aspects of utterances are considered is PRAGMATICS, concerned with the use of sentences in actual communication. Pragmatic features of utterances will be discussed in Chapter 7.

We see, therefore, that even a very simple sentence such as this can provide us with a whole range of different kinds of structure—phonetic, phonological, grammatical, semantic, pragmatic. The central levels, however, dealing with linguistic form at its most formal, are phonology and grammar. In fact, the simultaneous existence of these two levels of linguistic form—pronunciation and grammar—is often regarded as one of the most significant characteristics of human language, which distinguishes it from other kinds of communication systems. Language has what has been called a DOUBLE ARTICULATION or DOUBLE STRUCTURE. At the level of the first articulation (the grammatical structure) there are certain symbols (words, phrases, etc.) standing for certain meanings—in our example the words *es* and *schneit*. But the symbols of the first articulation are themselves structured at the level of the second articulation (the phonological structure), although this time the symbols (the sound-units of the language—in our example *e, s, sch*, etc.) do not have meanings in themselves, but merely serve to make up the symbols of the first articulation, which do.

Exactly how many levels of language should be recognized, and what their status is, are matters on which there are different views. But regardless of the number, how are they to be analysed? When we speak of 'levels of structure', what do we mean by 'structure'?

To begin with, let us consider the following simple sentence:

Gerd schreibt Briefe.

Analysing this sentence at the grammatical level, we can say that it consists of three words: *Gerd, schreibt,* and *Briefe*. But sentences are, of course, more than just collections of words; the words have relationships with one another. Again Saussure provides a starting point for the investigation of these relationships with yet another of his dichotomies. He pointed out that the relations that an element such as a word has may belong to two quite different dimensions. On the one hand there are relations between the elements actually present (here the three words of this sentence)—for example, that they occur in this particular order, that *Gerd* is the subject and *Briefe* the object, etc.; but on the other hand there are relations existing between these elements and others not actually present but which could replace them. For example, *Gerd* could be replaced by *Maria, der Student, mein Vater, der Mann mit dem roten Gesicht*, and the like; *schreibt* could be replaced by *liest, unterschreibt*, etc.; and *Briefe* by *Romane, ein schönes Gedicht*, and so on. The point here is that in order to describe the structure of a given sentence we must take into account both kinds of relationships: the relationship between actually occurring elements provides us with a structural framework, a kind of pattern, while that between elements present and those that are not gives us sets of elements that can fit into this framework.

Analysing linguistic structure in terms of these two dimensions of co-occurrence and replacement (known as the SYNTAGMATIC and PARADIGMATIC dimensions respectively) gives us some appreciation of the structural possibilities available in a language, but it is naturally rather rudimentary. These general headings embrace a wide variety of different kinds of relationship, which will need to be explored if we are to do justice to the richness and complexity of linguistic structure. The nature of these various relationships will be considered in more detail in our examination of specific aspects of German in later chapters.

The Description of German

Universals

From our discussion so far of some basic linguistic principles, many of the general characteristics of our approach to the description of German will already have become clear. We shall not be concerned with the diachronic (historical) dimension of the language, nor with providing a model to be followed by the learner, but rather with investigating modern German in order to determine the nature of the structures involved. As we have noted, it is a fundamental principle that each language should be described in its own terms, and hence in describing German we should guard against unquestioningly adopting concepts and categories which are familiar from other languages. Our traditional school grammar recognizes a number of such categories which are appropriate enough for Greek and Latin, but which have no justification at all in modern German—the 'vocative' case being a good example. However, this principle must to some extent be qualified; we must also bear in mind that we are attempting to describe the language in terms of current linguistics, which involves a particular perspective and a particular set of assumptions (a 'theory') about the nature of language. It is neither possible nor desirable to analyse a language without such initial assumptions. Hence, it is inevitable that we should find—indeed that we should actively look for—parallels between languages, in the form of similar features, comparable structures, analogous categories, etc. It is only through recognition of such parallels that a *general* linguistic theory can be formulated which gives some insight into the nature of language itself.

In current linguistics, therefore, considerable attention is paid not merely to the description of individual languages in their own terms but also to what they have in common. Though each language is, of course, unique, this uniqueness has its limits, and many features—so-called UNIVERSALS—are found to be the common property of all languages. Even where there are clear differences, it appears that languages can differ in only a rather limited number of ways, allowing us to establish TYPOLOGIES of languages—

languages can be assigned to a limited number of types. There are, of course, dangers here; we must beware not only of making illegitimate assumptions about the phenomena to be described but also, in our desire to identify universals and to assign languages to a limited number of types, of forcing languages into an inappropriate mould and ignoring the observable facts.

In our study of German, therefore, we must strike a balance between the open mind required by the principle of objectivity on the one hand, and the legitimately preconceived ideas which will allow us to relate the facts of the language to a general linguistic framework on the other. In aiming for this balance, linguistic description is of course in no way unique; all disciplines which concern themselves both with the description of specific phenomena and with a general theory to account for them must achieve a similar balance.

Idealization

We have noted that the subject matter of our enquiry will be the linguistic *system* of German, i.e. the underlying principles and structures which determine acts of speech by speakers of the language. The implication of this is that characteristics of the acts of speech themselves may be of interest to us only in so far as they reflect this underlying system, and hence that some features might need to be excluded from consideration. For example, our German speaker might well be interrupted, forget what he or she was going to say, or switch to a different construction in the middle of his or her sentence. We would feel justified in excluding such fragmented or distorted utterances, and confining ourselves to 'legitimate' utterances which we feel to be in conformity with the system we are trying to describe, this system being (in terms of our earlier discussion) the 'langue' of the community rather than the 'parole' of the individual, or the 'competence' rather than merely the 'performance' of the speaker.

Our description of German will therefore inevitably involve a certain amount of idealization and abstraction: 'real' language is not quite as consistent, regular, or systematic as we might wish. In noting that idealizations are necessary we are not, of course, conceding that our descriptions and theories are necessarily false or illegitimate. On the contrary, any description or theory which purports to make generally valid statements—whether in linguistics or in any other discipline—must look beyond the observable facts to the underlying principles which determine them. In the process it is inevitable that certain aspects of these observable facts must be systematically excluded, or at least relegated to secondary importance. To take a simple example from everyday experience, we know that water boils at 100 degrees Celsius, but if we take measurements under a variety of different circumstances we shall find that this statement is never true in actual practice. Other factors, such as the atmospheric pressure, intervene to affect the result, and these must be discounted if we are to make our general statement. This does not mean that the statement about the boiling point of water is untrue, but merely that it is true only under ideal conditions, which may in practice never occur.

Such idealizations are also necessary in linguistics, though linguists do not always agree about what kind of idealizations should be made, and hence about which features should be excluded and in what way. The inconsistencies that we encounter in the utterances of German speakers are not all due to the kind of random, external factors just mentioned; some of the variation may be systematic and may, as we noted above, have social significance. Speakers differ from one another in their systems, and the same speaker may use different systems on different occasions; this variety may be correlated with factors such as the geographical origin of the speaker, social class, and situation. While exclusion of random or insignificant variation is clearly legitimate, the appropriateness of excluding such systematic variation is more debatable. Whatever idealizations we undertake, and however well justified they may be, we must not lose sight of the real facts of our investigation, and must ultimately relate our abstract structures to these facts in an appropriate way. In short, we must examine and take due account of the various factors that we have excluded in the process of our idealization.

'Hochdeutsch'

In most, if not all, languages we encounter different regional forms of the language, differing in pronunciation, grammar, and vocabulary: dialects.[9] In many cases one particular variety has become institutionalized as the STAND-ARD form; it may be recognized for official purposes (perhaps even given legal status), used in the media and literature, promoted through the educational system, and may have the greatest prestige. Standard forms commonly develop for a variety of historical, political, social, and cultural reasons; they do not in principle have any inherent superiority over other forms, but, since they are required to fulfil a wider range of functions, they may acquire a greater variety of grammatical structures, and a more extensive vocabulary.

Such a standard is usually identified for German, namely that variety of the language generally referred to as HOCHDEUTSCH. Though regional in origin, Hochdeutsch has arguably become the standard for the whole of the German-

---

[9] Note that differences of pronunciation alone are not sufficient for us to recognize distinct dialects. Varieties of a language which differ only in pronunciation are regarded as different *accents* rather than *dialects*.

speaking area, and thus contrasts with the regional dialects, which are geographically restricted.[10] It is the only form to be regularly used in writing, and hence virtually all literature and newspapers are written in it. In its written form it is also often called the *Schriftsprache*, but this is unduly restrictive, since it is not exclusively a written variety, and most educated speakers of German use it—or something approximating to it—as their normal form of speech.[11] It is furthermore the form that is codified in grammar books and dictionaries, taught in schools, and presented as the model for foreign learners.

The concept of 'Standard German' is, however, not without its problems. Though we may say that *Hochdeutsch* is recognized as a standard throughout all the German-speaking area, this requires some qualification, since there are also regional standards of less general validity. In Austria, for instance, we may recognize a 'Standard Austrian German', differing from the standard of Germany in a number of respects, especially in vocabulary, while in Switzerland, where Standard German is rather less used than elsewhere, we may identify regional standards based on the speech of the major cities, Basle, Zürich, and Berne. Even in Germany itself, where the standardization process has gone furthest, *Hochdeutsch* cannot be considered totally uniform; there are important differences of vocabulary and grammar, notably between North and South.

The question may indeed be raised whether there is such a form as Standard German at all. In the first place, given the existence of Standard Austrian and other regional varieties, is it accurate to speak of a single standard language or should we not recognize several different standards? Such a claim has in fact been made: German has been described as PLURI-CENTRIC, i.e. as having a number of different norms, valid for different areas where the language is spoken.[12] This description can certainly be accepted for English, since British and American English, for instance, must be regarded as equally 'standard' within their own spheres of relevance, and neither can be given priority over the other. This double standard is also reflected in the

---

[10] The 'hoch' of *Hochdeutsch* originally served to differentiate it from *Niederdeutsch*; in this sense all southern forms of German, including dialects, are varieties of *Hochdeutsch*. However, the term is now more commonly used to refer to the standard form, an interpretation that is no doubt reinforced by the sense of quality implied by 'hoch'.

[11] Dialects are also occasionally written, but dialect literature remains a rather artificial curiosity, and there is also little agreement on how to write the dialects, even in those parts of the German-speaking area where semi-official spelling systems have been devised, e.g. Luxembourg. In Switzerland dialects have a status not found elsewhere, and even educated people will regularly use their local dialect for all but the most formal purposes.

[12] On this point see particularly the work of M. Clyne—see Further Reading.

norms acceptable to foreign learners of English: British English is generally taught in Europe, Africa, and South Asia, American English in Latin America and the Pacific. But is this also true of German? Despite the existence of regional standards, there can be little doubt that the Standard German of Germany itself enjoys a prestige and influence which sets it apart from the other varieties. The German standard is tacitly, if reluctantly, treated as more highly valued than other more local standards, not only by Germans but also by speakers from elsewhere. It can therefore with some justification be treated as *the* standard for the whole of the German-speaking area. Its prestige does not, admittedly, guarantee its popularity, and German linguistic dominance is certainly resented as much as German economic dominance, but it would be hard to claim that this dominance does not exist. Thus the 'pluricentric' model, though valid in the sense that there clearly are regional standards, is certainly not valid in quite the same sense for German as it is for English.

But, as noted above, the German standard is itself not uniform: considerable regional diversity is tolerated from 'standard'-speakers, even within Germany.[13] This diversity extends to grammatical forms (such as the use of *haben* or *sein* in forming the perfect of verbs such as *stehen*, and the use of the simple past) and to many items of vocabulary (the variety of different words for 'butcher' is a classic example). And in the matter of accents too there is no form which could be regarded as completely free from regional associations (see Chapter 2). We must conclude, therefore, that *Hochdeutsch* in the sense in which this term is generally used, referring to an invariable non-regional standard, is not so much an actual form of language used by German speakers as an *ideal* which is, in a sense, abstracted from actual usage. This does not necessarily mean that it is not valid as a standard, but simply that it is a standard in a slightly different sense from, say, 'Standard English'.

Given that 'Standard German' in this sense is something of an ideal form, how are we to describe actual usage? In order to achieve this, German linguists generally identify a further speech form here, which stands between the standard *Hochdeutsch* and the dialects: the UMGANGSSPRACHE, which might be defined as 'colloquial speech'. However, the status of this form is rather doubtful. The *Umgangssprache* is said to deviate from the standard in that it makes 'concessions' to regional usage without, however, becoming dialectal. But this implies that there is, in fact, a standard with no regional implications from which it deviates, and it could be argued that such a form does not actually exist: as we have noted, the standard itself is an ideal rather than a real

---

[13] Paradoxically, English is more standardized within Britain than German is within Germany; but English as a whole, with its worldwide distribution, is less standardized than German.

form. The concept of *Umgangssprache* in this sense could therefore be seen as redundant; the facts might be better accommodated by accepting a more realistic standard which includes a degree of regional variation *within* the standard itself. This in turn naturally makes the dividing line between standard and dialect fluid and ill-defined—which, indeed, it is.[14] A standard defined in these terms is not a matter of prescription by some authority, but a question of the usage and attitudes of speakers themselves; a form is standard if it is accepted and used as such by German speakers.

This situation imposes further constraints on our description of German. It would clearly be impractical to attempt to embrace all the geographically different forms of German in a single book. A more realistic approach is to select a representative form of the language by way of illustration, and *Hochdeutsch*, despite its status as a somewhat idealized form, is the natural and inevitable choice as the representative variety of German to be described. However, its status as an ideal must be borne in mind,[15] and the assumption of regularity and consistency which appears to underlie our discussion is a practical convenience and not a claim about the nature of German itself.

Although we shall here be concerned with *Hochdeutsch*, we must nevertheless bear in mind that this is not the only form of German worthy of description, nor is it to be considered as the only 'correct' form. The necessity of seeing each language or variety in its own terms has been emphasized above, and this applies as much to regional dialects as it does to Standard German: each dialect has its own system, and must on no account be seen as a deviant or debased form of the standard.[16]

Social and Stylistic Variation

The range of variation that we have so far considered has been primarily geographical; dialects are varieties of the language that have arisen in particular localities or regions. But this is not the only kind of variation found in German. It is not the case that all speakers residing at the same place or in the same region speak in the same way, as language is differentiated according to *who* one is as well as *where* one is, and particularly according to which *group* of speakers one belongs to.

---

[14] The reader is warned that this view of the *Umgangssprache* is not typical of the majority of writers on German.

[15] One could reduce the variety to some extent by regarding only North German usage as standard here. But it seems more realistic to accept some regional variation within *Hochdeutsch*.

[16] The continuing decline of regional dialects, in German-speaking areas as elsewhere, means that the dialects in their 'pure' form are rarely found. Most so-called dialect speakers are very inconsistent, often switching between dialect and standard in a random manner. To this extent the 'system' of the dialect (as, indeed, that of the standard) is something of an idealization.

Societies are seldom uniform; there exist within them a number of different groups, differentiated by a variety of social and other criteria. One of the characteristics which often distinguishes different groups is the sort of language they use, though language is only rarely the basis of group differentiation and is merely a reflection of it. The study of geographical varieties is a long-established discipline,[17] but the systematic investigation of social variation is relatively recent.

Social variation in language is of many different kinds, reflecting the complexity of social groupings. There are features, for example, which reflect the age of the speaker; the younger generation feels the need to distance itself from its predecessor, and delights in using its own linguistic forms—of which, predictably, the older generation does not approve. Similarly, the sex of the speaker may be reflected in linguistic features, e.g. the tendency of some men to indulge in 'macho' language, incorporating vulgarities or obscenities, while women may use vocabulary which some men would consider effeminate. There are also features which reflect the occupation of the speaker, especially the technical jargon of trades or professions, or the slang of, say, students, soldiers, or criminals.

The most significant area of social variation, however, is that which relates to socio-economic class, and this has a clear reflection in language; the language a person uses is usually a good indicator of the social class to which he or she can be said to belong. Important factors that are involved here are status and prestige, and language varieties can be ranked on a high–low scale, the speech of the lower class being of low prestige and status, that of the middle and upper classes having higher prestige and status. It must be said, however, that social class is by no means as pervasive in modern German society as it is elsewhere, for example in England, and the social stigma associated with low-class-based linguistic forms is correspondingly less strong.

Despite its importance, variation of this kind, like dialectal variation, will not be considered systematically in our discussions, as the topic deserves a much deeper and broader treatment than would be possible here. Readers are therefore referred to works which focus on this area of the study of German (see Further Reading). Nevertheless, it must constantly be borne in mind that this variation exists, and that, in so far as it is excluded from our discussion, we are again resorting to idealization and abstraction from the true facts of the language.

---

[17] Considerable study of regional dialects was undertaken from a historical perspective in the late 19th century.

The same reservations must also be made in respect of another dimension of variation: STYLE. This is a very loose term which covers differences which can be ascribed to how, when, and for what purpose the language is used. Even a single speaker does not maintain a constant form of the language, but adjusts his or her style according to the circumstances. The factors involved here are many and various, and they can be systematized in a number of different ways. No attempt is made to provide a comprehensive treatment here.

We find differences, for example, according to the *medium* through which the language is conveyed, i.e. whether it is spoken or written. A written text sounds stilted when spoken, and spoken language appears unacceptable when written. A further way in which varieties typically differ depends on the *topic* with which the language is concerned. The main differences here relate to vocabulary, with technical terms appropriate to the subject matter, but they are not necessarily restricted to such differences, as technical language may also have its own specific grammatical features, too.

Lastly—but by no means exhausting the possibilities here—we may note differences which depend on the *persons* involved, and their relationship to one another. The form of address used in a letter, for example, may differ, depending on the relationship between the writer and the addressee. An informal mode of address may cause offence when a formal mode is appropriate, and vice versa.

All these factors create different forms of German which a comprehensive description of the language should attempt to cover. However, since no such comprehensive description is being attempted in this book, it will be possible to take only occasional account of this dimension of variation in our discussions.

FURTHER READING

Introductory and General Works on Linguistics

Crystal (1997); Fromkin, Rodman, and Hyams (2003); Yule (1996a).

History and Schools of Linguistics

Robins (1997); Seuren (1998).

German Linguistics

Beedham (1995); Bergmann, Pauly, and Schlaefer (2001); Boase-Beier and Lodge (2003); Bünting (1996); Herbst, Heath, and Dederding (1979); Johnson (1998); König (1998); Lühr (2000); Meibauer et al. (2002); Russ (1994).

German Dialects

Keller (1961); König (1998); Löffler (2003); Russ (1990, 1994: chs. 2–5); Seibicke (1972).

Social Varieties of German

Barbour and Stevenson (1990); Clyne (1984, 1995); Stevenson (1995, 1997).

EXERCISES AND DISCUSSION QUESTIONS

1. Explain the difference between the *synchronic* and *diachronic* dimensions of language and discuss the nature of the relationship between the two, with reference to German.
2. Explain what is meant by linguistic *levels*. How are these levels related to one another? Give examples from German.
3. Is it possible to recognize a 'Standard German' which is valid throughout the German-speaking area?
4. It has been claimed that German is *pluricentric*, i.e. that it has more than one regional standard. To what extent do you consider that this is true?
5. In what ways, if any, does the status of 'Hochdeutsch' differ from that of 'Standard English', or from that of the standard form of any other language you know?
6. Explain what is meant by the 'Umgangssprache' and discuss its possible usefulness in describing German.
7. Find out what you can about any non-standard regional variety of German. In what ways does it differ from the Standard form of the language?
8. Discuss some of the ways in which German varies socially, for example according to class, age, etc. What are the implications of this variation for (i) describing, and (ii) learning the language?

2

Phonology

Introduction

Phonetics and Phonology

In Chapter 1 phonology was introduced as that part of linguistics which is concerned with pronunciation. In this chapter we shall be examining in some detail the phonology of German, but in order to do this we shall need to make a little more precise the scope and meaning of the term 'phonology' itself.

It is important to draw a distinction between speech as a physical activity on the one hand and speech as language on the other. Speaking involves making bodily movements and producing sounds, and these can be described in much the same way that any movements or sounds can be described, in physiological and acoustic terms. The investigation and description of speech sounds and articulations from this point of view is called *phonetics*; it forms the indispensable starting point for the linguistic study of pronunciation. We shall therefore have to begin our consideration of German phonology with a brief explanation of some of the basic principles of phonetic theory. But in considering the role of sounds in language we must go beyond the purely articulatory and acoustic facts and take into account the patterns of sounds in the language in question, the relationships between the sounds, and the way in which these relationships are exploited in the expression of meaning. It is this approach to which the term 'phonology' is applied. The terms *phonetic* and *phonological* are generally used in contrasting and complementary senses: we may speak of the 'phonological' as opposed to the 'phonetic' characteristics of speech sounds. Just how a phonological description differs from a phonetic one will be demonstrated in the course of this chapter.

The Production of Speech[1]

Speech is produced by air coming from the lungs, through the larynx (situated at the top of the windpipe), and out through the mouth and/or the nose.[2] The different kinds of sounds produced depend on how this air is affected during its passage. 2.1 gives a sketch of the relevant parts of the mouth to clarify how this is achieved.

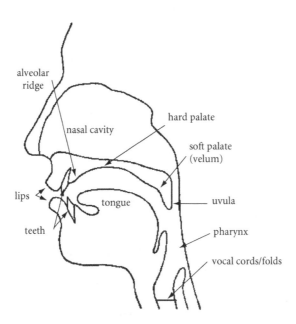

(2.1)   *The 'organs of speech'*

A major distinction is between those sounds made with an obstruction to the outgoing air on the one hand, and those in which there is merely a modification of the shape of the mouth, which affects its resonance, and therefore the sound quality, on the other. The former are CONSONANTS, the latter VOWELS. The dividing line between them is not completely sharp.

---

[1] The outline of phonetic theory presented in this section is very brief, and should be supplemented by one of the standard phonetics textbooks (see Further Reading).

[2] In some languages sounds are used which are produced in other ways, but as this is not the case in German or English they will be ignored here.

Consonants   In the production of consonants there is some form of obstruction or impediment to the flow of air through the mouth. Consonant sounds are classified according to where the obstruction to the airflow is located (= PLACE OF ARTICULATION), what kind of obstruction is involved (= MANNER OF ARTICULATION), and whether or not VOICE is also produced in the larynx. We shall consider each of these in turn.

Place of Articulation   Generally speaking, there are two articulators involved in the production of consonants, which together contribute to the obstruction, one of which is in most—but not all—cases a particular part of the roof of the mouth, and the other—again in most but not all cases—a part of the tongue. The categories most useful for description, listed here from front to back of the mouth, are:

bilabial: both lips (e.g. *b* in *Bein*)
labiodental: the upper teeth and lower lip (e.g. *f* in *fein*)
dental: the front of the tongue and the teeth (e.g. English *th* in *thing*)
alveolar: the front of the tongue and the alveolar ridge (e.g. *s* in *los*)
postalveolar: the tongue and the area just behind the alveolar ridge (e.g. *sch* in *schön*)
palatal: the tongue and the hard palate (e.g. *ch* in *ich*)
velar: the back of the tongue and the soft palate (velum) (e.g. *k* in *kein*)
uvular: the back of the tongue and the uvula (e.g. *r* in *ruhen*)
glottal: the obstruction is in the glottis (larynx) itself, the vocal folds ('vocal cords') being brought together (e.g. *h*)

Manner of Articulation   'Manner of articulation' refers to the way in which the airstream is obstructed during its passage through the mouth or nose. The most important manners are:

plosive: there is a complete blockage of air followed by a release (e.g. *p* in *Pein*)
fricative: a small gap is left between the articulators, creating a noise of friction as the air comes through (e.g. *f* in *fein*)
affricate: like a plosive except that there is a slow release resulting in friction (e.g. *z* in *zu*)
nasal: there is a complete closure in the mouth but the soft palate (the 'velum'—a soft flap at the back of the roof of the mouth) is lowered and the air escapes through the nose (e.g. *m* in *mein*)

lateral:	a gap is left at one or both sides of the tongue for the air to escape (e.g. *l* in *Luft*)
trill (roll):	part of the mouth (usually the tongue-tip or the uvula) is allowed to vibrate, repeatedly interrupting the airstream (e.g. some forms of *r* in *rot*)
semivowel *(frictionless continuant, approximant):*	as the names suggest, this is a consonant which involves a narrowing of the mouth but no appreciable friction, hence it is vowel-like (e.g. *j* in *jung*)

Voice   The larynx, a complex valve situated at the top of the windpipe, may be adjusted in a variety of ways by the speaker. It consists mainly of two small pieces of ligament—the 'vocal folds' (or 'vocal cords')—which are normally apart but can be brought together so as to obstruct the airflow. They can close the windpipe completely, preventing the air from flowing at all; they can narrow the passage so as to cause friction (the glottal fricative *h* is produced in this way); or they can be brought together in such a way that they open and close very rapidly in the airstream, giving a note of a distinct pitch. Sounds made in the last of these ways are known as *voiced* (e.g. *l, a*); those made in other ways are known as *voiceless* (e.g. *f, t*). (We can test whether a sound is voiced by placing a finger on the throat or putting our fingers in our ears during its articulation; we will feel or hear a buzz if the sound is voiced, but not if it is voiceless—compare English *zzzzz* with *sssss*, which are voiced and voiceless respectively).

Labels and Symbols   A given consonant sound can be described in terms of the three dimensions discussed above: whether it is voiced or voiceless, what its place of articulation is, and what its manner of articulation is. This gives a threefold label for each sound. Examples are: 'voiceless velar fricative' (German *ch* in *Bach*), 'voiced alveolar lateral' (German or English *l* in *viel* or *feel*), 'voiced bilabial nasal' (German or English *m* in *mein* or *mine*), etc. The chart in 2.2 shows the most important types of consonants and the symbols used for them. Symbols for voiceless sounds appear on the left of each pair and those for voiced sounds on the right; a space indicates either that the sound is not found or that it does not warrant a symbol of its own.

(2.2)	Plosive		Fricative		Nasal	Lateral	Trill	Semivowel
Bilabial	p	b			m			w
Labiodental			f	v				
Dental	t	d	θ	ð	n	l	r	
Alveolar			s	z				

Postalveolar			ʃ	ʒ			ɹ
Palatal			ç				j
Velar	k	ɡ	x	ɣ	ŋ		
Uvular			ʁ				
Glottal	ʔ		h				

Note that no symbols are provided for affricates, as these can be constructed out of the corresponding plosive and fricative symbols, e.g. *ts*. It is also rarely necessary to distinguish between dental and alveolar categories, except in the case of the fricatives. It should be noted that a few categories and symbols that are not required for Standard German have been included, but it is in no way a complete list of possible phonetic categories for consonants.

Vowels   Vowels do not involve an obstruction to the flow of air through the mouth—in this case there is none—but rather modifications to the shape of the mouth itself, principally produced by changes in the position of the tongue and the shape of the lips, and these affect the resonance characteristics of the mouth. The tongue can be moved in two dimensions—FRONT to BACK and HIGH to LOW—and since both of these allow virtually infinite gradations a very large number of different vowels can in theory be produced. In addition, the sound is affected by the degree of rounding of the lips, though in practice it is usually enough to distinguish simply between ROUNDED and UNROUNDED ('spread'). Furthermore, the velum (soft palate) can be lowered, as in the production of nasal consonants, to give NASALIZED vowels.

As far as the front–back and high–low dimensions are concerned, the area within which the tongue can move has roughly the shape given in 2.3 (the lines indicate the position of the highest point of the tongue).

The most accurate system of description and notation for vowels involves the use of so-called 'cardinal vowels', sounds of known quality to which other vowels can be referred. Two fixed points can be easily determined from the diagram of 2.3: where the tongue is as far forward and as high as possible, and where it is as far back and as low as possible, consistent in each case with no friction being produced. Other cardinal vowels are located at points which are judged to be auditorily equidistant from these points and from one another. The standard scheme establishes eight such points for the 'primary' cardinal vowels.

To make the chart more usable it is distorted into a quadrilateral figure, on which the primary cardinal vowels are located as in 2.4.

Of these, numbers 1 to 5 have unrounded lips, while numbers 6 to 8 are rounded, reflecting the types of vowels commonly found in languages. A further set of eight 'secondary' cardinal vowels is obtained by reversing these

(2.3)

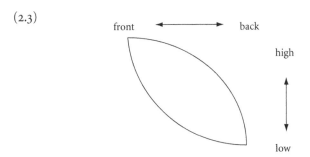

lip postures, numbers 9 to 13 being rounded and 14 to 16 unrounded, as in 2.5. A number of additional cardinal vowels are sometimes added in the central part of the chart, but they will be ignored here.

The system is employed as follows. The phonetician, who has learnt through extensive training and practice the values of the cardinal vowels, both auditorily and in terms of their tongue positions, determines the pos-

(2.4)

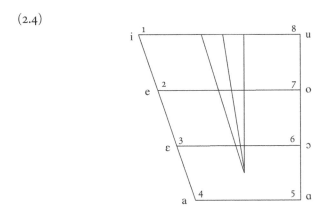

ition on the chart of a vowel sound by judging the distance and direction of the tongue from the nearest cardinal vowel when pronouncing the vowel. An appropriate vowel sound can be produced from a mark on the chart in a similar manner by the reverse procedure. A symbol can be allocated to a vowel by adding 'diacritics' (accents and other marks) to the nearest cardinal symbol as necessary. Thus, the vowel of 2.6, which is 'retracted' and 'raised' from cardinal vowel no. 2, can be given the symbol ẹ, where the diacritics indicate in what ways the vowel differs from cardinal vowel no. 2 (*e*).

(2.5)

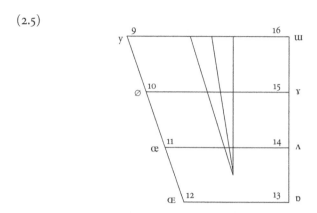

This system is quite accurate, but its use requires considerable training and experience, since the auditory quality and the tongue position of each of the cardinal vowels has to be learnt through extensive practice.

Other Sound Attributes Both consonant- and vowel-symbols may have additional diacritics, some specifying more accurately the characteristics of the sound, others indicating additional optional attributes (SECONDARY ARTICULATIONS) which are the result of the activity of other articulators. The following are the most common:

advanced	[₊]	the consonant or vowel has a more 'forward' or 'front' articulation than the symbol used would indicate, e.g. [o̟], [k̟]
retracted	[₋]	the consonant or vowel has a more 'back' articulation than the symbol used would indicate, e.g. [e̠], [k̠]

(2.6)

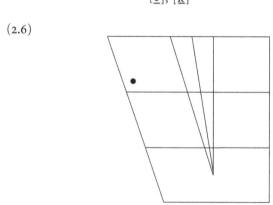

raised	[ˌ]	the vowel has a higher articulation than the cardinal vowel symbol would indicate, e.g. [e̝]
lowered	[ˍ]	the vowel has a lower articulation than the cardinal vowel symbol would indicate, e.g. [e̞]
aspirated	[ʰ]	the onset of voice is delayed after a consonant, giving a brief h-sound, e.g. [tʰ]
nasalized	[˜]	the soft palate is lowered during articulation of the sound, allowing the air to come out through the nose, e.g. [ã]
dental	[ˌ]	used to distinguish dental sounds from alveolar sounds, e.g. [t̪]
labialized	[ʷ]	pronounced with rounded lips, e.g. [tʷ]
palatalized	[ʲ]	pronounced with the front of the tongue raised to the palate, e.g. [lʲ]
velarized	[~]	pronounced with the back of the tongue raised towards the soft palate, e.g. [ɫ]
long	[ː]	e.g. [eː]
half-long	[ˑ]	e.g. [eˑ]
voiceless	[ˌ]	used to indicate voiceless pronunciation of a normally voiced sound, e.g. [l̥]
syllabic	[ˌ]	a consonant pronounced as a syllable in its own right, e.g. [n̩] in English *button* or German *bitten*.

The Phoneme

The phonetic description of speech sounds is, as we noted earlier, merely the starting point for a consideration of the linguistic role of these sounds: phonology. As an initial demonstration of the distinction between phonetic and phonological description consider the notion of speech sound. We may speak of 'the German *r*-sound', 'the German *t*-sound', etc., but closer inspection shows that such an entity is not really a 'sound' at all. The German words *rot* and *Tor*, for example, may be thought of as containing the same sounds in reverse order, but this is not in fact the case. For most German speakers the *r* in *rot* is a uvular fricative (phonetic symbol [ʁ]), produced by constricting the back of the mouth in such a way that audible friction is produced as the air coming from the lungs is forced between the uvula and the back of the tongue. The final *r* of *Tor*, on the other hand, has far less constriction and no appreciable friction, the tongue being drawn back to give a rather 'dark' quality to the end of the vowel. Similarly, the *t* of *rot* is by no means the same as the *t* of *Tor*. The latter is *aspirated*: it is followed by a short *h*-like sound before the vowel begins (phonetic symbol [tʰ]). Less or even no aspiration follows the *t* of *rot*. What we thought of as 'the same sound' in each case turns out to be rather different. These examples are in no way exceptional, and comparable phenomena are found throughout the language.

Does this mean, therefore, that we are wrong to think of these two *t*s and two *r*s as 'the same sound'? In one sense, of course, yes; they are actually different sounds. But in another sense no; as far as the speakers of the language are concerned they are the same: they are used in such a way that the difference, though noticeable if we stop to observe, is quite irrelevant to the language and how it works. To use the terminology introduced earlier, we might say that the two *t*s or the two *r*s are phonetically different, but phonologically the same.

The ambiguity of the term 'sound'—it may refer to the actual (phonetic) sound or to the phonological 'sound'—is inconvenient, and because of the importance of this distinction we must be rather more precise in our terminology. In linguistics the term PHONEME is used to describe the phonological 'sound', so that the term 'sound' itself is usually to be understood in a phonetic sense.[3] Thus, we may say that although the *r* of *rot* and the *r* of *Tor* are different sounds, they are (or they 'belong to') the same phoneme; we can now speak of the '*r*-phoneme' rather than the '*r*-sound'. Another useful term is ALLOPHONE. This is applied to the various sounds which are associated with (are 'members' or 'realizations' of) a particular phoneme. Thus, the aspirated and unaspirated *t*-sounds are both allophones of the German *t*-phoneme, while the fricative and non-fricative types of *r* are allophones of the German *r*-phoneme. It is customary to place symbols for phonemes within slanting lines, i.e. /t/, /r/, etc., while symbols for sounds or allophones are enclosed in square brackets: [tʰ], [ʁ]. We shall use the terms 'phoneme' and 'allophone' extensively throughout this chapter.

Phonemic Procedures

The wide range of actual sounds and articulations occurring in a language can be reduced to a much smaller and more manageable set by means of the phoneme concept. But we must not assume that this can always be done in exactly the same way. Different languages have different phonemes, and may

---

[3] The term 'phonemics' has also been used for what we have called 'phonology', but this term reflects an earlier stage of phonological theory, when the phoneme was the *only* phonological unit recognized. Nowadays the scope of phonology has been considerably broadened, and this term is less than appropriate.

treat sounds differently. For example, although in German the unaspirated and aspirated *t*-sounds are allophones of the same phoneme, this is not true in Hindi, where they are allophones of different phonemes. On the other hand, *b* and *v* are distinct phonemes in German and English, but are allophones of a single phoneme in Spanish. In describing the phonology of a language we must therefore have some means of deciding what the phonemes are.

Most speakers of a language will probably not realize that there are such variations in the sounds, and will think merely of 'the *t*-sound', 'the *r*-sound', etc. In fact, they are usually aware of the differences between phonemes but not of the differences between allophones of the same phoneme. In order to find out what the phonemes of a particular language are, therefore, it might be enough to rely on the speaker's feelings or intuition about the sounds of his or her language. Unfortunately, although these intuitions can be of value and importance, speakers' judgements are too variable and imprecise to be satisfactory, and we need to supplement them by more objective tests. A variety of such phonemic procedures have been devised, and, although none of them individually is entirely reliable under all circumstances, together they do give us more objective methods for determining the phonemes of the language than merely appealing to the speaker's feelings.

One characteristic of the different allophones of a phoneme that has already been noted is that they occur in different places in a word. In German the aspirated *t* occurs at the beginning of a syllable immediately before a vowel, while the unaspirated *t* occurs elsewhere. Allophones can thus be seen as different representatives or realizations of the same phoneme under different circumstances. Since they are always found in different places they are said to be in COMPLEMENTARY DISTRIBUTION. This means that one way of determining what the phonemes of a language are is to look at where they occur; if we find two similar sounds which are in complementary distribution they are likely to be allophones of the same phoneme.

Another criterion for determining the phonemes relies on meaning. Different allophones of the same phoneme can never constitute the only difference between words which are different in meaning (no two words in German, for example, could be distinguished only by the presence of an unaspirated *t* in one and an aspirated *t* in the other—if only because these two sounds never occur in the same place). Different phonemes, on the other hand (for example *r* and *t*), *can* distinguish words of different meaning (e.g. *rot* and *tot*). We can therefore use this as a test to determine whether different sounds are allophones of the same phoneme or not: if different words can be distinguished by them, they must be allophones of different phonemes. This is the criterion of CONTRAST.

The relative merits of distribution and contrast as criteria for determining the phonemes of a language have been much debated. Since contrast depends on the speaker's intuitive awareness of differences of meaning, those who wish to exclude totally such subjective principles have favoured the distributional approach, while those who are more concerned with phonemes from the point of view of their role in distinguishing different words have preferred the criterion of contrast.[4] In practice, however, both distribution and contrast are valid criteria, and we may need to use either as the occasion demands.

Variation

An important task in phonological description is the establishment of the set, or *system*, of phonemes appropriate to the language. But we are immediately faced with a difficulty: not only do different languages have different systems but different varieties of the same language also differ. In fact, even the same speaker may vary in this respect, using different systems on different occasions or in different styles of speech. In what sense, then, can we speak of *the* system of German phonemes?

The question of different varieties of German, and their significance for linguistic description, was considered in general terms in the previous chapter, and the relationship between the standard *Hochdeutsch* and regional forms was discussed. But even if we confine ourselves to the standard form we find considerable variation in how it is pronounced in different areas. It is these different pronunciations of the standard that are called ACCENTS. We could say, therefore, that whereas a dialect is a regional variety of the language which may differ from other dialects and from the standard form in phonology, grammar, or vocabulary (or in all of these), an accent is a regional variety of pronunciation of the standard form; different accents differ *only* in pronunciation.[5]

Just as we may often identify a 'standard' dialect of a language, we may also be able to identify a 'standard' accent. In the same way that a standard dialect enjoys a special status for speakers of a language, so a particular pronunciation of this standard may acquire a similar prestige. In the German-speaking countries, however, unlike England,[6] no such standard has evolved as the natural speech of any one social group. In the absence of such a norm, it has

---

[4] These two positions are those of the American Structuralist school and the Prague School, respectively.

[5] Accents are not merely regional, but may also be social, since, as we saw above, they may vary according to social class, even in the same geographical area.

[6] In England one form of pronunciation of Standard English has gained currency as the 'approved' pronunciation for such official purposes as broadcasting. This accent, known to linguists as 'Received Pronunciation' (where 'received' means 'acceptable in the best circles'), is not confined to a single geographical area, but is the speech of a particular social class. It has served as a model for foreigners

been thought necessary to establish one. At the end of the nineteenth century a commission was set up under the direction of Theodor Siebs which made recommendations for a standard accent for German, based on the pronunciation in use on the stage, and these recommendations have been quite influential. The 'Siebs pronunciation'—originally called 'Deutsche Bühnensprache' because it was based on, and recommended for, the stage, but later called 'Deutsche Hochsprache'—is the one that is generally described in books on the pronunciation of German,[7] and which has acquired something of the status of an official standard, even outside Germany itself.[8]

This standard accent of German is not the actual speech of any group of speakers, but is entirely artificial. It is not, therefore, a norm of pronunciation, but rather an ideal. Further, since it is based on a very formal style of speaking it is of rather limited value as a model for general use, and even its proponents do not regard it, in its pure form, as an accent to be acquired for everyday speech. For normal purposes a more moderate form ('gemäßigte Hochlautung') is advocated, which makes concessions to actual usage, but even this remains an artificial ideal.

The Siebs pronunciation, whether in its pure or more moderate form, cannot therefore be regarded as a standard accent in the sense of a norm of usage, and we cannot base a description on it if we wish to take account of how German speakers actually pronounce their language. Nevertheless, it would of course be quite impracticable, and beyond the scope of this book, to describe all the accents of Standard German, and the selection of some form as the basis for a description, whatever its theoretical drawbacks, is a practical necessity. The most useful type of accent for such a purpose is without doubt the kind of pronunciation found among North German speakers. Not only do North German pronunciations have, on the whole, greater prestige within Germany itself than Southern German, Austrian, or Swiss ones, but they are also somewhat more conservative and closer to the written form.[9] They are also closer to the Siebs model, since this too was largely based on a Northern kind of pronunciation. If we take such an accent as the 'standard', however, we must bear in mind that it is standard only in this rather arbitrary sense, and that it is not a single, homogeneous accent but a set

---

learning English as well as for those of other social groups who wish to obtain the social advantages which often accrue from using it. There is no German accent with a comparable status.

[7] For the latest version see De Boor et al. (2000) (see Further Reading).

[8] There is, for example, a Swiss 'Siebs Commission', which has adopted, often in modified form, some of the recommendations of Siebs.

[9] There are historical reasons for this. High German was originally acquired by Low German-speaking North Germans as a foreign language, largely through the written form.

of related pronunciations, differing according to region, social class, and style of speech. We must also note that there are other 'standards' of more restricted regional scope, e.g. in Austria and Switzerland, and there is of course no implication that such standards are inferior or invalid.

Foreign Words

There is a further problem that must be faced in attempting to establish the system of phonemes for German, even if we restrict ourselves to a standard pronunciation. Although we may identify such a system for native German words, words of foreign origin may not quite conform to it, or may have characteristics which are not found in native words. The words *Restaurant* or *Teint*, for example, as pronounced by German speakers, usually have a number of features which we do not normally find in native words, in particular nasalized vowels.

Such cases present difficulties for phonological description, and there are various ways of dealing with them. We could, of course, simply treat the nasal vowels of words such as *Restaurant, Teint*, etc. as vowels of German, on a par with native vowels, without worrying about the fact that they occur in only a few words of foreign origin. The problem with this is that virtually any foreign sound can be used by German speakers when incorporating foreign words into their speech, such as the English vowels of *lunch* or *surfing*. Clearly, it cannot be the case that any foreign sound can be part of the German system merely because German speakers have been heard to use it. At the other extreme we could simply eliminate all foreign words from consideration. This too is not entirely satisfactory, since foreign words have become an integral part of the German vocabulary and are widely used in everyday speech. Simply to ignore these words would give a distorted and partial picture of German phonology.

Foreign words differ in the extent to which they conform to the native pattern. While some such words have been completely assimilated and are indistinguishable from native ones, their foreign origin being a purely historical matter, others have retained features of their foreign identity to various extents.[10] In either case, the majority of foreign words do not in fact contain phonemes that are not also found in the native part of the vocabulary, largely because speakers tend to substitute native phonemes for unpronounceable foreign sounds. The English vowel of *surfing*, for example, is generally replaced by *ö*. But where foreign words differ from native ones is in the

---

[10] It is customary to distinguish *Lehnwörter*—borrowed words whose foreign origin is no longer discernible—from *Fremdwörter*—words which still appear foreign to German speakers. This distinction is, of course, not absolute, but is a matter of degree.

combination of phonemes, and in other characteristics such as stress. The word *Restaurant* has stress on the final syllable, which is typical of foreign words but not of the majority of native ones.

The most satisfactory approach is to separate, as far as is necessary and practicable, the system of native words (including foreign words that are completely assimilated into the German system) from that of words of recognizably foreign origin. We may distinguish a *central* system, which will include the former, from a more *peripheral* one, containing only the latter. In fact, the peripheral system can hardly be called a 'system' at all, since it varies from speaker to speaker, and from speech style to speech style. The central system is more stable, though even here there may be variations of a stylistic kind.

The German Phonemes

Bearing in mind the various reservations and problems noted above, we can provisionally establish for Standard German the system of phonemes presented in 2.7. The word 'provisionally' is significant, as it is important to recognize that our system cannot lay claim to being *the* definitive system. This is due not only to the difficulties outlined above, but also to the fact that the criteria for determining the phonemes do not necessarily lead to a single, unique solution. In some cases alternative analyses are possible, and our choice of a particular analysis depends on the weight we give to the different factors involved.

(2.7) **Vowels**

Symbol	as in	Symbol	as in	Symbol	as in
/iː/	s*ie*h	/uː/	g*u*t	/yː/	k*üh*l
/ɪ/	T*i*sch	/ʊ/	m*u*ss	/ʏ/	h*ü*bsch
/eː/	S*ee*	/oː/	s*o*	/øː/	sch*ö*n
/ɛ/	B*e*tt	/ɔ/	St*o*ck	/œ/	zw*ö*lf
/ɑː/	s*a*h	/a/	M*a*nn	/æː/	B*ä*r
/ai/	s*ei*	/au/	S*au*	/ɔi/	n*eu*
/ə/	G*e*bäud*e*				

Consonants

Symbol	as in	Symbol	as in	Symbol	as in
/p/	P*ein*	/b/	B*ein*	/m/	m*ein*
/t/	T*au*	/d/	d*ein*	/n/	n*ein*
/k/	k*ein*	/g/	g*ut*	/ŋ/	ju*ng*

/f/	*f*ein	/v/	*W*ein	/pf/	*Pf*au
/s/	mu*ss*	/z/	*s*ein	/ts/	*z*u
/ʃ/	*Sch*ein	/x/	Ba*ch*, i*ch*	/h/	*H*ain
/l/	*l*assen	/r/	*r*ein	/j/	*j*a

It must be emphasized that the symbols of 2.7 represent *phonemes* and not *sounds* (hence they are enclosed in slanting lines); each of these phonemes will correspond to a variety of actual sounds or allophones. The symbols are not, therefore, to be given any absolute phonetic value. Although the symbols themselves are chosen partly to reflect the typical pronunciations of the phonemes, they are essentially arbitrary, and could be replaced by other symbols of equal validity. This applies particularly to the vowel phonemes, for which a number of different systems of notation are in use. This issue will be taken up again shortly.

Though the phonemes themselves are not describable in phonetic terms, it is possible to give an approximate phonetic characterization of their typical allophones in terms of the general phonetic categories outlined above. In the case of the vowels, a major distinction is whether they are MONOPHTHONGS or DIPHTHONGS (i.e. whether the sound is relatively static throughout its articulation or whether the tongue moves and the sound changes). The monophthongs (i.e. all vowels except /ai/, /au/, and /ɔi/) can be given a fairly accurate representation by locating them on a vowel chart, as in 2.8, which indicates the height and backness of the vowels. Information about whether the lips are rounded or unrounded is also included: the squares represent unrounded vowels and the circles indicate rounded vowels. Information not shown on the chart relates to whether the vowels are typically long or short: the vowels /iː/, /eː/, /æː/, /uː/, /oː/, /aː/, /yː/, and /øː/ are typically long (the mark ː represents length); the others are typically short. (The length of vowels will be discussed below.)

(2.8)

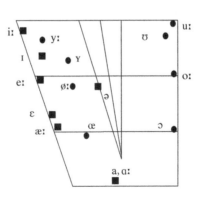

Since they are not static, diphthongs need to be represented by arrows rather than dots, as in 2.9. /ai/is unrounded throughout, /ɔi/ is rounded throughout, while /au/ starts unrounded and becomes rounded. All the diphthongs are relatively long.

(2.9)

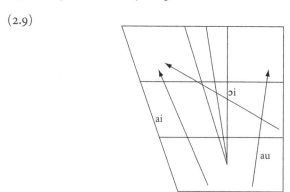

Note that the symbols used for representing the end points of the diphthongs are to some extent arbitrary; none of them ends as high as the corresponding monophthongs represented by the same symbols. The starting point of /au/ is further back than that of /ai/, and the end of /ɔi/, unlike /i/, is somewhat rounded.

Typical allophones of the consonants can be described in terms of the place and manner of articulation, and whether the sounds are voiced or voiceless. We obtain the chart of 2.10.

(2.10)

	Affricate	*Plosive*		*Fricative*		*Nasal*	*Lateral*	*Semivowel*
Bilabial		p	b			m		
Labiodental	pf			f	v			
Alveolar	ts	t	d	s	z	n	l	
Postalveolar				ʃ				j
Palatal								
Velar		k	g	x		ŋ		
Uvular					r			
Glottal			h					

The plosives and fricatives may be voiced or voiceless; those on the left of each pair (e.g. /p/ and /f/) are voiceless and those on the right (e.g. /b/ and /v/) are voiced. The affricates are voiceless; the nasals, lateral, and semivowel all voiced.

This chart gives only one typical allophone for each phoneme. In the majority of cases the allophones of a particular phoneme do not differ significantly in terms of the categories used here (e.g. all the allophones of /p/ are voiceless bilabial plosives), but in a few cases inclusion of even the most important allophones would require additional symbols to be placed on the chart. The phoneme /x/, for example, has an important allophone which is not velar, but palatal (phonetic symbol [ç]), while /r/ is particularly variable, and its allophones would need to be included in several different places.[11] Where this variation is significant it will be discussed below.

The System

The set of phonemes of a language is not just an arbitrary collection of sound-types; the phonemes form an ordered system in which there are certain kinds of regular relationships. A notable characteristic of the vowels is that the majority of them occur in pairs of similar quality but differing in length, as we see from 2.11. The short vowels tend to be somewhat more open and central than their long counterparts. The only vowels that are unpaired are /æː/, /ə/, and the diphthongs; the status of these will be considered shortly.

(2.11)	*Long*	*Short*			
	/iː/	/ɪ/	bieten	~	bitten
	/eː/	/ɛ/	beten	~	Betten
	/uː/	/ʊ/	spuken	~	spucken
	/oː/	/ɔ/	Ofen	~	offen
	/ɑː/	/a/	Staat	~	Stadt
	/yː/	/ʏ/	fühlen	~	füllen
	/øː/	/œ/	Flöße	~	flösse

There is also a certain regularity with the place of articulation of these pairs of vowels. They are basically of three heights (high, mid, and low), and, with the exception of the low pair, they are either front or back, the front ones being either rounded or unrounded. The whole system can thus—again with the exception of the unpaired vowels—be presented in the rather simpler form of 2.12.

---

[11] The symbols used in this chart are also the standard phonetic symbols for the relevant sounds, with the exception of /r/. The standard symbol for the voiced uvular fricative is [ʁ].

(2.12)

	Front		Central	Back
	Unrounded	*Rounded*	*Unrounded*	*Rounded*
High	iː, ɪ	yː, ʏ		uː, ʊ
Mid	eː, ɛ	øː, œ		oː, ɔ
Low			aː, a	

Such regularity is harder to find in the consonant system, but some general characteristics can be observed. Notice that the bilabial and labiodental consonants are complementary: the former set has plosives and a nasal, while the latter has fricatives and an affricate. It is more useful to group these two sets together as a single 'labial' category. Having done this, we shall see that the labial, alveolar, and velar categories are similar in having an affricate, voiced and voiceless plosives, voiced and voiceless fricatives, and a nasal, though there are gaps in the velar set (see 2.13). The remaining phonemes—/l, ʃ, j, r, h/—do not fit this scheme, and must be considered separately.[12]

(2.13)

	Affricate	Plosive		Fricative		Nasal
	Vcl.	*Vcl.*	*Vcd.*	*Vcl.*	*Vcd.*	*Vcd.*
Labial	pf	p	b	f	v	m
Alveolar	ts	t	d	s	z	n
Velar		k	g	x		ŋ

It is important to note that what is significant about these relationships between the phonemes is not the phonetic features as such, but rather the *contrasts*. The phonetic features that distinguish the phonemes may in fact be rather variable, but what is significant from a phonological point of view is that the phonemes are distinct from one another. As an example consider the case of the vowels. In the various charts of German vowel phonemes given here, the 'long' and 'short' vowels are distinguished in two ways: by using different symbols and by using the length mark (ː). This is intended to reflect the fact that the two sets of vowels tend to differ in both *quality* and *length*: the 'short' vowels are not only usually shorter than the 'long' ones but they are also generally articulated slightly more to the centre of the mouth. What is more, the 'long' vowels are not, in fact, always actually longer in duration than

---

[12] The voiced velar fricative is lacking, but one suggestion is to regard the voiced uvular fricative /r/ as part of the same series, equivalent to a velar consonant. This would remove two anomalies: the gap in the system of voiced fricatives, and the rather isolated position of /r/. However, /r/ differs in a number of respects from the other fricatives, in particular in where it occurs in words, and this proposal is therefore not altogether satisfactory.

the corresponding 'short' ones. The word *Philosophie* (/fiːloːsoːˈfiː/)[13] has 'long' vowels throughout, but the two cases of /oː/, which are in unstressed syllables, are quite short. Nevertheless, it would not do to regard these as the 'short' vowel /ɔ/. The shortened, unstressed /oː/ of *Kolonne* (/koːˈlɔnə/) is not identical to the 'short' /ɔ/ of *Kollege* (/kɔˈleːgə/), but what distinguishes them is not length but quality, i.e. tongue position. The contrast between the 'long' and the 'short' vowels is, paradoxically, not always one of length.

On the other hand, in the case of the pair /aː/–/a/ there is often no difference of quality between the 'short' and 'long' vowels for many speakers of the standard accent, so that the difference is only one of length. This means that in cases where the 'long' vowel is shortened (i.e. when it is unstressed), it is indistinguishable from the short vowel, and it is difficult to decide which phoneme is actually present. This is borne out by the representation of some words in German pronouncing dictionaries. The words *Araber, arabisch,* and *Arabist,* for example, are given the following pronunciations in the Duden pronouncing dictionary (the dictionary uses the same symbols for 'long' and 'short' vowels, distinguished only by the length mark): /ˈaːrabər/, /aˈraːbɪʃ/, /araˈbɪst/. It can be seen that the /aː/ (= ɑː) of the stressed syllable is represented as the short phoneme /a/ when shortened in an unstressed syllable. A similar situation exists with the vowels /æː/ and /ɛ/, which may likewise become indistinguishable when short (the symbol /ɛ/ is used for /æː/): /ˈɛːtər/ (*Äther*) but /ɛˈteːrɪʃ/ (*ätherisch*). The transcriptions /ˈaːraːbər/, /aˈraːbɪʃ/, /aːraːˈbɪst/ and /ˈɛːtər/, /ɛːˈteːrɪʃ/, with 'long' vowel phonemes throughout, would be equivalent and equally valid, since /aː/ and /ɛː/ (= ɑː and æ) are indistinguishable from /a/ and /ɛ/, respectively, in this position. Indeed, these transcriptions would probably be preferable, since they preserve the phonemic shape of the roots in the related words.

These difficulties raise some practical problems for the way we represent the vowels. As we have noted, the set of symbols used here represents the differences in terms of *both* length *and* quality. But since what is significant here is not these properties as such but rather the fact that the two sets of vowels are distinct, any set of symbols would be theoretically adequate as long as it kept the two sets of vowels apart, and alternative systems of transcription are found in books on German (and, we may add, on English, where a similar situation occurs), which represent the distinction in terms of *either* quality *or* quantity (length). The different systems are illustrated in 2.14: the first system reflects the differences of quality, the second quantity, and the third both of these.[14]

---

[13] ' indicates stress on the following syllable.

[14] The first edition of this book in fact used the qualitative system, without length marks for the 'long' vowels.

(2.13)

	Qualitative		Quantitative		Both	
	'Long'	'Short'	'Long'	'Short'	'Long'	'Short'
	/i/	/ɪ/	/iː/	/i/	/iː/	/ɪ/
	/e/	/ɛ/	/eː/	/e/	/eː/	/ɛ/
	/u/	/ʊ/	/uː/	/u/	/uː/	/ʊ/
	/o/	/ɔ/	/oː/	/o/	/oː/	/ɔ/
	/ɑ/	/a/	/aː/	/a/	/ɑː/	/a/
	/y/	/ʏ/	/yː/	/y/	/yː/	/ʏ/
	/ø/	/œ/	/øː/	/ø/	/øː/	/œ/

The qualitative system has the advantage that it does not use length marks, and thus does not imply that the difference between the two sets of vowels is always one of length; on the other hand, it wrongly implies that the distinction between /ɑː/ and /a/ is one of quality. The quantitative system has the benefit of using a smaller set of symbols, and reduces the number of 'exotic' symbols, but it wrongly implies that the 'long' vowels are always longer than the 'short' ones. The third system combines the virtues (and the vices) of the other two. But it is important to stress that all three sets of symbols represent the same set of vowel phonemes and therefore that all three are, in phonological terms, perfectly adequate; the differences are a matter of convention and convenience only.

Because the distinction here is not always one of length it is perhaps unsatisfactory to use the terms 'long' and 'short' for these vowels, and some linguists prefer to refer to them as TENSE and LAX respectively. Exactly what physical or physiological reality attaches to these terms is not quite certain (it is claimed that in the former group the muscles of the tongue are tenser), but they do at least give us a way of referring to this particular distinction without the potentially misleading ambiguity of the terms 'long' and 'short', and without the paradox of having short 'long' vowels.

One further problem of vowel length in German deserves mention. Some linguists have noted a difference in the length of the 'same' vowel which is not due to its position in the word or whether it is stressed or not. Take, for example, the following pairs: *liest–liehst* (from *leihen*); *Blüte–blühte; Braut–braut; Rute–ruhte; reißt–reist; heute* ('today')–*heute* (from *heuen* 'to make hay'). It has been claimed that the vowel of the second word in each case is longer than that of the first word. This difference would relate to a difference of grammatical structure: in the second word of each pair the vowel in question is at the end of the verb stem, and is followed by an inflectional ending; in the first words of each pair the consonant following the vowel is part of the stem itself. If this claim is true (and it appears to be true for some

North German dialects), then we would need *three* distinct degrees of length for the vowel—'short', 'long', and 'overlong'—and hence an extra set of 'overlong' vowel phonemes. The validity of this claim is, however, in dispute. The majority of Standard German speakers probably do not normally make any difference of length here at all, though some *might* be able to make it if required to do so. In any event it is clearly a very marginal phenomenon, which cannot be regarded as properly characteristic of the Standard German system.

A similar problem to that of the 'short' versus 'long' distinction arises with the consonants. The phonetic description of typical allophones given in 2.7 has assumed that /p/, /t/, and /k/ are distinguished from /b/, /d/, and /g/ by the absence of voice in the former and its presence in the latter. However, this is not always true, and the 'voiced' set are not infrequently pronounced with no voice at all, e.g. *Bein* is pronounced [pain].[15] In what way, then, do they differ from the 'voiceless' set?

We have in fact already observed one characteristic of the 'voiceless' plosives at the beginning of a word: aspiration. These consonants are regularly aspirated in initial position before a vowel, whereas the 'voiced' plosives are not. We could therefore see the contrast between these sets in this position in the word as one of aspiration rather than of voice.[16] There are problems, however, since the vowels of the 'voiceless' set are not always aspirated. They remain unaspirated after /ʃ/ in words like *Span, Stein*, etc., and often in final position, too (though here the situation is a little more variable). However, it is noteworthy that it is precisely in these positions that the 'voiced' consonants do not occur. The only place where the contrast is primarily one of voice is between vowels, e.g. *Laken* (/lɑːkən/) versus *lagen* (/lɑːgən/), though even here contrasts are not frequent.

The problem of variability in the phonetic nature of this contrast is parallel to the problem of 'long' and 'short' vowels, and some linguists have adopted an analogous solution, using a label such as FORTIS ('strong') for the 'voiceless' set and LENIS ('weak') for the 'voiced'. Again it is not entirely clear what the phonetic reality behind such labels is, but they are useful as general

[15] The [p] here is not necessarily identical with allophones of the phoneme /p/, since it may preserve the somewhat 'laxer' articulation of a [b]. We might therefore prefer to call it a devoiced [b] rather than a [p], and transcribe it [b̥].

[16] Another proposal here is to treat the aspiration as an allophone of /h/, i.e. [pʰ] in *Pein* is to be analysed as /ph/, while [p] in *Bein* is /p/. We would then presumably not need the voiced plosives as phonemes at all! But the variability of the aspiration speaks against this approach: in other positions— in particular finally or in combinations such as that of the word *Akt*—the aspiration may be optional and variable in intensity, and it therefore seems more sensible to treat it as a property of the plosive consonant rather than as an independent phoneme.

classificatory terms. From the phonological point of view it is the *contrast* that is important here, not the precise manner in which it is manifested.

As mentioned above, any analysis must be justified by objective procedures. The list of words given in 2.7 to illustrate the phonemes also gives us some evidence for their validity, since *See, sah, so, sei,* and *Sau* all contain different vowels in the same position or 'context', so that the words are differentiated solely by the vowels. This is sufficient to show that all these vowels must be distinct phonemes. Unfortunately, it is rarely possible to find one particular context into which we can insert every vowel; there are, for example, no words *＊Suh, ＊Seu,* or *＊Süh,*[17] nor any single-syllable words ending in one of the short vowels (though these syllables can of course occur as parts of longer words). Similarly, /s/ (at least in the native vocabulary) is not found at the beginning of words[18] (in 'initial' position), and /z/ is not found at the end (in 'final' position): we have *sehen* (/ze:ən/) and *los* (/lo:s/) but no /*se:ən/ or /*lo:z/. Thus, these sounds do not contrast with one another in either of these positions. The only place where they can both occur is in the middle of a word between vowels (in 'intervocalic' position), e.g. *reisen* (/raizən/), *reißen* (/raisən/). This is sufficient proof that these are two distinct phonemes.

Some Problems in the Phonemic Analysis of German

Apart from these problems of demonstrating the validity of the contrasts between phonemes, there are also a number of controversial areas of the system where alternative analyses are possible. Consider first the diphthongs: /ai/, /au/, and /ɔi/.[19] Not only are these phonetically different from the other vowels in not having a static articulation, but they also do not have a 'long' versus 'short' (or 'tense' versus 'lax') distinction.

Since these vowels change their quality in the course of pronunciation, an obvious alternative to treating them as distinct vowel phonemes is to regard them as combinations of two phonemes: /a/ + /iː/, /a/ + /uː/, and /ɔ/ + /iː/. (The fact that our transcription uses a double symbol for each of these is not to be taken to imply this analysis, however; it is merely a convenience.) An advantage of treating the diphthongs as combinations is that we do not need to include them as extra phonemes; the vowel system becomes simpler, and the anomaly of these unpaired vowels is removed. Other things being equal, a simpler analysis is always favoured over a more complex one, and we

---

[17] The asterisk indicates a form which does not exist.

[18] /s/ may occur initially in some foreign loans, such as *Sex* and *City,* and it is normal in this position in Southern German in words such as *sehen* and *so.*

[19] There is a further diphthong /ʊi/ which occurs in only a few words, such as the interjection *Pfui!* It will be ignored here.

must therefore examine whether this approach actually does lead to a simplification.

But what are the phonemes which make up these diphthongs? Our transcription has opted for /a/ or /ɔ/ followed by /i/ or /u/ (the length mark has been omitted for convenience), but this is somewhat arbitrary, and it was pointed out in connection with 2.3 above that the ending points of the diphthongs are not the same as the simple vowels /iː/ and /uː/, but may be closer in quality to /eː/, /oː/, or /øː/. Furthermore, the second component is not really long, so that we could consider it to be the 'short' vowel in each case. These diphthongs could thus be seen as /aiː/, /auː/, /ɔiː/; /aeː/, /aoː/, /ɔøː/; /aɪ/, /aʊ/, /ɔɪ/; or /aɛ/, /aɔ/, /ɔœ/, among other possibilities. It would be difficult to decide which of these alternative analyses is to be preferred, and our transcription of these vowels as /ai/, /au/, /ɔi/ is something of a compromise.

The simplification of the vowel system produced by breaking the diphthongs into two separate parts must also be set against complications introduced elsewhere. The interpretation as single vowels ensures that each syllable has at most one vowel, but an analysis which divides them into two vowels entails accepting that the syllable may contain more than one vowel—an increase in the complexity of the structure of the syllable. A simplification in one part of our analysis (the vowel system) may thus introduce more complexity elsewhere (the structure of the syllable). This kind of dilemma is typical, and makes it clear that our analysis is always a compromise between competing requirements.

There is yet another analysis of the diphthongs which would avoid excessively complicating the syllable structure, but this involves further complications of a different kind. This would be to see the second part of these diphthongs not as vowels but as consonants. The boundary between vowels and consonants is not a sharp one, as it depends on the degree of constriction in the mouth, and certain sound-types (traditionally, and appropriately, called SEMIVOWELS) straddle the boundary between the two. Whether we treat them as vowels or as consonants is often not a matter of their phonetic characteristics at all, but of their phonological characteristics, i.e. how they are used in the language.[20] The initial sound of *jung* is a case in point; we could

---

[20] There is a terminological problem here with 'consonant' and 'vowel'. These can be defined in purely phonetic terms according to the presence or absence, respectively, of a constriction in the mouth, but we could also approach them phonologically, in terms of their role in the structure of syllables, vowels occurring in the 'centre' and consonants in the 'periphery' of the syllable. The problem with the 'semivowels' is that in these terms they are phonetically vowels but phonologically consonants. Some phoneticians find a terminological solution to this problem by using 'contoid' and

see it as a close front vowel [iː] or as a frictionless continuant consonant [j]. The same principle could be applied to the end points of the diphthongs: /ai/ could equally well be analysed as /aj/.

The analysis we favour in such cases will depend on the kinds of regularities which the language displays. Analysing German *jung* as /iːʊŋ/ or /ɪʊŋ/ is inappropriate, because it assumes a quite different kind of structure from what would otherwise be needed to describe German; it would introduce a new kind of diphthong with the main prominence on the second part (a so-called 'rising' diphthong) whereas the other German diphthongs have the prominence on the first part (they are 'falling' diphthongs). Treating this sound as a consonant, on the other hand, makes it conform to an existing kind of syllable structure consisting of vowel + consonant.

Since German syllables may end in a consonant, treating diphthongs as vowel + consonant constitutes a simplification, both of the vowel system (the diphthongs are no longer needed as separate phonemes) and of the range of syllable structures (we do not need to allow for syllables with more than one vowel). Unfortunately, this approach too brings unforeseen difficulties. Analysing [ai] as /a/ + /j/ will work well enough, but the consonant corresponding to [u] (the end point of /au/) is [w] (as in English *will*), and that corresponding to [y] (the end point of /ɔi/) is the 'labiopalatal' semivowel [ɥ] (the first sound of French *huit)*, and neither of these exists as an independent consonant in German. We are thus forced to introduce two more phonemes into the German consonant system, with no other motivation than to avoid having diphthongs in the vowel system.[21] On balance, it does not seem worth it.

Some time has been spent on the question of the appropriate analysis of the diphthongs, not because any of the solutions proposed are necessarily an improvement on simply regarding them as independent phonemes (indeed, treating them in this way seems after all to be the most straightforward and satisfactory) but because this is a good illustration of the kinds of procedures that are involved, and the kinds of arguments that must be deployed, in determining the system of phonemes of a language. It also demonstrates that it is hardly possible to establish, once and for all, *the* system of phonemes; a number of different possibilities exist, and there is not necessarily any one system that is obviously 'correct'. The system that we adopt is usually a

---

'vocoid' for phonetic description, so that 'consonant' and 'vowel' become purely phonological terms. The initial sound of *jung* is thus phonetically a vocoid but phonologically a consonant. This does not altogether solve the problems, however, as the distinction between the two categories is not completely sharp, either phonologically or phonetically.

[21] The final part of /ɔi/ could be identified with /j/, but this still leaves /w/ as an additional phoneme.

compromise between the demands of competing criteria. We look for the 'simplest' solution, but simplicity in one part of our analysis may entail a complication in another.

The affricates present a parallel problem: these sounds are complex, changing in the course of their articulation, and it is possible to see them either as single entities or as combinations. Thus, /pf/ and /ts/ can be analysed as /p/ + /f/ and as /t/ + /s/. The arguments here must again depend on the general pattern of phonemes in the language. We could see /pf/ and /ts/ as being parallel to other combinations: the pairs *hüpf* (/hʏpf/) and *hübsch* (/hʏpʃ/), or *Topfc* /tɔpf/) and *Torf* (/tɔrf/), show that the [p] and the [f] are independent in this position in the word, and this would justify treating /pf/ as a combination of phonemes. In initial position, however, this is not true to the same extent; the fact that the [f] cannot be replaced by anything else in words such as *Pflug* or *Pfropf* suggests that /pf/ should be treated as a single unit.

The arguments for a unitary treatment of /ts/ are analogous, though complications arise in final position because of the inflectional ending -*s*. If we treat the final affricate of *Graz* (/grɑːts/) as a single unit, what do we do with the identical sound of *Rats* (/rɑːts/), genitive of *Rat*, where the two components belong to different grammatical parts, and the /s/ is clearly an addition to the stem-final /t/? This suggests that there are two phonemic analyses of [ts]: as a single affricate in words such as *zu*, and as a sequence of /t/ and /s/ in *Rats*.

There is a further affricate that occurs in German but which has not been given phonemic status in 2.7. This is the postalveolar affricate [tʃ] in words like *deutsch* (/dɔitʃ/) or *rutschen* (/rʊtʃən/). This sound has a rather different status from /pf/ or /ts/, since its occurrence in initial position is restricted to foreign words such as *Tscheche* (/tʃɛxə/). In this position, therefore, it is probably best treated as a 'peripheral' part of the system. In other positions the arguments for treating the affricates as single phonemes are in any case less strong, and it can be seen as /t/ + /ʃ/.

The difficulties posed by diphthongs and affricates are very general in the phonemic analysis of languages. There are also a number of rather more specific questions raised by certain German sounds. Let us examine first of all the phoneme /ə/. This vowel is unpaired, occurring only short, and it also has other exceptional features. Its main characteristic is that it only occurs in unstressed syllables. Since the other vowels occur in stressed syllables, the question that arises here is whether this vowel is actually a separate phoneme, or whether it could be regarded as an allophone of one of the other vowels, occurring only in an unstressed position. The obvious vowel to link it with would be /ɛ/, since both are short, unrounded, mid vowels (the fact that both are spelt *e* should not really influence us here). The only way to disprove this hypothesis is to find cases where unstressed /ɛ/ contrasts with /ə/, but these are actually hard to find. Perhaps the nearest we can come are pairs such as *elend* (/ˈeːlɛnt/) ~ *Abend* (/ˈaːbənt/). This contrast would suggest that /ə/ should be regarded as a separate phoneme, distinct from /ɛ/.

There is a further difficulty when /ə/ occurs before /r/. The pronunciation of initial and final /r/ was mentioned earlier in order to exemplify the concept of the phoneme, and it was noted that in final position the /r/ is pronounced with very little constriction; final /r/ is more like a low back vowel. In combination with /ə/ the effect is to produce a more open variety of the /ə/, which we can represent as [ɐ]. Thus, *gute* and *bitte* are pronounced [guːtə] and [bɪtə], while *guter* and *bitter* are [guːtɐ] and [bɪtɐ]. Perhaps the simplest approach here is to regard the [ɐ] as the combined realization of the sequence of phonemes /ər/. But since [ɐ] is more like a vowel than a consonant, and since it contrasts with [ə], another possible analysis would be to consider [ɐ] to be a separate vowel phoneme. Thus, *gute* and *guter* would be /guːtə/ and /guːtɐ/ respectively. This avoids having the anomaly of a single sound representing two phonemes, but it complicates the system of phonemes.

Another solution can also be suggested here. A further characteristic of /ə/ is that it is frequently not pronounced at all when in combination with nasals (especially /n/) and with /l/, depending on the style of speech. There are alternative pronunciations of words such as those given in 2.15.

(2.15)	*geben*	/geːbən/ — /geːbm/	*Suppen*	/zʊpən/ — /zʊpm/
	Boden	/boːdən/ — /boːdn/	*reiten*	/raitən/ — /raitn/
	reißen	/raisən/ — /raisn/	*reisen*	/raizən/ — /raizn/
	eitel	/aitəl/ — /aitl/	*edel*	/eːdəl/ — /eːdl/
	Regen	/reːgən/ — /reːgŋ/	*Socken*	/zɔkən/ — /zɔkŋ/

In these cases the word may be pronounced with a /ə/ in a rather formal style, but more usually there is no /ə/, and the following nasal or lateral consonant is pronounced as a syllable by itself (a SYLLABIC CONSONANT).[22] (Note that a final /n/ may change its place of articulation, 'assimilating' to that of the preceding sound, when the /ə/ is omitted: see below.)

To some extent the situation with final [ɐ] is parallel to that which we find with the nasals and /l/, since in both cases a single sound occurs in place of a sequence of phonemes. Just as we find a syllabic version of /m/, /n/, /ŋ/, or /l/,

---

[22] A more elaborate proposal would be to treat the 'syllabicity' of the syllabic consonant as an 'allophone' of the /ə/. But this solution requires a rather unorthodox view of the nature of phonemes and allophones.

we could see the [ɐ] as a syllabic version of /r/, and consider *guter* to be phonemically /guːtr/.

The problem raised by the /r/ is actually wider than this, and affects virtually every German vowel. In the speech of many Standard German speakers such words as *hier, der, Tür, Wort*, etc. have no appreciable friction in the /r/, and the result is a diphthong, whose second part can be represented as [ɐ]. We thus find pronunciations such as those given in 2.16. We could recognize a whole new set of diphthongs ending in the vowel [ɐ], which would include both 'long' and 'short' varieties.[23]

(2.16)	*hier*	[hiːɐ]	*der*	[deːɐ]
	Tür	[tyːɐ]	*hört*	[høːɐt]
	irrt	[ɪɐt]	*sperrt*	[ʃpɛɐt]
	türkisch	[tʏɐkiʃ]	*Wörter*	[vœɐtɐ]

However, whereas it seemed preferable in the case of /ai/, /au/, and /ɔi/ to treat the second part as a vowel rather than as a consonant, here the most convincing analysis would be to regard it as a consonant, namely /r/, despite the fact that the sound is vowel-like, as this would otherwise entail an enormous increase in the complexity of the system. Thus [hiːɐ] can be represented as /hiːr/, [høːɐt] as /høːrt/, and so on.

Another area of difficulty is the relationship between the velar and palatal fricatives, [x] and [ç], both of which are spelt 'ch'. This is in fact one of the 'classic' problems of phonemic theory. Some examples of the distribution of these two sounds are given in 2.17.

(2.17)	*(i)*	*(ii)*	*(iii)*	*(iv)*
	[ç]	[ç]	[ç]	[x]
	riechen	Milch	Chemie	suchen
	nicht	welcher	Chirurg	Flucht
	rechnen	solcher	China	mochten
	rächen	Kirche		Rache
	leuchten	Lerche		rauchen
	reichen	durch		
	Bücher	Storch		
	flüchten	schnarchen		
	möchten	mancher		
		Mönch		

---

[23] If we accepted /ɐ/ as a phoneme, these would of course be susceptible to an alternative analysis as a sequence of two phonemes, the second being /ɐ/, in the same manner as the other diphthongs.

On the face of it, the solution is simple: these two sounds appear to be in complementary distribution and are therefore allophones of the same phoneme. It can be seen that [ç] occurs (i) after front vowels, (ii) after a consonant, and (iii) in initial position (though only in foreign words),[24] while [x] occurs only (iv) after a back or low vowel. On this evidence, the distribution of these two sounds is completely complementary, and they can be regarded as a single phoneme.

But there is one case where the two sounds appear to contrast. Consider the examples of 2.18.

(2.18) [ç]   [x]
        Kuhchen   *Kuchen*
        Frauchen   *rauchen*
        Pfauchen   *pfauchen*

All the words in this table with [ç] are diminutive forms with the ending -*chen*, and they contrast with the forms on the right with [x]. It must be said, of course, that these diminutive forms are somewhat unusual, since diminutives normally have 'Umlaut' of the stem vowel (see below), but some, at least are acceptable German words. Do these contrasts constitute evidence for regarding [ç] and [x] as distinct phonemes?

Some analysts do indeed find this evidence convincing, and establish /ç/ as a separate phoneme in the system, but it seems undesirable and, one might add, against the feeling of the native German speaker, to complicate our analysis in this way, especially as the relationship between these two sounds is otherwise such a clear case of complementary distribution. It is natural, therefore, that we should look for other explanations of these contrasts which would not necessitate recognizing /ç/ as a separate phoneme.

One way out is already suggested by the distribution of these sounds: we note that [ç], but not [x], occurs initially. An explanation for the difference between the [ç] of *Kuhchen* and the [x] of *Kuchen* would be that the sound is initial in the former but final in the latter, and that they are the regular allophones of /x/ in these positions; *Kuhchen* is /kuː + /xən/, while *Kuchen* is /kuːx/ + /ən/. But the problem here is that from the point of view of pronunciation both sounds are in an identical position: in both cases the

[24] Words with initial [ç], such as *Chemie* or *Chirurg*, are all foreign loans. Not all standard German speakers use [ç] here; some use /k/ instead. /k/ is also the pronunciation of initial *Ch*- in Greek loanwords for all speakers before back and low vowels and before consonants, e.g. *Charakter, Chor, Christ*. Some recent loanwords from Russian may also have [x] in initial position.

sound in question begins the second syllable ([kuː-çən], [kuː-xən]). There is a difference of word structure here, but it is a *grammatical* one: in *Kuchen* the fricative is part of the 'stem' of the word (see Ch. 3), while in *Kuhchen* it is part of the ending -*chen*.

This raises a number of very general questions about the nature of phonology which are of wider significance than merely determining the consonant phonemes of German. One view of phonology is that it is solely a matter of sounds and their relations; it must therefore be completely independent of grammar, and in describing phonological structure one must not bring in grammatical features of the sentences involved.[25] With this approach, we could not treat the [ç] as initial and the [x] as final solely on the basis of the grammatical structure of the word; we must demonstrate that they are also initial or final in some phonological sense. If we cannot do this, then we are forced to conclude that these two sounds are indeed separate phonemes. One ingenious proposal here is to introduce a special phonological device, a JUNCTURE, in effect the phonological equivalent of a grammatical boundary. The presence of such a juncture, by some phonologists considered to be a phoneme in its own right, but one lacking any independent sounds as its allophones, would thus distinguish the two cases of 2.18: *Kuhchen* would be /kuː + xən/ and *Kuchen* would be /kuːxən/, where /+/ is a juncture. Since they now occur in different contexts, [ç] and [x] can be treated as a single phoneme.

It would take us too far into matters of phonological theory to consider in detail the status of junctures. But it can be seen that such a concept follows naturally from the principle that phonological structure must be described in its own terms, without reference to grammar. But not all linguists accept the validity of this principle; most are prepared to bring grammatical considerations into phonological analysis. Provided we do this, we can find a solution to this problem: -*chen* is a word-like entity, and [ç] is the regular allophone occurring in initial position in the word. However, it still remains an anomaly, since the other instances of initial [ç] are all in foreign words, which –*chen* certainly is not.

Before leaving the problem of the palatal and velar fricatives, we may consider briefly another proposal that has been made. If we treat [ç] and [x] as distinct phonemes we shall find that the phoneme /x/ is now rather restricted in its distribution: it can never occur in initial position. Another phoneme, not too dissimilar in its phonetic manifestation, which also has a restricted distribution, is /h/, but this time it can occur *only* in initial position.

---

[25] Strict avoidance of such 'mixing of levels' was characteristic of American stucturalist linguistics. It is motivated by a desire to be completely objective and to avoid methodological circularity.

In this case, then, since [h] and [x] are in complementary distribution, we could establish a single phoneme with these two sounds as its allophones, the former occurring initially, the latter elsewhere. We could not do this if [ç] and [x] are regarded as the same phoneme, however, as both [ç] and [h] can occur in initial position.

A further area of controversy is the velar nasal /ŋ/. As noted in 2.13, this phoneme fits neatly into the system, and there would therefore appear to be no reason to question its status. It does differ from the other nasal consonants in its distribution, however, as we see from 2.19.

(2.19)	Initial	Intervocalic	Final
/m/	*müssen*	*summen*	*gutem*
/n/	*Nüsse*	*Brunnen*	*guten*
/ŋ/	—	*gesungen*	*Buchung*

But the absence of /ŋ/ in initial position is no mere accident; it is simply impossible here. Why should this be so? One suggestion is that [ŋ] should be analysed phonemically as /ng/, parallel to the spelling. In this case, it would hardly be surprising that it does not occur initially, since comparable combinations in other places of articulation do not occur here either: there is no initial /mb-/ or /nd-/, so why should there be initial /ng-/?

Two points can be made here. First, the interpretation of [ŋ] as /ng/ only works if there is no contrast between [ŋ] and [ŋg]. Certainly [ŋg] does occur in words such as *Kongo, Tango, Linguistik,* etc., but these are foreign words whose relevance for the German system is debatable. The sequence [ŋg] does not appear to occur in native German words (except in compounds such as *Junggeselle*, where the two sounds belong to different syllables).[26] This would lend credibility to this analysis. The second point, however, is that [ŋ] occurs not only by itself but also in combination with /k/, as in *Anker, Schrank* (/aŋkər/, /ʃraŋk/), etc. If /ŋ/ is not a phoneme in its own right, we would want to interpret the [ŋ] here as an allophone of /n/ rather than the realization of /ng/, as the sequence /ngk/ is implausible. This would mean, however, that [ŋ] would have two possible interpretations: as /n/ before /k/ and as /ng/ elsewhere. This overlapping of phonemes would not be acceptable to all phonologists. All in all, then, such an analysis does not seem convincing.

One final sound of German may be mentioned which does not appear on the consonant chart at all: the 'glottal stop' (phonetic symbol [ʔ]), produced

---

[26] English differs from German in this respect. Most English speakers have a /g/ in words such as *finger* and *longer*, but none in *singer*, whereas there is no /g/ in the Standard German pronunciation of *Finger, länger,* or *Sänger*.

by completely closing the glottis (vocal folds). This normally occurs before vowels which are initial in words or stems, e.g. in *erinnern* ([ʔɛrʔɪnərn]), but also occasionally elsewhere. Why is it not considered to be a German phoneme? One could certainly cite contrasts such as *verreisen* ~ *vereisen*~ ([fɛrraizən] ~ [fɛrʔaizən]), and it could also be seen as the plosive equivalent of the glottal fricative /h/ (which similarly occurs only in initial position). However, its status is quite different from that of /h/; it is variable and often disappears—compare *über* and *vorüber* (where the glottal stop disappears in the compound) with *her* and *vorher* (where the /h/ is preserved)—and it is automatic and predictable. It is therefore best treated not as a phoneme in its own right, but as an auxiliary and non-phonological feature which appears before initial vowels.

Peripheral Phonemes

Our discussion so far has been concerned only with what we have called the 'central' phoneme system of German, i.e. with those phonemes used by German speakers in their native vocabulary (or in foreign words that are fully assimilated into the language). It was pointed out above that other sounds may also be used by German speakers, especially in words of foreign origin. Although these 'peripheral' phonemes cannot be entirely excluded from the phonology of the language, they do not have the same status as the central phonemes, and do not form a comparable system.

It is not only foreign sounds that can be anomalous, however, as even the sounds of native words may not be thoroughly integrated with the rest of the system. A case in point is the vowel /æː/, which is a little unusual since, though long, it is not paired with a short vowel.[27] Its existence thus seems to disturb the regularity of the system. However, this vowel turns out to be rather marginal in other respects, too. Many speakers, even those who can be said to speak a variety of the standard pronunciation, use it only very infrequently, or indeed, not at all, and employ /eː/ instead. It could thus be seen as a 'peripheral' phoneme.

This vowel is not necessarily peripheral for all speakers; for those who use it consistently it is a central part of the system. But many speakers are inconsistent, using it only in those very few cases where there is a need to contrast it with /eː/. Pairs of words where this might be necessary are, for example, *gebe* and *gäbe*, or *sehe* and *sähe*.

---

[27] In 2.5 /ɛ/ is paired with /eː/, though in fact it is closer in quality to /æː/ than it is to /eː/. An alternative pairing would be /ɛ/ and /æː/, leaving /eː/ unpaired. But this is less satisfactory, since /eː/ is a central part of the standard vowel system, while /æː/ is marginal and more variable in occurrence.

Somewhat different is the case where a vowel of this quality is used before /r/, as in *Bär, wäre*, etc. For some speakers this sound appears to occur only before /r/, and the closer vowel does not occur in this position: words like *sehr, Ehre*, etc. also have the more open vowel. Such speakers do not have two distinct phonemes in their system, since [æː] and [eː] are in complementary distribution and are therefore allophones of the same phoneme. But this is not typical of Standard German speakers. Note also that speakers with a more open allophone of /eː/ before /r/ are also likely to have a more open allophone of /oː/ in the same position (e.g. in *Ohr, Tor*, etc.), though this does not cause the same sort of phonological problem, since there is no back vowel phoneme comparable to /æː/.

A more serious problem is posed by foreign sounds, as discussed earlier. Some sounds used in foreign words are indisputably foreign, and would only be used by German speakers if they happened to be quite familiar with the language from which the words are borrowed. These include the English vowel of *lunch* (phonetic symbol [ʌ]). A more German pronunciation of this word would use the German vowel /a/.

In other cases, however, there may be no German alternatives to foreign sounds. One such case is presented by the French nasal vowels. We find pronunciations such as [ʃɑ̃sə] (*Chance*), [tɛ̃] (*Teint*), [pardɔ̃] (*Pardon*), or [parfœ̃] (*Parfum*). Attempts are often made to 'Germanize' these vowels, e.g. in *Pardon* /pardɔŋ/ or *Salon* /zalɔŋ/, and in Austria final *-on* is regularly pronounced /oːn/, e.g. /balkoːn/ (*Balkon*). But in the majority of cases the words remain recognizably foreign, and the nasal vowels must be treated as peripheral phonemes in the German system.

Another case of a foreign sound which is widely used by German speakers is /ʒ/, which is found in a number of words of French origin, such as *Genie, Garage* (/ʒeːniː/, /garɑːʒə/), etc. This sound is perhaps not quite as isolated from the native system as the nasal vowels, as it can be fitted comfortably into the central system as the voiced counterpart of /ʃ/, but the fact that it is frequently replaced by its voiceless equivalent native phoneme (/ʃeːniː/, /garɑːʃə/) suggests that it is not fully integrated.

Another problem is presented by un-German vowel combinations, which are found in many words from Greek or Latin. Some examples are given in 2.20.

(2.20)				
	speziell	/iːɛ/	*asiatisch*	/iːɑː/
	Nation	/iːoː/	*Kloake*	/oːɑː/
	poetisch	/oːeː/	*ritual*	/uːɑː/
	virtuos	/uːoː/	*Hyäne*	/yːæː/

Vowel combinations of this kind are not normal in native words, as, if they are diphthongs, they are of a different kind from the native ones (they are 'rising' diphthongs, i.e. the second part is more prominent). We could treat the first element as a consonant— /ʃpeːtsjɛl/, /aːzjaːtɪʃ/, etc.—though this will only do for those starting with [iː], as there is no corresponding consonant for those starting with other sounds. Again it would unduly complicate the analysis to attempt to include such vowels as additional phonemes in the native system; in so far as they are genuine diphthongs and not merely sequences of vowels, they are best treated as part of the peripheral system.

Phonemic Structure

So far we have considered the system of German phonemes and the problems that arise in demonstrating its validity. Another aspect of phonology is the *use* of this system in the formation of the words of the language, i.e. how these phonemes can be combined into larger structures. This part of phonology is concerned with the PHONEMIC STRUCTURE of words (sometimes called PHO-NOTACTICS). Just as different languages may have different systems of phon-emes, they may also have different phonemic structures. For example, although both English and German have voiced plosives (/b/, /d/, /g/), these may occur at the end of a word in English, but not in German.

We have already had reason to examine the distribution of phonemes in words as a way of determining possible contrasts, and we noted that not all phonemes occur in all positions. There are, however, different kinds of restrictions on the occurrence of phonemes. The absence of some words, e.g. *Suh or *Seu, is entirely fortuitous; it is an accidental gap, as these would be perfectly good German words if they happened to exist (they can always be invented, e.g. as brand names for washing powders). The absence of stressed short vowels at the end of a word, however, is not accidental; words such as /*zɛ/ or /*za/ are simply impossible in modern German; the gap here is *systematic* rather than accidental.[28] Accidental gaps are of no significance for the possible combinations of sounds, while systematic gaps reflect genuine restrictions on the occurrence of phonemes. In investigating the phonemic structure of German words we may discount accidental gaps; systematic gaps, restrictions on *possible* structures, are what concern us here.

---

[28] Short /a/ occurs finally in foreign words such as *rosa* and also in some place names such as *Jena* and *Fulda*, but here it is unstressed. /ə/ also occurs finally, but again it is never stressed.

The Syllable

The most important stretch of speech to consider in determining the possible combinations of phonemes is the SYLLABLE. There are, however, different kinds of syllables, such as 'stressed' and 'unstressed' (see below), and syllables which are 'roots' and those which are 'affixes' (i.e. prefixes or suffixes—see Chapter 3), and these may differ in their structure. Roots may also have a different structure in isolation from when they are followed by affixes. The most useful starting point is the stressed monosyllabic root, spoken in isolation. We shall also restrict ourselves initially to the native German part of the vocabulary.

At the simplest level of description, we could describe the structure of stressed root-syllables in terms of the *number* of phonemes they contain, but this would not be very revealing. If we are to determine the regularities underlying this structure we must consider the *class* of phonemes involved. As an initial classification we shall use consonants (C) and vowels (V), but our classification will ultimately need to become more detailed than this.

A formula to describe the possible structures of stressed monosyllabic roots would be the following:

(C)(C)(C)V(C)(C)(C)(C)

What this formula means is simply that all such syllables must have a vowel, which may be preceded by up to three consonants and followed by up to four consonants (the optional elements are enclosed in brackets). Most of the possibilities are exemplified in 2.21.

(2.21)

V	*Ei*	VC	*Uhr*	VCC	*Art*	VCCC	*Angst*	VCCCC	*Ernst*
CV	*Kuh*	CVC	*Buch*	CVCC	*Wolf*	CVCCC	*Dunst*	CVCCCC	*Herbst*
CCV	*Schnee*	CCVC	*Stein*	CCVCC	*Stern*	CCVCCC	*Brunst*		
CCCV	*Stroh*	CCCVC	*Strick*	CCCVCC	*Strand*				

Not all the theoretically possible structures are represented here, as there are some accidental gaps with the more complex structures. Though there may in principle be up to three consonants before the vowel, and up to four consonants after it, the words *Ernst* and *Herbst* seem to be the only words (other than inflected forms) which have four final consonants. Similarly, no example has been found of the structure CCCVCCC.

Such a description does not tell us very much about the permissible structures of German words, since it is clear that it is not possible to have just any combination of three consonants initially or four finally. Words such as *Rtschick* or *Hetspr* are not mere accidental gaps in the German vocabulary, despite the fact that they are apparently of the same structure, and contain the same consonants, as *Strick* and *Herbst* respectively. We need, therefore, to consider in more detail the kinds of consonants and vowels that are possible in the various positions in the syllable.

It is important to note here that the syllable is not simply a string of phonemes; it has a *structure*, i.e. it is made up of different parts. As we have seen, the syllable can potentially consist of a vowel, preceded and followed by a number of consonants. This gives us three basic parts: the initial consonant(s), known as the ONSET, the vowel, called the NUCLEUS (or PEAK), and the final consonant(s), called the CODA. Thus, in *Frist* /fr/ is the onset, /ɪ/ the nucleus, and /st/ the coda. The nucleus and the coda appear to be more closely linked to each other than they are to the onset, since, for example, rhyme depends on words having the same combination of the two: *Frist* rhymes with *List* and *ist*, but not with *Fritz* or *Frost*. The nucleus and coda therefore together form a constituent part of the syllable, known as the RHYME, and the structure of the syllable /frɪst/ can be represented as in 2.22, where O = Onset, R = Rhyme, N = Nucleus, and Co = Coda.

(2.22)

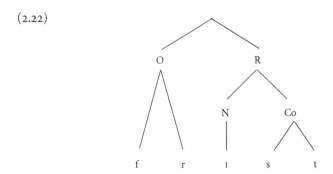

As far as the vowels are concerned (i.e. those phonemes that can occur in the nucleus of the syllable), all are found in stressed monosyllables with the exception of [ə], though they cannot all occur in all kinds of syllable. We may distinguish between OPEN and CLOSED syllables, the latter having a coda, the former not (we may say that the coda is 'empty' or that such syllables have 'zero coda'). All of these vowels can occur in closed syllables, but only the 'long' vowels can occur in open syllables. Thus, we may have /zeː/, /zoː/, /zaː/, and so on, but not /*zɛ/, /*zɔ/, or /*za/. The distinction between long and short vowels is therefore not just a matter of phonetic difference within the vowel system, but is also one of how the sounds are used in the construction of words. There is also a relationship between vowel length and the number of final consonants:

long vowels are more often found before single consonants and short ones before consonant clusters. But this is only a tendency, not an absolute restriction.[29] There are also a number of more specific restrictions which defy generalization: long vowels are rare before /ŋ/, /pf/, /ts/, and /ʃ/, and diphthongs do not occur before /ŋ/ or /r/.[30] These restrictions and tendencies are a further indication of the close relationship between the nucleus and the coda within the rhyme of the syllable.

This relationship may lead to a rather more radical analysis of the structure of the syllable. If short vowels cannot occur without a coda, but long vowels can, then we might conclude that long vowels have, in a sense, an inbuilt coda, which makes a further coda unnecessary. We could therefore regard a long vowel as consisting of two parts, as in 2.23(i). More radical still would be to regard the second part of the vowel as equivalent to a coda consonant, and to analyse the syllable as in 2.23(ii). This would mean that all syllables have a coda—a nice generalization. However, this analysis is open to the objection that it treats part of the vowel as a consonant, and thus appears to violate the phonetic facts.[31]

(2.23)

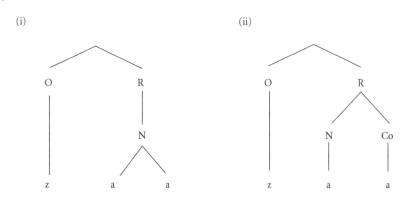

(i)   (ii)

---

[29] In some cases there are historical explanations for the restrictions. In the development of modern German from Middle High German, the short vowels were lengthened in open syllables and the long vowels shortened in closed syllables; hence the present distribution. However, other developments, such as the simplification of double consonants, dialect mixture, foreign loans, analogical lengthening of vowels, etc., have complicated the picture. We are not concerned with historical explanations here, of course, but only with the current distribution of the phonemes.

[30] These distributional restrictions may offer some support for certain of the analyses presented earlier. Since long vowels are infrequent before consonant clusters, the fact that they are also infrequent before the affricates and /ŋ/ might be regarded as evidence that these sounds should also be analysed as consonant clusters.

[31] It could also be claimed that all syllables have an onset, since independent syllables beginning with a vowel are preceded by a glottal stop, filling the onset position. However, as we have noted, this is a purely *phonetic* phenomenon; *phonologically* speaking we could still maintain that such syllables have no onset.

In the case of the consonants there are much stricter limitations on occurrence in specific positions in the syllable. Most consonants can occur alone in the onset, the only exceptions being /ŋ/ and /s/. /x/ (pronounced [ç]) occurs initially only in words of foreign origin, and even /s/ may occasionally be found here, e.g. in *City* (/sɪti/). But in groups of two or more consonants their occurrence is more restricted. Two-consonant onset clusters fall into two basic types, as we see from 2.24.

(2.24) (i)   pl-   *Platz*   pr-   *Preis*   tr-   *treu*
              bl-   *blau*   br-   *braun*   dr-   *drei*
              kl-   *klein*   kr-   *Kreis*
              gl-   *Glut*   gr-   *grau*
              pfl- *Pflaume*   pfr- *pfropfen*
              fl-   *Floh*   fr-   *frei*
        (ii) ʃp-   *Span*   ʃt-   *Stein*   ʃm-   *Schmuck*
              ʃn-   *Schnee*   ʃl-   *schlau*   ʃr-   *Schrank*
              ʃv-   *schwer*

Combinations of group (i) consist of a plosive, affricate, or fricative followed by /l/ or /r/; those of group (ii) consist of /ʃ/ followed by another consonant. (There are also a few other miscellaneous combinations: /kn-/, /kv-/, /gn-/, and /tsv-/.) Note that in the first group /l/ does not occur after the alveolar consonants /t/, /d/, and /ts/, and in the second group /ʃ/ does not occur before /k/. It would be possible to place /ʃl-/ and /ʃr-/ in either of groups (i) and (ii).

Onset clusters consisting of three consonants could in theory be very numerous, but in fact there are only three possibilities.

ʃpl-(*Splitter*)   ʃpr-(*Spritze*)   ʃtr-(*Strick*)

These are all of the same type: /ʃ/ followed by a voiceless plosive (apart from /k/, which does not occur after /ʃ/), followed by /l/ or /r/ (as with the two-consonant clusters, /l/ does not occur after /t/).

These combinations of two and three consonants are not at all arbitrary, since, with few exceptions, only consonants of certain kinds can occur in specific positions. The plosives, fricatives, and affricates form one group, which can occur initially in conjunction with /l/ and /r/, while the latter two phonemes form another group which can combine with these. /ʃ/ has a special status, both in two-consonant clusters and in three-consonant clusters. Because they tend to be used in similar ways in many languages, /l/ and /r/ are sometimes grouped together under the traditional term LIQUID, though this is not a technical term of phonetics. Plosives, fricatives, and affricates can similarly be included in a general category of OBSTRUENTS.

Coda clusters (occurring after the nucleus) may contain up to four phonemes, and the possibilities are a little more complex than in onset position,
though we shall not examine them in detail as the principles are the same. In
monosyllabic roots without any affixes (endings) we find all the consonants
except /b/, /d/, /g/, /v/, /z/, /j/, and /h/. Apart from /j/ and /h/, which are
somewhat isolated in the system, the others are the voiced obstruents, which
are also those voiced consonants that are paired with voiceless ones. The only
voiced consonants that can occur here are the liquids and nasals—which do
not have voiceless counterparts.

Two-consonant coda clusters are very varied and difficult to systematize.
Those consonants that cannot occur alone here (the voiced obstruents, and /j/
and /h/) do not occur in these clusters either. The occurring clusters fall
largely into three groups (there are also a few others, such as a plosive
followed by a fricative /-ks/, /-tʃ/, etc.):

(i)   /l/ or /r/ followed by an obstruent or nasal (e.g. -lt, -rt, -rm, -rpf, -rf, -lx,
      -ls, etc.);
(ii) a nasal followed by an obstruent (e.g. -mt, -ŋk, -mpf, -nx, etc.);
(iii) an obstruent followed by /t/ (e.g. -kt, -tst, -st, -xt).

It is notable that many of the most common coda clusters are mirror images
of onset clusters. Thus, we find pr- and -rp, pl- and -lp, pfr- and -rpf, ʃt- and
-tʃ, ʃr- and -rʃ, etc. Not all clusters are reversible in this way, however; those of
the third group (obstruent + /t/) cannot occur in reverse order in the onset
position.

Three-consonant coda clusters are much more restricted. With the exception of marginal cases such as the /-rps/ of *Knirps* or the /-rks/ of *Marx*, the
final consonant is always /-t/. The most common are given in 2.25.

(2.25)	-pst	*Obst*	-kst	*Axt*	-nst	*Gunst*
	-ŋst	*Angst*	-nft	*sanft*	-lst	*Schwulst*
	-rst	*Wurst*	-rkt	*Markt*	-rxt	*Furcht*
	-rtst	*Arzt*	-rft	*Werft*		

Four-consonant coda clusters are very rare. There really are only two:

-rpst   *Herbst*   -rnst   *ernst*

These are simply three-consonant clusters preceded by /r/.

On the basis of these combinations of two, three, and four final consonants
it is to some extent possible to establish a general scheme for the order of
consonants in coda clusters: 'liquids' (/r/ and /l/) precede nasals, and both

of these precede obstruents. /r/ also precedes /l/ (e.g. *Kerl*). The order is thus:

r—l—nasal—obstruent

But it is difficult to order the nasals or obstruents among themselves; the nasals do not occur together, while plosives and fricatives occur in various orders.

This sequence of phonemes proceeds—more or less—from the more 'vowel-like' to the more 'consonant-like'. Since, as we have seen, it is also in some respects a mirror image of the onset consonant clusters, the structure of the syllable as a whole could be said to reflect a SONORITY SCALE of phonemes. The nucleus of the syllable (the vowel) is the most 'sonorous', and it is flanked by progressively less sonorous phonemes. However, this principle is not without exceptions; onset clusters such as /ʃp-/ or /ʃt-/, and coda clusters such as /-ps/, violate it, since the plosives /p/ and /t/ are evidently less sonorous than the fricatives /ʃ/ and /s/.

German roots may also be disyllabic (with two syllables), e.g. *Vater, Apfel*. The most complex structure found in these words is:

$(C)(C)(C)V_1(C)(C)(C)V_2(C)(C)$

Some typical examples are given in 2.26.

(2.26)	VV	*Ehe*	CVV(C)	*Ruhe, Feuer*
	VCV(C)	*Affe, Ofen*	CVCV(C)	*Henne, Messer*
	VCCV(C)	*Erbe, After*	CVCCV(C)	*Gurke, Kerker*
	VCCCV(C)	*Ernte, Elster*	CVCCCV(C)	*Bürste, Fenster*
	CCVV(C)	*Brühe, Schleier*		
	CCVCV(C)	*Stange, Klammer*	CCCVCV(C)	*Straße, Sprudel*
	CCVCCV(C)	*Schlampe, Pflaster*	CCCVCCVC	*Sprenkel*

The consonants that can occur in the middle of such words are very similar to those that occur word-finally in monosyllabic roots, but with two important differences: the number of consonants is limited to three, and, more importantly, it is possible to have voiced obstruents. There are still some restrictions, however: the voiced plosives are very rare here after the short vowels. Words such as *Roggen, baggern, schmuggeln* are somewhat exceptional (they are, in fact, loanwords from Low German). Because voiced obstruents are no longer excluded, we can add two-consonant clusters consisting of a liquid or nasal followed by voiced plosives or fricatives, e.g. /-rb-/ (*Erbe*), /-nd-/ (*Sünde*), /-mz-/ (*Bremse*), etc.

There are one or two simple roots in German with more than two syllables, e.g. *Holunder, Wacholder, Hornisse*, but such forms are very rare, and the structure of the syllables is in all these cases fairly simple.

There are a number of possible ways of describing the syllable structures involved in words of more than one syllable. Each syllable naturally has a nucleus, but the main question is how we should analyse the consonants occurring between the nuclei (the 'intervocalic' consonants), since they could be the coda of the first syllable, the onset of the second, or be shared between the two syllables. There is some evidence for a PRINCIPLE OF MAXIMAL ONSETS, according to which as many consonants as possible are made part of the onset of the second syllable, as long as this does not create onsets which could not occur in independent syllables. Thus, for example, *Affe* and *Henne* will be analysed as /a- fə/ and /hɛ- nə/, but *Kerker* and *Schlampe* as /kɛr-kər/ and /ʃlam-pə/, since */rkər/ and */mpə/ are not possible syllables. However, there are some difficulties here, since although for the sake of consistency we would want to analyse *Messer, Fenster,* and *Finger* as /mɛ-sər/, /fɛn-stər/, and /fɪ-ŋər/, respectively, */s-/, */st-/, and */ŋ-/ are all impossible onsets in independent syllables in German. It will also be noted that in the case of *Messer* and *Finger*, the first syllable has a short vowel with no coda, which is not possible in isolated syllables. Evidently, then, if these analyses are correct, then the structure of syllables *within* words is not necessarily the same as that found in words in isolation.

One solution to this is to regard the intervocalic consonants as shared between syllables (AMBISYLLABIC), and therefore simultaneously the coda of the first syllable and the onset of the second. Under this analysis, *Messer* would be represented as in 2.27. Against this is the fact that the resulting structure is rather curious, since it is not clear where the boundary between the syllables is, or, indeed, if there is one at all.

(2.27)

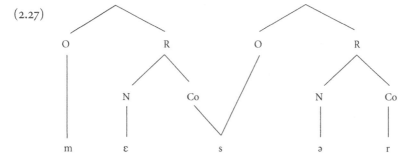

As an inflecting language (see Chapter 3), German has many *affixes* (suffixes and prefixes) that are added to these roots and which may further increase the phonological complexity of the word. The affixes themselves are generally very simple in structure, however. Some affixes consist merely of consonants (/-s/, /-t/, /-n/, /-st/, /-nt/), others of a vowel (/-ə/), a vowel and one or two consonants (/-ər/, /- ən/, /-əs/, /-əm/, /- ət/, /ɛr-/, /-əst/, /- ənt/), a consonant and a vowel (/bə-/, /gə-/), or consonant, vowel, and consonant (/fɛr-/). Since several of these can be strung together to form complex words, the structure of the word as a whole can become quite complex (e.g. *er— inn—er—t—est*), but the structure of the syllables of which it is composed remains fairly simple. When suffixes consisting only of consonants are added to a root, they naturally increase the complexity of the structure of its final syllable. In these circumstances we can have final consonant clusters that are still more complex than those we have seen so far, e.g. in *des Herbsts*,[32] *Ernsts Hut*, etc., with five final consonants in each case.

Phonological Features

We have so far assumed that all words and syllables can ultimately be broken down into phonemes, and that these are the smallest elements out of which the words are composed. But phonemes are not completely indivisible. In describing typical allophones of the German phonemes we have used phonetic categories such as tongue height, backness, and lip rounding for the vowels, and place and manner of articulation and voice for the consonants. Although phonemes can be seen in terms of minimal contrasts between words, we could in a sense say that it is not so much the phonemes that distinguish different words as these phonetic attributes. What distinguishes *Bein* from *Pein* is not that one has /b/ and the other /p/, but rather that the first consonant of *Bein* is voiced and that of *Pein* voiceless; what distinguishes *Bein* from *dein* is that it has a labial as opposed to an alveolar articulation at the beginning; what distinguishes it from *Wein* is the plosive rather than the fricative articulation, and what distinguishes it from *mein* is that it has an oral (i.e. non-nasal) as opposed to a nasal articulation. Far from being a minimal unit, therefore, the phoneme /b/ is seen to be a collection of simultaneous contrasting characteristics.

This principle lies at the heart of the theory of DISTINCTIVE FEATURES. According to this theory, it is contrasting features such as these, rather than phonemes, that are the basic phonological units of a language. Just as an analysis in terms of phonemes must establish a set of phonemes for a given language and examine their relationships, so an analysis in terms of distinct-

---

[32] A form such as *Herbsts* is, of course, likely to be replaced by *Herbstes*.

ive features must determine what the appropriate features are, and how they may be combined.

It must be emphasized that distinctive features are not simply phonetic properties of the allophones of the phonemes; as with other phonological concepts, they are somewhat abstract. As we have seen in our consideration of the German phoneme system, phonology is concerned not so much with the sounds themselves as with their relationships, and distinctive features are to be interpreted as products of such relationships.

To see what this means consider the phoneme /l/. A typical allophone of this phoneme might be described phonetically as a voiced alveolar lateral. But when we examine the other phonemes with which /l/ contrasts we do not really need to take account of all these phonetic characteristics. There is no voiceless lateral consonant in German, nor, indeed, any other lateral consonant at any other place of articulation. To identify this phoneme it is sufficient to refer to its lateral articulation; it is this characteristic which distinguishes /l/ from other phonemes. Although /l/ has a variety of phonetic features associated with it, only one, its lateral articulation, is DISTINCTIVE.[33]

Phonemes can thus be decomposed into a number of distinctive features, but they will also contain other features which do not serve to distinguish them from other phonemes. In the case of the German /l/, these will include such features as voice and the alveolar articulation. Since these features do not contribute to distinguishing the /l/ from other phonemes they are said to be REDUNDANT.

We see, therefore, that distinctive features are a corollary of the contrasts (technically called OPPOSITIONS) between the phonemes of the system. Which particular features are needed to identify the various phonemes of the language, and which are redundant, will depend on the system as a whole, as it is this system which determines the oppositions. A language in which a voiceless lateral exists as a separate phoneme from the voiced lateral will require 'voice' to be regarded as a distinctive feature of the latter; if there is a palatal lateral phoneme in addition to the alveolar lateral then the feature 'alveolar' will also become distinctive.

Since distinctive features are derived from phonological contrasts it also follows that their phonetic content is relative, rather than absolute. We have already noted that the contrast between 'voiced' and 'voiceless' plosives is variable, being sometimes a matter of voice and sometimes of aspiration. What is significant is the contrast itself, not its phonetic nature. Nevertheless,

---

[33] In fact, we shall present a somewhat different analysis of /l/ below, in terms of the set of features to be introduced shortly.

we can still see the contrast as involving the same distinctive feature in all its manifestations, since the features are products of oppositions, and therefore relative. Though in one position there may be a difference of voice (e.g. [p] versus [b]), and in another position a difference of aspiration ([pʰ] versus [p]), there is only one opposition, which we might characterize as *fortis* ('strong') versus *lenis* ('weak').

A further, though more controversial, consequence of deriving distinctive features from phonological oppositions is that features are matters of 'yes' or 'no': a phoneme either has or does not have the feature in question, with no other possibilities. This is because the relationships between phonemes that we are dealing with are basically those of sameness or difference; we want to know whether two given sounds are the same phoneme or not, and the answer to this question can only be 'yes' or 'no', with nothing in between. The features are therefore regarded as BINARY, and can be represented as either + or −. Thus, if we take the opposition between /z/ and /s/ to be one of voice, /z/ can be classified as [+voice], and /s/ as [−voice].

Binary features work well enough for oppositions such as those of voice, length, nasality, etc., where only two values are required, but they are less plausible for those oppositions where more than two phonemes are arranged along a single phonetic scale, in particular distinctions of tongue height for the vowels and place of articulation for the consonants. In these cases, though it follows logically from the nature of oppositions, the restriction to two values is less convenient. In order to maintain the principle of binarity in such cases, more than one feature will be required to distinguish the phonemes along a single phonetic parameter. For example, if we have the vowels /iː/, /eː/, and /ɑː/, differing in tongue height, we cannot distinguish them simply by using the feature [+high] versus [−high], as this allows only two values; we shall need an additional feature, such as [+low]/[−low], in order to distinguish them.

Although the theory of distinctive features has been widely adopted, there are different views as to the nature of the features themselves. The features we have referred to so far have been based on the standard phonetic classification of consonants and vowels, i.e. on articulatory categories. An alternative approach uses acoustic or auditory labels, such as 'strident', 'grave', 'sharp', etc. This has some advantages, as it allows certain sounds to be grouped together as sharing the same feature value which, in articulatory terms, would have to be regarded as different. This acoustic or auditory approach will not, however, be adopted here.

Feature Analysis of the German Phonemes

We may now consider the appropriate feature analysis of the German phonemes. This is not altogether straightforward, and the analysis presented here is just one of several different possible alternatives. In the interests of clarity we shall also take little account of the various alternative solutions to the phonemic analysis of German.

Taking the system as a whole, we find that the major opposition is between those sounds which have a CONSONANTAL articulation (i.e. some form of constriction in the mouth) and those which do not. The former are [+consonantal], the latter [−consonantal]. This distinction corresponds to the classification into consonants and vowels that has been adopted above, except that /j/ has no such constriction, and is phonetically like a vowel. /j/ differs from the vowels proper, however, in not being syllabic, i.e. in not forming the centre of a syllable; the vowels are therefore [+syllabic], while the consonants (including /j/) are [−syllabic]. A further major distinction is between those sounds that are obstruents (the plosives, fricatives, and affricates) and those that are not; the latter, including the nasal consonants, /l/, /j/, and the vowels, may be called SONORANTS; they are [+sonorant], while obstruents are [−sonorant]. /r/ is problematical; in some of its allophones it is a fricative (and therefore an obstruent) but in others it is more vowel-like (and therefore sonorant). The distribution of this phoneme in words is, as we saw above, similar to that of /l/ (they are both 'liquids'), and this too supports the [+sonorant] interpretation.

These features give us the basic classes of phonemes given in 2.28 ('consonantal' can be abbreviated to [cns], 'syllabic' to [syll], and 'sonorant' to [son]).

(2.28)   [−cns, +syll, +son]:   all the vowels
         [−cns, −syll, +son]:   the semivowel: /j/
         [+cns, −syll, +son]:   nasals and 'liquids': /m, n, ŋ, l, r/
         [+cns, −syll, −son]:   all the remaining consonants

Since all the sounds that are [−cns] (the vowels and /j/) are also [+son], the latter feature is redundant for them, and need not be included in their specification. Moreover, since /j/ is the only sound that is both [−cns] and [−syll] (i.e. it is the only semivowel) it requires no further specification whatever.

The 'true' consonants (i.e. those that are [+cns]) must be further differentiated according to place and manner of articulation, and, for the obstruent ([-son]) consonants, according to whether they are voiced or not (assuming that 'voice' is the distinction involved). As far as manner of articulation is concerned, there is an opposition in the case of the non-sonorants between 'stop' consonants (with a complete closure of the air passage, i.e. plosives and affricates) and CONTINUANT consonants (fricatives). The former are [−continuant], the latter [+continuant]. The feature AFFRICATE can be used to distinguish the two categories of stops: affricates are [+affricate], stops are [−affricate].[34] The sonorant consonants are, like the fricatives, continuants, but since this applies to all of them the feature [+continuant] is redundant here. They can be further divided, using the feature NASAL, into [+nasal]) and [−nasal]. We thus obtain the specifications of 2.29, where 'continuant' is abbreviated to [cnt], 'affricate' to [aff], and 'nasal' to [nas].

(2.29) [−son, −cnt, −aff]:   the plosives: /p, t, k, b, d, g/
        [−son, −cnt, +aff]:   the affricates: /pf, ts/
        [−son, +cnt]:   the fricatives: /f, v, s, z, ʃ, x, h/
        [+son, +nas]:   the nasals: /m, n, ŋ/
        [+son, −nas]:   the 'liquids' /l, r/

The characterization of oppositions involving place of articulation raises problems, since, from the phonetic point of view, there are several different contrasts along a single dimension, and, as noted above, these are difficult to specify using only binary distinctions. One solution is to distinguish 'front' consonants, which are given the feature ANTERIOR ([+ant]), from those pronounced further back, and those involving the 'central' part of the mouth, called CORONAL consonants ([+cor]), from the others. Most of the continuum of places of articulation can therefore be broken down into these two binary oppositions. The only opposition that is not covered by these features is that between the velar consonants (/k/, /g/, and /x/) and the glottal fricative /h/, all of which are [−ant, −cor] (the uvular /r/ has already been taken care of as it is [+son], and merely needs to be distinguished from /l/ by being [−ant]). /h/ can be distinguished from the velars as a LOW ([+lo]) consonant. This gives us the categories of 2.30.

(2.30) [+ant, −cor]:   labials
        [+ant, +cor]:   alveolars
        [−ant, +cor]:   postalveolar (/ʃ/)
        [−ant, −cor, −lo]:   velars
        [−ant, −cor, +lo]:   glottal (/h/)

The only remaining opposition within the consonant system involves VOICE, giving [+vce] and [−vce] consonants (though we may prefer a more general feature such as *fortis*).

---

[34] A label for this feature which has also been used is [+delayed release].

The vowel system is rather simpler and more symmetrical than the consonant system, but again we must analyse a phonetic continuum into a number of binary phonological oppositions. The three contrasting heights of the German vowel system (high, mid, low) can be described in terms of the features HIGH and LOW, where the high vowels (/iː/, /ɪ/, /uː/, /ʊ/, /yː/, /ʏ/) are [+hi, −lo], the low vowels (/ɑː/, /a/) are [−hi, +lo], and mid vowels (/eː/, /ɛ/, /oː/, /ɔ/, /øː/, /œ/) are [−lo, −hi]. The 'long' versus 'short' distinction can be accommodated by the feature LONG (or, since length is not always the distinguishing characteristic, TENSE ([tns])), and the features BACK and ROUND ([ba, ro]) will cover the remaining oppositions for all the paired vowels, though the former is redundant for the low vowels (there is only one pair, /ɑː/, /a/), and the latter is redundant for both the back and the low vowels (where there is no rounding contrast—all the back vowels are rounded and the low pair is unrounded).

Difficulties arise with the unpaired vowels (/æː/, /ə/, and the diphthongs). Those speakers who have /æː/ as a phoneme in their system have an additional opposition between /eː/ and /æː/ which must be accommodated. The four vowel heights of such a system (/iː/, /eː/, /æː/, and /ɑː/) cannot be specified with the two features [high] and [low] (the remaining combination (+high, +low) is impossible!), but could be specified if we replaced [low] by a new feature MID. We would obtain the classification of 2.31.

(2.31) [+hi, −mid]:   /iː/, /ɪ/
        [+hi, +mid]:   /eː/, /ɛ/
        [−hi, +mid]:   /æː/
        [−hi, −mid]:   /ɑː/, /a/

But a better alternative is to regard the low vowels /ɑː/ and /a/ as [+back] and /æː/ as the front vowel corresponding to /ɑː/, giving the classification of 2.32.

(2.32) [+hi, −lo, −ba]:   /iː/, /ɪ/, /yː/, /ʏ/
        [+hi, −lo, +ba]:   /uː/, /ʊ/
        [−hi, −lo, −ba]:   /eː/, /ɛ/, /øː/, /œ/
        [−hi, −lo, +ba]:   /oː/, /ɔ/
        [−hi, +lo, −ba]:   /æː/
        [−hi, +lo, +ba]:   /ɑː/, /a/

This classification is supported by other facts, such as the occurrence of the velar allophone of /x/ after /ɑː/ and /a/ as well as the back vowels, and the fact that low as well as back vowels are subject to Umlaut, and in the same way: Umlaut involves replacing a back vowel by the corresponding front one (see below), and the 'umlauted' version of /ɑː/ is /æː/.

The vowel /ə/ is also a problem. As a lax, mid, unrounded vowel it shares the specification of /ɛ/, namely as [−hi, −lo, −ba, −ro]. One way to distinguish them is to use two features for the front–back dimension, giving an additional 'central' category. We could employ the feature ANTERIOR ([+ant]), as with the consonants, to identify the front vowels, so that they become [−ba, +ant], the back vowels become [+ba, −ant], and /ə/ becomes [−ba, −ant]. /ə/ then differs from /ɛ/ in being [−ant].

The diphthongs are also difficult to accommodate in this framework. From the point of view of distinctive-feature theory, the analysis of the diphthongs as combinations of two phonemes makes classification easier, since we can then describe them in terms of their component parts, with no additional phonemes or features. If we prefer to see them as single phonemes, we need a feature such as DIPHTHONG to oppose them to monophthongs. One possibility would be to see /ai/ and /au/ as diphthongized versions of /ɑː/, differentiated from each other by the feature [+ba], and /ɔi/ as the diphthongized version of /o/.

A summary of the feature specifications of the German phonemes is given in 2.33. It will be clear from the foregoing discussion that such an analysis has many points of difficulty and uncertainty, and cannot claim to be the only possible solution. For the sake of simplicity, the diphthongs have been excluded.

(2.33)

	p	pf	b	t	ts	d	k	g	f	v	s	z	ʃ	x	h	l	r	m	n	ŋ	j
cns	+	+	+	+	+	+	+	+	+	+	+	+	+	+	+	+	+	+	+	+	−
syll																					−
son	−	−	−	−	−	−	−	−	−	−	−	−	−	−	−	+	+	+	+	+	
cnt	−	−	−	−	−	−	−	−	+	+	+	+	+	+	+						
nas																−	−	+	+	+	
ant	+	+	+	+	+	+	−	−	+	+	+	+	−	−	−	+	−	+	+	−	
cor	−	−	−	+	+	+			−	−	+	+	+	−	−			−	+		
lo														−	+						
vce	−	−	+	−	−	+	−	+	−	+	−	+									
aff	−	+		−	+																

	iː	ɪ	yː	ʏ	uː	ʊ	eː	ɛ	øː	œ	ə	oː	ɔ	æː	ɑː	a
cns	−	−	−	−	−	−	−	−	−	−	−	−	−	−	−	−
syll	+	+	+	+	+	+	+	+	+	+	+	+	+	+	+	+
hi	+	+	+	+	+	+	−	−	−	−	−	−	−	−	−	−
lo							−	−	−	−	−	−	−	+	+	+
ba	−	−	−	−	+	+	−	−	−	−	−	+	+	−	+	+
ant							+	+	+	+	−					
ro	−	−	+	+			−	−	+	+						
tns	+	−	+	−	+	−	+	−	+	−		+	−		+	−

In 2.33 each phoneme is given feature specifications which ensure that it is different from every other phoneme in at least one feature, reflecting the fact that these features are characterizations of oppositions between the phonemes. But each phoneme is also *minimally* specified in the sense that only those specifications are included which serve to distinguish the phonemes, and redundant features are excluded. In some cases alternative specifications are possible, depending on which features we take to be distinctive and which redundant. For instance, we could oppose /uː/ to /iː/ and /yː/ as [+ba] versus [−ba], in which case the feature [+ro] is redundant for /uː/; or we could oppose /iː/ to /yː/ and /uː/ as [−ro], in which case the feature [−ba] is redundant for /iː/.

The approach to phonological description through distinctive features may appear to be an unnecessary complication, and both less straightforward and less useful than simply establishing a system of phonemes, as well as permitting too many different analyses. But the aims of distinctive-feature theory are rather different from those of phoneme theory, since it attempts to go beyond the phonemes to the distinctive properties of which they are composed. In a number of respects, too, despite its apparent complexity, this theory does allow a simpler statement of the facts of the language. To demonstrate this, let us consider the description of phonemic structure in the previous section, where we noted that there are restrictions on the phonemes that can occur in specific positions in the word. One such restriction is that those voiced sounds which have a voiceless counterpart may not occur at the end of a word. In a theory in which phonemes are the only units, such a restriction can only be expressed by listing the phonemes involved: /b/, /d/, /g/, /v/, and /z/. In distinctive-feature theory, however, such a generalization is easily expressed: these are the consonants that are [−son, +vce]. Distinctive features are thus not simply a way of describing phonemes; they are also a way of grouping phonemes into classes which share certain characteristics, and thus they enable generalizations to be made. What is more, it will be evident that the larger the class of phonemes involved, and hence the more inclusive the generalization, the smaller the number of features will be, and hence the simpler will be the description. In phoneme theory, on the other hand, the greater the generalization to be made, the more symbols will be required, since each phoneme has to be listed separately. The use of features to group phonemes together will only result in simplification if the group actually does constitute a legitimate class, as it is only in the case of phonemes which have features in common that a saving of features is achieved. Features are thus said to reflect *natural classes* of sounds.

Distinctive features can also go beyond phoneme theory in other respects. Features are intended to be distinctive, i.e. they reflect oppositions between phonemes; but since some phonemes do not occur in some positions it follows that the oppositions between phonemes will vary according to the position in the word. Hence, the features required will also vary. For example, we have observed that voiced, non-sonorant consonants do not occur in final position; that being so, there is no opposition between voiced and voiceless non-sonorants in this position (it is *neutralized*), and the feature [vce] is not distinctive here.

Redundancy of features is also not just a matter of the system itself but depends on the phonemic structure of the words of the language. Consider the possible clusters of three consonants that may occur initially in German words: /ʃpr-/, /ʃtr-/, and ʃpl-/. Giving a full specification of these clusters, we can set up a table (a MATRIX), as in 2.34*a* (the values of [ant] and [cor] for the second and third phonemes depend on whether they are /p/ or /t/, and /r/ or /l/, respectively). Many of these features are, however, redundant: all conson-ants are [−syll]; all sonorants are [+cnt]; if phonemes are not continuants they cannot be [+nas]; neither sonorants nor anterior or coronal consonants can be [+lo]; all sonorants are [+vce], but non-anterior, non-sonorant continuants are all [−vce]; and continuants cannot be [+aff]. Omitting these redundant features, we obtain the matrix of 2.34*b*. When we take into account the possible structures, however, we can eliminate still more specifi-cations. A sequence of three [+cns] sounds at the beginning of a word must begin with /ʃ/, the second consonant must be /p/ or /t/, and the third must be /r/ or /l/. The only features that need to be specified are those which identify these three sounds as consonants, and those that determine whether we have /p/ or /t/, and /r/ or /l/. The result is the matrix of 2.34*c*.

(2.34)		(a) ʃ	p/t	r/l	(b) ʃ	p/t	r/l	(c) ʃ	p/t	r/l
	cns	+	+	+	+	+	+	+	+	+
	syll	−	−	−						
	son	−	−	+	−	−	+			
	cnt	+	−	+	+	−				
	nas	−	−	−				−		
	ant	−	+	−/+	−	+	−/+			−/+
	cor	+	−/+	−/+	+	−/+			−/+	
	lo	−	−	−						
	vce	−	−	+	−					
	aff	−	−	−	−					

Thus, though distinctive-feature notation is certainly more complex and more cumbersome than a simple phonemic transcription, it can nevertheless be argued that, by applying to whole classes of sounds and by omitting reference to redundant characteristics, it can achieve a simpler and more general description of word structure.

Phonological Alternations

In our discussion of German phonology so far, relationships between sounds (rather than the sounds themselves) have had a crucial role: there are complementary relationships between the allophones of a phoneme, and relationships of contrast or opposition between the phonemes themselves. These relationships allow us to establish the system of phonemes appropriate to the language in question.

Relationships between phonemes are not only matters of contrast, however. In some cases phonemes may complement one another in the same way that allophones do, and this means that we must extend our discussion from the *phonetic* alternations between allophones to the *phonological* alternations between phonemes.

We have in fact already noted some of the alternations of phonemes. In discussing the contrast between long and short vowels it was observed that, whereas for the majority of pairs the contrast is not lost when the long vowel is shortened, this does not hold for /ɑː/ and /a/, since /ɑː/ in stressed syllables alternates with /a/ in unstressed syllables. Another alternation was observed with /ə/: the combination /ən/, for example, may alternate with simple /n/.

These are simple instances of a much wider phenomenon. Since these alternations may affect the phonemic structure of words and their grammatical parts (*morphemes*—see Chapter 3), they are not just a matter of phonology, but overlap with morphology, the study of word structure. For this reason such phonological alternations are often included in an area of linguistics called MORPHOPHONEMICS or MORPHOPHONOLOGY. They form a kind of bridge between phonology and morphology, and their role in the latter will be taken up again in the next chapter.

Phonological alternations fall into a number of types, according to the particular factors that determine them, and according to whether they have primarily a phonological or a grammatical motivation. Among the phonological characteristics that can result in alternative forms of words or morphemes are dynamic factors, particularly those dependent on stress and rhythm, and articulatory factors, to do with the nature of the sounds themselves and their interaction in specific contexts.

The main dynamic principle is that phonemes in unstressed syllables are likely to be subject to various forms of weakening. With vowels, this is manifested mainly as a shortening process, as we have already seen, though in the majority of cases this produces only allophonic, rather than phonological, alternations, i.e. we have short allophones instead of long ones. In the case of /ə/ the situation is somewhat different, since, as the examples of 2.15 showed, the weakening may result in the complete elimination, or ELISION, of the phoneme in question (when a phoneme is subject to elision, we might say that it alternates with zero). As those examples showed, this may affect both the unstressed syllables of roots (e.g. in *Boden*) and the many suffixes which are added to the roots, and it produces alternative forms with and without /ə/.

Take, for example, a two-syllable word such as *edel*. Spoken by itself, this form is likely to lose its /ə/, giving a syllabic /l/: /eːdl/. The /ə/ of the root also disappears when it is inflected, though the /ə/ of the inflexions is preserved: *edle, edlen, edlem, edles, edler*. But the verb *veredeln*, derived from it, behaves differently: here the /ə/ of the root is kept, while that of the inflexions is lost: *veredeln, veredelt, veredelnd* (in *Veredlung* the /ə/ of the root is lost; in the first-person singular both *veredele* and *veredle* are found). Another well-known case is the /ə/ of the genitive form -(*e*)*s*, which is normally lost after roots of more than one syllable (*des Vaters, des Bodens,* etc.), but may be kept after single-syllable roots (*des Tag(e)s, des Kopf(e)s,* etc.).[35]

Consonants too may be subject to elision, through articulatory rather than dynamic factors. Complex consonant clusters may be simplified by the omission of one of the phonemes: *hältst* may become /hɛlst/, *ganz* may become indistinguishable from *Gans*, and so on.

Another kind of articulatorily determined factor that affects the phonemic structure of German words is ASSIMILATION. As the name suggests, it involves changing a phoneme to make it more similar to a neighbouring phoneme. The motivation for this is clear: like elision, it entails an articulatory simplification. For example, the phrase *das Schiff*, which is pronounced /das ʃif/ in a relatively careful style of speech, may in a more normal style be pronounced /daʃ ʃif/, with /s/ replaced by /ʃ/ in anticipation of the following /ʃ/. Similarly, the careful pronunciation of *geben* is /geːbən/, but the more normal pronunciation is /geːbm/, in which the loss of /ə/ brings /n/ into contact with the preceding /b/, whereupon it is replaced by /m/. It will be noted that assimilation can go in either direction; in the first example (/daʃ ʃif/) the influence was backwards (REGRESSIVE assimilation) and in the second (/geːbm/) forwards (PROGRESSIVE assimilation). The effect of the assimilation in the above cases is to change the place of articulation, but we also find

---

[35] The situation is, of course, more complex than this, and the presence or absence of /ə/ depends on other factors, such as whether the word is native or foreign and the nature of the final consonant of the root. In many cases both possibilities exist, the choice being a matter of speech style.

changes in voicing, e.g. in *das selbe* (/das zɛlbə/—/das sɛlbə/), where /z/ alternates with /s/.

Assimilation is a very widespread phenomenon. It can perhaps be seen as an extension of normal allophonic variation in phonemes, but its phonological implications are different, since it involves a different *phoneme* rather than merely a different sound in a particular context. It may also result in a difference of structure, since certain combinations of phonemes (here /s + ʃ/ and /b + n/) are eliminated in favour of other ones (here /ʃ + ʃ/ and /b + m/). In the case of /das sɛlbə/ a new structure may be produced in which, contrary to the usual rule, /s/ may occur in initial position in the word, though this will only be the case if the assimilation is total.

The overall effect of these various processes is to produce slightly different forms of the words in question. In the case of words that are in any case short and usually unstressed (such as pronouns, articles, etc.) the effects may be more marked, since the whole word may be drastically simplified and abbreviated. The article *den*, for example, which when pronounced by itself would have the form /deːn/, may appear as /dɛn/, /dən/, /dn/, or /n/, and so on. These various alternative pronunciations are called WEAK FORMS of the word in question. Weak forms are not as common in German as they are in English, but they are nevertheless widely used.[36] Some have even found their way into written German, e.g. *im* (for *in dem*), *ans* (for *an das*), and, less commonly, *überm, unterm, durchs*, etc.

Alternations due to dynamic and articulatory factors are fairly general in languages, since their source is probably ultimately physiological. Other alternations are found which depend not so much on general human traits as on specific features of particular languages. It is, in fact, difficult to draw the line between general, universal processes, found in all or at least most languages, and features peculiar to specific languages. Some processes, such as assimilation, are not only very widespread but also easily explicable on phonetic grounds, and they can legitimately be regarded as universal; others, for example the devoicing of final obstruents in German, are less widely found and they may appear arbitrary and idiosyncratic, but they may nevertheless be attributable to general and natural tendencies, which are manifested in some languages but not others. If devoicing of word-final obstruents is such a process, then German, in a sense, behaves more 'naturally' than English,

---

[36] In English a word such as *and* is always reduced to /ənd/, /ən/, /nd/, /n/, etc. in certain contexts. In German, however, though *und* is often reduced, it need not be, and the pronunciation /ʊnt/ is always possible.

since in the latter this process is apparently suppressed. (One way of dealing with such tendencies is discussed under 'Phonological Constraints', below.)

The absence of the voiced obstruents /b/, /d/, /g/, /v/, and /z/ in the final position in the word in German is important, since it results in phonological alternations. Since these consonants cannot occur finally, but can occur between vowels, many roots appear in two forms, one with these phonemes and one with their voiceless equivalents. *Lob*, for example, has the form /loːb/ if a vowel follows (*Lobes*), but /loːp/ if it does not. Similar alternations are found with the other voiced and voiceless pairs: *Rades* (/d/) and *Rad* (/t/), *lagen* (/g/) and *lag* (/k/), *braver* (/v/) and *brav* (/f/), *lose* (/z/) and *los* (/s/), etc. This may also mean that some roots which are distinguishable when followed by a suffix become identical in sound when there is no suffix. The words *Rat* and *Rad* are distinct in their genitive forms *Rates* and *Rades*, but in the nominative they are both pronounced /raːt/.

One particular case of alternation which deserves special mention is that which involves the velar obstruents /g/, /k/, and /x/. In most cases the alternations of /g/ and /k/ are comparable to those of the other plosives (e.g. *Tag* with /k/, and *Tage* with /g/), but there are special forms involving the suffix *-ig*. There are important regional variations here; Southern German accents treat this suffix regularly, so that the alternation here is between /k/ and /g/ (*wenig~wenige*; /veːnɪk/ ~ /veːnɪgə/). Standard North German accents have different forms, however, with final *-ig* being pronounced /ɪx/ (phonetically [ɪç]). The alternation here is thus between /x/ and /g/: /veːnɪx/ ~ /veːnɪgə/. For many North German speakers this alternation is not restricted to this particular suffix, and /x/ is found alternating with /g/ in any root following a front vowel, as in *Krieg* (/kriːx/) ~ *Kriege* (/kriːgə/), *Weg* (/veːx/) ~ *Wege* (/veːgə/), etc. But these pronunciations, though very common in the North, are probably to be regarded as falling outside the 'standard' accent.

Alternations like the ones exemplified so far raise some interesting theoretical questions. It will be recalled that the phonetic alternations between sounds in different contexts justified our establishing the phoneme as the basic unit of phonological description; since certain sounds are found to replace one another in appropriate contexts they can be seen as realizations of the same more general and abstract entity: the phoneme. In the case of the phonological alternations described here we have a parallel situation, except that the alternation is between phonemes rather than allophones: certain phonemes are found to replace one another in specific contexts. It would be possible, therefore, to see these phonemes as realizations of something more general and abstract. For example, the /k/ of *Tag* and the /g/ of *Tage* could be seen as variants of one another, and as realizations of some more general entity, say {G}. This {G} cannot, of course, be a sound or a phoneme (hence it is enclosed in curly brackets rather than square brackets or slanting lines), but must be more abstract. This kind of entity is given the name MORPHOPHO-NEME.

The theoretical implications of morphophonemes will not be pursued here, though more will be said of them below. We may note, however, that words such as *Rat* and *Rad*, though pronounced identically, could be analysed differently in terms of morphophonemes, since they differ in their inflected forms. We could, for example, represent *Rat* as {rɑːT} and *Rad* as {rɑːD}, where {T} represents a morphophoneme which is always phonemically /t/, and {D} represents a morphophoneme which is phonemically /t/ in final position and /d/ when between vowels (it will be noticed that this is actually the way German is spelt; the spelling is morphophonemic rather than phonemic).

These alternations are phonological, partly in the sense that they involve phonemes rather than allophones, but also because they are determined by characteristics of the phonological structure of the language. Other alterna-tions are found in German which have a more grammatical basis, and their phonological status is therefore less certain. The alternations to be considered here are covered by the terms UMLAUT and ABLAUT. In both cases we are dealing with processes which are perhaps more relevant for an understanding of the historical development of German, but both of these also have impli-cations for the description of modern German from a synchronic (non-historical) point of view.

Popularly, the term 'Umlaut' is used to describe a sign used in writing German: the two dots over the vowels *ü, ö,* and *ä.* In the first two cases this serves as a way of distinguishing the vowels /yː/, /ʏ/, /øː/, and /œ/ from /uː/, /ʊ/, /oː/, and /ɔ/; in the last case it enables /æː/ to be distinguished from /eː/, for those who have the former vowel in their system, but serves no distinctive purpose in the case of the short *ä,* which is identical to *e* (both are pro-nounced /ɛ/), nor in the case of *äu,* which is identical in pronunciation to *eu.* Like the spelling of final obstruents, however, the written Umlaut is indicative of a morphophonemic relationship between back and front vowels (or, in the case of *a* and *ä,* between low and mid front vowels).[37]

The alternation between what might be called the 'plain' vowels and the 'umlauted' (or 'mutated') vowels is restricted to certain grammatical contexts,

---

[37] The fact that the alternation with the other vowels is between back and front offers additional support for the phonological treatment of /æː/ as the 'front' equivalent of /ɑː/, and therefore as a 'low' vowel. See above.

and is therefore not predictable from the phonological structure.[38] In general, plain vowels are found in the basic forms of words, and these are replaced by the mutated vowels in the stressed syllables of the roots when certain grammatical affixes are added. However, in some words, such as *grün, Stück, schön, Löffel, spät*, etc., the mutated vowel is found in the basic form and does not alternate at all.

Umlaut may occur in the plural of nouns (*Löcher*), in the past subjunctive (*käme*) and the second- and third-person singular of the present indicative of 'strong' verbs (*fährst, fährt*), in the comparative and superlative of adjectives (*länger*), and in many derived[39] forms with a variety of suffixes (*täglich, Häuschen, Güte*). In some of these cases (e.g. the past subjunctive) it is entirely regular, but in others there are many exceptions, e.g. diminutive forms such as *Kuhchen* cited earlier, and words like *gastlich* (contrast *täglich*). The alternation is thus not always predictable, even in grammatical terms. Nevertheless, the relationship between each pair of vowels is a consistent one (back versus front—or, in the case of the low vowels, low versus mid), and we may be justified in treating it as a phonological matter.

A further type of alternation is Ablaut. Ablaut is a very ancient phenomenon in the Indo-European languages[40] but its effects are still present in modern German, in the forms of 'strong' verbs and in certain word-formative processes. It is, however, even less regular than Umlaut, and the claim for treating it as phonological is much less strong.

The alternations which fall into this category are those involving the root vowels of certain verbal stems. While most verbs ('weak' verbs) form their various parts by the addition of prefixes and suffixes without changing the root (e.g. *lach-en, lach-te, ge-lach-t*), others (the 'strong' verbs)—fewer in number but much more frequent in use—modify the root vowel, either instead of or in addition to adding prefixes and suffixes (e.g. *sing-en, sang, ge-sung-en*). Ablaut is also found in certain other words containing 'strong' verbal roots, such as *Gabe* (cf. *geben*), *Flug* (cf. *fliegen*), *Gang* (cf. *gehen*), *führen* (cf. *fahren*), and many more. (For further discussion of the role of Umlaut and Ablaut in word formation see Chapter 3.)

Although many words take part in these alternations, the relationships between the vowels are very inconsistent, unlike those of Umlaut. In the case of strong verb-forms, there are some twenty-five different patterns of

---

[38] Historically, the mutated vowels arose from the plain ones by a process of fronting when followed by a high front vowel, though generally the latter has since been lost or has become /ə/.

[39] The significance of this term will be discussed in the next chapter.

[40] It is found, for example, in Greek and Latin, though in neither of these cases was it employed in such a systematic way as in the Germanic languages.

alternation, which defy generalization. Furthermore, the relationships are phonetically completely arbitrary—again in contrast to those of Umlaut, where there is a regular back versus front relationship. Ablaut also differs from Umlaut in being no longer a productive process: we cannot invent new words which are subject to this kind of alternation, whereas Umlaut is still, to a limited extent, active (e.g. new diminutive forms with Umlaut can be formed from unfamiliar names). For all these reasons, then, Ablaut cannot really be described as a phonological phenomenon.

Phonological Processes

Our description of the various relationships between the sounds of German has so far been a static one, taking account of the distribution of sounds and phonemes in different contexts and different forms of words. Pronunciation is, however, a dynamic activity, and it is possible to reinterpret the distributional facts that we have so far observed not as mere static alternations but as phonological *processes*, in which sounds are modified and word structures transformed.

In the preceding discussion of phonological alternations we have in fact occasionally found it convenient to talk in more dynamic terms, as, for example, in the case of assimilation, where we could say that one sound is *replaced* by another, or in the case of elision, when a sound is *omitted*. In a purely static interpretation these expressions could perhaps be regarded as illegitimate; we are not really entitled to say that sounds are 'changed' or 'lost' but only that one form of a word has one phoneme and another form has another phoneme (or has no phoneme at all). What right have we to say, for example, that in /geːbm̩/ the /ə/ has been omitted and the /n/ changed to /m/, and not simply that the word *geben* appears in two forms: /geːbm̩/ and /geːbən/?

We shall now examine in more detail the consequences of a dynamic approach to phonological description, in which we can see the actually occurring sounds of the language as the result of a variety of interacting phonological processes. This approach is not, however, merely a restatement of the various relationships and alternations already discussed in different terms. It entails a rather different conception of the nature of phonology and phonological description, and raises questions of a fundamental and theoretical nature.

Let us consider first of all the alternation between voiced and voiceless obstruents discussed above. It will be recalled that the phonemes /b/, /d/, /g/, /v/, and /z/ do not occur in final position in a word, but may occur between vowels, and this means that many words have alternative forms according to whether they have affixes or not *(Rad ~ Rades* etc.). The correspondences are given in 2.35.

(2.35)   *initially and between vowels:* /b/ /d/ /g/ /v/ /z/
                        finally: /p/ /t/ /k/ /f/ /s/

These relationships are rather one-sided; although every case of a voiced obstruent between vowels corresponds to a voiceless obstruent in final position, the reverse is not the case, as some final voiceless obstruents do not alternate with intervocalic voiced ones *(Rat ~ Rates)*. It is possible, therefore, to derive the phonemes of the second row of 2.35 from those of the first row, but not vice versa. For this purpose we can formulate phonological *rules*, to the effect that voiced obstruents are replaced by voiceless obstruents in final position, as in 2.36.

(2.36)   b → p   / __ #
          d → t   / __ #
          g → k   / __ #
          v → f   / __ #
          z → s   / __ #

These rules are to be interpreted as follows: the sound to be changed is placed on the left of the arrow; what it is to be changed into comes on the right of the arrow; where the change is to take place is indicated after the sign '/' (to be read as 'in the context'), where '__' indicates the position of the affected sound, and any preceding or following symbols indicate the context. In the present case, therefore, the rules will apply before '#', which is the symbol for the end of a word. The first rule thus describes the process whereby /b/ becomes /p/ in final position.

It will be clear, of course, that all the rules of 2.36 are part of the same general process, in which voiced obstruents become voiceless in final position. It would therefore be better to express these rules as one single and more general rule. For this purpose distinctive features are useful, as they can apply to whole classes of phonemes. In the present case it is the class of [−son, +vce] consonants that are affected, and they become [−vce] in this context. The rule could thus be expressed as:

(Rule 1) $\begin{bmatrix} -\text{son} \\ +\text{vce} \end{bmatrix}$ → [−vce] / __ #

or more simply, since voiceless consonants would not be affected by this rule:

(Rule 2) $[-son] \rightarrow [-vce] / \_\_ \#$

Similarly, the rule eliding /ə/ in words such as *geben, Boden,* etc. can be expressed as follows:

(Rule 3) $\begin{bmatrix} +syll \\ -ba \\ -ant \end{bmatrix} \rightarrow \emptyset \ / \ [+cns] \_\_ \begin{bmatrix} +cns \\ +son \end{bmatrix} \#$

(/ə/ is identified by the features [+syll, −ba, −ant], and it is replaced by ∅ (= zero)—i.e. deleted—after a consonant and before a final sonorant consonant.)

Rules such as these express dynamically the relationships between different phonemes or different forms of a word. But they also imply a rather different kind of phonological description from that which we have hitherto envisaged. Instead of describing relationships between alternative occurring forms, we have more abstract structures and rules which specify the various alternative realizations of these structures in specific contexts. Instead, for example, of saying that *Rad* has two different phonological forms (/raːt/ and /raːd/) we may describe it as having only one form (/raːd/) and as being subject to a phonological rule (Rule 2 above) which converts the /d/ to /t/ in final position. One of the alternative forms is therefore given priority as a 'base' from which the other may be derived. The base for *Rad* and *Rat* will, of course, be different, even though they are both pronounced alike when they have no suffix; the final /t/ of the former, though not that of the latter, is derived from an original /d/. Such base-sounds are, in effect, the morphophonemes discussed above, since they have a variety of phonemic realizations.

This approach is characteristic of the important and influential theory known as GENERATIVE PHONOLOGY. As in the case of the other theoretical approaches touched on so far, we shall not go too deeply into the theory itself, but rather note some of its consequences for the phonological description of German.

One useful characteristic of this approach is that it allows us to overcome some of the problems that we have encountered in establishing the phonemes of German. One difficulty that was noted above is that in some cases a single sound corresponds to a combination of phonemes. We would like, for example, to analyse the sound [ɐ] in words such as *guter* as the realization of the sequence of phonemes /ər/, although the contrast between [guːtə] and [guːtɐ] implies that we should recognize a separate phoneme /ɐ/. Using rules to describe processes applying to more abstract forms, however, we have no problem, since such rules can easily amalgamate two phonemes (or morpho-phonemes) into a single sound, as in Rule 4:[41]

(*Rule* 4)   /ə/ + /r/ → [ɐ]

Rule 4 shows that it is possible to use rules not only for describing alternations of phonemes but also in the specification of allophones. Thus, two of the major allophones of /t/, [t] and [tʰ], could be specified by a rule aspirating voiceless plosives when in initial position before a vowel; the palatal and velar allophones of /x/ could be specified by palatalizing the velar fricative initially and after a front vowel or a consonant. If we expressed these rules in terms of features we would, of course, need to use more features than those given earlier, since we are no longer confining ourselves to distinctive properties (allophonic characteristics are by definition not distinctive).

The fact that similar rules can be used for specifying alternations of allophones and alternations of phonemes brings with it a number of important consequences. To see what these are, let us examine the rule that might be required to cover the processes of assimilation described earlier, and which are illustrated in 2.37.

(2.37) /t/ → /p/ / __ /b/   *ist blau:* [p–b]
        /t/ → /p/ / — /p/   *wird parken:* [p–p]
        /t/ → /p/ / — /m/   *hat mich:* [p–m]
        /t/ → /k/ / __ /g/   *wird gehen:* [k–g]
        /t/ → /k/ / __ /k/   *hat keine:* [k–k]
        /n/ → /m/ / __ /b/   *ein Buch:* [m–b]
        /n/ → /m/ / __ /p/   *ein Platz:* [m–p]
        /n/ → /m/ / __ /m/   *ein Mann:* [m–m]
        /n/ → /ŋ/ / __ /g/   *kann gehen:* [ŋ–g]
        /n/ → /ŋ/ / __ /k/   *ein Kind:* [ŋ–k]

As in the case of 2.35, we have a number of specific changes, and these processes can again be generalized by means of features. It is impossible to do this, however, without introducing a new device in our rules. We wish to

---

[41] For the sake of clarity this has not been expressed in terms of features. This process is actually best expressed by two rules, one which deletes the /ə/ before /r/, and the other which produces [ɐ] as the syllabic version of /r/. This enables these rules to be generalized with others, the first with Rule 3, the second with the process producing [ɐ] from /r/ after vowels (cf. 2.16).

incorporate the fact that the values of the features [ant] and [cor] for the one sound (these being the features of /t/ and /n/ which change) must agree with those of the other: if the value is '+' in one case it must be '+' in the other, if '−' in one case then it must be '−' in the other. This is achieved by replacing the '+' or '−' by a variable which must be the same in all its occurrences. Letters of the Greek alphabet are used for this purpose. We thus obtain the formulation of Rule 5, which corresponds to all the cases of 2.36.[42]

(*Rule* 5)

$$
\begin{bmatrix} +\text{ant} \\ +\text{cor} \end{bmatrix} \rightarrow \begin{bmatrix} \alpha\text{ant} \\ \beta\text{cor} \end{bmatrix} \; / \underline{\hspace{1em}} \begin{bmatrix} \alpha\text{ant} \\ \beta\text{cor} \end{bmatrix}
$$

But consider now the examples of 2.38. These are cases of allophonic variation, with different allophones of /n/ occurring in different contexts ([ɱ] is a labiodental nasal, [n̠] a postalveolar nasal, and [ɲ] a palatal nasal).

(2.38)

/n/→/ɱ//__/f/	*ein Fluss*: [ɱ—f]
/n/→/ɱ//__/v/	*ein Wein*: [ɱ—f]
/n/→/n̠/ /__/ʃ/	*ein Schiff*: [n̠—f]
/n/→/ɲ//__/j/	*ein Junge*: [ɲ—f]

These are not cases of assimilation, since no change of phoneme is involved, but they are clearly part of exactly the same process as that described by Rule 5, and could be included in it with only minor modifications to the rule. This suggests that there is no real difference between rules which change phonemes and rules which specify allophones; to separate the two processes would mean duplicating our rules unnecessarily.

The fact that there is no distinction between these two kinds of rules has far-reaching implications. Rule 5 specifies the phoneme to be used in particular contexts, and hence its starting point, the sound it applies to, must be something more general and abstract than the phoneme itself, namely a morphophoneme. But the fact that Rule 5 also specifies allophones means that, in effect, it converts morphophonemes into allophones without regard to what the phonemes are. The rather surprising conclusion from this is that the phoneme has no place in this particular theory; we have morpho- phonemes and sounds, and rules which convert one to the other, but the

---

[42] Rule 5 would need to be a little more restricted than this, since as it stands it applies to all alveolar consonants. But /l/, for example, does not assimilate in the same manner. The context of this rule should also be more precisely specified.

phoneme is both unnecessary and undesirable. It is unnecessary because we do not need to say which phoneme is involved in the rules of 2.38, and undesirable because to do so would involve breaking a single process into two parts, and having two rules rather than one.

The conception of phonology that emerges from the discussion of phonological processes, therefore, is somewhat different from that which was presented earlier in this chapter. We have so far assumed that speech can be represented phonologically as a succession of phonemes, each phoneme corresponding to a segment of the sound of the utterance. The possibility of changing or even removing parts of the utterance by phonological rules means that the representation of the utterance in phonological terms may not correspond to the actual sounds in any direct way at all. Words like *geben*, for example, may be represented as /geːbən/ even if the pronunciation is [geːbm], since we can derive the latter from the former by means of rules. The phonological form of words may thus become rather abstract and remote from the actual pronunciation.

This case also shows another characteristic of rules in phonology. Two such rules must apply to /geːbən/ to convert it into [geːbm], one to remove the [ə], the other to assimilate the [n] to the [m] (the assimilation rule given above needs to be made a little more general if it is to apply here, since in this case the /n/ *follows* the /b/). It is also clear that these rules must apply in this order if the correct result is to be obtained. We cannot apply the rule of assimilation until the [ə] has been removed, since the conditions under which assimilation takes place do not arise until the two consonants are juxtaposed. The rules are therefore *ordered* so as to apply in a particular sequence.

The possibility of applying a succession of rules to a word increases still more the possibilities for abstract phonological forms. To see what the dangers of such abstractness might be, consider another form of the phonological alternations discussed in the last section: Umlaut. As mentioned earlier, the relationship between the 'plain' and the mutated vowels is very easy to describe in phonetic terms, since the former are back and the latter front. We could provide a phonological rule for this purpose, which 'fronts' back vowels:

(Rule 6)   [+syll] → [+ant]

The problem is, however, to establish the context in which this rule would apply. To a large extent Umlaut is determined grammatically, i.e. certain grammatical forms (plural, past subjunctive of strong verbs, etc.) require Umlaut. We could therefore provide a grammatical context for this rule, using a grammatical feature such as [plural] instead of a phonetic feature (this approach does not require grammatical facts to be kept strictly apart from phonological facts). Given the possibility of abstract phonological forms and a sequence of rules to apply to them, however, it might even be possible to provide a purely phonological context. Historically, Umlaut is the result of a following high front vowel which was subsequently often lost or weakened to /ə/. It would be possible to mirror these historical events in a description of modern German phonology by representing those words where Umlaut takes place with such a vowel in the following syllable, and by applying suitable rules to effect the Umlaut and the vowel reduction. Thus, we might represent the word *Männer* phonologically as /manɪr/, and derive the actually occurring form [mɛnər] by means of the two ordered Rules 7 and 8 (V and C are informal abbreviations for the set of features required for vowels and consonants respectively):

(Rule 7)

$$V \rightarrow \quad [+ant] \ / \_\_ \ (C) \begin{bmatrix} -ba \\ +hi \\ V \end{bmatrix}$$

(i.e. a vowel becomes front before a high front vowel).

(Rule 8)

$$\begin{bmatrix} -ba \\ +hi \\ V \end{bmatrix} \rightarrow \begin{bmatrix} -ant \\ -hi \\ -lo \end{bmatrix} / \text{ when unstressed}$$

(i.e. an unstressed high front vowel becomes [ə]—again this rule needs to be restricted, as not all cases of unstressed [ɪ] become [ə]).

A form such as /manɪr/ is rather remote from the actual pronunciation [mɛnər], and for this reason few linguists would endorse descriptions of this kind. They are, however, merely an extreme form of the general principle according to which the actual pronunciation is seen as the result of interacting phonological processes. A certain amount of abstraction is unavoidable, indeed desirable, if we are to describe pronunciation in a systematic fashion; the question is, however, how far this abstraction can go without becoming unnatural.[43]

---

[43] The approach illustrated here is characteristic of so-called 'classical' generative phonology, which dominated the theory of phonology from the 1960s, though it was taken much further and applied to a

Phonological Constraints

It was noted in Chapter 1 that a fundamental principle of the approach adopted by the structuralist tradition is that each language must be described in its own terms and not in terms of another language or an earlier stage of its history. On the other hand, it was also pointed out that we must base our description on a general theory of language, taking account of universal characteristics of language. These two apparently contradictory principles reflect the fact that on the one hand all languages are different and must be described separately, but on the other hand they have many things in common—not surprisingly, since they are all spoken by the same species and all have the same role in communication and in society.

We have so far described German phonology mostly in terms of the first of these principles, identifying the particular features of the German phoneme system and the structures and processes occurring in the language. We may conclude this part of our discussion with a brief explanation of one way in which the other principle—which sees German phonology in a more general context—has been implemented. This approach, which goes by the name of OPTIMALITY THEORY, describes the language in terms of CONSTRAINTS: restrictions on the phonetic form of the words and sentences of languages.[44]

As an illustration let us consider again possible syllable structures in German. As we saw above, German permits up to three consonants in the onset position of the syllable and up to four (five if inflections are taken into account) in the coda position. However, there are many restrictions; in particular, voiced obstruents are not permitted in the coda. Looking at languages worldwide, however, we find a somewhat different picture: many languages permit only very simple structures, with only one onset consonant and no codas at all. (Interestingly, it appears that no language allows a coda but no onset.) At the other extreme, English allows syllables with the same degree of complexity as German, but does not prohibit voiced obstruents in the coda.

How are we to describe this situation? We could, of course, simply note that different languages are subject to different constraints on possible sound-types and syllable structures and leave it at that. We may be able to recognize a limited number of absolute, universal principles, such as the prohibition on

wider range of phenomena than can be exemplified here (see especially Chomsky and Halle (1968)). The problems inherent in this approach—in particular the difficulty of curbing its excessive abstractness—led to the abandonment of the theory in its classical form, though the principle of deriving pronunciations from abstract forms by means of rules is still implicit in more recent approaches.

[44] Optimality Theory (OT) arose in the early 1990s and had become very popular by the end of the century, especially in America. See, for example, Archangeli and Langendoen (1997).

languages having only coda consonants with no onset ones, but this does not take us very far.

There are, in fact, a number of different types of phonological constraints that can be recognized here:

(i) *language-specific restrictions*: 'Hawaiian has no voiced obstruents', 'German does not permit voiced obstruents in syllable codas'

(ii) *universals*: principles that apply to all languages, e.g. 'all languages have vowels', 'all languages have some voiceless consonants'

(iii) *universal tendencies*: 'nasal consonants tend to agree in their place of articulation with the following plosive', 'non-low back vowels tend to be rounded'

The only one of these that has been incorporated into our description so far is the first, and this merely by describing German in its own terms. But the second and third are presumably in some way significant for a general theory of language, and we therefore need to see how we can take account of them. This can be achieved by making two assumptions about the constraints involved: first, that they are *universal*, and second, that they can be *violated*. It is then assumed that differences between languages arise not because they are subject to different constraints but because these constraints are differently *ranked* in individual languages.

To make this clear let us consider a number of constraints on sound types and syllable structure. Some languages, such as Hawaiian, have no voiced obstruents. Let us account for this by means of a universal constraint (1):

(1) *VOICED OBSTRUENTS (languages do not have voiced obstruents—the '*' indicates a negative constraint, i.e. a prohibition)

This constraint is satisfied in Hawaiian, but it is clearly violated in many other languages, including German and English. However, the absence of voiced obstruents in syllable codas in German can be assumed to reflect another constraint (2):

(2) *VOICED CODA OBSTRUENTS (languages do not have voiced obstruents in the coda)

This time German complies with the constraint, though English does not.

Given these two constraints, therefore, we see that Hawaiian satisfies both of them, since it does not have voiced obstruents and it also follows from this that they do not occur in codas in the language. German, on the other hand, violates the constraint on voiced obstruents but complies with the constraint on their occurrence in codas. English violates both these constraints. We could, of course, simply say that the different languages follow different principles in the types of sound they allow and where they occur, but this would fail to account for the fact that (*a*) there is a tendency in languages not to have voiced obstruents, and (*b*) that in languages with such sounds they tend not to occur in syllable codas.

The answer to this problem lies in the ranking of constraints. The constraints are assumed to be ranked differently in different languages; high-ranking constraints will be complied with, but lower-ranking constraints can be violated in order to satisfy a higher-ranking one. To clarify this, we need to add another constraint:

(3) FAITH(Voice) (the output will be the same as the input in terms of voice)

This approach assumes that, as we saw in discussing phonological processes, the forms of words will initially be quite abstract and they will need to be converted into a specific phonetic form. The FAITH(Voice) constraint (one of a set of 'faithfulness' constraints covering not just voice but other properties of sounds) requires that the value of the feature [voice] be preserved during this process. So, for example, if we take an input such as /band/, its output in English will be [band] (*band*) but in German it will be [bant] (*band*)—English complies with the faithfulness constraint but German does not. Thus, FAITH(Voice) ranks *higher* than *VOICED CODA OBSTRUENT in English but *lower* in German; in each case the language violates a lower-ranking constraint in order to satisfy a high-ranking one. In both languages, the constraint *VOICED OBSTRUENT ranks lower than either of these, since it is violated in order to satisfy FAITH(Voice), preserving the initial voiced obstruent.

The interactions between the different constraints are conventionally represented in the form of a *tableau*, as in 2.39.

(2.39)   English

/band/	FAITH(Voice)	*VOICED CODA OBSTRUENT	*VOICED OBSTRUENT
☞ [band]		*	* *
[bant]	*!		*
[pand]	*!	*	*
[pant]	*! *!		

German

/band/	*VOICED CODA OBSTRUENT	FAITH(Voice)	*VOICED OBSTRUENT
[band]	*!		* *
☞ [bant]		*	*
[pand]	*!	*	*
[pant]		*! *	

These tableaux are to be interpreted as follows. The form /band/ in the top left-hand corner is the 'input' (the abstract form from which the actual pronunciation is derived), and the phonetic forms in the left-hand column are potential outputs ('candidates'). The constraints are listed in decreasing order of rank across the top and the stars in each box represent a violation of the constraint by the form concerned. The ! indicates a crucial or 'fatal' failure for a candidate, and the shading indicates that the cell concerned is irrelevant to the evaluation. The candidate [band] in both languages is the only one not to violate the FAITH(Voice) constraint (because it is identical to the input); candidates ending in a voiced obstruent violate the *VOICED CODA OBSTRUENT constraint, and all candidates containing a voiced obstruent will violate the *VOICED OBSTRUENT constraint (the only form not to do so is [pant]).

It can be seen, therefore, that in each language one candidate emerges from this as the 'best' or 'optimal' output, given this input and the particular ranking, and this is indicated by the pointing hand (☞). In English it is [band] (the same as the input), which is the only form not to violate the FAITH(Voice) constraint, but in German it is [bant], with a devoiced final obstruent. Both [bant] and [pant] satisfy the *VOICED CODA OBSTRUENT constraint, and both violate the FAITH(Voice) constraint, but the violation is more serious in the case of [pant], leaving [bant] as the optimal form.

It has not been possible to indicate more than the bare outline of this approach here, but the intention is clear: the particular characteristics of German are to be seen in the context of overall properties of language. These properties (in this case the constraints and tendencies to which languages are subject) are assumed to be the same for all languages; where languages differ is the degree of importance (ranking) which is attached to each constraint.

Suprasegmental Phonology

There is more to the pronunciation of a language than merely the vowels and consonants. As we have seen, these are combined together into more complex entities such as syllables, and these too have phonetic properties which are susceptible to systematic analysis. The study of such properties is called SUPRASEGMENTAL phonology, in contrast to the study of the 'segmental' units, i.e. the vowels and consonants.

In our discussion so far we have not altogether ignored features of larger units of speech; we found it convenient to describe the various permissible combinations of vowels and consonants with reference to the syllable and its structure. But the syllable is not just a combination of vowels and consonants; it has properties of its own, the most important of which is STRESS. Another major feature of longer stretches of speech is INTONATION. Both of these deserve closer attention.

Stress

In German speech—as in English—some syllables stand out as being more prominent than others: the first syllable of *machen* is more prominent than the second, while in *gemacht* it is the second syllable that is the more prominent. This phenomenon is referred to as *stress*. It is usually easy enough to identify the stressed syllable in a word, but it is rather more difficult to identify exactly what phonetic features are involved. Though stress is sometimes thought of as a matter of loudness, and explained as the result of greater physical effort in the articulation of syllables, detailed phonetic experimentation has shown that the physical nature of the phenomenon is extremely variable. Nevertheless, speakers and hearers do perceive one syllable in a word to be more prominent than the others, whatever the phonetic properties are. As in the case of certain of the distinctive properties of phonemes, therefore, it is best to treat stress as a somewhat abstract phonological property of syllables, whose phonetic manifestation may take on a variety of different forms in different contexts and on different occasions.

We shall be concerned here with the principles which determine the particular syllable of the word on which the stress falls. Here it is especially important to distinguish between native and foreign words, as the principles involved in the two cases are quite different. As before, this distinction is based not just on the origin of a word but also on the degree to which the word has been assimilated into the German system. For example, the word *Kaffee* can be heard pronounced as /ka'fe/ or as /'kafe/,[45] the former, with

[45] See above, n. 13.

final stress, being an approximation to the original French, the latter, with initial stress, a 'Germanized' version.

In order to determine the position of the stressed syllable we must also take into account the grammatical structure of the word itself. As we shall see in more detail in Chapter 3, words consist of *roots* (the basic meaningful elements) and *affixes* (the various grammatical parts, such as endings, which are added to the roots). The first important principle that determines the position of the stress in native German words is that the stress falls on the root rather than on the affixes, e.g. in *'gute, ge'sagt, ver'reisen,* etc. There are some exceptions, however, of which the most important is the case of the 'separable' verbal prefixes *(ein-, aus-, auf-, hin-, her-, vor-,* etc.), which take the stress, e.g. *'einbrechen, 'ausgehen, 'herkommen.* Inseparable prefixes *(ent-, ver-, ge-,* etc.) do not take the stress, e.g. *ver'kaufen, ge'stehen.* There are contrasts in a number of cases where a prefix can be either separable or inseparable with a different meaning, e.g. *über-* in *übertreten: 'übertreten =* 'step over', *über'treten =* 'overstep' (notice the comparable phenomenon in English). Another exception is the prefix *un-,* which is usually stressed, e.g. in *'Unkraut, 'unschön,* etc., though in some common words the stress may also appear on the root, e.g. in *unmöglich ('unmöglich* or *un'möglich).*

Many German roots have two syllables, and here the stress falls on the first syllable of the root,[46] e.g. in *'Boden, 'Tafel, 'Schwester,* or, with affixes, *'väterlich, 'Brüderlein,* etc. In compound words, which have more than one root (see Chapter 3), the general rule is that the stress falls on the first element. Examples are *'Schreibtisch, 'Vaterland,* though again there are exceptions, such as double names like *Österreich-'Ungarn, Schleswig-'Holstein,* or certain adjectives like *stock'finster, riesen'groß,* etc.[47] In fact, words of the latter type are generally pronounced with two stressed syllables, one on each root, but the second is more prominent. The first stress in such cases is often called a 'secondary stress' and marked with a subscript stress mark, e.g. *₁riesen'groß* (see also below).

These principles apply only to native German words. Foreign words are in general subject to a quite different rule. Here, the stress falls on the *final* syllable. This is especially the case with many foreign words which have suffixes, such as *-ant (Demon'strant), -eur (Ingeni'eur), -ist (Ar'tist), -ität (Universi'tät),* and the like. Some foreign endings, such as *-us ('Zirkus), -o ('Konto), -a ('Drama),* etc., do not usually take the stress. Some suffixes, e.g.

---

[46] The very few simple roots with three syllables, such as *Holunder* and *Hornisse,* have the stress on the second syllable.

[47] Some words of this last type provide a stress contrast: *blut'arm* means 'very poor', while *'blutarm* means 'anaemic'; similarly, *stein'reich* means 'very rich', while *'steinreich* means 'stony'.

-ik, are variable; compare *Lin' guistik* with *Mu' sik*; also, Austrian *Mathe' matik* corresponds to German *Mathema' tik*.

It is interesting to see what happens when there is a conflict between the basically initial stress (within the root) of the native vocabulary and the basically final stress of foreign words. Where the root is foreign and the affix native there is generally no problem, since both principles can be satisfied simultaneously. In *na' türlich*, for example, the foreign root *Na' tur* has final stress according to the 'foreign' rule, and this is unaffected by the addition of the native suffix *-lich*, which, following the 'native' rule, does not take the stress. In words such as *Liefe' rant* or *Wäsche' rei*, however, there is a conflict between the initial stress of the native root and the final stress of the foreign suffix; here the latter wins, though this is not always the case (cf. *' anmarschieren*, where the stress of the separable prefix overcomes that of the foreign suffix). All these examples show that in the majority of German words—native or foreign—the position of the stressed syllable is predictable from a few general principles, though these principles are different for the two categories of words. It is only in a small number of cases (such as the verbs with variable prefixes) that stress can actually distinguish pairs of words.

For this reason we might conclude that stress has a relatively minor role to play in German phonology. Stress is not just a matter of distinguishing different words, however; it is part of the rhythmical and accentual structure of the language, and must be seen in the context of whole utterances. If we take a stretch of speech of any length, we will find that it has several stressed syllables, and these will tend to be spaced out evenly, creating a rhythmical framework for the utterance. For example, in the utterance

Mein 'Vater fährt 'morgen 'früh zum 'Frankfurter 'Flughafen

we are likely to find stresses on *Va-*, *mor-*, *früh*, *Frank-*, and *Flug-*, and the time interval between the stresses will be approximately the same. In a slower style of speech more stresses are likely, and in a more rapid style there will be fewer, but the same rhythmical principle is observed:

(slow)   'Mein 'Vater 'fährt 'morgen 'früh zum 'Frank'furter 'Flug'hafen
(fast)   Mein 'Vater fährt morgen 'früh zum Frankfurter 'Flughafen

Naturally, the spacing between the stressed syllables is not *exactly* the same, but it is sufficiently similar to create a rhythmical impression.

The rhythmical principle of which stress is a manifestation has an important influence on other aspects of utterances. We have already noted that unstressed syllables tend to be weakened, by shortening or eliding the vowel for instance, and that some words which are regularly unstressed may be subject to even more drastic reduction. For the most part it is words such as nouns, verbs, and adjectives ('lexical' or 'content' words) that are stressed, and articles, prepositions, conjunctions, etc. ('grammatical' or 'form' words) that remain unstressed, but this depends on the speed of speech and upon the needs of the rhythm. The preposition *auf*, for example, is usually unstressed, as in an expression such as

Er 'steht auf der 'Straße

but it may well acquire a stress for rhythmical reasons in

Der 'Mann, der 'auf der 'Straße 'steht...

For the same reason, longer words, such as the compounds mentioned above, may often have two, or even more, stressed syllables, exemplified in 2.40.

(2.40) *'Bahnhofs'vorsteher*
        'Fernsehappa'rat
        'Landesbiblio'thek
        'Universi'tätsdo'zent
        'Hauptver'waltungsge'bäude

In words containing more than one stress it will be observed that one of the stressed syllables is more prominent than the others. The first stress of both *Fernsehapparat* and *Landesbibliothek* is the more prominent, while *Universitätsdozent* has a more prominent second stress. This difference is explained by the fact that, as a non-native word, *Universität* has its main stress on the final syllable. In all these cases, however, it is the first element of the compound that has the main stress.[48] Syllables with the prominent stress are said to have *primary stress* (notation'); the other stressed syllables are said to have *secondary stress* (notation˛). These words may thus be represented as *'Fernsehappa˛rat*, *'Landesbiblio˛thek* and *˛Universi'tätsdo˛zent*. In faster speech the secondary stresses will tend to disappear, while in very slow speech even more secondary stresses may be introduced, e.g. *'Fern˛seh˛appa˛rat*, *'Landes˛biblio˛thek* and *˛Uni˛versi'tätsdo˛zent*.

The same principle applies to whole utterances: one of the stressed syllables is picked out as especially prominent. In the examples of 2.41, this syllable is printed in capitals. (These are not the only possibilities, as the position of the prominent stress is variable—see below.)

---

[48] For further discussion of stress in compounds, see Chapter 3.

(2.41)   Meine 'Frau hat ein 'neues 'KLEID ge'kauft.
         Er 'hat sich 'wirklich 'LÄcherlich be'nommen.
         Ich 'kann die 'ZEItung nicht 'finden.

Stress, therefore, can be of two kinds. Firstly, we have the prominence associated with one syllable in the word (or in some cases two); this is often called WORD STRESS. Secondly, we have the extra prominence associated with one of the stressed syllables in the phrase or sentence; this is often called PHRASE STRESS or SENTENCE STRESS.[49] However, the group of syllables with one 'word stress' will not necessarily coincide with a word; it may contain some words with no stress at all (*'gib mir das, ich 'weiß es nicht, auf der 'Straße,* etc.), or, if the word has more than one stress, it may be less than a word. A more satisfactory term for a unit containing a stressed syllable is therefore STRESS GROUP or FOOT.[50] Similarly, the stretch of speech characterized by a sentence stress may not be a sentence in the grammatical sense; we may call it an ACCENT PHRASE.

As we can see, an utterance is built up in 'layers' or 'levels' of different sizes. At the bottom we have the smallest segments of speech: phonemes (though these can be broken down into features); higher up there are syllables, stress groups, and accent phrases. The phonological structure of German, as indeed of other languages, is thus hierarchical, with larger units made up of smaller ones, which are in turn made up of still smaller ones. The phonemes are grouped into syllables, which constitute the smallest independently pro-nounceable units; the syllables are grouped into feet, giving a rhythmical framework for the utterance, and the feet are grouped into accent phrases, which, as we shall see shortly, form the basic units of intonation. In this way the suprasegmental characteristics of an utterance are integrated into a uni-fied structure. This is exemplified as follows, where the syllables are separated by ., the feet by |, and the accent phrases by ||.

||Als . er . nach |Hau.se |kam ||stand . der |Mann. schon . vor . der |Tür ||

Another way of representing both the stress pattern of utterances and the hierarchical structure of the utterance itself is in the form of a METRICAL TREE. Consider the word *Garten.* In terms of our analysis so far, this has a stress on the first syllable: *'Garten,* constituting a foot. If the first (stressed) syllable of the foot is regarded as 'strong', and the second as 'weak', then this word can be represented as in 2.42.

---

[49] Some linguists go further, and recognize another degree of stress, making (with the inclusion of 'unstressed') four degrees in all.

[50] The meaning of the term 'foot' is not quite the same here as when it is used in the description of verse. Although speech has a rhythmical structure, this differs in important respects from that of verse.

(2.42)

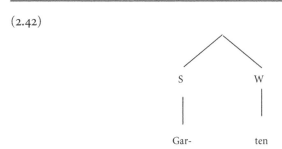

Consider now the word *Gartenzwerge* ('garden gnomes'), whose stress pattern could be given as '*Garten zwerge*, with two feet. The stress of the first foot is more prominent than that of the second, and we can again regard the distinction as 'strong' versus 'weak'. The result is the diagram given in 2.43. The syllable bearing the main stress of the whole word is now identifiable as that syllable which is 'strong' at both levels.

(2.43)

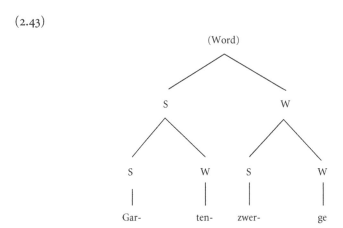

The advantage of this approach is that it correctly treats 'stress' not as an absolute phonetic property but as a *relative* property: 'stress' is merely the stronger of two entities at each level. Since the utterance—or even, as here, a single word—consists of several levels, a hierarchy of 'stress' is built up. There remain, however, some difficulties. First, the 'metrical' approach assumes that 'strong' versus 'weak' is essentially a binary relationship; this works for this example, where the foot contains only two syllables, but it creates problems if there are more, e.g. '*bessere* or '*laufende*. Here we must either accept non-binary feet, as in 2.44(*a*), or we must introduce a second, possibly spurious, level, as in 2.44(*b*).

(2.44)

    (*a*)   (*b*)

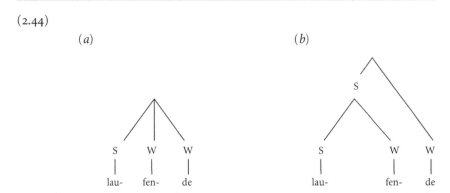

The second problem arises with unstressed syllables which occur *before* the stressed syllable, as in *ge'geben* or *verge'wissern*. Here we must assume either an 'empty' stressed syllable to attach the unstressed syllable(s) to (2.45*a*), or attach them at a higher level (2.45*b*), again creating spurious structures.

(2.45)

    (*a*)   (*b*)

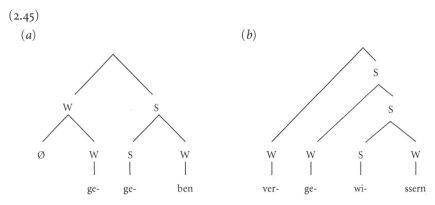

Which, if any, of these structures best captures the nature and organization of stress in German utterances is a matter of dispute.

Intonation

One further important suprasegmental characteristic of utterances is *intonation*, by which we mean modifications of the pitch of the voice. No utterance is spoken on a monotone; the pitch is constantly rising and falling, and these variations in pitch are not arbitrary and uncontrolled, but systematic and meaningful. We can thus attempt to subject the intonation of German utterances to a phonological analysis, i.e. to determine its linguistically significant features.

Although the pitch of an utterance may rise and fall, it does not do so in the same manner as in singing, in which there is a fixed set of notes forming a musical scale, and in a particular key (i.e. the scale starts at a specific pitch). Intonation is much more variable; there are no fixed notes, scales, or keys. Different speakers may have a wider or narrower pitch range, or a lower or higher voice. In describing the intonation of an utterance, therefore, the standard musical notation is inappropriate; for the phonetic description of voice pitch it is preferable simply to represent the upper and lower limits of the speaker's range by two parallel lines, and the pitch by a continuous line or a series of dots and lines in the middle, which moves up as the pitch rises, and down as it falls. An example of this notation is given in 2.46.

(2.46)

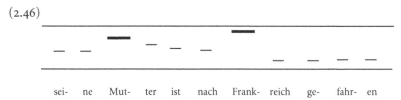

sei-   ne   Mut-   ter   ist   nach   Frank-   reich   ge-   fahr-   en

The diagram in 2.46 is merely a *phonetic* representation of the pitch of this utterance; to understand how it can be analysed *phonologically* we must examine its structure. The pitch of an utterance such as that of 2.46 can be regarded as a complete pattern, a kind of 'tune'; the pitch of a longer utterance, such as 2.47, may well consist of more than one pattern. Thus, we can recognize each such pattern—here separated by '||'—as a basic INTONATION UNIT—in fact it corresponds to the accent phrase discussed above.

(2.47)

sei-ne Mut- ter ist nach Frank-reich ge- fah- ren ||a- ber sein Va- ter bleibt zu Hau- se

In the pronunciation given here (which is, of course, merely one of many ways in which this utterance could be spoken) it is noticeable that there is one point in each phrase where the pitch is particularly prominent. This point is the pivot of the pitch of the utterance, and it is called the NUCLEUS[51] or NUCLEAR STRESS; in 2.46 it is the syllable *Frank-*, and in 2.47, which has two such phrases, the nuclei are *Frank-* and *Hau-*. The nucleus of the utterance

---

[51] Not to be confused with the nucleus of the *syllable*—see above.

coincides with what we have called the phrase stress or sentence stress; it is the most prominent point in the phrase. In fact, what gives it the extra prominence that distinguishes it from other stressed syllables is precisely that it has a special role in the intonation pattern.

Consider now the pitch of the utterances represented in 2.48. It will be clear that the actual shape of the intonation pattern is exactly the same in each case; where they all differ is in the point at which the pitch falls, i.e. in the place of the nucleus (printed in capitals).

(2.48)

(i)   seine MUTter ist gestern nach Frankreich gefahren

(ii)   seine Mutter ist GEStern nach Frankreich gefahren

(iii)   seine Mutter ist gestern nach FRANKreich gefahren

In 2.48(i) the nucleus is on *Mut-*, in 2.48(ii) on *ges-*, and in 2.48(iii) on *Frank-*. In each case the meaning is slightly different, not in the basic state of affairs that is reported on, but rather in the emphasis given to the different parts of the utterance. One could imagine these utterances as replies to slightly different questions: 2.48(i) might be a response to the question 'Wer ist gestern nach Frankreich gefahren?' and 2.48(ii) to the question 'Wann ist seine Mutter nach Frankreich gefahren?'

The examples of 2.48 show the same pattern but with the nucleus in different places. Those of 2.49 both have the nucleus in the same place but with different patterns. While in 2.48 the pitch falls immediately after the nucleus, here it rises (2.49(i)), or rises and then falls (2.49(ii)). The meaning is slightly different in each case, though again the basic content is unchanged. The differences here are not, as in 2.48, a matter of emphasis, but rather of implication: 2.49(i) is more questioning, 2.49(ii) more exclamatory.

(2.49)

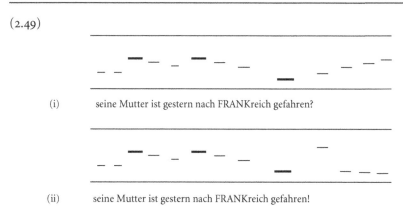

(i)   seine Mutter ist gestern nach FRANKreich gefahren?

(ii)   seine Mutter ist gestern nach FRANKreich gefahren!

Thus, we can see the basic structure of the intonation of utterances: there is a series of intonation units, each of which has an intonation pattern centred on the prominent nucleus, the position of the latter being variable. Shifting the nucleus can change the emphasis; altering the pattern can change the implication.[52]

The kinds of entities required in order to describe the intonation patterns phonologically are, however, rather difficult to identify. A variety of different concepts and categories have been proposed, but there is considerable disagreement among scholars as to which of these are to be preferred. One approach is to divide the pattern into sections, or segments, each of which can have a different shape (e.g. falling, rising, rising–falling, etc.). In the above examples we could divide the intonation pattern into two main parts, one consisting of everything preceding the nucleus and the other consisting of the nucleus and everything coming after it. Various terms have been used to describe these parts, but we shall call them the HEAD and the NUCLEAR PATTERN respectively.[53] The pattern of 2.48 can thus be described as a falling nuclear pattern preceded by a high head, that of 2.49(i) as a high head with a rising nuclear pattern, and so on.

There are many other details of the patterns which are ignored by this description, e.g. the slight undulations in the pattern due to the stressed syllables, or the slightly lower pitch before the first stress at the beginning, but all these can be regarded as not distinctive, and therefore not part of the phonological description itself.

One of the difficulties in analysing intonation is that the forms themselves are not necessarily completely distinct from one another in the way that,

[52] For further discussion of the significance of intonation see Ch. 7.
[53] Other terms are 'pretonic' for the head, and 'tonic' for the nuclear pattern. The different shapes of nuclear patterns are often called 'nuclear tones'.

say, phonemes are. Though each phoneme may correspond to a range of different sounds, the phonemes themselves are assumed to be distinct. But with intonation there may be a range of different pitch patterns—for example, a falling pitch may start higher or lower and fall further or less far—and this variation is actually meaningful: a high, wide fall does not mean quite the same thing as a low, narrow one. This makes it difficult to establish a definitive set of phonologically distinct nuclear patterns. Nevertheless, it is possible to group the various pitch patterns into a number of major types. In German we need, at the very least, to recognize three different nuclear patterns, which might be labelled 'falling', 'rising', and 'level', and which are exemplified in 2.50.

(2.50)

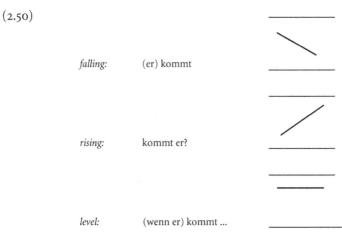

falling: (er) kommt

rising: kommt er?

level: (wenn er) kommt ...

The rising type tends to be used in certain kinds of questions (those which can be answered by *ja* or *nein*); the level type is frequently found in non-final intonation units, i.e. those which are followed by something else; the falling type is likely to be used everywhere else.

It is possible to produce stronger or more emphatic versions of these patterns which differ in the range of pitch movement, or in the presence of further glides. One common variant of the rising nuclear pattern, for example, has a preceding fall before the rise, as in 2.51.

(2.51)

falling–rising: kommt er?

As we have seen, other patterns, such as that of 2.49(ii), are also found, and we could regard this 'rising–falling' pattern as a further nuclear pattern, but it is difficult to say which of these should be regarded as variants or modifications of the others, and which are independent patterns in their own right.

Our description of German intonation so far has been rather informal, in the sense that it provides only a superficial phonological analysis. It is possible to go further than this though, as in the case of vowels and consonants, it is difficult to know where to stop in our search for generalization and abstraction.

Just as a vowel or consonant phoneme can be broken down into distinctive features, pitch patterns, too, are not necessarily indivisible. Any gliding pitch, such as a fall or a rise, can be described in terms of its end points: a falling pitch can be described as 'high' + 'low', and a rising pitch as 'low' + 'high'. Arguably, therefore, pitch patterns such as those described above could be seen phonologically as a sequence of high (H) and low (L) pitches, or 'tones'. These tones are not completely independent, but are grouped together to form patterns: H–L, L–H, L–H–L, etc. In German it will be observed that stressed syllables have a particularly important role in these patterns; if the location of the stress is indicated by '*', then we could describe these patterns as H*–L, L*–H, L*–H–L, for falling, rising, and rising–falling patterns and, by extending the principle a little, a level pattern can be analysed as H*–H.

These principles form the basis of an influential approach to intonation called AUTOSEGMENTAL-METRICAL theory.[54] In terms of this approach, the intonation patterns of phrases such as those we have discussed so far could be regarded as a sequence of PITCH ACCENTS (i.e. patterns such as H*–L). Since the nucleus of the pattern is also characterized by stress, it, too, can be interpreted as a pitch accent. However, the final pitch of the phrase can be separated from the pitch accent as it is more a property of the end of the unit rather than the accent; it is regarded as a BOUNDARY TONE, represented as H% (high) or L% (low). In these terms we can therefore describe the pattern of 2.48(iii) as H*–L H*–L H*–L L%.

One characteristic of the pitch accents of the head is that, where there is more than one, they are identical. From a phonological perspective, therefore, we may argue that specifying *all* the stressed syllables is redundant, and a single pitch accent, applied repeatedly according to the number of stressed syllables, would be more satisfactory, though this principle is not, in fact, built in to the autosegmental–metrical analysis.

It will be clear even from this very brief discussion of German intonation that this is a rather complex and elusive part of the language. There is far more

---

[54] The term derives from the fact that it is based on two theories: Autosegmental Phonology and Metrical Phonology. The first of these was originally devised for pitch in 'tone languages'; the latter is, as we have already seen, an approach to stress. We shall not pursue these theories further here, however.

to this area of phonology than can be dealt with adequately here; for more detailed discussion see the works listed under this topic in the Further Reading.

FURTHER READING

General Phonetics

Abercrombie (1968); Ball and Rahilly (1999); Clark and Yallop (1995); Ladefoged (2001); Laver (1994).

Phonological Theory

Anderson (1985); Davenport and Hannahs (1998); Gussenhoven and Jakobs (1998); Hawkins (1984); Katamba (1989); Lass (1984); Roca and Johnson (1999); Spencer (1996).

German Phonetics and Phonology

Boase-Beier and Lodge (2003: chs. 4 and 5); De Boor, Moser, and Winkler (2000); Hall (1992); Kohler (1995); MacCarthy (1975); Moulton (1962); Philipp (1974); Wängler (1983); Werner (1972); Wiese (1996).

German Stress and Intonation

Féry (1993); Fox (1984); Giegerich (1985); Pheby (1975).

EXERCISES AND DISCUSSION QUESTIONS

1. Explain how consonants and vowels are produced and how they are classified.
2. Give a phonetic label for the following German sounds: h, m, v, d, ŋ, tʃ, j, l, ʁ, ç.
3. Transcribe the following German words phonemically, marking stress: *Sprachwissenschaft, Landeszentralbank, Einnahmequelle, Pferdefuhrwerk, Kaffeebohnen, Dolchstoß, unabhängig, mutmaßlich, schüchtern, Fingerknöchel, Bücherschränke, Junggeselle, hübsch, überraschend, bösartig, Bauernhäuschen, Pförtnerloge, salonfähig, Chirurg, Tschechin.*
4. Explain the concept of the 'phoneme', and discuss its application and usefulness in describing the phonology of German.
5. Discuss the problems encountered in establishing a 'standard' pronunciation of German. To what extent do you consider the 'Siebs' pronunciation to be a satisfactory solution?

6. Discuss any areas of uncertainty or difficulty in establishing the phoneme system of German with respect to (i) vowels and (ii) consonants.

7. Compare the possibilities for final consonant clusters in English and German.

8. Evaluate the significance and usefulness of *distinctive features* in German phonology.

9. What advantages, if any, are there in a rule-based description of German phonology, as opposed to one using phonemes?

10. Outline the main principles that determine the location of the stressed syllable in German words. In what way do these rules need to be modified to apply to words in connected speech?

3

Morphology

Introduction

One complaint often made by learners of German is that it has 'a lot of grammar'. This is, of course, somewhat misleading, since all languages are complex and difficult for foreigners to learn, and there is no evidence that, taken as a whole, any language is significantly more or less complex than any other; *all* languages have 'a lot of grammar'. What is usually meant by this remark is that German has a particularly complex word structure, and in this respect certainly it may be said to be rather more complex than some other languages, including English. There are, of course, also many languages, especially outside the Indo-European family, that have more complex word structures than German.

As we noted in Chapter 1, it is customary to divide grammar into two basic parts, morphology and syntax, the former dealing with word structure, the latter with the structure of sentences. Since German words may be quite complex, morphology is an important part of the description of the language, and we shall need to examine these complexities in some detail. In this chapter we shall attempt to identify the various components of German word structure, and consider the ways in which these components may be combined.

The Word

Before examining the structure of words we must first consider what we mean by a *word*. For literate speakers, this is not normally felt to be a problem: a word is that stretch of language which is conventionally written with a space on either side. But we cannot really be content with this definition, as it does not tell us what a word actually is, but only how we represent it in writing. Unfortunately, it is not altogether easy to give a satisfactory definition; speakers, at least literate ones, feel they *know* what the words of their language are, with only marginal exceptions (should we write 'book mark', 'book-mark', or 'bookmark'?), but it is difficult to make this knowledge explicit, or to justify it according to linguistic criteria.

Attempts are sometimes made to define the word on semantic grounds, as a *unit of meaning*. This is not satisfactory, as it is impossible to say what we mean by such a unit. If *Mann* is one word, and *der Mann* is two because it has two units of meaning (MAN and DEFINITE), why is *Männer* only one word, even though it could be said to contain the meanings MAN and PLURAL? Another approach might be to identify the word in spoken language by phonological criteria, i.e. by aspects of pronunciation. Unfortunately, we do not split up our utterance into word-sized units in speech, pausing between the words, but run them together into whole phrases, and there are rarely any features which will tell us how many words there are.[1]

Definition of the word in terms of its meaning or its pronunciation is thus not satisfactory. However, the word is a unit of *grammar*, not of meaning or pronunciation, and we are more likely to be able to identify it in grammatical, rather than semantic or phonological, terms. If the word is an important grammatical unit, then this should be evident from its grammatical characteristics. One criterion we could use is what might be called its *grammatical integrity*. This is partly reflected in the fact that it is *not interruptable*. *Der Mann* is not a word, since we can insert an adjective in the middle of it (*der kleine Mann*); *Mann*, on the other hand, cannot be split up in this way. This is unfortunately not quite enough, since we could divide up the word *kleine* by the addition of the comparative *er* to give *kleinere*. We could hardly argue that forms such as *er* do not count because they are not proper words but merely 'endings', as it is precisely the nature of the 'word' that is at issue. A second reflection of the integrity of the word is its relative *independence;* it could be regarded as the smallest grammatical unit that can occur alone. Unfortunately, such words as *in, ist*, etc., could hardly be regarded as independent of other words, and would be unlikely to occur alone; conversely, it is sometimes possible to give even parts of words an independent status, as was done, for example, in discussing the comparative *er* earlier in this paragraph.

In short, definition of the word, even in grammatical terms, is difficult, and the criteria involved tend to depend on the identification of the word in the

---

[1] There may nevertheless sometimes be clues to the number of words in an utterance, or to the boundaries between one word and the next, especially in slower speech. For example, *finde Treue* and *findet Reue* can be distinguished, if need be, by the timing and length of the individual sounds. Similarly, the glottal stop before the second word might distinguish *sein Urgroßvater* from *sei nur Großvater*. Such boundary phenomena are covered by the term JUNCTURE (cf. the discussion of this term in Ch. 2). But such features are seldom completely reliable as a guide to the words involved.

first place. Such circularity, frustrating though it may be, is normal, indeed inevitable, in the definition of many linguistic units and categories. If we are to make any progress in linguistic description we must often take certain units, such as the 'word', for granted at the outset. As our description proceeds, our definitions may become more refined and precise, but they will nevertheless remain dependent both upon one another and upon the general theory of language structure which we adopt. In the remainder of this chapter, therefore, we shall assume that we can identify words, and our aim will be to determine their structure. As we proceed, the nature of the word will become clearer, since we in part define it in terms of this structure.[2]

Morphological Units

Despite the difficulties involved in defining the word, it nevertheless remains a basic unit of German grammar in terms of which many of the grammatical features and structures of the language can best be described. However, it is not the only unit, nor is it the smallest one. The word has a structure: it consists of smaller parts which occur in various combinations. Words such as *Möglichkeiten* or *Einbildungskraft* are clearly not indivisible, but contain a number of parts:

Mög-lich-keit-en

Ein-bild-ung-s-kraft

These individual parts are not further divisible into smaller grammatical units; they are the *minimal* units of word structure. By analogy with the term 'phoneme', which is the minimal unit of phonological structure, these minimal units of morphological structure are called MORPHEMES. Any German word can in principle be described in terms of such morphemes. Simple words, such as *Mann, komm, schnell*, etc., will consist of a single morpheme, while *Möglichkeiten* contains four, and *Einbildungskraft* five. Morphemes are, of course, analysable into phonemes on the phonological level,[3] but from the grammatical point of view they are indivisible. Such elements as *Mög-, -keit-, -bild-*, and so on are also clearly meaningful, and it would be possible to see the morpheme as the minimum unit of meaning. But although such a definition is sometimes put foward it is not quite accurate. It would be hard

---

[2] The usefulness and validity of the word may also vary from language to language. Even if we decide that all languages have such a unit, it cannot necessarily be defined in the same way in all cases.

[3] Cf. the mention of the 'double articulation' of language in Ch. 1. Morphemes belong to the 'first articulation', phonemes to the 'second'. Strictly speaking, we cannot say that morphemes 'consist of' phonemes, since they are on a different level; they are 'represented' or 'realized' by them.

to identify a meaning for the -*s*- of *Einbildungskraft*, for instance, though it does have a role in linking together the parts of the word. The morpheme, though generally meaningful, is not a unit of meaning as such, but of grammar; it is the minimal grammatical unit out of which words are built.

Let us begin our examination of German morphology by considering the words of 3.1.

(3.1)   *liebe*   *Liebe*
        liebt   *lieblich*
        lieben   *Liebchen*
        geliebt   *Liebling*

We have no difficulty in recognizing a common element in the form of all these words: *lieb*. We can say that the morpheme *lieb* is the basis of these and a number of other words, unifying them under the same heading, as it were. Apart from this basic morpheme *lieb*, these words contain other morphemes: *e*, *t*, *en*, *lich*, *chen*, etc., and we could find sets of words which have these morphemes in common, too. Some examples are given in 3.2.

(3.2)   (i)   (ii)   (iii)
        möglich   *Häuschen*   *lache*
        deutlich   *Mädchen*   *singe*
        freundlich *Küsschen*   *komme*
        gelblich   *Städtchen*   *schreibe*

There is, however, a difference between the sets of words in 3.1 and 3.2. While it makes sense to say that the words of 3.1 are all based on the morpheme *lieb* with various additions, we would find it rather odd to say that the basic morphemes of 3.2(i), 3.2(ii), and 3.2(iii) are *lich*, *chen*, and *e*, to which various other morphemes have been added. In other words, the status of *lieb* is somewhat different from that of *lich*, *chen*, and *e*; the former can legitimately be regarded as the main part of the words in which it occurs, since it contains the central component of meaning, while the latter have a less important role, indicating merely the grammatical function or the type of word. For this reason, then, we can distinguish between different kinds of morphemes—ROOTS (e.g. *lieb*) and AFFIXES (e.g. *lich*, *chen*, *e*, etc.)—and a word such as *lieben* can be analysed as *root* + *affix*. Though for the most part the affixes follow the root, a word such as *geliebt* shows that this is not always the case. A distinction can be made between different kinds of affixes according to where they occur in relation to the root, and especially between

SUFFIXES (affixes which follow the root), e.g. *-e, -t, -lich, -chen,* etc., and PREFIXES (affixes which precede the root), e.g. *ver-, ab-,* etc. As we shall see later, there are other possibilities too.

One obvious difference between roots and affixes is that the latter do not occur alone as independent words, while the former may do so. Thus, in addition to *Liebchen, lieblich,* etc., we also find just *lieb,* but not *chen* or *lich.* Affixes therefore occur only in conjunction with a root, while roots do not depend on affixes. Affixes are thus said to be BOUND, while roots are typically FREE. We must say 'typically' free, as not all roots can in fact occur alone. Examples are found in the words *vergessen* and *verlieren,* which contain the roots *gess* and *lier* respectively, although these roots never occur without the accompanying affix *ver-.* Because of examples like these, it is not possible to define roots as free morphemes and affixes as bound morphemes; some roots may be free, others bound.

Roots are the fundamental building blocks of the vocabulary of the language, and are therefore sometimes called LEXICAL MORPHEMES. Affixes, on the other hand, are more grammatical in character, and are combined with roots in order to fulfil a variety of grammatical functions. They are often called GRAMMATICAL MORPHEMES. The grammatical functions of affixes may be of different kinds. Words such as *liebe, liebt, lieben, liebte, geliebt,* etc. are generally thought of as forms of *lieben;* we would not expect to find them all listed separately in a dictionary, but only the one form *lieben* which is conventionally used to represent the whole set. Any other form of this word could represent the set just as well; in Latin and Greek dictionaries it is usual to give the first-person singular form of the verb (e.g. *amo* 'I love'), while in grammars of Sanskrit (the classical language of India) just the root is listed. In German the infinitive form is taken as a representative of all the other forms of this word, and these other forms are to be derived from it. This is not the case with all forms containing the root *lieb,* however. We would expect to find *Liebe, lieblich, Liebchen,* and so on, not as different grammatical forms of *lieben* but as independent words in their own right, words which themselves have a variety of different forms: *Liebe, Lieben; lieblich, lieblicher, liebliches, lieblichen,* and so on. Not all combinations of root and affix are quite the same, therefore, and the role of the affixes may thus be different in different cases. Some affixes distinguish different forms of the same word, others distinguish different words.

It will be noted that 'word' is being used in two different senses here, giving rise to a certain amount of ambiguity. There is a sense in which *liebe* and *liebte* are different 'words': they are written and pronounced differently, and they have a different meaning. But there is also a sense in which they are both forms of the same 'word'. These are clearly two different meanings of 'word', which it is important to keep apart. It is sometimes helpful to distinguish the two different senses by using different terms, WORD FORM and LEXEME, the first of these referring to individual 'words' such as *liebe, lieben, liebte*, etc., the latter to the whole set, the more general 'word' of which these are different manifestations. Thus, the lexeme LIEBEN (it is sometimes useful to print lexemes in capitals, though this practice will not always be followed here) has the word forms *lieben, liebe, liebte*, and so on. 'Words' such as *Liebe, lieblich, Liebling*, and so on are of course distinct lexemes in their own right.

Looking at the various affixes given so far in the light of this distinction, we can group them into two different categories. Some, such as those of the first column of 3.1, serve to distinguish different word forms belonging to the same lexeme, while others, such as those of the second column of 3.1, distinguish different lexemes. It will also be noticed that affixes of the first type are associated with certain regular grammatical categories of German—tense, number, etc. (these will be discussed in Chapter 4)—while those of the second type have no such regular grammatical role; their function is to create new lexemes from the same root. Affixes can therefore be added to roots for two different purposes: INFLECTION, producing different word forms of a lexeme with different grammatical functions, and DERIVATION, producing different lexemes from the same root. We can also classify the affixes themselves into inflectional and derivational types. Since they create new lexemes, the latter are also called LEXICAL affixes.[4]

It should perhaps be noted here that 'derivation', 'derive', and so on are not to be taken literally. Such terms are not necessarily meant to imply that speakers of the language take a root and actually derive a lexeme from it. Nor should the terms be understood in a historical sense, although derived forms will for the most part have evolved from simpler ones at some time in the past.[5] 'Derivational' and 'derive' must rather be interpreted as purely descriptive terms; *lieblich* is derived from *lieb* merely in the sense that it is a lexeme which contains the root *lieb* with an additional affix.

---

[4] There are many pitfalls in the terminology here. Although affixes are grammatical rather than lexical morphemes, we can nevertheless speak of 'lexical affixes'. Some scholars use the term 'lexeme' to refer to what we have here called the root, and restrict the term 'morpheme' to what we have called affixes; the term 'derivation' is occasionally used to include both derivation and inflection. In view of this confusion, it is important when consulting works on this subject to note carefully how the terms are defined.

[5] There are exceptions. New words may occasionally be formed from more complex forms (so-called *back formation*). An example is *Freimut*, derived from the form *freimütig*. In synchronic (non-historical) terms *freimütig* is 'derived' from *Freimut*.

It is possible to have more than one affix simultaneously in a word. However, not all words which appear to have more than one affix actually do so. The combination of prefix and suffix in the 'ge—t' or 'ge—en' of the past participle (*geliebt, getragen*), for example, is not a case of two affixes but of a single affix which has two parts, since these parts occur together with a single function. In this case we speak of a DISCONTINUOUS affix. But there are many genuine instances where there are two or more affixes in a word. Thus, *liebten* has two inflectional affixes (*t* and *en*); *Möglichkeit* has two lexical (derivational) affixes (*lich* and *keit*), while *mögliche* has a lexical affix (*lich*) and an inflectional one (*e*). In cases like the last of these, where we have both lexical and inflectional suffixes, the lexical ones come first,[6] and the inflectional ones are added to this combination of root + lexical affix. What is inflected, therefore, is not the root as such but this combination, which is called the STEM. The structure of the word *mögliche* is thus *stem + inflectional affix*, where the stem consists of *root + lexical affix*. Similarly, in *liebten* we could say that the inflectional affix -*en* is added to the past stem *liebt-*, though in this case the structure of the stem is *root + inflectional affix*. We can distinguish between the two kinds of stem, one formed with a lexical affix, the other with an inflectional affix, by calling the former a LEXICAL STEM and the latter an INFLECTIONAL STEM. In complex words such as *reinigten* the inflectional stem *reinigt-* is itself formed from the lexical stem *reinig-*, which contains the root *rein*.

In both inflection and derivation we are concerned with words containing a root morpheme and one or more affixes. There is also another possibility: words may contain more than one root, as exemplified in 3.3.

(3.3)   Bahnhof   Ankunftszeit
         Tischlampe   Parkanlage
         Kühlschrank   Gastarbeiter
         Haustür   Weltmeisterschaft

Words (lexemes) such as these are COMPOUNDS. Those in the first column of 3.3 consist of two roots, those of the second also have affixes, attached to either the first or the second root. Compounds may be much more complex than this, with such formations as *Bundesforstverwaltungsamt, Lastkraftwagenversicherungsgesellschaft*, and so on, which contain several roots and

---

[6] There are only isolated examples of the opposite order, such as *Kinderchen*, where the inflectional affix precedes the lexical one. But these must be considered exceptional, and this word is hardly standard German.

accompanying affixes. German is notorious for its propensity to form such long compounds.[7]

Compounding, like derivation, involves different lexemes; the roots of a compound together form a different lexeme from the roots themselves: *Bahnhof* is a different lexeme from *Bahn* or *Hof.* Both compounding and derivation are therefore sometimes grouped together as aspects of WORD FORMATION. All three of these—inflection, derivation, and compounding—will receive closer attention below.

Morphological Alternations

We have so far described word structure in terms of morphemes, and classified morphemes into roots and affixes, of which the latter may be either inflectional or derivational (lexical). Words can consist of one or more roots, either alone or in combination with one or more affixes.

Matters are more complex than this, however, the main difficulties being due to morphological alternations. In Chapter 2 we examined alternations between sounds, which made it necessary to distinguish between sound and phoneme, and indeed alternations between phonemes themselves, which could lead us to propose still more abstract phonological entities. Comparable problems arise in connection with morphology.

Just as phonemes have a variety of different realizations (allophones), so do morphemes. Consider a pair of words such as *Straßen* and *Menschen*. These could be divided up into two morphemes each: *Mensch-en* and *Straße-n*, the second morpheme in each case being the plural ending. Most books on German grammar rightly regard these two endings as variant forms of the same affix, and list it as (*e*)*n*, standing for both *en* and *n*. By analogy with phonemes and allophones, such variants of a morpheme are called its ALLO-MORPHS. Both -*n* and -*en* (or, in phonemic terms, /n/ and /ən/) are thus allomorphs of the same morpheme.

Roots, too, may be subject to alternation. *Tag* and *Tage* contain two different allomorphs of the same root: /taːk/ and /taːg/; similarly, we find *gelb* (/gɛlp/) and *gelbe* (/gɛlb/), *Rad* (/raːt/) and *Rades* (/raːd/), and so on.

All these alternations are entirely regular and predictable; they happen as a result of the combinations of sounds and their position in words. The plural ending is /ən/ after the final consonant of *Mensch*, but simply /n/ after the

---

[7] It should be noted that English has a similar tendency, but this is less evident since the compounds are not written as single words, e.g. 'community centre finance committee meeting', 'Science Research Council Student Award Scheme', and the like.

final /ə/ of *Straße*. Voiced obstruent consonants cannot occur at the end of German words, hence we find /g/ in *Tage* but /k/ in *Tag*, etc. These alternations are thus automatic, and are determined purely by phonological factors when morphemes are combined. It will be noticed that these are precisely the cases where we might introduce abstract phonological units such as 'morphophonemes', and devise phonological rules to modify them in specific contexts (see Chapter 2).

Not all alternations between different forms of the same morpheme are of this type, however. Consider the pairs of 3.4.

(3.4) *der Tag*   *die Tage*
       der Mensch   *die Menschen*
       das Kind   *die Kinder*
       die Oma   *die Omas*

The suffixes of the nouns in the right-hand column of 3.4 all have the same grammatical function: they indicate that the nouns are plural. They can therefore all be regarded as different allomorphs of the morpheme 'plural'. But in these cases the alternations do not depend on phonological factors at all. The particular allomorph of the plural morpheme that appears with each root is to a large extent arbitrary, and must often be learnt separately for each individual word. It would be difficult, and indeed pointless, to propose a 'morphophoneme' here, and to attempt to devise phonological rules to derive the allomorphs from it, since the relationship between the allomorphs is not phonologically regular.

Alternations of this kind, where the different allomorphs are not related in a phonologically regular way, are also found with roots, but they are less common, and indeed are usually treated as exceptions. Examples from German are the adjective *gut*, with its comparative and superlative forms *besser* and *best*, and the verb *sein*, with its present forms *ist*, etc., and its past form *war*. Here we can identify an alternation between phonologically unrelated roots: gut ~ bess-; sei ~ is- ~ war; etc. This phenomenon is called SUPPLETION. In cases of this kind, one or other of the alternating roots (here *bess-* and *is-*) is likely to be bound, since it may occur only in conjunction with specific affixes.[8]

Since the allomorphs of a given morpheme may sometimes be rather different from one another, it is clear that the morpheme itself cannot

---

[8] Historically, suppletion arises through the merging of different lexemes, so that what were originally quite separate roots come to be used in different word forms of a single lexeme. An English example is *go* with its past form *went*.

necessarily be identified with any one form. The reverse is also true: the same form need not always be identified with the same morpheme. For example, the morphological structure of the words of 3.5 is clear enough, and we have no difficulty here in isolating the minimal morphological components.

(3.5)   *Menschen*   =   *Mensch + en*
      kommen   =   *komm + en*
      Tage   =   *Tag + e*

Such components, unanalysable parts of words, are generally called MORPHS. But it is not possible, in the absence of further information, to identify the morphs as allomorphs of particular morphemes. The *en* of *Menschen* could be either plural or else accusative, genitive, or dative singular; the *en* of *kommen* could be the infinitive or the plural ending; the *e* of *Tage* could be plural or dative singular; and so on. Only in particular grammatical contexts can these ambiguities be resolved: in *des Menschen* the *en* is clearly genitive singular; in *der Menschen* it is genitive plural.

    Consider now the forms of 3.6. In grammar books such words are said to have 'no ending in the plural', but what does this mean in terms of morphological structure?

(3.6)   *der Lehrer*   *die Lehrer*
      das Mädchen   *die Mädchen*
      das Muster   *die Muster*
      der Onkel   *die Onkel*

At first sight it looks as if there is no plural morpheme in such words, but this is not necessarily the case. Contrasts such as *der Lehrer schreibt* versus *die Lehrer schreiben* show that there is a difference between *Lehrer* (singular) and *Lehrer* (plural), since both the article and the verb are different in each case, agreeing with the noun. Thus, we must conclude that the two forms of *Lehrer* are grammatically different: *Lehrer* and *Lehrer* + 'plural'. Following on from this, we can say that among the allomorphs of the plural morpheme in German (*-e, -er, -(e)n*, etc.) there is one which has no overt form: 'zero'. From the grammatical point of view, it makes sense to say that there is a difference between *Lehrer* and *Lehrer* + 'zero', since 'zero' is here an allomorph of the plural morpheme.

    The use of zero allomorphs is open to the objection that it is difficult to know where to stop. If the plural of *Lehrer* contains a zero allomorph, then why should we not treat the singular in the same way, as *Lehrer* + 'zero', where 'zero' is here an allomorph of the singular morpheme? The answer is that German nouns never have an affix to indicate the singular; if they did, then we could certainly treat cases where there is no overt affix as having a zero allomorph. But in German the singular is regularly indicated by the absence of an affix (we say that the singular is 'unmarked'). 'Singular' certainly is a relevant grammatical category of German, but it is not one that is indicated morphologically, except negatively. Thus, odd though it may seem, it is justifiable to distinguish between 'nothing' (the absence of a morpheme) and 'zero' (the 'presence' of a zero allomorph of a morpheme).

Consider now the pairs of singular and plural given in 3.7.

(3.7) *der Sohn*   *die Söhne*
       die Hand   *die Hände*
       der Mann   *die Männer*
       das Buch   *die Bücher*
       die Mutter   *die Mütter*
       das Kloster   *die Klöster*

How are these to be analysed morphologically? We note that the plural is not formed simply by adding an affix; the root also differs. One way of dealing with these plurals would be to divide them into two parts, corresponding to the root morpheme and the plural morpheme, where the root has a different allomorph in the singular and the plural, as in 3.8.

(3.8) Singular   Plural
       Sohn   *Söhn* + *e*
       Mann   *Männ* + *er*
       Hand   *Händ* + *e*
       Buch   *Büch* + *er*

But this is not entirely satisfactory, since there is no phonological factor to determine the alternation of roots, which must therefore be seen as a case of suppletion. This is even less satisfactory with plurals such as *Mütter* and *Klöster*, since here we have zero allomorphs of the plural morpheme, and therefore no obvious factor to determine the use of a different root.

Grammars of German generally find a simpler and more sensible solution: they regard the plural forms of 3.7 as being formed from the singular not merely by the addition of an ending but also by the modification or 'mutation' of the vowel (Umlaut), and in the case of *Mütter* and *Klöster* by Umlaut alone. The plural of these words is thus indicated in dictionaries by such means as '⸚ e', '⸚ er', and '⸚'. This is, of course, merely a graphic device, but it also has some linguistic justification. The relationship between the different forms of the root in the singular and plural is not an arbitrary one, but is phonologically regular. Forming the plural of words of this kind, therefore, consists not only in the addition of an affix but in modifying the root in a regular and predictable fashion, replacing one phoneme of the root by another. If we wish, we can regard such a modification (with or without the addition of an affix) as an allomorph of the plural morpheme, a REPLACIVE morph, though this is evidently a rather different kind of morph from those we have recognized so far, and it makes the notion of a morph itself perhaps rather less clear.

This phenomenon is not restricted to noun plurals in German. Consider the verb forms of 3.9 (so-called 'strong' verbs), in which the vowel of the root morpheme for a given verb is different in each column (Ablaut: see Chapter 2).

(3.9)	*beginnt*	*begann*	*begonnen*
	bittet	*bat*	*gebeten*
	singt	*sang*	*gesungen*
	liegt	*lag*	*gelegen*
	nimmt	*nahm*	*genommen*
	wächst	*wuchs*	*gewachsen*

The first and third columns of 3.9 are formed with the help of affixes, but the middle column relies solely on this difference of vowel as a means of identifying the form. The alternations here can again be described in terms of the replacement of one phoneme of the morpheme by a different one. In the forms of the second column of 3.9 such replacement could be seen as an allomorph of the 'past' morpheme. In regular (weak) verbs, this morpheme has a different allomorph, -t- (*liebte, machte,* etc.).

Morphological Models

From the above discussion it will be clear that German word structure is quite complex, and its description requires a variety of concepts and categories. It is also possible to look at it in several ways, from different perspectives, using a variety of descriptive frameworks, or MODELS. The traditional approach to describing and learning the forms of German words—as indeed those of other languages with a complex morphology, such as Latin or Greek—is to set out a PARADIGM, a list of the various forms of the words. Thus, in grammars of

German we find the forms for the masculine singular of the definite article given in 3.10 (i), and the forms of the present tense of *werden* given in 3.10 (ii). This is the WORD-AND-PARADIGM approach.

(3.10)   (i) (Nom.) *der*   (ii) (*ich*) *werde* (*wir*) *werden*
               (Acc.)   *den*   (du) *wirst*   (*ihr*) *werdet*
               (Gen.)   *des*   (er) *wird*   (*sie*) *werden*
               (Dat.)   *dem*

Although this model has proved invaluable for generations of language-learners, it does not really examine the structure of the words as such. No attempt is made to solve the problems raised by, for example, a form such as *wird* (which part of this word is the stem, which the inflectional affix?). The words are listed as wholes, and the problem of their structure does not arise. Though such paradigms of forms play a significant part in the learning of German by speakers of other languages, there is therefore some doubt as to their role in the structure of the language itself.

A second approach, sketched out in the above discussion, divides words into morphs, grouping different morphs together as allomorphs of the same morpheme. This is the ITEM-AND-ARRANGEMENT model, since it describes word structure in terms of morphs and their combinations. This model is characteristic of the 'structuralist' approach to language description (see Chapter 1). Unlike the word-and-paradigm model, it obviously does consider the question of word structure, and for many cases works well enough. But it is also not without its problems, since, as we have seen, not all aspects of word structure can be dealt with satisfactorily in these terms, notable difficulties being those associated with zero allomorphs and replacive morphs.

A third framework is the ITEM-AND-PROCESS model, which describes word structure not merely as an arrangement of morphs, but in terms of modifications to forms. As we have seen, this model seems particularly appropriate for certain types of plural and tense forms in German, where processes such as Umlaut and Ablaut are found, but it does demand a rather more elaborate descriptive framework, with more abstract base forms which are converted into others. A word like *Mütter*, for example, must be deemed to contain a root *Mutter* and the process of Umlaut, which modifies the vowel of the root. Such terms as 'process' and 'modify' must not, of course, be taken literally; there is no suggestion that speakers actually take a root and modify it in some way. They are part of a *descriptive model*, where the model makes use of processes rather than just static relationships. The item-and-process model can therefore best be interpreted within a 'generative' approach to linguistic description, since this incorporates processes as part of its formalism (cf. the discussion of generative phonology in Chapter 2). The abstractions inherent in this model are not acceptable to all linguists.

None of these models is necessarily to be regarded as the only correct one; each has its strengths and its weaknesses, and each may be appropriate for different aspects of morphological structure. The declension of articles and pronouns is often most conveniently represented in terms of the word-and-paradigm model; many aspects of German word structure can be usefully described in an item-and-arrangement model; while Umlaut and Ablaut seem to be more appropriately dealt with in terms of the item-and-process framework. Furthermore, different languages have different kinds and degrees of complexity of word structure, and may call for different descriptive frameworks.[9]

In addition to these three basic models, there are many different ways in which the structures and processes involved in the morphology of languages can be described, and a variety of different theories which attempt to account for the phenomena observed. We shall take up some of these issues again below.

Inflectional Mophology

As we have seen, affixes can be inflectional or lexical (derivational), according to their function, the former reflecting different grammatical forms of a lexeme, the latter serving to distinguish different lexemes. German makes extensive use of inflection, and we must consider in some detail the resulting word structures.

Since inflection involves the indication of certain grammatical categories, these must also be identified, though we shall postpone a detailed consideration of the categories themselves and of their functions until the next chapter. We must also bear in mind that word structure cannot be totally isolated from sentence structure, since the categories have important syntactic functions. And since the grammatical categories involved also depend on the kind of word (noun, verb, etc.), we must also pre-empt to some extent the more detailed discussion of word types also to be undertaken in the next chapter. This interdependence of the various linguistic levels and categories is,

---

[9] The traditional typology of languages, established in the 19th century., divides languages into three groups using morphological criteria: (a) ISOLATING languages, in which lexical words consist only of roots; (b) INFLECTING languages, with affixes representing a number of categories simultaneously; and (c) AGGLUTINATING languages, with affixes strung together in sequence. German falls into the 'inflecting' type. (See also below, n. 17.)

as already noted, a typical problem in the description of a language: each category tends to presuppose and define the others, so that wherever we commence our description we must take certain other categories for granted, and in order to explore one aspect of language in depth we must in the interests of clarity give it an independence and autonomy which, in the context of the language as a whole, it clearly does not have.

Traditionally, especially in descriptions of the classical languages (Greek and Latin), two types of inflection are distinguished, CONJUGATION and DECLENSION, the former applying to verbs, the latter especially to nouns, pronouns, and adjectives. Such a scheme is largely justifiable in German too, as it reflects the kinds of grammatical categories that are indicated by the inflectional affixes.

Conjugation

Grammars of German typically list a large number of different forms of the verb. For example, for the verb *tragen* we might find such forms as those of 3.11.[10]

(3.11)

ich trage		*wir tragen*	
du trägst		*ihr tragt*	
er			
sie	*trägt*	*sie tragen*	
es			

Sets of such forms can be given for all the different tenses, moods, etc. One edition of the Duden grammar, for example, lists no fewer than forty-two sets, each of which has these six forms. A representative selection is given in 3.12.

(3.12)   *er trägt*   *er trage*
          er trug   *er trüge*
          er hat getragen   *er habe getragen*

---

[10] The verb forms with the formal pronoun *Sie* are not included in the following tables. They are formally identical to the third-person plural forms, though they are, of course, second person in function. Since we are concerned here only with the formal structure of words, it is simpler to omit these forms.

er hatte getragen	*er hätte getragen*
er wird tragen	*er werde tragen*
er würde tragen	*er würde getragen haben*
er wird getragen haben	*er werde getragen haben*
er wird getragen	*er werde getragen*
er wurde getragen	*er würde getragen*
er ist getragen worden	*er sei getragen worden*
er war getragen worden	*er wäre getragen worden*
er wird getragen werden	*er werde getragen werden*
er würde getragen werden	*er wird getragen worden sein*
er werde getragen worden sein	*er würde getragen worden sein*

Such lists are familiar to all those who have learnt German by the word-and-paradigm method. A number of verbs are 'conjugated', giving all their various forms, and these are intended to serve as models for other verbs of the same type.

Since these are different forms of the same verb (i.e. of the same lexeme), the variety of different forms reflects the different grammatical categories involved. For example, the forms of 3.11 differ from one another in two respects: those in the left-hand column are 'singular' and those on the right are 'plural', and we can say, therefore, that NUMBER is a relevant grammatical category here. The distinctions within each column indicate PERSON ('first', 'second', and 'third'). Note, however, that although we may use pronouns of different genders in the third-person singular, no distinction of gender is made in the form of the verb itself; gender, though obviously important for nouns and adjectives, is not a relevant category for the verb.

In a similar way, the forms of 3.12 reflect a variety of other grammatical categories: TENSE ('present', 'past'), MOOD ('indicative', 'subjunctive'), VOICE ('active', 'passive'), etc. The large number of different forms results from combinations of these categories. Thus, *trägt* differs in tense from *trug* and in mood from *trage;* it differs from *trüge* in both these respects.

It will be noted that very few of the forms of 3.12 are actually single words. If morphology is concerned with word structure, then the analysis of these more complex forms is evidently no longer a morphological matter, but belongs to the study of syntax. However, it is precisely in cases such as these that the definition of the 'word' is open to question. It might seem odd, for example, that *trug* is regarded as a single word whereas *hat getragen*, which is similar in meaning, is regarded as two. But there are actually good reasons for endorsing this traditional analysis. Firstly, whereas *trug* is not interruptable, *hat getragen* is, since we can insert material between the two parts: *er hat es getragen* versus *er trug es.*[11] Secondly, an analysis of all these verb forms will demonstrate that the parts of which these complex forms are composed have a word-like structure, and are best treated as words in their own right.

To clarify this let us examine the structure of the forms given in 3.12. Forms such as *trägt* or *trage* consist of the verb stem *trag* and an affix (in the first of these with modification of the root itself). Given the kind of analysis set out earlier, in which morphemes are rather abstract entities whose allomorphs may also be zero or replacive processes, *trug* and *trüge* can be described in a similar way. The structure of all these forms can be given as

VERB STEM + TENSE AFFIX

(where *tense affix* stands for all the various morphs indicating such categories as 'tense', 'mood', 'person', and 'number': see below). The forms *hat getragen, hätte getragen,* etc., as well as *wird getragen, würde getragen,* and so on, all contain the verb stem, but this time with a discontinuous morph *ge—en,* which forms the past participle, and also an additional ('auxiliary') verb stem, either *hab-* or *werd-,* which is also accompanied by affixes. The resulting structure could be given as

AUXILIARY VERB + TENSE AFFIX — MAIN VERB + PAST PARTICIPLE AFFIX

Similar structures are found with other forms: *wird tragen* has the structure

AUXILIARY VERB + TENSE AFFIX — MAIN VERB + INFINITIVE AFFIX

while the most complex structure, exemplified by *wird getragen worden sein,* can be analysed as

AUXILIARY VERB + TENSE AFFIX — MAIN VERB + PAST PARTICIPLE AFFIX — AUXILIARY VERB + PAST PARTICIPLE AFFIX — AUXILIARY VERB + INFINITIVE AFFIX

Summarizing all these possibilities we arrive at the table of 3.13, where $v =$ main verb stem, AUX = auxiliary verb stem, AFF_1 = tense/person/number/mood morpheme, AFF_2 = past participle morpheme, and AFF_3 = infinitive morpheme.

(3.13)   *Structure*   *Example*
         $V+AFF_1$ *trägt*
         $AUX+AFF_1$ $V+AFF_2$ *hat getragen*
         $AUX+AFF_1$ $V+AFF_3$ *wird tragen*

---

[11] 'Separable' verbs are, of course, interruptable in a different way: *vortragen* but *er trug es vor.*

AUX+AFF₁	V+AFF₂	AUX+AFF₂		*ist getragen worden*
AUX+AFF₁	V+AFF₂	AUX+AFF₃		*wird getragen werden*
AUX+AFF₁	V+AFF₂	AUX+AFF₂	AUX+AFF₃	*wird getragen worden sein*

It will be evident from 3.13 that although some of the verbal forms are very complex, they can easily be broken down into parts, all of which have a similar, and rather simple, structure: they consist of a verb stem (either the main verb or an auxiliary verb) with an affix (or other morph) indicating either tense, mood, person, or number, or past participle, or infinitive. No matter how complex the form, the component parts can all be described in these terms. Since this simple structure of stem + affix is characteristic of the word, it makes sense to divide these complex forms into a sequence of words. Indeed, to treat the whole of such a form as a 'word' simply because, like *trägt*, it is a 'form of the verb', would complicate the description.

From the morphological point of view, therefore, these various verb forms consist of one or more words, the number of words and their structure depending on the particular grammatical categories involved. The 'perfect' and 'passive' have an auxiliary verb with the past participle of the main verb, while the 'future' has an auxiliary verb and the infinitive of the main verb.[12] Since all these categories can occur simultaneously, they interact in a complex but regular fashion to produce the forms listed above: the perfect passive has an auxiliary verb and the past participle of the main verb, but the auxiliary verb is itself made perfect with a second auxiliary verb: *ist getragen worden*. Should we need the future of this perfect passive, then this second auxiliary is made future with a third auxiliary and the infinitive of the second auxiliary: *wird getragen worden sein*.

Common to all of these forms is the presence of a word which contains the affixes for the categories of number and person, etc. This word (in the construction given here it is the first) is traditionally called the FINITE verb. Simple verb forms such as *trägt* or *trugen* consist solely of such forms, but the more complex forms also contain NON-FINITE verbs (participles or infinitives).

As for the type of morph involved, the majority are suffixes, attached *after* the stem. This is the case with all the forms of 3.11, where we can identify a number of different endings: *-e, -t, -en*, etc. The infinitive is likewise formed by the addition of a suffix *-(e)n*. The simple past form of weak verbs also has a suffix *-te* (*liebte*), but that of strong verbs, e.g. *trug*, involves a replacive morph, with a different form of the root itself, though in some cases, such

---

[12] The nature and validity of such categories as 'perfect', 'future', etc. will be considered in Ch. 4. These terms are used here simply because they are traditional designations of the forms in question.

as the plural, a suffix is added too: *trugen*. The past subjunctive of strong verbs has a further process of replacement, the root being subject to Umlaut: *trüge*. The past participle is characterized by a variety of means. With the regular (weak) verbs there is the discontinuous morph *ge—t* (*geliebt*), but strong verbs have a different allomorph *ge—en*, and generally also a replacive morph (*geschrieben*).[13] Derived verb stems with 'inseparable' prefixes (*ver-, er-, zer-,* etc.) dispense with the *ge-* prefix: *verliebt, verschrieben*.

But it is notable that, although the structure of some of the verb forms is quite complex, that of their component words is rather simple. Furthermore, if we examine the finite forms of 3.12, we find that they are few in number and restricted in type. As we see from 3.14, for any of these verbs, whether main or auxiliary, there are only four distinct forms for each person/number of the verb, and these reflect two grammatical categories, tense and mood, the traditional labels being 'present' and 'past' for the former, and 'indicative' and 'subjunctive' for the latter.

(3.14)   MAIN VERB

trägt	*trug*				
trage	*trüge*				

AUXILIARY VERB

hat	*hatte*	*wird*	*wurde*	*ist*	*war*
habe	*hätte*	*werde*	*würde*	*sei*	*wäre*

Of course, the forms of 3.12 are only examples, representing a set of six forms such as those given for the present indicative in 3.11, which, as we have seen, can be described in terms of person and number. Moreover, the auxiliary verbs tend to be irregular in many of their forms (the forms of *sein*, in particular, involve suppletion), and their morphological structure can hardly be taken as typical; they will be largely ignored in what follows.

Thus, if we restrict ourselves to the finite verbs, we find that we require four grammatical categories: person, number, tense, and mood (there are also other categories, which will be discussed in the next chapter). In order to determine what the various affixes associated with these categories are, and how they are organized in the structure of the finite verb, let us examine the individual word forms in more detail. For the present indicative and present subjunctive we can isolate the suffixes of 3.15.[14]

---

[13] No attempt will be made to describe the various changes in the verb stem that occur in the strong verbs. Cf. also the discussion of Ablaut in Ch. 2.

[14] The present subjunctive (Konjunktiv I) is, of course, not common, and is regarded as rather literary. However, we are not concerned here with its use but merely with its form.

(3.15) INDICATIVE   SUBJUNCTIVE
   lieb-e lieb-en *lieb-e lieb-en*
   lieb-st lieb-t *lieb-est lieb-et*
   lieb-t lieb-en *lieb-e lieb-en*

These are merely typical allomorphs. In a number of cases there are automatic, phonologically determined alternations, which for the sake of simplicity will be taken for granted here. Thus, in the indicative the second- and third-person singular and the second-person plural have an additional *e* when the verb stem ends in *t* or *d* (*reitet, leidest*); the second-person singular loses its *s* after a stem-final *s* (*reist, reißt*); and there is no *e* in the endings of the first- and third-persons plural after the lexical suffixes *-er* and *-el* (*erinnern, klingeln*).

It will be noticed that some of the suffixes of 3.15 are ambiguous: in the indicative, *-t* represents either the third-person singular or the second-person plural, while in the subjunctive the first- and third-persons singular are identical. In both moods *-en* could be either first- or third-person plural. The syntactic context is often necessary to determine what the form is (though with some strong verbs, such as *tragen*, the third-person singular is distinguished from the second-person plural by Umlaut: *trägt—tragt*). It will also be noticed that the forms of the subjunctive differ from those of the indicative only in the second- and third-persons singular and the second-person plural.[15]

For the past forms, both indicative and subjunctive, we must divide the verbs into 'weak' and 'strong' classes. As we see from 3.16, the weak verbs have the same forms for both moods (there are also some automatic alternations here with stems ending in *t* or *d*), while the forms of the strong verbs have a change of stem vowel, and, in some cases in the indicative, no ending at all. The subjunctive has Umlaut of the stem vowel, where appropriate, and the *e* of the second-person singular and plural is optional.

(3.16) WEAK
     INDICATIVE AND SUBJUNCTIVE
     lieb-te   *lieb-ten*
     lieb-test *lieb-tet*
     lieb-te   *lieb-ten*

---

[15] Since the indicative and subjunctive are distinct in only a minority of instances (in the past tense of weak verbs they are not distinct at all), it is arguable that we should not even attempt to draw up a complete set of forms here. But the existence of a distinction with certain verbs, such as *sein* and the 'modal' verbs, as well as in the past tense of strong verbs, makes it legitimate to do so. The subjunctive is clearly somewhat marginal in modern German, both in its forms and in its use.

STRONG

INDICATIVE		SUBJUNCTIVE	
trug	*trug-en*	*trüg-e*	*trüg-en*
trug-st	*trug-t*	*trüg-(e)st*	*trüg-(e)t*
trug	*trug-en*	*trüg-e*	*trüg-en*

These paradigms can be found in any German grammar book. But here we are interested in the possibility of analysing them further. Since there are two grammatical categories involved (tense and mood), each of which has two possibilities (present and past, indicative and subjunctive), we must ask first of all whether it is possible to identify morphs associated with each of these.

A number of such morphs do appear to be identifiable. In the past form of the weak verbs there is a *-t-* which does not appear in the present form, while the past of the strong verbs regularly has a different form of the stem. Somewhat less clear is the representation of the subjunctive. In the present, the subjunctive differs from the indicative only in three of the six forms (*-est* versus *-st*, *-e* versus *-t*, and *-et* versus *-t*), with a characteristic *e*; in the past, it can be identified in the case of the strong verbs partly by Umlaut (where the stem has a vowel which is susceptible to this process), and partly by differences in the endings, but in the weak verbs it is not distinct at all.

Thus, although we can in the majority of cases identify the paradigm to which a particular form belongs, it is clear that there is no such thing as *the* morph for past or for subjunctive. The actual morph used to indicate these categories varies according to what other categories are involved. In order to determine the morph for subjunctive we need to know whether the form is past or present, singular or plural, and first, second, or third person. This applies even more to the remaining categories, number and person. There is clearly no consistent morph for plural, as the morph used depends on whether the form is first or third person, in which case the morph is *-(e)n*, or second person, in which case it is *-t*. None of the persons has a consistent morph either; even where the forms are consistent in the different paradigms, as in the second person, the choice of morph depends on whether the form is singular or plural: *-st* versus *-t*.

In fact, the affixes for number and person are not just mutually dependent, they are inseparable. We can hardly speak of an affix for either of these at all, since a single affix represents both categories. Though both number and person are independent categories of the verb, they have a combined realization in a single affix. There are also relationships between the person/number affix and those of tense and mood, as we shall see.

Both tense and mood involve a contrast between two sets of forms: present and past in the first case, and indicative and subjunctive in the second. The contrast is not, however, an equal one; in each case one of the sets is given priority in the sense that it has no overt representation at all, but is indicated by default, as it were, by the *absence* of a morpheme (we saw above a similar situation with the singular of nouns, which is indicated by the absence of the plural morpheme). Thus, *liebten* contrasts with *lieben,* and *liebet* contrasts with *liebt,* the second form in each case lacking an element that is present in the former. We may say that present and indicative are UNMARKED for tense and mood respectively, while past and subjunctive are MARKED for these categories. This does not mean, of course, that there are no such categories as present and indicative, just as it does not mean that nouns have no singular. Nor is it the same as saying that they have zero allomorphs; this would imply that there exist other allomorphs for these categories which are *not* zero, and this is not the case, since present and indicative never have any overt manifestation. The present indicative is unmarked on two counts, while the past subjunctive is doubly marked. It may also be that there is no unmarked category for the person/number category; all of the six forms have some overt marker, though not necessarily in all the paradigms: the first- and third-persons singular lack a person/number affix in the past indicative of strong verbs (*trug*). But since there is a marker in other cases, the absence of a marker here can be treated as a zero allomorph of the respective morphemes.

Where tense and mood are marked, they may interact with the person/number affix, resulting in some difficulties of analysis. Consider, for example, the present subjunctive of a verb such as *lieben*. The first-person singular of this paradigm has the form *liebe,* for which there would appear to be only one possible analysis: *lieb + e*. Allowing for the possibility of zero allomorphs, however, we find that the assignment of the affix *e* to the appropriate category is not altogether straightforward. If we compare this subjunctive form with the corresponding indicative *liebe* they appear to be identical. We might say, therefore, that subjunctive has no overt realization here, but since subjunctive is a marked category we would expect a zero allomorph rather than merely the absence of a morpheme. Since the order of the affixes in cases where both mood and person/number affixes are present is stem + mood + person/number, the structure of the subjunctive *liebe* could plausibly be seen as

lieb + Ø + e

where Ø represents the position of the zero allomorph of the mood morpheme. When we inspect the whole paradigm of the present subjunctive, however, we find that *e* is a constant element in all its forms. It might be better, therefore, to see the affix of the subjunctive *liebe* as an instance of the mood morpheme, with *liebe-* as the subjunctive stem; in this case it is the person/number morpheme that has the zero allomorph, and the structure of this form is

lieb + e + Ø

Yet another analysis of this form could be devised. If we take *e* to be the regular marker of *both* first-person singular *and* present subjunctive, we would expect the first-person singular present subjunctive to have the form:

lieb + e + e

If we take this to be the 'underlying' form, we may derive the actually occurring form by means of a phonological process or rule of vowel reduction or coalescence (a similar rule could also be used to deal with the absence of *e* in the ending (*e*)*n* after /ə/):

/ə/ + /ə/ → /ə/

We are faced with the same kind of dilemma in other forms of the verb, too. Consider the relationship between the past indicative and past subjunctive of weak verbs. Outwardly, these two paradigms are indistinguishable, but the fact that there is a clear distinction in the strong verbs makes us reluctant to say that the weak verbs have no subjunctive; we assume that they have, but that the forms are identical with those of the indicative.[16]

Consider now how we might dissect a form such as *liebten*. The indicative mood is unmarked, and therefore we do not need to look for an affix for it. The marker of the past would appear to be *t*, since it occurs in all the past forms but is absent from the present forms (the *t* of the third-person singular and the second-person plural of the present is a person/number affix). This gives the past stem *liebt-*, which leaves the remainder of this word as the person/number affix; we arrive at the following analysis for the indicative form:

lieb + t + en

with *verb stem + tense + person/number*. As with the present forms, however, the subjunctive allows a number of different analyses. Since subjunctive is a marked category elsewhere, we might choose to regard the *e* as the mood affix, in which case we have a past-subjunctive stem *liebte-*, and simply *-n* as the

---

[16] This is, of course, a challengeable assumption (see n. 15). It draws some support from the fact that this form is frequently replaced by one with an overt subjunctive marker (*würde lieben*) and that certain verbs which have the weak past suffix (*bräuchte, könnte*) *do* indicate the subjunctive.

allomorph of the person/number affix, the other *e* being automatically lost. The subjunctive might thus be given the following structure:

lieb + t + e + n

with *verb stem + tense + mood + person/number*. Given such an analysis, the indicative and subjunctive of weak verbs would *not* be identical in structure, even though they are identical in pronunciation. Again, this is not the only possible analysis, nor is it necessarily the most plausible, but it does illustrate the kind of solution that is available.

The difficulties encountered here in segmenting verbs into their component morphemes are, in fact, typical of languages like German, which make extensive use of inflections. Affixes are frequently fused together in such a way that it is not possible to identify specific morphs as manifestations of individual grammatical functions or categories.[17] In many words a clear morphological structure is evident; they may be divided up with relative ease into morphs which can be assigned unambiguously to specific morphemes. But many other words do not have such a clear structure, and the analysis either breaks down or permits too many different possibilities. In such cases we have no alternative but to list the inflectional endings as wholes.

Declension

The traditional term *declension* covers a second type of inflection for a range of different word types—nouns, adjectives, pronouns, and articles—which can be conveniently grouped together, since they involve the same grammatical categories. These words share many of the principles and problems encountered in the analysis of the verb forms, and we shall not need to examine them in such detail.

As with the verbs, we must determine which grammatical categories are involved, and how the various morphs interact. As a point of departure let us consider the set of forms given in 3.17, which can be found in many German grammar books.

(3.17) (i) *der gute Mann*   *die gute Frau*   *das gute Kind*
              den guten Mann   *die gute Frau*   *das gute Kind*
              des guten Mannes   *der guten Frau*   *des guten Kindes*
              dem guten Mann   *der guten Frau*   *dem guten Kind*

---

[17] This is, in fact, the crucial difference between 'inflecting' and 'agglutinating' languages in the traditional typology referred to in n. 9, above. In the former, various categories are represented by a single affix, while the latter has separate affixes for each category. A frequently cited example of an agglutinating language is Turkish.

(ii)   *die guten Männer   die guten Frauen   die guten Kinder*
       die guten Männer   die guten Frauen   die guten Kinder
       der guten Männer   der guten Frauen   der guten Kinder
       den guten Männern   den guten Frauen   den guten Kindern

The categorization of these forms presents little difficulty: those of (i) are singular and those of (ii) are plural, the three columns being 'masculine', 'feminine', and 'neuter'. The four rows of (i) and (ii) are 'nominative', 'accusative', 'genitive', and 'dative'.

The grammatical categories involved here—number, gender, and case—apply to the declension of all the relevant word types (article, pronoun, adjective, and noun), though in slightly different ways, and a number of general points can be made about all of them. First, the fusion of categories that we observed with the verb is even more in evidence here: just as it was not possible to separate the morphs for person and number in the verb, in the pronouns, adjectives, and articles the three categories of number, gender, and case cannot be morphologically dissociated: a single affix indicates all three simultaneously. For example, the form *der* represents the masculine nominative singular of the definite article, but it is not possible to determine any part of it that indicates masculine or nominative or singular individually; the ending *-er* must be taken as a whole. This does not apply to the noun, where there is generally a separate morph to indicate the plural, so that here only gender and case are represented together, e.g. in the *-es* affix of the masculine and neuter genitive singular.

That there are no separate morphs for number, gender, and case in adjectives, pronouns, and articles does not mean that these are not independent grammatical categories for these words. The form of the article differs according to the number or gender or case of the noun, and hence all three categories are grammatically relevant, even if we cannot always isolate them morphologically.

A second general point is that not all the actually occurring forms are distinct. Since there are two numbers (singular and plural), three genders (masculine, feminine, and neuter), and four cases (nominative, accusative, genitive, and dative), the number of potentially different forms of each word is $2 \times 3 \times 4$, which is 24. In fact, however, there are only six forms of the article (*der, die, das, den, des,* and *dem*), two forms of the adjective (*gute* and *guten*—though this is only true after the definite article; elsewhere there are more), and the maximum number of forms of the nouns is four[18] (*Mann, Mannes,*

---

[18] This excludes the *-e* ending of the dative singular in the masculine and neuter (*dem Manne, dem Kinde*). This affix is only marginal in modern German; it can only be used with certain kinds of words, and even then it is rare, being inserted for stylistic reasons. It also occurs in a few fixed expressions, e.g. *im Grunde genommen.*

Männer, Männern). As a result, there is inevitably considerable ambiguity in the forms if taken in isolation. The word *der* may be masculine nominative singular, feminine genitive or dative singular, or genitive plural of all three genders; *den* could be masculine accusative singular or dative plural; and so on. And a form like *guten* is hardly interpretable at all, since it can represent every combination of categories apart from masculine nominative singular, and feminine or neuter nominative or accusative singular.

On the other hand, a number of distinctions exist which are apparently unconnected with grammatical categories as such. Thus, as exemplified in 3.18, the adjective has a slightly different set of forms from the above when it follows the indefinite article or words such as *kein*, etc., and a further set when there is no preceding word at all. This gives us so-called 'strong', 'weak', and 'mixed' declensions.

(3.18)		'STRONG'	'WEAK'	'MIXED'
	(NOM.)	*guter* Wein	der *gute* Wein	ein *guter* Wein
	(DAT.)	*gutem* Wein	dem *guten* Wein	einem *guten* Wein

All this makes the declension of German nouns, articles, pronouns, and adjectives seem rather arbitrary. If most of the categories cannot be identified because the forms are not distinguishable, while further distinctions are made which apparently have no function at all, this suggests that the whole system is so inefficient as to be unworkable.

Before attempting to counter this argument, let us examine in a little more detail the forms of the individual word types. As far as the noun is concerned, the major inflection is, as we have just noted, that of number: the singular is unmarked, while the plural is characterized by a range of different morphs, including a variety of different suffixes (-*e*, -*er*, -(*e*)*n*, -*s*, and 'zero'),[19] with or without Umlaut (-*er* is always accompanied by Umlaut if the stem has a susceptible vowel; -*e* and 'zero' have Umlaut in some words but not in others; -(*e*)*n* and -*s* never have Umlaut). Examples are given in 3.19.

(3.19)	(-*e*)	*Tag*	*Tage*
	(-*e* + Umlaut)	*Rat*	*Räte*
	(-*er* + Umlaut)	*Rad*	*Räder*
	(zero)	*Wagen*	*Wagen*
	(zero + Umlaut)	*Boden*	*Böden*
	(-*en*)	*Mensch*	*Menschen*
	(-*s*)	*Oma*	*Omas*

[19] This excludes, of course, the plural formations of foreign loanwords, such as *Celli, Examina*, etc.

Apart from the plural, the only regular inflections of any note in the German noun are the -(*e*)*s* of the genitive in the masculine and neuter singular, and the -*n* of the dative plural (all genders). There is also one class of so-called weak nouns which has -(*e*)*n* in all forms except the nominative singular, e.g. *Mensch ~ Menschen, Affe ~ Affen*.

On the whole, therefore, the declension of nouns is rather simple. Moreover, the possibility for conflicting analyses of the same form (such as we saw in the verb) only arises in the dative plural, which may have both a case affix and a plural affix. Different analyses are in fact possible where the plural allomorph is the suffix -(*e*)*n*, and we might be uncertain whether the final -*n* of *Straßen* in *auf den Straßen* is actually the plural ending, or the mark of the dative, or both.[20]

The articles and pronouns can be taken together, as they are morphologically very similar. Their forms are rather more elaborate than those of the nouns, as they make more distinctions of grammatical categories, though even here there are ambiguities, as we shall see. There are many different pronouns, including *demonstrative* (*der, dieser, jener*), *relative* (*der, welcher*), *interrogative* (*wer, welcher*), *possessive* (*meiner*, etc.), and *personal* (*ich, du, er, sie, es*, etc.), as well as others such as *jeder, solcher, keiner*, etc. Apart from the personal pronouns, they inflect in a very similar way to the definite article, except for some forms of the genitive (e.g. *dessen, wessen*). Many of the pronouns have corresponding adjectives, with a slightly different inflection (e.g. *mein Wagen* versus *der Wagen ist meiner*). The indefinite article has similar forms to these adjectives, with no ending in the masculine nominative singular, or the neuter nominative and accusative singular (*ein*); it also has no plural forms. In what follows we shall for the sake of simplicity largely confine ourselves to the forms of the definite article.

The personal pronouns stand somewhat apart from the other forms, and are more difficult to analyse consistently. The most obvious difference from the other pronouns (though shared with the possessive pronouns) is the additional category of person (1, 2, and 3), which, as we have seen, is also found with the verb. With these pronouns, too, gender is only relevant in the third-person singular. A further peculiarity is that they use a variety of different stems. While a pronoun such as *jeder* has the same stem throughout, in all cases, numbers, and genders, the third-person pronouns have at least three quite different stems, and even these are not quite consistent. *Ihn, ihr,* and *ihm* seem to suggest a stem *ih-*, but this will not do for *ihrer* or *ihnen,*

---

[20] Various solutions to this problem are possible along similar lines to those put forward for the verb, using zero allomorphs or rules deleting an 'underlying' *n*.

where the stem would need to be *ihr-* and *ihn-* respectively. Again, there is little alternative but to regard them as morphological anomalies.

The forms of 3.17 show that all four cases are distinguished in the masculine singular of the definite article. The feminine singular is less differentiated, with only two forms, one for the nominative and accusative, the other for the genitive and dative, while the neuter has a single form for the nominative and accusative, and is identical to the masculine in the other two cases. In the plural, it is immediately noticeable that the forms are the same for all genders. This is no mere coincidence; it is a systematic feature of German declension that there are no gender distinctions in the plural. It is sometimes said, borrowing the terminology of phonology, that the distinctions are *neutralized* in the plural. A similar situation, though on a smaller scale, is found in other forms. As we have seen, the distinction between nominative and accusative is relevant only for the masculine singular, while the distinction between masculine and neuter is applicable only in the nominative and accusative singular.

But not all instances where forms are the same can be regarded as neutralization of distinctions. The masculine nominative singular *der* is identical to the feminine genitive and dative singular, and also to the genitive plural, but the categories themselves remain distinct, and can usually be identified with the help of other forms (see below). The same is true of the form *die*, which is identical in the nominative and accusative for the feminine singular on the one hand and the plural of all genders on the other.

The adjective declensions are complex, not particularly in the forms themselves but in the choice of different sets of forms in different contexts. As noted above, adjectives have no fewer than three different paradigms, sometimes called *weak, strong,* and *mixed.* As the forms given in 3.18 show, the 'strong' and 'weak' forms differ in both the nominative and dative cases. The 'mixed' forms are like the 'strong' in the nominative but the 'weak' in the dative.

These have characteristic uses: the weak declension is used after the definite article and *dieser* etc.; the strong declension where no article is present; and the mixed declension after certain words such as the indefinite article and *kein.* However, it is not the uses but the forms that interest us here. The forms of the strong declension are similar to those of the definite article, except in the genitive singular; in contrast, the weak declension distinguishes only two different forms, while the mixed declension has characteristics of both the other two. This variety of forms raises a number of more general questions, particularly about the way in which the grammatical distinctions are indicated morphologically. Here we may recall the question posed earlier: to what extent are the morphs able to indicate the various grammatical categories, when so many of the distinctions are obscured, especially by the wholesale neutralization of forms in the adjective?

In order to answer this question we must take account of a number of other features of the morphological structure of sentences. Firstly it will be observed that although we have considered the grammatical categories purely in terms of the structure of the individual words, the words do not occur in isolation, and the affixes of one word are not independent of those in neighbouring words. There is CONCORD or AGREEMENT among the words of the whole phrase. Thus, in a phrase such as *des guten Weins* all three words share the same grammatical characteristics: they are all masculine genitive singular. We can say, therefore, that these words *agree* in gender, case, and number. The gender of the phrase is, of course, determined by the noun; it is *intrinsic* to the noun, but *extrinsic* to other words. The gender is also *fixed* for a given noun, but the other categories are *variable,* in the sense that they change with the particular use to which the phrase is put. If we change this use, so that the phrase is plural, or dative, the forms will change accordingly, but we are not free to make it, say, feminine.

It is usual to say that the article and adjectives agree with the noun, i.e. that the noun determines the forms of the other words in the phrase, but this is only clearly the case with regard to gender, since this is an intrinsic property of the noun. There is a sense in which we could claim that a category such as 'plural' or 'dative' is a property of the whole phrase. This is in fact borne out by the forms themselves. Consider the problem of ambiguity referred to above. Although we may say that case is an important grammatical category for nouns in German, the forms of the nouns themselves hardly indicate it at all. As we have seen, the singular of most masculine and neuter nouns has an affix to indicate the case only in the genitive; the nominative, accusative, and dative are indistinguishable. In the plural only the dative has a distinct form, while the feminine singular has no affixes at all. When there is a definite article, however, its forms come to the rescue: although *Mann* is ambiguous as to case, *der Mann* is certainly not. Paradoxically, although the noun is supposed to determine the case, and the article is said to agree with it, it is only through the form of the article that the case of the noun can be determined.

On the other hand, the articles themselves contain ambiguities. As we have noted, the masculine nominative singular is indistinguishable from the feminine genitive and dative singular and from the genitive plural: all have the form *der.* In the context of the whole phrase, however, ambiguities are actually very few. We have no difficulty in assigning the phrases of 3.20 to the appropriate categories, even though the article is identical in each: (i) is clearly masculine nominative singular because the noun itself is masculine and singular, and in the masculine singular *der* characterizes the nominative. This would be clear without the adjective, but the form of the latter reinforces the interpretation, as the only other possibilities for *der* would be followed by *großen*, as in (ii) and (iii).

(3.20) (i)   *der große Mann*
       (ii) *der großen Frau*
       (iii) *der großen Frauen*

The interpretation of these latter two forms as singular or plural depends on the form of the noun. The ambiguity of *die*, as nominative or accusative feminine singular, or as plural of any gender, can be resolved in a similar way: *die große Frau* and *die großen Frauen* are singular and plural respectively because of the form of both the noun and the adjective. With nouns which have a zero allomorph in the plural there could be difficulties without an adjective, but, perhaps significantly, such difficulties do not arise because no nouns of this type are feminine! The only ambiguities that might occur here would be with nouns which are themselves ambiguous, e.g. *Leiter*. *Die Leiter* may be the plural of *der Leiter* ('leader') or the singular of *die Leiter* ('ladder').

What is evident here, and it could easily be further exemplified, is that the morphological interpretations of the affixes involved in declension may often depend on the forms found elsewhere in the phrase, so that the phrase must be taken *as a whole*. In this way, most of the potential ambiguities of the individual forms turn out not to be ambiguities at all. Some ambiguities will, of course, remain, especially when not all the words are present which could give the clues: *der Leiter*, for example, is still ambiguous as to nominative singular or genitive plural of the masculine noun, or genitive singular of the feminine noun, but in the wider context of the sentence as a whole even these ambiguities will be resolved. If *der Leiter* is the subject of the sentence, it must be masculine nominative singular; if it follows a preposition, e.g. *mit der Leiter*, it must be feminine dative singular.

The various different forms of the adjective must also be seen in the light of this. The fact that we find *der gute Wein* but *guter Wein* can hardly be unrelated to the importance of the *-er* suffix as an indicator of masculine nominative singular. In *der gute Wein* this affix, combined with that of the adjective, is a clear marker of the form; without the article, the affix passes to the adjective, and the interpretation remains unambiguous. Naturally, we cannot take this idea too far; both ambiguities and redundancies will always remain. But it does seem clear that significant distinctions are maintained by the interaction of various parts of the phrase. This interaction, and the role of the whole phrase in distinguishing grammatical categories, shows both the significance, and the limitations, of German inflectional morphology.

Lexical Morphology

Derivation and Inflection

Derivational, or lexical, morphology differs from inflectional morphology in being concerned with the formation of different lexemes from the same root, rather than with different grammatical forms of the same lexeme. As we saw earlier, words such as *liebe, liebt, liebte,* etc. all belong to the same lexeme, the different forms reflecting the various grammatical roles that this lexeme has to play, and the different grammatical categories that can be associated with it. By contrast, words such as *Liebe, lieblich, Liebchen,* and so on, though containing the same root, are not grammatical variants of a single lexeme, but are lexemes in their own right, and their affixes do not reflect grammatical categories such as number, tense, etc., but serve to distinguish the lexemes from one another.

Inflectional and lexical morphology also differ in their role in the structure of sentences. Inflectional categories such as case have an important syntactic function, and agreement between words which share the same categories plays a significant part in the establishment of syntactic relationships. Lexical affixes, on the other hand, are of more importance for the vocabulary, since they allow the creation of new lexemes out of existing resources.

There are other characteristics, too, which tend to differentiate the two kinds of morphological structure. One feature of word forms of the same lexeme is that they all belong to the same class of words. The words *liebe, liebt, liebte,* etc. are all verbs, whereas *Liebe, lieblich,* and *Liebchen* are nouns or adjectives. It is an important function of lexical affixes that they can create not just different lexemes but words belonging to different classes. This in turn allows them to be used in different ways in sentences. Thus, in the examples of 3.21 the different lexemes formed from the same root belong to different types of word, and they have a different syntactic role in each case.[21]

(3.21)	(adjective)	Der Garten ist sehr *schön*
	(noun)	Die auffallende *Schönheit* des Gartens
	(verb)	Der Gärtner *verschönert* den Garten

---

[21] The syntactic role of derivational morphology will be further discussed below.

A further difference between lexical and inflectional affixes is that the latter are far freer in their potential combinations with roots. Given a stem of a particular type (noun, verb, etc.), the appropriate inflectional affixes or morphological processes can usually be applied to it without difficulty. If we take any German weak verb, it will generally be possible to form its third-person singular or past subjunctive, etc. even if we have never heard the form before. For example, we may well not have heard of the verb *strotzen*, nor know what it means ('to abound in'), but this will not prevent us from forming the past *es strotzte*, or the perfect *es hat gestrotzt*. In the case of lexical morphology, however, this is rarely so, since the derived forms from a particular root may be quite idiosyncratic and unpredictable.

By way of illustration consider the adjectives and the corresponding nouns derived from the same root given in 3.22.

(3.22) *groß*   *Größe*
        feige   *Feigheit*
        sauber   *Sauberkeit*
        finster   *Finsternis*
        bereit   *Bereitschaft*
        deutsch   *Deutschtum*

Although each of these adjectives has a corresponding noun, the form of the noun is different in each case, and it is not possible to add just any affix to any root: there is no **Bereitnis*, **Saubertum*, or **Feigschaft* (the asterisk indicates a non-occurring form). Thus, we cannot simply invent new derived forms in the same way that we can create new inflected forms from a given stem.

These two kinds of morphological structure—inflection and derivation—thus differ in both their form and their function, and they must be kept apart. Nevertheless, the distinction is not without its problems. Consider, for example, the infinitive form of the verb. This involves the addition of an affix to the verb stem, but it is not regarded as an instance of derivation since it is merely a different grammatical form of the same lexeme. However, we can also derive another form from all verbs which is identical to the infinitive, e.g. *das Kommen, das Singen, das Essen*, etc. These are sometimes called SUBSTANTIVAL INFINITIVES, and, as the name makes clear, they are no longer verbs but nouns ('substantives'). They cannot, therefore, belong to the same lexeme as the verbal forms, but must be different lexemes, and hence cases of lexical, rather than inflectional, morphology. The problem here is that these forms are completely regular in exactly the same way that infinitive forms are: given any verb stem, we can automatically create not only a verbal infinitive but also a substantival one. We have no difficulty in producing such a form, even when the verb is unfamiliar: from *strotzen* we obtain *das Strotzen*.

A similar case is found with adjectives. As we have seen, German adjectives inflect in specific ways in various contexts when with an accompanying noun. But they also have similar affixes when the accompanying noun is not present, as in 3.23.

(3.23)	*alt*	*der alte Mann*	*der Alte*
	schlank	*eine schlanke Frau*	*eine Schlanke*
	blau	*mein blaues Hemd*	*mein Blaues*

Though using the same affixes as when there is a noun present, these forms *replace* the noun rather than accompany it, and must be considered to be nouns in their own right. Hence, they must be different lexemes from the corresponding adjectives. Here again, however, these forms are not only identical to the inflected forms, but they are also totally regular, and can be produced from almost any adjective stem. It should be noted that, where an 'adjective' occurs alone, it is not necessarily to be interpreted as a noun, since the phrase may be elliptical, i.e. the noun is simply omitted—e.g. 'das blaue Hemd oder das grüne'. German spelling here uses a small letter for the adjective. But in other cases, e.g. 'er sagt immer das Richtige', there is no omitted noun and the adjective must be regarded as nominalized. It is then written with a capital letter. But the dividing line between these two cases is not always clear, creating some orthographic uncertainty.

A more marginal case is presented by the comparative and superlative forms of the adjective. We may derive such forms from almost any adjective stem with the affixes *-er* and *-(e)st*, as in 3.24.

(3.24)	*der späte Zug*
	der spätere Zug
	der späteste Zug

These forms are completely regular, but here there is no change of word type: they are derived from adjectives, but they remain adjectives. We might question, therefore, whether such cases are inflectional or lexical. The regularity of these formations, and the fact that no change of word class is involved, would suggest the former. But we may also note that in many other cases whose status as lexical formation is not in doubt, such as those of 3.25, there is no change of word class either.

(3.25)   (noun—noun)   *Mensch*   *Menschheit*
         (adjective—adjective)   *gelb*   *gelblich*
         (verb—verb)   *kommen*   *verkommen*

Thus, the crucial difference between inflectional and lexical morphology appears to rest not on the regularity of the formation nor on the change of word class, but rather on the function of the affixes as indicators of certain grammatical categories.

Inflectional affixes have the role of associating the lexeme with one of these grammatical categories, whereas lexical affixes do not. Just what we regard as an appropriate grammatical category in this sense is open to discussion, and hence so is the dividing line between these two morphological types. Such categories as 'plural', 'past', 'verbal infinitive', etc. evidently qualify for inflectional status in German, whereas 'substantival infinitive' or 'substantival adjective' do not. But whether 'comparative' or 'superlative' fall into the former or the latter category is debatable.

Types of Derivation

Despite the problems of classification just noted, the distinction between inflectional and lexical morphology remains generally viable and useful. It will be clear, however, that there are several different kinds of derivation, some of which are rather closer to inflection than others.

An important concept here is that of *productivity*. As we have noted, some forms may be created rather freely (e.g. substantival infinitives and adjectives), while others are more restricted (e.g. nouns ending in -*tum*). We may distinguish between PRODUCTIVE and UNPRODUCTIVE affixes, the former being those which can be used by speakers to form new lexemes, the latter being those which cannot. For instance, the suffix -*er* in such words as *Leser, Fahrer*, etc. is productive, since it is possible for speakers to create new forms from existing verbs virtually without restriction. On the other hand, the suffix -*t* in *Fahrt, Flucht*, etc. is unproductive: it is no longer possible for German speakers to create new nouns by adding this suffix to a verbal stem. The productive affixes are clearly those which come closest to inflections, since it is a general characteristic of all inflections that they are productive in this sense.

The distinction between productive and unproductive affixes is not an absolute one; there are degrees of productivity of affixes, such that certain words could in principle be coined with them for special purposes (e.g. as technical or scientific terms) but not as a general rule. The suffix -*tum*, for instance, could not generally be used to form new nouns in the productive way in which -*er* can be, but a non-existent word such as *Händlertum* would be more or less comprehensible, and not an impossible formation should the need ever arise to coin it. Such affixes are sometimes called SEMI-PRODUCTIVE. Furthermore, even highly productive affixes cannot necessarily be used with every root. We might reasonably assert that the suffix -*heit* (or the related -*keit*) is productive in the creation of new nouns from adjectives. But, as noted in 3.22 above, it cannot be used with, for example, *groß*. One suggestion here is that the existence of established forms containing unproductive or less productive affixes—here 'Umlaut + -*e*'—may 'block' the creation of a regular form with a productive affix—here -*heit*. This blocking does not always take place, however, since a form such as *Blassheit*, though not normal, would not be completely impossible as an alternative to the regular *Blässe*.

There is inevitably a historical dimension to the notion of productivity, since unproductive affixes were obviously productive at the time the words containing them were formed, but now no longer are, whereas productive ones are productive at the present time. However, it must be stressed again that 'derivation' is not a historical concept, but a descriptive term designating structural characteristics of words in the modern language. Words such as *Fahrt, Flucht,* etc. are still 'derived' from the corresponding roots *fahr* and *flieh* in modern German, even though the suffix is no longer productive. The -*t* suffix differs from productive suffixes like -*er* in modern German simply in occurring in a fixed set of words, to which no more words can be added.

There are, furthermore, cases of historical derivation which are no longer to be regarded as derivation in the modern language. The words *Blume* and *Samen*, for example, are historically derived from *blühen* and *säen* respectively, by the addition of a suffix (-*me* and -*men*, respectively). But this suffix is not merely unproductive in modern German, it is also unidentifiable without a knowledge of the history of the language. In modern German *Blume* and *Samen* must be seen as containing only a single morpheme, with no affix at all.[22]

We saw earlier that the forms of a lexeme all belong to the same class of words, whereas different lexemes formed from the same root may be of different word classes. Some lexical affixes have the function of converting one type of word to another—e.g. -*er,* which converts verbs to nouns (*fahren ~ Fahrer*), or -*heit,* which converts adjectives to nouns (*schön ~ Schönheit*). On the other hand, there are lexical affixes which do not affect the word class,

---

[22] The extent to which speakers make explicit connections between such words and their historical bases is inevitably individual and variable. It is not impossible that some German speakers, even those without the necessary historical knowledge, might feel these nouns to be derived from the appropriate verbs.

such as *-chen* (*Tisch* ~ *Tischchen*), or *ver-* (*lieben* ~ *verlieben*). The first type are called CLASS-CHANGING affixes, the second CLASS-MAINTAINING affixes. Whereas the role of class-changing affixes is generally that of allowing a stem to be used in different syntactic ways, the second produces a different kind of word within the same class. For example, while *Mensch* refers to an individual, *Menschheit* refers to all humans and is a 'collective' form; *Tisch* is the general word for 'table', while *Tischchen* is a 'diminutive' form. It will be clear that while class-changing affixes have important syntactic implications, class-maintaining affixes generally do not.

Most German affixes do not fall exclusively into one of these classes or the other, however, but may apply to a number of word types. The suffix *-lich*, for example, forms adjectives, but from a variety of sources, as we see from the examples of 3.26, of which the first two rows are class-changing and the last is class-maintaining.

(3.26) (noun)   *sprachlich, weiblich*
        (verb)   *beweglich, möglich*
        (adjective)   *gelblich, reichlich*

Cases such as this allow us to apply further classificatory criteria, especially with the class-changing category. We may describe the role of lexical affixes either in terms of the *source* or in terms of the *target*. By 'source' is meant the type of word from which the new lexeme is formed—principally nouns, verbs, or adjectives. The source is indicated terminologically by the (lexical) prefix 'de-': words formed from nouns (e.g. *weiblich*) are called *denominal* derivations; those formed from verbs (*beweglich*) are *deverbal*, and those formed from adjectives (*gelblich*) are *deadjectival*. By 'target' is meant the type of word that is produced, whatever its source, again principally nouns, verbs, and adjectives. The most frequently produced word type is the noun, and the process is called *nominalization*. Less elegant, though fortunately less frequently found, are the terms used for the formation of verbs and adjectives: *verbalization* and *adjectivalization* respectively.[23] Any particular class-changing formation, therefore, can be described in terms of both its source and its target. *Schönheit* is the result of a 'deadjectival nominalization', and *brauchbar* of a 'deverbal adjectivalization', and so on. In practice, however, it is rarely necessary to use these clumsy terms.

---

[23] The reader who has followed the discussion so far might like to try a morphological analysis of these complex English words!

Determining the source of a derived lexeme is not always straightforward, however. In the first place, there are many cases of multiple derivation, where the stem to which the lexical affix is added is itself a derived form. Take, for example, the word *Möglichkeit*. This is a nominalized form of the adjective *möglich*, which itself is derived from the verbal root *mög-*. The ultimate source of the word is thus a verb, but *Möglichkeit* is actually a deadjectival rather than a deverbal formation.

The complexities that may ensue from such multiple derivations can be illustrated with the verbal root *fahr-* and its derivatives. In 3.27 we see merely a sample of the many lexemes that are derived from this root by a variety of means.

(3.27)   *fahren Fahrt Fahrer Fahrerin*
          einfahren Einfahrt
          Gefahr gefahrlos Gefahrlosigkeit
          gefährden Gefährdung gefährlich Gefährlichkeit
          Fähre Gefährte Gefährtin
          Fuhre Abfuhr
          führen Führer Führung
          verführen Verführer verführerisch

As can be seen, a number of stems are derived from the original root, and then serve as the basis for further derivations. The eventual form may be related to the original root only indirectly, through several stages of derivation.

Furthermore, the ultimate source of a derived form may in some cases be ambiguous as to its word class. Although there is usually no doubt about the class of words to which a root should be assigned, especially when it also occurs alone as a word (the *schön* of *Schönheit* is unmistakably an adjective), in some cases we might at least have doubts. For example, is the root *teil* of *Vorteil* and *teilbar* a noun or a verb? *Vorteil* seems to be a derivative of *Teil*, which is a noun, while *teilbar* seems related to *teilen*, which is a verb. Presumably we shall wish to identify the same root in both *teilen* and *Teil*, but which of these is the source of the other? Since there is no derivational affix involved here (the -*en* of *teilen* is inflectional) we cannot appeal to morphological structure in order to settle the issue.

To throw more light on this kind of problem, it is worth examining the kinds of derivational processes available to the language. Although we may distinguish the roles of inflectional and lexical morphology, the structures and processes involved in both are very similar: derived lexemes are formed by means of suffixes, prefixes, discontinuous and replacive morphs, and zero affixes, or by means of combinations of these. Some examples are given in 3.28.

(3.28)	(suffix)	*schön*	*Schönheit*
	(prefix)	*sagen*	*versagen*
	(discontinuous morph)	*reden*	*Gerede*
	(replacive morph)	*greifen*	*Griff*
	(zero morph)	*laufen*	*Lauf*
	(prefix + replacive morph)	*stehen*	*Verstand*
	(suffix + replacive morph)	*Stadt*	*Städtchen*
	(discontinuous + replacive morph)	*Berg*	*Gebirge*

Of special importance is the type without an affix, called ZERO DERIVATION or CONVERSION. It is this type that causes the problem of identifying the source referred to above, since we cannot distinguish the source from the target on the basis of the absence versus the presence of a lexical affix. Some of the problem cases for the differentiation of inflection from derivation are also of this type; difficulties arise with substantival infinitives and adjectives precisely because there are no lexical affixes to identify them as derivational. Thus, the noun *Gehen* is derived directly from the verbal infinitive *gehen* without modification, as is the noun stem *Alt-* from the adjective *alt*, and so on. In the case of pairs such as *laufen ~ Lauf, fallen ~ Fall*, where verbs and the corresponding nouns have the same stem, it is usual to regard the verb as the source of the noun in most cases, though with *teilen ~ Teil* the noun seems more appropriate as the source of the verb. In either case we have conversion, but since the stems are identical it is hard to find evidence for the direction of derivation in the word structure itself.

Replacive processes are of two basic types: Umlaut and Ablaut (cf. Chapter 2). In the examples given in 3.27 the root *fahr-* produces *fähr-* by means of the first, and *fuhr-* by the second. The two processes can be combined to give the stem *führ-*. All of these then serve as the basis of further derivations. In a few cases replacement is more radical: *gehen ~ Gang* and *stehen ~ Stand*, where the derived form uses the same stem as the past participle.

As we can see, it is possible to classify the various structures and processes involved in German lexical morphology in a variety of different ways. To conclude our discussion, we shall present some examples of the different types. No attempt will be made to list all the possibilities, as this would be beyond the scope of this book; more complete lists will be found in the works referred to under Further Reading at the end of this chapter.

Nominalization accounts for the majority of lexical formations in German. Most nominalizations involve the addition of suffixes, but other means are, as we have seen, discontinuous and replacive morphs, and conversion. Few of these are restricted in their application to one particular word type, though many tend to have one major source. Apart from describing the various forms in terms of their structure, we can also attempt to classify them according to the function of the nominalization. Thus, deverbal nouns in *-er* could be said to be largely 'agentive', since they designate the doer of the action; denominal forms in *-heit* are 'collective' (*Menschheit*); deadjectival forms in *-e* (*Blässe, Kürze*) are 'abstract'; and so on. It is often difficult, however, to find a suitably general label to cover all the words produced by a particular means, and such categorization will not be undertaken here. The reader may like to pursue this further. Typical examples of nominalization are given in 3.29.

(3.29)   DEVERBAL

-e	*Liege*
—(+ Ablaut)	*Lage*
-erei	*Fahrerei*
-ung	*Drohung*
-er	*Fahrer*
-nis	*Erlaubnis*
—(+ Umlaut)	*Gefängnis*
-ling (+ Umlaut)	*Sträfling*
-schaft	*Leidenschaft*
-t	*Fahrt*
Ge- (+ Ablaut)	*Geruch*
—(+ Umlaut)	*Geräusch*
Ge—e	*Geschreibe*
—(+ Ablaut)	*Getriebe*
—(+ Umlaut)	*Gebläse*
(Ablaut)	*Sprung*
(conversion)	*Essen*

DENOMINAL

-ei	*Gärtnerei*
-er	*Frachter*
—(+ Umlaut)	*Bürger*
-ler	*Sportler*
—(+ Umlaut)	*Künstler*

-ner	*Harfner*
—(+ Umlaut)	*Pförtner*
-heit	*Menschheit*
-schaft	*Freundschaft*
-chen (+ Umlaut)	*Pünktchen*
-lein (+ Umlaut)	*Bächlein*
-in (+ Umlaut)	*Ärztin*
Ge- (+ Umlaut)	*Gebüsch*
Ge—e (+ Umlaut)	*Gestühle*
Erz-	*Erzbischof*
Ur-	*Urzeit*
Miss-	*Missklang*
Un-	*Unkraut*

DEADJECTIVAL

-e (+ Umlaut)	*Nässe*
-heit	*Schönheit*
-keit	*Sauberkeit*
-igkeit	*Genauigkeit*
-ling (+ Umlaut)	*Schwächling*
-nis	*Finsternis*
(conversion)	*Gut*

The majority of nominalizing affixes and processes also determine the gender of the noun: nouns in *-ung, -heit, -schaft, -t,* etc. are all feminine; diminutive forms in *-chen* and *-lein* are neuter; nouns derived from verbs by Ablaut are masculine; and so on.[24] There are also some that are more variable: nouns in *-nis* are either feminine (*die Finsternis*) or neuter (*das Erlebnis*).

The derivation of adjectives, of which some examples are given in 3.30, is neither as varied nor as complex as that of nouns, but there are nevertheless several different possibilities.

(3.30)   DEVERBAL

-bar	*brauchbar*
-ig (+ Ablaut)	*bissig*
-lich	*verzeihlich*

---

[24] Some of these regularities account for the native German speaker's intuitions about gender. One widely used German grammar suggests that *Schrank* must be masculine because 'der Schrank' *sounds right* (Hammer 1971: 1). An explanation might be that this word looks like a typical deverbal Ablaut formation, and such forms are all masculine.

—(+ Umlaut)	*käuflich*
-sam	*biegsam*
-haft	*lebhaft*

DEADJECTIVAL

-lich (+ Umlaut)	*kränklich*
-sam	*langsam*
-haft	*krankhaft*
-ig (+ Umlaut)	*völlig*
ge-	*getreu*
un-	*untreu*

DENOMINAL

-bar	*fruchtbar*
-lich	*sprachlich*
—(+ Umlaut)	*täglich*
-sam	*gewaltsam*
-ern (+ Umlaut)	*hölzern*
-er	*Berliner*
-haft	*zweifelhaft*
-ig	*staubig*
—(+ Umlaut)	*bärtig*
-isch	*modisch*
—(+ Umlaut)	*bäurisch*
-los	*mühelos*
-mäßig	*schulmäßig*

The possibilities for lexical derivation of verbs are more restricted, and they are of a different kind from those encountered so far. Whereas nominalizations and adjectivalizations are primarily a matter of suffixes or of change in the root, verbs can be formed with only a few suffixes, but with a wide range of prefixes. The principal suffixes are listed in 3.31, but verbs are also formed without affixes: *ehren, fetten,* etc. A 'causative' type of verb is formed from nouns or adjectives, usually by means of Umlaut (*färben, kürzen, töten*), and from other verbs often by other vowel changes: *tränken* (cf. *trinken*), *senken* (cf. *sinken*), *führen* (cf. *fahren*), and so on.

(3.31)	*-ieren*	*hausieren*
	-igen	*reinigen*
	-eln (+ Umlaut)	*näseln, kränkeln*
	-ern	*steigern*

The major lexical device with verbs is, however, the addition of prefixes. These fall into two types, with both syntactic and phonological implications: 'inseparable' and 'separable'. The former include *be-, ent-, er-, ge-, ver-, zer-,* etc.; the latter include *ab-, an-, auf-, aus-, ein-,* among others. The separable prefixes are characterized syntactically by not being bound to the verb stem. In most constructions, but not in all, they are treated as independent words: *ich nehme es auf* but *ich kann es aufnehmen;* further, they have the property of occurring before the inflectional *ge-* of the discontinuous past-participle morphs *ge—en* and *ge—t: aufgenommen, ausgemacht.* Phonologically, these prefixes are stressed. The inseparable prefixes, on the other hand, are like other prefixes in being unstressed and inseparable from the rest of the stem; they replace the first part of the discontinuous past-participle morph: *vernommen, besagt.* A few affixes can be used in either way (*durch, über, um, unter*), resulting in some well-known contrasts of meaning, e.g. with *übersetzen,* which can mean 'carry over' (separable) or 'translate' (inseparable).

With other word classes the possibilities for lexical derivation are rare. There are a few suffixes which regularly characterize adverbs (*-s* in *morgens, -maßen* in *gewissermaßen, -weise* in *glücklicherweise,* etc.), and the prepositional use of nouns such as *Dank, Trotz, Statt,* etc. could be regarded as a case of conversion.

In the above list no account has been taken of foreign affixes. A number of the 'native' ones are actually of foreign origin (e.g. *-ei, -er, -ieren*), but they have been integrated into the language to various extents, and are no longer felt to be un-German. But there are also many affixes which remain foreign. These are generally added to foreign rather than native roots, as in 3.32, but we also find some hybrids, e.g. *Lieferant,* which contain a native stem. For the most part, too, native affixes are not added to foreign roots, but again there are exceptions, e.g. *natürlich.*

(3.32)   *-ant*   *Fabrikant*
          -eur   *Friseur*
          -ität   *Universität*

One further characterization of foreign affixes can also be pointed out: their effect on stress. As we noted in Chapter 2, the main stress in native words is normally on the root, the affixes remaining unstressed. Usually, then, derivational affixes will not affect the location of the stressed syllable (this is not true of the prefixes of separable verbs, however, which, as we have just noted, are stressed). But in words containing affixes of foreign origin the situation is rather different, since a number of these affixes are regularly stressed. We thus find sets of words such as those of 3.33, where the location of the stress varies according to the affix.

(3.33)   *Or'gan*
          Orga'nismus
          organi'sieren
          Organisati'on

Since some of these affixes can also be added to native German roots, these can also be affected, as we see from the words of 3.34.

(3.34)   *'waschen*   *Wäsche'rei*
          'Haus   *hau'sieren*
          'liefern   *Liefe'rant*

This discussion of German derivational morphology is not, of course, exhaustive, and the above lists are by no means complete. There are also many more problems than have been considered here, and different theoretical approaches which attempt to solve them. It will be clear even from the limited discussion here, however, that this area of German is both very significant for its role in the grammar of the language and very complex.

Compounding

Like derivation, compounding is concerned with the formation of lexemes from existing roots, but while derivation achieves this by affixes, in compounding it involves roots. The possibilities that this gives are somewhat different from those of derivation. As we have seen, class-changing lexical affixes convert lexemes of one class into those of another, enabling the root to fulfil a variety of syntactic functions, while class-maintaining lexical affixes provide a means of differentiating lexemes into semantic subclasses. Compounding serves functions similar to these, and especially to the latter, since it may also differentiate lexemes within a given word class, but this differentiation goes far beyond what can be achieved by affixes alone.[25]

As an example, consider the root *fahr-* illustrated in 3.27 above. We saw there that a large number of lexemes can be derived from this root, belonging to all the major classes of words, and this can be achieved by means of lexical affixes or other morphs. In some cases a derived form may itself be the source of further

---

[25] Compounding has only a limited class-changing role. Examples are provided by cases such as *Taugenichts* or *Vergissmeinnicht*, where the resulting class of the word is not the same as that of its parts.

derivations: *Fahrt* gives *Vorfahrt, Einfahrt, Ausfahrt,* etc. The prefixes in these last examples do not involve change of word class, but rather serve to specify more narrowly the meaning of the stem to which they were added. But we may also take this same stem and combine it with other roots, to give *Autofahrt, Bahnfahrt, Schifffahrt, Kreuzfahrt, Heimfahrt,* and the like. Again, the meaning of the stem *fahrt* is made more specific, but this is done in a very different way. While affixes allow only a limited range of very general subclassifications of the stem morpheme, these being of a grammatical kind, the range permitted by compounding is enormous, since it is achieved by drawing on the resources of the vocabulary rather than those of the grammar.

Important though the difference between derivation and compounding is, it is not absolute, as the status of individual morphemes as roots or affixes may occasionally be in doubt. Consider, for example, the morpheme *Zeug*. This occurs as a lexeme in its own right, but it is also found as the second part of more complex forms such as *Werkzeug, Fahrzeug, Schlagzeug, Spielzeug, Bettzeug, Nähzeug,* etc. Since *Zeug* is an independent lexeme, we might consider these words to be compounds, but the meaning of *zeug* is here so general that it is hardly more than an affix. The same is true of a number of other morphemes, such as the adjective-forming *fähig*; this is again a word in its own right, but it is used as an affix in forms such as *zahlfähig, gebrauchsfähig,* etc. Similarly, *weise* can be attached to many adjective-stems to form adverbs, e.g. *notwendigerweise, möglicherweise, glücklicherweise,* and so on. It could be regarded as a lexical affix in such cases, even though it is also a word in its own right.

Exactly where we draw the line between root and affix here, and what criteria we can use to do so, is not easy to decide. The main factor seems to be the kind of meaning that the morpheme conveys. The meaning of an affix is normally so general that it can only be described in terms of its effect on other morphemes, e.g. 'creates agentive nouns from verbs', 'makes the meaning of the noun collective', etc. Hence, we are justified in seeing affixes as grammatical devices. The meaning of roots, on the other hand, is more independent, and can be given—however inadequately—in a dictionary. But a number of morphemes remain somewhat marginal; it might be possible to discern in the *zeug* of *Werkzeug* something of the (admittedly rather vague) meaning of the independent word *Zeug*, though its meaning is here so general as to qualify for grammatical status.

The Structure of Compounds

We have defined a compound as a lexeme containing more than one root. This is in principle true, but it requires some elaboration. Consider the examples of 3.35.

(3.35) *Bleistift*   *Tischtuch*
        Lehrerzimmer   *Gesellschaftsspiel*
        Buchhandlung   *Rotkehlchen*
        Schönheitsfehler   *Verkehrshindernis*

Some of these words contain only roots, while the remainder also have affixes, attached to the first root, the second root, or both. In the case of these more complex compounds, the component parts are not single roots, but stems, consisting of a root and one or more lexical affixes. Thus, though it is certainly true to say that compounds contain one or more *roots*, it might be more appropriate to say that they consist of one or more *stems*.

There are, however, a number of additional complexities, since the component parts of a compound cannot always be identified with stems. In some cases we find that compounds contain inflections or other elements that do not appear to be part of the stems themselves. Compound nouns, for example, may be plural (e.g. *Fahrräder, Teppichböden*), with a plural affix at the end and/or a replacive morph. It will be noticed that it is the *last* element of the compound that is inflected, and which determines the affix to be added. If the compound is a noun it also determines the gender. There is a sense, however, in which the whole word is plural, so that the structure of a word like *Fahrräder* is not

$$(\text{stem}) + (\text{stem})^{\text{plural}}$$

but rather

$$(\text{stem} + \text{stem})^{\text{plural}}$$

where the superscript affix applies to what is inside the brackets which it follows. What is inflected, in other words, and what therefore constitutes the stem of the compound, is the combination of component stems. It would not really be accurate to say that a compound consists of stems, since there may also be inflections, but we can say that the *stem* of a compound will consist of stems.

The point can be made even more strongly with certain lexical affixes. As we have already observed, lexical affixes can be attached not only to roots but also to derived stems, and the same applies to compound stems. A word such as *schöngeistig* may appear to have a two-part structure, *schön* + *geistig*, but a more plausible analysis is $(\textit{schön} + \textit{geist})^{\text{ig}}$, since the word is not directly derived from *geistig*; it is in effect an adjective formed from *schöner Geist*. Similarly, *Schwerverbrecher* is not to be analysed as *schwer* + *Verbrecher*; it cannot be paraphrased as 'ein Verbrecher, der schwer ist', but rather as 'jemand, der etwas Schweres verbrochen hat'. The analysis (*schwer* + *verbrech*)^{er} might therefore be more justifiable. In all these cases a compound stem is formed to which are added either inflectional affixes or lexical affixes, in the latter case producing a further stem.

There are also a number of instances where the first component of the compound is inflected, either for number (plural) or for case (genitive), e.g.

Bücherschrank   *Wörterbuch*
Landesgrenze   *Bundeswehr*

In these cases it is not possible to treat the inflection as applying to the whole word; here we must accept that the first component is neither a root nor a stem but a whole word form. A similar problem is created by LINKING MORPHEMES. In a number of instances the component stems of a compound are linked together by a more or less 'empty' morpheme. Some examples are:

Einbildungskraft   *Sonnenschein*
Arbeitsplatz   *Warteraum*

Though ostensibly attached to the stem of the initial element of the compound, this linking morpheme is not really an inflectional ending of the initial stem. The *s* of *Einbildungskraft* and *Arbeitsplatz* has no real justification here as an inflection, since the first component is a feminine noun, for which *s* is not an appropriate inflection. Even in the other examples it would be difficult to interpret the function of this linking morpheme in inflectional terms.

We have so far considered only compounds containing two roots, but more complex formations, with more components, are frequent. To a large extent these more complex forms can be analysed in the same way as those containing only two components, but the addition of more parts increases the structural possibilities. Take, for example, the word *Autobahnbrücke*. This word has three roots (*Auto, bahn,* and *brücke*), but the structure is not a simple linear one, as the first two roots belong more closely together:

(*Auto-bahn*) + (*brücke*)

The word *Hauptbahnhof,* on the other hand, though also containing three roots, has a different structure, with the second and third elements more closely related:

(*Haupt*) + (*bahn-hof*)

As the number of components increases, so do the possible structures, and it becomes imperative to have some means of determining what the structure is.

A useful test, as with words like *schöngeistig* or *Schwerverbrecher* discussed above, is to paraphrase the compound, splitting it up into two parts. Thus, *Autobahnbrücke* is a 'Brücke über die Autobahn' and not a 'Bahnbrücke für ein Auto', while *Hauptbahnhof* is not a 'Hof für die Hauptbahn' but rather a 'Haupt(art) eines Bahnhofs'. With longer words such tests become rather elaborate: *Bundeslandwirtschaftsforschungsamt* is the 'Landwirtschafts-forschungsamt des Bundes'; the *Landwirtschaftsforschungsamt* is the 'Amt für Landwirtschaftsforschung', while *Landwirtschaftsforschung* is 'Forschung über die Landwirtschaft'. We thus obtain the structure of 3.36.

There may sometimes be difficulties in determining the appropriate structure. For example, is a *Windschutzscheibe* a 'Schutzscheibe vor dem Wind' or a 'Scheibe zum Windschutz'? We can also find different interpretations of a given compound according to how it may be paraphrased. *Wintersportanzug*, for example, is ambiguous: it may be an 'Anzug für den Wintersport' or a 'Sportanzug für den Winter'.

(3.36)

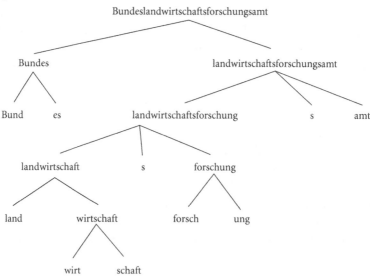

In some cases the structural problems of compounds may go beyond the word itself. Consider the phrases of 3.37.

(3.37)   *die medizinische Buchhandlung*
          das bürgerliche Gesetzbuch
          das geheime Wahlrecht

Paraphrases give a 'Handlung für medizinische Bücher', a 'Buch der bürger-
lichen Gesetze', and a 'Recht auf eine geheime Wahl'. The *Handlung* is not
medizinisch, nor is the *Buch bürgerlich*, or the *Recht geheim*.

Here the syntactic structure of the phrase, which divides the phrase into
adjective + compound noun, does not correspond to the relationship between the stems, which associates the first part of the compound more closely
with the adjective than with the second part of the compound. The structure
of *geheime Wahlrecht* is thus (*geheime-Wahl*) + (*recht*). In other cases alternative interpretations may be possible: *deutsche Sprachwissenschaft* may be
either (*deutsche*) + (*Sprachwissenschaft*) or (*deutsche-Sprach*) + (*wis-
senschaft*), according to the meaning.[26]

Types of Compounds

Compounds can be classified in a number of ways. As with derivation, the
formations may be subdivided according to the type of word that results—
compound nouns, compound verbs, compound adjectives, etc.—but the
source words are too various to give a simple set of categories. More useful
is a classification according to the relationship between the component parts.

Consider the examples of 3.38, which display a variety of different relationships between the components.

(3.38)   *Arbeitszimmer*   *Hochhaus*
         Strumpfhose   *Radiowecker*
         Taugenichts   *Handvoll*
         Schleswig-Holstein   *Baden-Württemberg*

Arbeitszimmer and *Hochhaus* are compounds of the kind discussed above,
where the first element qualifies the second: an *Arbeitszimmer* is a kind of
Zimmer, a *Hochhaus* a kind of *Haus*. This is not true of *Strumpfhose* or
Radiowecker, however; a *Strumpfhose* is not a kind of *Hose*, but rather both
a *Strumpf* and a *Hose*; a *Radiowecker* is both a *Radio* and a *Wecker*. *Taugenichts*
and *Handvoll* are different again; they are more like whole phrases, and again
neither part can be regarded as a qualification of the other. *Schleswig-Holstein*
and *Baden-Wurttemberg* are likewise of a different kind, denoting an entity
which is the result of combining the two parts.

A number of terms are in use to designate these and other types of
compounds. The first type (*Arbeitszimmer*), in which one part qualifies
another, is called a SUBORDINATING compound; the second (*Strumpfhose*),

---

[26] There are also a number of humorous possibilities here, such as *der vierstöckige Hausbesitzer, der
siebenköpfige Familienvater*, or even *der geruchlose Klosettfabrikant*.

where the two parts are equal, is a COORDINATING compound. The third type (*Taugenichts*), more akin to a whole phrase, is known in German as ZUSAM-MENRÜCKUNG,[27] while the fourth type (*Schleswig-Holstein*) is a COPULATIVE compound. These are not the only types, nor are these the only terms used to describe them.[28]

Most compounding involves nouns, and the most common and most productive kind of compounding is subordination. We shall therefore examine some aspects of this type of compounding as an illustration of the typical problems and principles involved. Subordinating compound nouns with an adjective as the first component (i.e. with the structure *adjective + noun*) are perhaps the most straightforward. Examples are:

Großstadt   *Sauerkraut*
Edelmann   *Hochhaus*

For the most part the relationship between the components of these compounds is clear, and can be expressed by the approximate paraphrase 'N which is A' (N = Noun, A = Adjective): a *Großstadt* is 'eine Stadt, die groß ist'.[29] This interpretation will work for the majority of such compounds. Slightly more variable in interpretation are nouns with a verbal stem in the first position (V + N). In some cases the interpretation could be stated as 'the N which V-s' (V = Verb), e.g.

Glühwürmchen   *Rollstuhl*
Stinktier   *Poltergeist*

but in others it is 'the N which is for V-ing', e.g.

Fahrschein   *Kochtopf*
Gießkanne   *Streichholz*

though *Schlagsahne* and *Bratwurst* could also be interpreted—less plausibly— as 'the N which has been V-ed'. There are also some cases, such as *Gefrierpunkt,* which fall outside these possibilities and are difficult to reduce to a general formula.

---

[27] There does not appear to be a consistent English equivalent of this term. The term 'phrase compound' has been used.

[28] Other categories that can be found in discussions of word formation are *endocentric* and *exocentric*, and, as types of coordinating compounds, *additive* and *appositional*. For details of these see the books referred to under Further Reading.

[29] Such paraphrases are, of course, only approximate. There is a difference between 'eine Stadt, die groß ist' and 'eine Großstadt'—the latter, as one lexeme, having a unitary meaning which is not identical with the sum of its parts.

Noun compounds whose first element is also a noun ($N_1 + N_2$) are still more varied, with a range of different interpretations. As an example, consider the words of 3.39, which are some of the forms based on *Arbeit*.

(3.39) *Hausarbeit*   (place)
        Kinderarbeit   (agent)
        Handarbeit   (instrument)
        Lederarbeit   (object)
        Präzisionsarbeit   (quality)
        Doktorarbeit   (goal)

The label in brackets is intended to suggest the interpretation of the first noun in relation to the second. Not all of these labels are self-explanatory, but it would take us too far to justify them here. A paraphrase of these compounds would be rather elaborate, and different in each case: 'the N_2 which is done in N_1', 'the N_2 which is done by N_1', etc. (see below).

Compounds with other word types in the second position also occur, and a few examples may be given to illustrate them. Compound adjectives are formed especially with nouns and verbs, and with a variety of semantic relations. The following are a few illustrations:

herzkrank   *wasserdicht*
schreibfaul *bügelfest*

Compound verbs are not frequent,[30] but some are found. A few form stems from simple verb roots, e.g. *drehbohren, mähdreschen,* with the structure $(V_1 + V_2)^{en}$. Whether verbal constructions such as *sitzen bleiben* or *kennen lernen* should be treated as compounds is uncertain; if so, their structure would be different: $V_1^{en} + V_2^{en}$. These were formerly written as single words, but the recent spelling reform now requires them to be written as two, implying that they are not genuine compounds.[31] Unlike the *drehbohren* type, they are also separable verbs, with the first element detached from the second under appropriate circumstances, as in 3.40.

(3.40) *kennen lernen*   *er lernt sie kennen*
        sitzen bleiben   *er bleibt sitzen*
        spazieren gehen   *er geht spazieren*

Verbs compounded with other word classes, such as nouns and adjectives, are more common, but again their status as true compounds is uncertain, as are

---

[30] This is not true of technical vocabulary, where compound verbs are more common, especially as deverbal adjectives formed from past participles: *tiefgekühlt, feuerverzinkt,* etc.

[31] This change removes the distinction between *sitzenbleiben* ('to repeat a school year') and *sitzen bleiben* ('to remain seated').

the rules for writing them as single words, e.g. *teilnehmen, kundgeben,* but *Auto fahren, Fuß fassen,* though both types are separable ('er nimmt daran teil', 'er fährt Auto'), and both types are written together when nominalized ('das Teilnehmen', 'das Autofahren'). On the other hand, inseparable verbs such as *bauchreden* or *sonnenbaden* are certainly compounds. Verbs with separable prefixes (*hinzukommen, herablassen*) are, of course, derived forms rather than compounds.

Morphological Universals

In Chapter 2 we discussed some attempts to see the structure of German words in terms of general principles which are applicable to all languages. It will be recalled that, for example, the absence of voiced obstruents in final position in German words may be seen as a reflection of a general tendency in languages which is not always implemented. Can any such tendencies be observed in German morphology, too?

The forms of German inflections may seem to be too idiosyncratic for any such principles to apply, but there may nevertheless be some general principles involved here. One possibility relates to the discussion of both the conjugation of verbs and the declension of nouns and other types of words regarding 'marked' and 'unmarked' categories. It was suggested that 'present' and 'indicative' in the verbs and 'singular' in the nouns, etc. are 'unmarked' in the sense that they do not have any specific inflection associated with them; they are indicated by the *absence* of an inflection rather than by the presence of any affix. 'Past', 'subjunctive', and 'plural' are, on the other hand, 'marked'; they are typically indicated—in many cases, at least—by an additional affix or related process. Furthermore, we might consider that the morphologically unmarked categories are also more basic in their meaning, and that the marked categories add an extra element to this meaning. The principle could, of course, be extended: we could see 'nominative' as the unmarked case, not primarily on morphological grounds, since there are affixes associated with this case (though it may be significant that the only forms of such words as the indefinite article and possessive adjectives—*mein, ihr,* etc.—to occur without inflections are in the nominative singular), but on the grounds of their meaning. There would even be grounds for regarding 'masculine' as the unmarked gender, since such apparently sexless words as *wer, jemand,* etc. are masculine.[32] Among the verbal categories we could add 'active' to the 'unmarked' list.[33]

---

[32] This would add weight to the assertion made by some that German is biased in favour of the male sex.

[33] It has also been suggested that 'first person' should be regarded as the unmarked person, since the speaker is at the centre of linguistic activity.

We see, then, that there are two aspects to the unmarked/marked distinction. On the one hand, unmarked forms are morphologically more basic, lacking inflectional affixes; on the other hand, they are also semantically more basic, lacking an extra element of meaning. Underlying this there is an assumption that the natural state of affairs in languages is for one element of meaning to be associated with one morpheme. Furthermore, it implies that there is a natural tendency in languages to associate basic semantic categories with basic morphological forms. As we add elements of grammatical meaning to the basic meaning of a lexeme, we also add morphological elements to its basic form. If this is a universal principle—as to some extent it seems to be—then we can offer some sort of natural explanation for the morphological structure of inflected words in German.

We may also link this discussion with our search for a consistent affix for certain grammatical categories, such as the subjunctive or the past tense. If the natural state is to have an association of one morpheme with one element of meaning, then it would also be natural for each category to have its own, identifiable morpheme. The fact that this is not consistently true of German (we have seen, for example, that person and number share a single affix in the verb conjugation and that case and number share a single affix in declension) suggests that the language and, indeed, inflecting languages in general depart from 'naturalness' in this respect.

One could even take the association of form and meaning further, and see some sort of *iconic*[34] relationship between morphological and semantic markedness. Thus, for example, plurals are, in a sense, 'larger' than singulars (there is more of the entity concerned!) and hence plural forms will be longer than singulars. However, such an interpretation easily breaks down; in the area of German derivational morphology, diminutives are clearly semantically smaller than the basic lexeme, but morphologically they involve the *addition* of an affix (*Tier* ~ *Tierchen*, etc.). Evidently, there are limits to how far we can take the search for 'natural' explanations in morphology.

Morphology and Syntax

At various points in our discussion we have observed a relationship between morphology and syntax. We noted at the outset that, although both are concerned with grammatical structure, they differ in being concerned with two different kinds of grammatical unit: the word and sentence. Nevertheless,

---

[34] An *icon* is a symbol which not only *represents* what it symbolizes but also *resembles* it.

there are links between the two, and in some theoretical approaches these links are made explicit.

To begin with, we may recall that, as noted at the beginning of our discussion of derivational morphology (3.21), derivation—in this case of the class-changing variety—allows a given root to appear in a number of syntactic guises. Further examples are given in 3.41.

(3.41) (i)   *man hat das Haus total zerstört*
        (ii) *die totale Zerstörung des Hauses*
        (iii) *das total zerstörte Haus*

By converting words from one class to another, derivation allows them to be used in different syntactic contexts. In these examples TOTAL and ZERSTÖR assume different syntactic roles, and their morphological form is adjusted appropriately in each case: the former may—to use traditional grammatical terms—be either an adverb or an adjective, the latter a verb, a noun, or an adjective. In each case the three roots—HAUS, TOTAL, and ZERSTÖR—have the same basic meaning, and their relationships to one another remain essentially the same; only their morphological forms differ. Furthermore, we might consider that underlying all of these expressions is the same basic proposition: that someone totally destroyed the house, and that the morphological 'adjustments' follow automatically from the different syntactic uses to which the expression is put. Example (i) states the basic proposition, but examples (ii) and (iii) collapse the proposition into a phrase with a different noun as its 'head'—the word to which the other words are subordinated. In sentence (ii) the verb ZERSTÖR is nominalized, and TOTAL, which in (i) appears as a qualifying adverb, must now take the form of an adjective in order to qualify the noun. In example (iii), where the head HAUS is the original object of the verb, the verb itself must appear as a qualifying adjective, though in this case TOTAL must again take adverbial form in order to qualify it.

What is clear from these examples is first that there is an important syntactic dimension to the derived forms, and also that there is a sense in which the same syntactic relationships that are found in the underlying proposition are also preserved in the derived expressions. These principles are explicitly incorporated into some approaches to the description of morphology by deriving expressions such as (ii) and (iii) from an underlying syntactic structure corresponding to the basic proposition.[35] This would

---

[35] The parallel in the syntactic relationships in the different expressions can to some extent be accommodated by means of 'X-bar theory', which provides a general scheme for representing such relationships—see Ch. 5.

require rules, similar to those introduced for phonology in Chapter 2, which convert words from one class to another under appropriate syntactic conditions. For example, instead of merely stating that *Zerstörung* is a 'deverbal nominalization' (i.e. a noun derived from a verb) consisting of the stem *zerstör-* and the derivational suffix *–ung*, we could devise a nominalizing rule such as the following, where X is any verbal root:

$$[_V X]_V \rightarrow [_N [_V X]_V \text{-ung}]_N$$

Such a rule merely states that a verbal root (here X), identified as such by the brackets labelled V surrounding it, is converted into a noun (identified by the brackets labelled N) by the addition of the suffix *-ung*. (Note that this noun can be said still to contain the verbal root, as indicated by enclosing the verb brackets inside the noun brackets.) Such a rule would be part of a set of similar rules transforming the underlying proposition into the phrase of 3.41 (ii).

Whatever the theoretical interest of such an approach, it does encounter a number of difficulties, which impose some restrictions on its operation. We may recall the earlier discussion of substantival infinitives, where we noted that the derivation of such forms is so regular as to be virtually a matter of inflection. But by the side of such forms there are others of similar meaning whose formation is far less predictable. Consider the examples of 3.42, where those of (i) contain substantival infinitives and those of (ii) contain other derived forms.

(3.42) (i) *das Ankommen des Zuges*   (ii) *die Ankunft des Zuges*
         das Wiederholen der Sendung   *die Wiederholung der Sendung*
         das Aufnehmen ins Krankenhaus   *die Aufnahme ins Krankenhaus*

The expressions of 3.42 (ii) differ from those of 3.42 (i) in two respects: first, the particular affix used to form the derivative is not predictable, and second, the meaning of the derived form is not quite the same as that of the substantival infinitive, and is again unpredictable.

We may note that a parallel problem arises in English with so-called 'gerundives', such as *arriving* in *his arriving at that moment embarrassed me*. This is not the same as the present participle (e.g. *he was arriving at that moment*), which is arguably an inflected form of the verb;[36] the gerundive is a noun (hence the use of the possessive adjective *his* to qualify it),[37] and

---

[36] It could also be considered an adjective, as it appears in constructions such as *running water*, etc.

[37] That it still retains its verbal character is evident from the fact that in colloquial speech the possessive adjective is frequently replaced by a personal pronoun which serves as the 'subject' of the 'verb': *him arriving at that moment*).

therefore a derived form. But, like the German substantival infinitive, it is formed by a completely regular and productive process, and is therefore almost inflectional. On the other hand, the word *arrival,* in *his arrival at that moment,* is unequivocally a derived form. Gerundives may be derived from verbal constructions (*he arrived* → *his arriving*), but true derived nouns such as *arrival* cannot be, partly because there is no way of predicting which affix will be used in such cases (we say *arrival* but not **departal*), and partly because the meaning of affixes such as *-al* is not consistent. In a similar way, the German substantival infinitive *Ankommen* (e.g. *sein Ankommen war mir peinlich*) is syntactically regular and predictable, but *Ankunft,* in *seine Ankunft war mir peinlich,* is not.

The implication of this difference is that, should we wish to adopt a syntactic approach to the description of morphological structure, deriving derived forms from corresponding syntactic structures, then this is only possible with substantival infinitives such as *Ankommen, Wiederholen,* and *Aufnehmen* (and with nominalized adjectives such as *der Alte*), and *not* with true derived nouns such as *Ankunft, Wiederholung,* and *Aufnahme.* The difference is partly to do with the productivity of the formation (the former are completely productive processes) but primarily with the quasi-inflectional nature of the process.

Similar considerations apply in the case of compounding. As we have seen, one way of making the relationship between the roots in a compound clear is to expand the compound into a phrase or sentence. We have already noted that certain compounds can be expanded to 'N which is A', 'N which V-s', 'N which is for V-ing', 'N which has been V-ed', etc., while some of the compounds given in 3.39 could be expanded as in 3.43.

(3.43) *Hausarbeit*   *Arbeit, die man zu Hause macht*
        Kinderarbeit *Arbeit, die von Kindern gemacht wird*
        Handarbeit   *Arbeit, die man mit der Hand macht*

Again it would be possible to 'derive' compounds from such 'underlying' structures similar to these paraphrases. In effect, compound nouns are seen as having an affinity to nouns with appended relative clauses, and the structure of the compound can be described by relating them to such constructions by explicit rules. But apart from the problem that the wide variety of different types of compounds makes it difficult to achieve any significant degree of generalization, the use of rules to relate compounds to other grammatical structures implies that these relationships are of a grammatical kind. But the nature of the relationship between the first and second noun in such compounds is often so loose and indirect that any syntactic relationship is hard to identify, and it is difficult to justify this approach.

We must also bear in mind that a compound that can be paraphrased as a construction containing a relative clause is not identical in meaning to such a construction: *Sauerkraut* is not quite the same as 'saures Kraut' or 'Kraut, das sauer ist'. Compounds have a different status from such syntactic constructions: they are single lexemes, and hence have a semantic unity which is not characteristic of these larger structures.

Hence, although some theoretical models of morphology use such devices in order to describe the processes of word formation, this approach is arguably rather restricted in its application, and may not be able to account satisfactorily for the structure of the lexemes produced. Many morphologists therefore prefer to regard morphology as a separate component of the grammar of a language, independent of the syntax of the language.

This last point might serve as a general conclusion from our discussion of morphology in this chapter. We have seen something of the complexities of German word structure, and have examined some of the many categories, components, and relationships that characterize it. This will have made evident the fundamental importance of the word in German grammar: as a unit which carries the vital inflectional affixes of the language, as a unit of syntactic structure within the sentence, and as the grammatical embodiment of a basic unit of meaning.

FURTHER READING

Theory of Morphology

Bauer (2003); Carstairs-McCarthy (1992); Katamba (1993); Matthews (1991); Spencer (1991).

German Morphology

Boase-Beier and Lodge (2003: ch. 3); Donalies (2002); Durrell (1979: 55–89); Eichinger (2000); Eisenberg et al. (1998); Erben (2000); Fleischer and Barz (1995); Henzen (1983); Motsch (1999); Naumann (2000); Olsen (1990).

EXERCISES AND DISCUSSION QUESTIONS

1. In view of the problems encountered in defining the 'word', how useful do you think the concept is in the description of German morphology?
2. Analyse the following words into roots and affixes and indicate whether the affixes are derivational or inflectional: *fabelhaft, gewaltig, konnten, Heiter-*

keit, Männern, entkämen, Versunkenheit, mütterlicherseits, aufgeschlosse-
nere, Lebensbedingungen, Niederträchtigkeit.

3. List as many ways of forming the plural of native German nouns as you can. Is it possible to establish rules to determine which nouns form their plurals in which ways, e.g. according to gender, phonological form, meaning, etc.?

4. List as many forms of the verb *fahren* as you can, including those formed with auxiliary verbs. Identify the grammatical categories involved.

5. Find nominalized forms of the following verbs and adjectives (there may be more than one for each): *folgen, ankommen, reden, bleiben, hindern, graben, binden, schneiden, ziehen, flieaen, bleich, dick, lebhaft, tot, klein, wild, übel, tief, hoch, laut.*

6. Find as many derivatives as you can from the following roots: *grab(en)*, *zieh(en)*, *geh(en)*.

7. Draw trees to represent the structure of the following compounds: *Zweitaktmotor, Filmschauspieler, Elektrorasenmäher, Ersatzteilverkaufstelle, Stadtverwaltungsfinanzausschussprotokoll.*

4

Classes and Categories

Introduction

In our consideration of the word in the last chapter, we were concerned primarily with its structure, i.e. with the parts of which it is composed and their relationships to one another. In the course of our discussion a number of other features of the word were briefly touched on, but not developed. This chapter is devoted to two such features: the different types of words that are found in German, and the nature and significance of the various inflectional categories that are associated with them.

The first of these forms a basic part of traditional grammatical study; learners of 'grammar' have long been expected to 'parse' a sentence, which involves, among other things, being able to assign each word of the sentence to one of the 'parts of speech'[1]—noun, verb, etc. Many grammars, whatever language they are concerned with, pay considerable attention to this task. The second question to be considered here, the inflectional categories, also figures in traditional grammars, where we find discussion of the meanings of the various 'endings' of words.

In both these cases, however, traditional treatments tend to leave a great deal to be desired. In the first place, the assumption is generally made that all languages are in fact rather similar: all languages must, it is assumed, have nouns, verbs, and adjectives, and all languages must be able to distinguish between past, present, and future, and between singular and plural. One of the characteristics of modern linguistic study, however, particularly within a structuralist framework, has been an emphasis on seeing each language in its own terms, with the consequence that we should not impose the categories of one language on to another. Even apparently uncontroversial assumptions such as these cannot, therefore, be taken for granted, but must be justified for

---

[1] The term 'parse' in fact comes from the Latin grammatical expression 'pars orationis', of which 'part of speech' is a rough English translation.

every particular case. Indeed, when we apply them to a wider range of languages than merely the familiar ones of Europe, they are found to be not self-evident at all.

In spite of this, there has also been a trend in recent linguistics, as we have also noted in our earlier discussions, to look beyond the features of individual languages and attempt to identify 'universal' characteristics of language as such, so that features of individual languages are seen as a realization of these more general categories. Examples of this will be discussed below.

A second difficulty with traditional treatments of such phenomena is that they are often very inconsistent and unsystematic. Definitions of such categories as 'noun', for example, or 'present tense', are, as we shall see, inadequate in a number of important respects, largely because the criteria for their definition have not been clearly formulated. Again, discussion of these matters in terms of modern theory requires a rather more rigorous and consistent approach.

In the present chapter, therefore, we shall examine critically these two areas of the grammatical description of German, and attempt to assess the extent to which traditional treatments do justice to the phenomena concerned.

Word Classes

Introduction

The traditional term 'part of speech' is rather too vague to be useful, as speech can be divided into many kinds of parts. Since the parts that we are concerned with here are different types, or classes, of words, modern linguists prefer to use the term WORD CLASS instead of 'part of speech'. In traditional grammar, word classes are of crucial importance; the 'word' is taken to be a central, indeed *the* central, grammatical concept, and an understanding of grammar therefore demands an ability to identify the different kinds of words that are found in languages. Modern linguistic study is less dependent on the word, since it has identified other units, such as morphemes, phrases, etc. in terms of which the grammar of a language may be described, and the difficulties that linguists have had in defining the word (cf. Chapter 3) have further undermined its position. Nevertheless, the word is still a useful and important unit in grammatical description, and the attempt to classify words into different classes is still an instructive exercise, even if, as we shall see, it presents certain problems.

In our discussion of word structure in the preceding chapter we found frequent need to refer to different classes—nouns, verbs, adjectives, etc.—but made no attempt to draw up a complete list, still less to justify the categories themselves, which were simply taken for granted. This might be satisfactory if our grammatical tradition was clear about the classes to be recognized and about the criteria involved in recognizing them, but this is unfortunately not the case. Consider, for example, the traditional definition of nouns and verbs. The noun is popularly defined in words such as 'the name of a person, place, or thing', while a verb is typically defined as 'a doing-word'. Such definitions are based on the meaning of words in the class, and are thus *semantic*. Adjectives are sometimes defined in a similar way, e.g. as words which refer to 'qualities', but, since this is difficult to apply in all cases, they are also described as words which 'qualify a noun'. But such a definition is no longer semantic, it is *syntactic*. The semantic criterion breaks down totally for such words as prepositions, where it is hardly possible to find a consistent type of meaning for the whole class.

Furthermore, the semantic criterion, which is used for the 'major' word classes such as nouns, verbs, and adjectives, can easily be shown to be unsatisfactory even for these classes, since in many cases it is either wrong or completely circular. We might agree that words such as *go* in 'I go to the office every day', or *look* in 'she is looking through the window', are verbs because they are 'doing-words', but what about the same words in 'to have a go', or 'to take a look', where we would prefer to call them nouns? Either our definition is wrong, and not all 'doing-words' are verbs, or we must regard the *go* of 'have a go' and the *look* of 'take a look' as being somehow no longer 'doing-words', but rather 'names of a person, place, or thing'. If we adopt this latter course, against the semantic evidence, we have done so merely because we know the words are nouns for other reasons. We have not, in other words, called them nouns because they are the 'names' of something, but have called them 'names' because they are nouns—which brings us no nearer to defining a noun itself.

Semantic criteria are in fact not very satisfactory for defining word classes, and the reason is not difficult to find: the word is not really a semantic unit at all. Though, as we saw in the previous chapter, it is difficult to arrive at a satisfactory definition of the word, it is nevertheless clear that it is a grammatical entity, and hence the most appropriate criteria for establishing classes of words are similarly grammatical. This does not mean, of course, that semantic classification of linguistic items is either wrong or unhelpful; but it is appropriate for semantic rather than grammatical units.

It is nevertheless true that many types of meaning are particularly associated with a specific word class. The meaning of the root *lieb*, for example, is felt to be fundamentally verbal in character, while that of *gut* is felt to be basically adjectival. But such roots are not restricted to these 'natural' word classes, and a range of word-formative devices are available to make the root more widely usable. The root *lieb* also occurs in non-verbal lexemes, and the same flexibility is found with *gut*. This makes it inappropriate to define word classes in terms of such meanings, or indeed to define meanings in terms of word classes.

As further proof of the separate nature of these two, we may note that it is often possible to determine the word classes even where the meanings of the words are not known, provided that grammatical information is available. To illustrate this, we might make up a nonsense sentence, such as 'Der Graube steibt'. On hearing this sentence we would surely have no doubt here that *Graube* is a noun and *steibt* a verb, even though we have no idea what, if anything, these words could possibly mean. The article preceding the former, and the inflection -*t* of the latter, as well as the structure of the sentence, make the word classes clear.

But if the criteria that are important for distinguishing word classes are grammatical, there are several different grammatical characteristics of words which might be relevant. Since grammatical features may be morphological or syntactic (to do with word structure and sentence structure, respectively), word classes could differ in either of these. In a morphologically complex language such as German, morphological differences between different types of words are in many cases easily identifiable. In our nonsense sentence we used the affix -*t*, readily identifiable as part of the set of verb inflections, to conclude that *steibt* must be a verb. Even more clearly, derivational affixes frequently give an unambiguous clue to the word class: nonsense words such as *Graubheit*, *Preugschaft*, and *Stringtum* could hardly be anything other than nouns, while *graublich*, *preughaft*, and *stringbar* are immediately recognizable as adjectives. The syntactic classification of words rests on the principle that words of different classes have different syntactic roles, and are used differently in sentences. In the sentence 'Die Frau schreibt', for example, we could replace *schreibt* by *spricht, kommt, lacht,* etc. but not by *sehr, mit,* or *auf,* showing that *spricht, kommt,* and *lacht,* but not *sehr, mit,* and *auf,* are the same kind of word as *schreibt*.

Using morphological and syntactic criteria, then, it should in principle be possible to assign words to a limited set of classes. As mentioned at the beginning of this chapter, our grammatical tradition generally assumes that this set of classes will, with minor exceptions, be the same for all languages, but it should be clear that, since our classes are based on the morphological and syntactic features of the languages in question, and since languages may differ in these respects, there is no necessity for this to be so. It is also to be expected that, since the grammatical tradition itself derives from the study of the classical languages, the classes required for German might well differ from what traditional grammar prescribes.

These questions are confused, however, by the fact that the procedures for establishing classes in this way are not at all straightforward. One would perhaps imagine the tests to be objective enough to lead, for a given language, to a single, verifiable result, but this is unfortunately not the case; some fundamental problems arise here which make the establishment of the word classes of a language a rather complex, and indeed somewhat doubtful, undertaking. This will be clarified in the course of our discussion.

Establishing German Word Classes

The question of word classes in German has long concerned grammarians, and it still forms one of the major topics of discussion among modern writers on the language.[2] But it may come as a surprise to find that, despite the long grammatical tradition, there are still many disagreements among modern grammarians as to the specific classes to be established. To some extent these disagreements reflect uncertainty about the appropriate criteria in the light of the greater theoretical awareness of modern linguistic study, as discussed above, but they also reflect certain characteristics of German words themselves, and the problems which they pose for classification. These problems are worth investigating more closely.

One laudable aim of some German writers on the subject is to replace the rather meaningless grammatical terms of traditional grammar by native German words which are more indicative of the nature of the words themselves. Unfortunately, this has been undertaken on the assumption that the classes are in principle semantic, so that the terms reflect categories of meaning. The noun, for example, has been called a *Nennwort, Namenwort, Gegenstandswort*, or *Dingwort*, while the adjective has been given the labels *Eigenschaftswort* or *Artwort*.[3] For the reasons given earlier, such semantically based labels do not really help in clarifying the nature of the classes, as the classes themselves are not semantic. Most recent grammars do not employ them, but prefer the more traditional Latinate terms, whose comparative meaninglessness is perhaps an advantage, since it does not tie the categories to any preconceived notion of their nature.

Leaving aside semantic criteria, we may attempt to classify German words on a morphological or syntactic basis. As far as the former is concerned, we

---

[2] One edition of the Duden grammar, for example, devotes 300 pages—nearly half the book—to a discussion of word classes.

[3] Such terms are used in the works of the linguists Hans Glinz and Johannes Erben, among others.

may consider both inflection and derivation. In terms of inflection, we have already identified two main categories of words: those that are subject to declension, and those that are subject to conjugation. This gives us the threefold classification of 4.1.

(4.1)

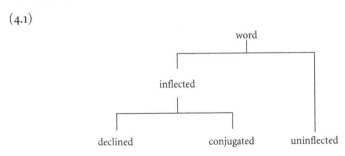

This is clearly of limited value. Not only does it provide us with only three 'classes', but the groupings are in some cases quite spurious. Morphological similarity does not guarantee that words are of the same class, as words may agree in their morphology but be otherwise quite different. For example, articles and adjectives have to agree with the nouns they accompany, but this does not make it sensible for nouns, articles, and adjectives to be treated as the same class of word. The category of 'uninflected word' is similarly very broad; it would include not only such traditional categories as prepositions, adverbs, and conjunctions, but also uninflected forms of verbs, nouns, and adjectives. The only traditional word type that this scheme allows us to establish without further criteria is the 'conjugated word', which we can largely identify with the traditional verb.

Derivational morphology adds a further means of classification, though generally only with 'lexical' (i.e. 'content') words, since 'grammatical' ('form') words are rarely derived.[4] Since one of the chief functions of such affixes is to convert words of one class to another, the affix used is often a good indicator of the class to which the word belongs. Nominalizing suffixes such as *-heit*, *-schaft* , *-tum*, *-nis*, etc. allow us to recognize the words concerned as nouns, while adjectivalizing suffixes such as *-lich*, *-bar*, or *-haft* show the words concerned to be adjectives. A limited number of derivational affixes are also available for other lexical word types, such as verbs (e.g. *-ieren*) and adverbs (e.g. *-weise*). Using this criterion, therefore, we obtain the classification of 4.2.

---

[4] There are nevertheless some examples of derived grammatical words, such as the prepositions *gemäß, zwecks*, etc.

(4.2)

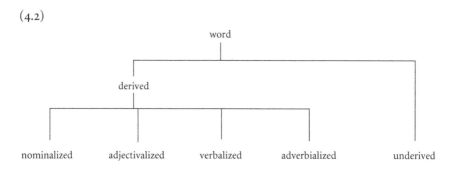

This scheme may be satisfactory as a representation of the types of derived forms, but it is not at all adequate for a discrimination of word classes in a helpful sense. This is partly because very many words, of a variety of classes, fall into the type of 'underived word'. Using this scheme, we would not be able to distinguish, for example, *komm*, *schön*, *und*, and *Mann*. Furthermore, even derived words may be formed by the process of 'conversion' (i.e. without any overt derivational affix). Infinitival nouns, such as *(das) Schreiben*, for example, are morphologically indistinguishable from the verbal infinitive form *schreiben* itself.

Thus, morphological criteria are not satisfactory for determining the word classes of German, since either they do not allow sufficient discrimination of word types or they group words together which otherwise have nothing in common. Although morphological features may sometimes help us to identify which class a word belongs to, they do not really constitute the most significant characteristics of these classes. The fact that many words are not unambiguously assignable to classes on morphological grounds alone suggests that word classes are not simply 'morphological classes', and that morphological differences are symptoms rather than causes of the differences between the classes.

We must thus turn to syntax in our search for suitable criteria for the establishment of German word classes. The main syntactic criterion is distribution. This depends on the fact that words of different types combine differently with other word types, and hence we can establish a classification based on these combinatory possibilities. We might, for example, set up a 'frame' such as the following:

_____ N

and test which words will fit into it. Given a noun such as *Bücher*, we could have phrases such as those of 4.3.

(4.3)   *die Bücher*
     diese Bücher
     keine Bücher
     ihre Bücher
     alle Bücher
     drei Bücher
     alte Bücher

In carrying out this test, however, we must bear in mind that we are concerned with classes of words and not individual words. If we were to replace the word *Bücher* here by *Buch*, the possibilities would not be quite the same; we could not, for example, have *drei Buch* or *die Buch*. The point is that, in principle, words like *drei* or *die* may combine with words like *Bücher* or *Buch*, even though certain specific forms of these words, or individual members of these classes, may not be readily combinable. Clearly, articles may precede nouns in German, but it is possible to find specific forms of the articles which do not combine with specific nouns. Both articles and nouns fall into certain subclasses (e.g. masculine singular) and not all subclasses of each can co-occur. But this does not invalidate the principle that words of the noun class can combine with words of the article class. Similarly, even where these grammatical subclasses are compatible, there may be semantic restrictions on co-occurrence. For example, colour-words such as *gelb* or *blau* do not normally co-occur with abstract nouns such as *Glück* or *Wahrheit*, but this naturally does not mean that, as a general rule, adjectives cannot co-occur with nouns.[5]

The examples of 4.3 allow us to establish a class of words which would include *die, diese, keine, ihre, alle, drei,* and *alte*, together with their variants. We might call this the class of NOUN QUALIFIERS. But we can go a little further, and examine the possibilities for combining these words among themselves. The expressions of 4.4 are all possible.

(4.4)   *die drei Bücher*   *die alten Bücher*
     diese drei Bücher   *diese alten Bücher*
     keine drei Bücher   *keine alten Bücher*
     ihre drei Bücher   *ihre alten Bücher*

---

[5] Of course this does not take account of metaphorical expressions such as *schwarze Sünde, heller Wahnsinn,* etc. The capacity for individual words (lexemes) to co-occur semantically is called COLLOCATION. Some linguists describe the co-occurrence of whole word types as COLLIGATION. Thus, the expression *gelbe Blume* shows that the lexeme *gelb* collocates with the lexeme *Blume*, and that adjectives colligate with nouns. This usage will not, however, be adopted here.

alle die Bücher	*alle diese Bücher*
alle ihre Bücher	*alle drei Bücher*
alle alten Bücher	*drei alte Bücher*
die drei alten Bücher	*diese drei alten Bücher*
keine drei alten Bücher	*ihre drei alten Bücher*
alle die drei Bücher	*alle die alten Bücher*
alle diese drei Bücher	*alle diese alten Bücher*
alle ihre drei Bücher	*alle drei alten Bücher*
alle die drei alten Bücher	*alle diese drei alten Bücher*
alle ihre drei alten Bücher	

On the other hand, combinations such as those of 4.5 are not found.

(4.5)   **die diese Bücher*   **die ihre Bücher*
        *diese keinen Bücher   **ihre alle Bücher*
        *drei ihre Bücher   etc.

   Though the pattern of occurrence is complex, it is possible to discern some general principles here. In the first place, the words *die, diese, keine,* and *ihre* do not occur together but are mutually exclusive alternatives. Such words (they include the traditional articles, and demonstrative, possessive, and interrogative adjectives) can therefore be grouped together as a single class of DETERMINERS. *Alle*, on the other hand, has rather different characteristics, since it may combine with these other words. It might be called a QUANTIFIER. Numbers such as *drei* are also different; they can co-occur with both determiners and quantifiers, though unlike the latter they occur after the determiner. They could be said to form a class of NUMERICAL ADJECTIVES.[6] Finally, we find words like *alte*, which combine freely with the other word types, and with other words of the same type (e.g. 'die alten, schweren, staubigen Bücher'). These constitute the 'true' ADJECTIVES.

   In addition to the possibility of distinguishing classes by virtue of their potential combinations, we may also invoke their different syntactic functions. This is often not really distinct from their distribution, since, as we shall see in the next chapter, syntactic function is largely concerned with where the elements of the sentence occur. However, syntactic function is rather broader than the distribution of individual words, since it is often a matter of whole phrases and their relationships to one another, and it is useful in some cases to

---

   [6] This class does not include *all* numerals, however, as numbers may fall into several different word classes (see below).

take this broader view. One frequently encountered description of the traditional word class 'pronoun', for example, is that it 'replaces a noun'. But this is not strictly true; if we compare the sentence 'Die nette Lehrerin gab meiner jungen Schwester das interessante Buch' with 'Sie gab es ihr', it will be clear that the pronouns *sie, es,* and *ihr* do not replace the nouns *Lehrerin, Buch,* and *Schwester* but rather the whole phrase in each case: *die nette Lehrerin, das interessante Buch,* and *meiner jungen Schwester.* This is reinforced by the observation that none of the 'noun qualifiers' discussed above can occur with such pronouns: we cannot have **die sie,* **mein ihr,* or **interessantes es.*

The syntactic criteria applied so far permit us to assign German words to classes, but there are unfortunately many problems here which make this procedure rather questionable. When applied to the noun phrases of 4.3, 4.4, and 4.5, our distributional tests revealed a number of differences within the original group of 'noun qualifiers' which allowed us to differentiate this group into smaller classes. Indeed, we could add still more types by taking into account words such as *solch, manch,* etc. which have distributions different from those already described. There are some difficulties, however. Firstly, the further we go in our examination of the properties of these words, especially of the non-lexical variety, the more we find that each word tends to have its own characteristic distribution. Taken to its logical conclusion, this procedure may result in classes with only a single member. No other word, for example, has exactly the same distribution as *alle.* The purpose of establishing classes is to make generalizations which go beyond individual words, but our analysis of the syntactic distribution of the words may result in there being no generalizations at all.

But the basic problem here is that words are not just syntactically the same or different, but may be *more or less* the same, and hence we may recognize more or fewer classes according to how far we take our discrimination. We may, for example, establish a class of words which may qualify nouns, and which would include all the words discussed here. But when we apply further criteria, we shall find that some of these 'noun qualifiers' have slightly different characteristics, which justify our recognizing classes such as 'determiners', 'quantifiers', and 'adjectives'. Nor do we need to stop here. Determiners may be subdivided into 'articles', 'possessive adjectives', 'demonstrative adjectives', etc. and among the 'articles' we could further recognize 'indefinite' and 'definite' varieties, which again have slightly different syntactic characteristics. The difficulty here is obvious: we simply do not know where to stop. We can establish larger or smaller classes with equal justification, and there is no sense in which any of these various alternatives can be regarded as factually incorrect.

Nor is it simply a matter of establishing more or less inclusive classes. A further problem is that classes are likely to overlap in their syntactic roles. We may decide, for example, to recognize a class of 'adjectives', and will note that among its syntactic characteristics are the ability to qualify nouns ('der *alte* Mann') and the ability to follow a verb ('der Mann ist *alt*'). However, neither of these characteristics is exclusive to the class of adjectives; the former is shared with articles, among other words, and the latter with adverbs ('das Auto fährt schnell'). Identification of a particular set of word classes is thus the result not merely of making more or fewer distinctions, but of giving appropriate weight to these distinctions. We might choose, for example, to treat the ability to qualify nouns as more significant than the occurrence after verbs, and thus group adjectives with articles; alternatively, we may prefer to ignore the first of these characteristics at the expense of the second, and group adjectives with adverbs.

These problems in selecting and applying the criteria make the discrimination of the different word classes of German a less objective task than one would imagine it to be. Indeed, they point to the inevitable conclusion that any set of word classes is bound to involve a degree of arbitrariness, and that the whole enterprise is an extremely doubtful one, which is difficult to justify in theoretical terms. But this does not mean that categories such as 'noun', 'verb', etc. are useless and entirely spurious. It would hardly be possible to discuss German at all without reference to such categories, as a glance at any of the chapters of this book will verify. The use of these categories is justified provided that we do not assume their absolute and universal validity. If we unquestioningly accept that all German words can be assigned unambiguously and once and for all to a handful of traditional word classes then we are clearly mistaken, but if we make the more modest claim that certain German words may, under certain circumstances, have some grammatical characteristics in common, then we shall come much nearer to the truth of the matter.

The recognition of such groups of words with common characteristics is clearly useful and justifiable in the case of lexical words such as nouns, verbs, and adjectives. These form OPEN classes, in the sense that the group can be readily expanded by the addition of further words with the same grammatical characteristics. (Grammatical words such as articles, conjunctions, prepositions, etc. constitute CLOSED classes which cannot be readily added to.) But even here we cannot be too rigid with our definition, as the limits of such classes are hard to specify. Exactly which words are deemed to belong to the various classes depends to a significant extent upon the purpose of the classification. In describing German morphology, for example, we found it useful, indeed essential, to group words together which are subject to declension, and to this extent they form a legitimate word class. But though words of this class will, from a morphological perspective, be quite homogeneous, from a syntactic point of view they will be grouped together quite arbitrarily. Syntactically too there are different points of view which may be quite legitimate and yet in conflict. If our concern is with the structure of phrases containing nouns, for example, we may legitimately see adjectives, quantifiers, articles, and other determiners as a single class of 'noun qualifiers'; if we are examining the role of adjectives as 'complements' (e.g. in sentences such as 'Meine Frau ist *schön*'), then they have no affinity with determiners and quantifiers at all, and may well be grouped together with adverbs in such sentences as 'Meine Frau singt *schön*'. Word classes are not, in other words, absolute, but depend on the particular focus of the investigation.

With these reservations, then, it is in practice not only possible but also useful to identify different classes of words. There is little likelihood of misrepresentation or misunderstanding when we say that 'German nouns are masculine, feminine, or neuter', or that 'in interrogative sentences the verb comes in first position', and so on. But we must nevertheless bear in mind that such statements beg a number of questions, and may in some cases even be positively misleading. To state that 'adverbs qualify verbs', for example, is unilluminating, given that the traditional class of 'adverb' is often considered to include such disparate words as *oft, sehr, ja,* and *weg.*

Some Word Classes of German

In the light of what has been said so far, it would clearly be inappropriate, as well as misleading, to give a definitive list of 'the' word classes of German. But it will help to clarify the nature of the problems involved in such a procedure if we conclude our discussion with a mention of some of the more interesting characteristics of the major types of word considered by German grammarians. No attempt is made to be exhaustive or to provide definitions of these classes; the purpose is merely to draw attention to some of the questions raised by the particular class.

Verb   The verb is one of the least controversial classes, and it is recognized by all German grammarians as an independent type. This is partly on account of its unique inflectional morphology ('conjugation'), which is shared with no other class, and partly because of its central syntactic role in the sentence. Nevertheless, not all verbs are identical in their forms or in their syntactic roles. Consider the examples of 4.6.

(4.6)   (i)   er *sieht* es nicht ~ er kann es nicht *sehen*
　　　 (ii)   er *sah* es nicht ~ er hat es nicht *gesehen*

Apart from the finite (inflected) forms—*sieht* and *sah*—we can here identify two other uninflected verbal word types, the INFINITIVE (4.6 (i)) and the PARTICIPLE (4.6 (ii)), which, though they share certain syntactic character-istics with finite forms (e.g. they may have 'objects'), differ from these in a number of other respects (e.g. their position in the sentence). Unlike the finite forms, these two word types have close connections with other word classes: as discussed above, the infinitive has a nominalized form, which, though it contains a verbal root, must be treated as a noun, while the participles—there are two types, the 'present' and the 'past' (usually called 'Partizip I' and 'Partizip II' respectively by German grammarians)—readily take on an adjec-tival form.

But even finite verbs are not all the same in their syntactic properties. Some may take objects ('transitive verbs'), others ('intransitive verbs') cannot; some have their objects in the accusative case, others in the dative or the genitive; and so on (these questions will be pursued further in the next chapter). The characteristics of 'modal' and 'auxiliary' verbs are also different from other verbs. Not surprisingly, grammarians differ in the categories (or subcategor-ies) of verbs that they consider it necessary to recognize.

A further difficulty for word-class assignment arises with separable verbs, such as *aufstehen, stattfinden*, etc. First, of course, the number of words involved is not constant, since in some cases, such as the infinitive, they constitute a single word, while in their separated forms they constitute two. But what type of word is the separated prefix in such cases? In words such as *aufstehen, ausgehen*, etc. the prefixes *auf* and *aus* look rather like prepositions, though they are hardly comparable to prepositions in their use, since they are not followed by nouns. The prefixes of *hinfahren* and *herholen* do not have such affinities with prepositions, however, while that of *stattfinden* looks rather like a noun, and seems comparable to *Auto* in *Auto fahren*.[7] Faced with this problem, many grammarians simply call such words 'particles', and leave it at that, though this label is hardly precise.

Noun   Like the verb, the noun is in the majority of instances readily recognizable, and is accepted as a word class by all grammarians, albeit under differing names. As we saw in Chapter 3, noun inflections are, apart

---

[7] The new spelling rules for German attempt to clarify this, but they still equivocate in these cases: they still prescribe *stattfinden* but *Auto fahren*.

from the plural affix, relatively few, but the syntactic distribution and role of this word type in the sentence are fairly distinct. The noun has, along with the pronoun, the capacity of functioning in a variety of syntactic roles, but unlike the pronoun it is frequently qualified by determiners, adjectives, and other words. Some difficulties nevertheless arise as a result of word-formative processes and elisions, illustrated in 4.7.

(4.7)   (i)   Der alte Mann ist gestorben.
          Das ist die richtige Antwort.
    (ii)   Der Alte ist gestorben.
          Das ist das Richtige.

There is no problem with the nouns of 4.7 (i), which are qualified by a determiner and an adjective, but there is some room for doubt in 4.7 (ii), where there is apparently no noun in either case. Such cases were mentioned in Chapter 3, where we considered the problem of deciding whether words such as *Alte* and *Richtige* are here adjectives (the accompanying noun having been elided) or whether they are nominalized, and therefore nouns. It is hardly possible to resolve this problem in a way which is not arbitrary.

Demarcation difficulties also arise between nouns and some other classes. Certain words, nouns in origin, are used prepositionally, as in 4.8.

(4.8)   *dank dieser Erfahrung*
      trotz der ungünstigen Situation
      kraft seiner Mitarbeit
      statt meiner Mutter

Here the words are undoubtedly prepositions, not nouns, but we may perhaps be less sure with the more complex forms of 4.9.[8]

(4.9)   *aufgrund/auf Grund seiner Krankheit*
      anstelle/an Stelle des ursprünglichen Plans

In these cases the noun element is still sufficiently recognizable for some doubt to be felt about whether these expressions are prepositional phrases (containing a noun) or genuine prepositions, and this doubt is reflected in the orthographical variation.

---

[8] The new spelling rules leave the choice in these cases to the writer.

Adjective　Syntactically, one main role of the adjective is to accompany a noun, when it is said to be used ATTRIBUTIVELY; but, as we have seen above, it shares this function with other word types. To define the adjective in terms of this role would thus group it with other words such as determiners and quantifiers. This is a perfectly plausible solution, though it is not the one usually adopted. It is possible, as we have seen, to distinguish the adjective 'proper' from the other noun qualifiers on the grounds that it is freely combinable, and comes last in the sequence of qualifiers. Another way of identifying the adjective, however, is in terms of another of its functions, its occurrence as the 'complement' of the sentence, in such expressions as 'Mein Vater ist alt', 'Das Wetter wird schön', etc. Here it is said to be used PREDICATIVELY. None of the other noun qualifiers can normally be used in this way.

There is, however, a problem here, which was touched on above. Consider the examples of 4.10.

(4.10)　(i)　Meine Frau ist *schön*.
　　　　　　　Seine Augen sind *schlecht*.
　　　　(ii)　Meine Frau singt *schön*.
　　　　　　　Seine Augen sehen *schlecht*.

The final word appears to have a very similar role in all the sentences of 4.10; it is, moreover, morphologically the same in each case: it is uninflected. Many words may therefore appear in sentences like those of (i) or (ii) without modification. Because of these characteristics, a number of scholars see no compelling reason to divide them into two classes,[9] even though this is at variance with traditional usage: the final words of 4.10 (i) are traditionally described as 'adjectives', while those of 4.10 (ii) are traditionally 'adverbs'. (Such an analysis would not work for English, where the equivalent of type (ii) would differ from type (i) in having the suffix *-ly*.)

But if words such as *schön* and *schlecht* in 4.10 are treated as a single adverb/ adjective class, then we encounter another problem in sentences such as those of 4.11.

(4.11)　Mein Vater fährt *oft*.
　　　　　Wir kommen *bald*.
　　　　　Er arbeitet *nie*.

---

[9] Kufner (1962: 57–60), for example, establishes a class of 'adjective-adverbs'. See Further Reading.

The 'adverbs' in these sentences differ from *schön* and *schlecht* in not being usable to qualify nouns. They would thus need to form a class of their own, distinct from the adjective/adverb class.

Adverb and Particle   In traditional accounts the adverb is said to qualify either a verb, an adjective, or another adverb, these three possibilities being illustrated in 4.12.

(4.12)   Der Wagen fährt *schnell.*
Er ist ein *sehr* berühmter Mann.
Das Orchester hat *wirklich* gut gespielt.

In practice, however, the class of 'adverb' covers a very wide area, and any word which cannot otherwise be accommodated tends to be called an adverb by default. Thus, many grammarians are happy to group together the highlighted words of 4.13 as a single class of adverbs, even though they have little in common.

(4.13)   Er wohnt *dort.*
Hoffentlich kommt er.
Er kommt *nicht.*
Das hat er *doch* gesagt.
Es ist *sehr* gut.

Others, however, make a number of distinctions here, especially between adverb and particle, the latter including particularly non-lexical words, though the distinction is rarely clear or consistent. Furthermore, the particle then merely takes over from the adverb its role as the class in which to put anything that does not fit anywhere else (we saw earlier that the prefixes of separable verbs are sometimes called particles).[10] The problem is evident: many such 'particles', such as *nicht,* have a virtually unique function and distribution in the sentence, and though it is possible to group them together with other words on the basis of a number of criteria, there is inevitably an element of arbitrariness involved, and the ensuing 'class' is hardly homogeneous.

Determiner, Quantifier, and Numeral   We have already considered the various words which can occur with a noun, and have identified a class of

---

[10] Confusingly, the *Duden* grammar recognizes a class of 'Partikeln' which includes not only various kinds of adverbs, but also prepositions and conjunctions. These are grouped together as a 'Rest- und Sammelklasse' on the grounds that they can be neither declined nor conjugated.

'determiners' and a class of 'quantifiers', though these cover groups of words which may differ in some respects among themselves. Some grammarians also establish a class of 'numerals', one of whose functions is to qualify a noun. However, 'numeral' is a purely semantic class, since numbers may have a variety of syntactic roles. This is clear from the examples of 4.14.

(4.14) (i)   *Zwei* Bücher waren auf dem Tisch.
        (ii) *Zwei* sind gekommen.
        (iii) *Hunderte* von Menschen waren dort.

Zwei in 4.14(i) qualifies the noun and could be considered to have an attributive function, comparable to that of an adjective; *Hunderte* in 4.14 (iii) would appear to be a noun, however, while *Zwei* in 4.14(ii) is ambivalent: it could be considered to be a noun or an adjective with the noun elided (cf. 4.7, above). We might, of course, see the latter two cases as derived words, and the noun-qualifying function of numerals to be primary, but this does not alter the fact that numbers as such do not constitute a single syntactic class.

Pronoun   It has already been remarked that pronouns have the same function in the sentence as noun phrases (not nouns as such). Semantically, and to some extent syntactically too, they fall into a wide range of subclasses, which traditional grammar rightly identifies. Thus, we find personal, demonstrative, reflexive, possessive, relative, interrogative, and indefinite pronouns, to give only the major types. Many of these have close morphological and semantic links with noun qualifiers, giving a partly parallel set of determiners (often treated as adjectives): demonstrative, possessive, interrogative, and indefinite. We may thus have 'Welches Tier ist das?' (determiner) or 'Welches ist das?' (pronoun); 'Das ist mein Buch' (determiner) or 'Das ist meines' (pronoun), etc.

If pronouns are seen as 'replacements' for noun phrases, we should also consider here other kinds of replacements. Consider the sentences of 4.15.

(4.15) (i)   Mein Onkel lebt in Indien.
              Mein Onkel fuhr letzte Woche weg.
        (ii) Mein Onkel lebt dort.
              Mein Onkel fuhr dann weg.

We could say that *dort* and *dann* in 4.15(ii) 'replace' (i.e. have the same syntactic role as) *in Indien* and *letzte Woche* respectively in 4.15(i). Since such words replace a part of the sentence their function is similar to that of pronouns, though they are not generally treated as such. In the case of the first sentence of 4.15(i), *dort* replaces a prepositional phrase (*in Indien*), but in the second sentence *dann* replaces a noun phrase (*letzte Woche*). But it is evidently not sufficient for a word to replace a noun phrase for it to be called a pronoun; it must also have an appropriate syntactic function. These words can be described as adverbs, but in view of their replacive role a case could be made for establishing a class of 'pro-adverbs'. The same category might include the corresponding interrogative words *wo* and *wann*. However, the status of all these words is not completely clear, since they can themselves be preceded by prepositions (*von dort, bis dann, seit wann*, etc.), a characteristic that is usually associated with nouns or pronouns. They are usually simply classed as adverbs, for want of a better solution.

Preposition and Conjunction   Prepositions and conjunctions have some syntactic affinities with one another, and some German grammarians group them together as *Fügewörter*. There are, furthermore, some forms which can appear as both (e.g. *statt, bis*). A significant difference, however, is that prepositions 'govern' cases, i.e. determine the case of a following noun, while conjunctions do not ('der Mann mit seiner Frau' versus 'der Mann und seine Frau').

One instance of possible difficulty was illustrated in 4.8 and 4.9. These are cases of prepositions which are derived from nouns, and which retain some of the characteristics of nouns. A further uncertainty can be identified with some of the prefixes of separable verbs (*auf, um, aus*, etc.), which look like prepositions but have quite different syntactic properties.

Interjection   The status of the interjection as a word class has always been in some doubt, in German as in other languages. One may perhaps feel that words such as *Pfui!* or *Ach!* are not 'real' words, but merely noises produced by human beings under the stress of particular emotions. This view is reinforced by the fact that such expressions may contain sounds not otherwise found in words of the language (compare the sounds represented by the English *ugh!* or *phew!*). *Pfui* is in fact a case in point, since it is virtually the only German word to contain the 'phoneme' /ʊi/.

Not surprisingly, then, the word class 'Interjektion', or its equivalent, is not recognized by a number of German grammarians. One argument put forward for its exclusion is that it represents a whole sentence, though this is not a very good argument since, if the point is that 'proper' words must all be of the same minimal scope, then we could equally well exclude pronouns on the ground that they represent whole phrases (see above). More cogent is the argument that interjections cannot be accommodated within the syntactic structure of the sentence: they have no real syntactic function and cannot, therefore, be assigned to a class on syntactic grounds. It might be reasonable, therefore, to regard such expressions as a somewhat peripheral and minor class of words, not fully integrated into the syntactic system of the language.

We must also bear in mind, however, that not all 'exclamations' are interjections in this sense. Very many expressions can be used for making exclamations, such as *Gott!, Herrlich!,* and the like (as well as many unprintable ones), but this does not make such words interjections in the sense of a class of words which are used only for this purpose.

Conclusion

This brief discussion of some of the widely accepted word classes of German will have served to demonstrate some of the difficulties involved here, and will have confirmed the doubtful nature of the traditional assignment of German words to classes. If we may draw some consolation from this state of affairs, however, it is that the concept of 'word class' is probably not as fundamental to grammatical theory as traditional grammar would have us believe, since, as noted in the introduction to this chapter, modern linguistics is less word-based than traditional grammar. Word classes can be seen as a reflection of the grammatical relations between the words of a sentence, and thus secondary to these relations. Since these relations are of a variety of kinds, and of varying degrees of closeness, it is not surprising that the establishment of a definitive set of classes, and the assignment of words to these classes, should be a complex and difficult problem, and one which does not necessarily have a simple, or a single, solution.

Grammatical Categories

Introduction

In the discussion of German morphology in Chapter 3, we identified a number of types of inflectional affixes which could be attached to roots. In the context of a morphological discussion it was not appropriate to consider the nature of these inflections beyond an examination of their role in the structure of German words. In the present chapter we shall investigate these inflections further.

The various inflectional affixes that we have identified are a reflection of a number of GRAMMATICAL CATEGORIES—grammatical features of words or phrases which have a range of different functions within the sentence. A precise definition of the term 'grammatical category' would be hard to formulate, but the concept can be loosely characterized as a feature of the morpheme, word, or phrase which has grammatical, as opposed to purely lexical, significance.

To illustrate this we may take the category of NUMBER. In English and German we make a distinction between SINGULAR and PLURAL: *book ~ books, Buch ~ Bücher*. It seems perfectly natural to speakers of English or German to make this distinction, and we may easily be misled into thinking that 'number' is simply a category of meaning; after all, objects in the world come either singly or in groups. But we must be careful to distinguish number as a category of meaning and number as a grammatical category. There are many languages which do not have number in a grammatical sense, where there is no distinction between singular nouns and plural nouns or singular verb-forms and plural verb-forms. In Chinese, for example, the sentence 'Shu zai zhuozi shang' contains the nouns *shu* 'book' and *zhuozi* 'table', but there is no indication of number here, and the sentence means 'The book is on the table', 'The books are on the table', or even 'The books are on the tables'. On the other hand, there are also languages which make more, rather than fewer, distinctions of number than English or German. Arabic, for example, distinguishes not 'one' and 'more than one', but 'one', 'two', and 'more than two', with an additional category of 'dual'. For example, *kitaab* means 'book', *kitabeen* means 'two books', and *kutub* means 'more than two books'.

It would be wrong, however, to regard these differences between languages as questions purely of the meanings that can be communicated. The fact that Chinese does not indicate the number of its nouns does not mean that speakers of Chinese cannot say whether there is one or more than one of an object, any more than the absence of a dual in English or German implies that the speakers of these languages cannot tell the difference between 'two' and 'more than two'. Should the need arise, English or German speakers (and, indeed, speakers of Chinese) can of course quantify their nouns to whatever degree of precision is required, merely by adding a numeral. The differences between languages here are not differences in the meanings that can be communicated (and still less are they differences in what speakers of these languages can perceive);[11] they are merely differences in the features of meaning that are given a *grammatical form* in the languages concerned. Speakers of all these languages have, conceptually and semantically, the same set of numbers, but grammatically English and German recognize a twofold distinction between singular and plural, Arabic makes a threefold grammatical distinction between singular, dual, and plural, while Chinese

---

[11] Some anthropological linguists have argued that we perceive the world through our own language, and hence that speakers of different languages have different perceptions of the world (the 'Sapir–Whorf hypothesis'). Though there may be some truth in this, it is difficult to determine how much. It does not follow from this, however, that speakers can only perceive what their language allows them to.

makes no grammatical distinctions of number at all. And other possibilities are also found among the languages of the world.

The distinction to be made here, therefore, is between grammatical categories on the one hand, and lexical categories on the other, i.e. between features which are given grammatical expression as opposed to those which are merely part of the meanings of individual words. When Arabic speakers distinguish between 'two' and 'more than two', they may do so grammatically, by the choice of a particular grammatical form; when English or German speakers make this distinction, they must do so lexically, by the choice of a particular number-word.[12]

This discussion should have made clear the difference between grammatical and lexical categories, but it does not solve all the problems. Consider the category of GENDER. Remembering the gender of German nouns is a particularly difficult task for learners of the language, as the gender often seems—and indeed generally is—completely arbitrary with regard to the semantic content of the words concerned. This makes it clear not only that (as in the case of number) grammatical categories may reflect meanings in a variety of different ways, but that they may even have no basis in lexical categories at all.

In English, of course, we are unable to make grammatical distinctions in the gender of nouns; there are no differences of forms in, for example, the articles or adjectives which accompany them, though a distinction is nevertheless made in the personal pronouns, where we have the forms *he, she,* and *it.* Since these pronouns are used to refer to males, females, and 'sexless' objects respectively, it is often said that English has *natural* gender rather than the *grammatical* gender of German. But this is misleading; it implies that both languages have gender, but that while in German the category that nouns belong to is arbitrary, in English it is based on the sex of the object referred to. The truth is, however, that whereas German has gender (seen as a grammatical category), English does not. The different personal pronouns of English relate not to the grammatical category of gender, but to the lexical category of *sex.* It is characteristics of the meanings of the words, not features of their grammar, that determine which pronoun to use.

The distinction between grammatical and lexical categories is admittedly not always a clear-cut one, however. In cases such as gender, which is to a large extent semantically arbitrary, there is really no doubt that the category that we are dealing with is a grammatical one; but where meaning is closely involved, e.g. with number or tense, the question may be somewhat less easy to decide,

---

[12] It has also been said that certain categories are *compulsory* in languages, and others not. Thus, number is compulsory in English and German, but not in Chinese.

though meaningfulness does not of itself make the category lexical.[13] If the category concerned is indicated morphologically, e.g. with an inflectional affix, then again we can legitimately consider it to be grammatical, but this is not always the case. Some German verb forms, for example, involve differences of syntax rather than of word structure (e.g. 'er *ist gekommen*', 'es *ist gesagt worden*'). But if we admit (as we should) such categories as 'perfect' or 'passive' to be grammatical, should we extend this to other complex forms such as 'er *soll kommen*', 'du *kannst* es *sagen*', and so on? The dividing line between the grammatical and the lexical is not always easy to draw.

A further characteristic of many grammatical categories is their susceptibility to agreement (concord). In German the gender, number, and case of a noun are obligatorily shared by the words which qualify it within the phrase—determiners, adjectives, etc. Similarly, the number and person of a noun or pronoun which is the subject of the sentence are shared with the verb. Such agreement, since it is dependent on grammatical relationships within the sentence, is clearly grammatical, and vouches for the grammatical nature of the categories themselves. However, not all grammatical categories can agree; in German the tense of the verb is not reflected in the form of any other word in the sentence. Agreement is not, therefore, a requirement for a particular category to be regarded as grammatical.

Agreement has a 'direction' to it: German articles and adjectives, for example, could be said to agree with the nouns they accompany, and not the reverse. Similarly, the verb could be said to agree with the subject of the sentence in its number, rather than the other way round. This means that the categories of one word may determine those of others. This being so, the categories associated with the words that are determined by others are EXTRINSIC to these words; the words acquire the categories in the course of agreement. The categories of the determining words, on the other hand, are INTRINSIC to those words. For example, gender and number are categories of the article in German, but they are extrinsic to it, since the article acquires its gender and number from the noun it accompanies. For the noun itself, gender and number are intrinsic categories. But categories can be intrinsic to words in one of two ways: they may be FIXED or VARIABLE. Gender is a fixed category for the German noun; nouns have a specific and unchanging gender. Number, on the other hand, though also intrinsic to nouns (the number of the noun

---

[13] To distinguish (as does Kufner (1962): see Further Reading) compulsory *grammatical* categories (e.g. gender) from compulsory *semantic* categories (e.g. tense), on the grounds that the former are automatic and meaningless and the latter meaningful, is problematical, as the dividing line between 'meaningful' and 'meaningless' is not clear. Even apparently meaningful categories may be a matter of automatic rules.

can be said to determine the number of the article and other noun qualifiers), is variable: a given noun may be singular or plural.

The various grammatical categories of German require us to classify particular forms grammatically, as 'singular' or 'plural', as 'masculine', 'feminine', or 'neuter', and so on. But it is sometimes possible to think of a particular category as being present or absent. For example, plural nouns generally differ from the singular in having an additional plural affix; there is no singular affix. It would be justifiable, therefore, to regard the singular form as the basic form, lacking the category of number, and the plural as having this category. We could say that singular is the *unmarked* number and that plural is the *marked* number. Here, what we regard as marked or unmarked is simply a reflection of the morphological features. But we might also extend this principle to categories where there is no morphological reason to regard one form as unmarked. With case, for example, the 'absolute' form (which is used in isolation) is the nominative, and this might justify considering this case to be unmarked and all the others marked. With gender, we might consider the masculine to be unmarked, on the grounds that pronouns such as *wer* are masculine in form even where they refer to females, and that in pairs such as *Lehrer* ~ *Lehrerin* it is the masculine that serves as the basic form to which the feminine suffix is added, and not the reverse.[14] But although unmarked categories can sometimes be established in this way, the concept is not often very helpful.

The Grammatical Categories of German

In an inflecting language such as German it is inevitable, and indeed sensible, to commence our discussion of grammatical categories with the kinds of inflections that are found in the language (though, as we have noted, not all categories will necessarily be manifested through inflections). In Chapter 3 we recognized two basic inflectional patterns, declension and conjugation, associated primarily with nouns and verbs respectively. Consequently, the grammatical categories that are to be recognized can be grouped into nominal and

[14] There are some exceptions, where the masculine form is derived from the feminine—e.g. *Gänserich*. This topic raises political and social questions which it is inappropriate to pursue further here. It has been claimed that many languages, including German, are in fact formally biased against the female sex. Though it can hardly be denied that most societies, including those of Western Europe, are inexcusably discriminatory in their attitude towards women, and that this discrimination, along with other social attitudes, is inevitably reflected in the language which these societies use, it does not necessarily follow that the responsibility for these attitudes should be laid at the door of language itself. It is also relevant to our present discussion to note that some of the difficulty here arises from the failure to distinguish between the *grammatical* category of gender and the *lexical* category of sex, a confusion that is aggravated by the application of the biological terms 'masculine' and 'feminine' to the grammatical category, and the grammatical term 'gender' to the biological category of sex.

verbal types. Though these two groups overlap in a number of instances (e.g. *number* characterizes both types), each category can nevertheless be regarded, in terms of the above discussion, as intrinsic either to nouns or to verbs.

As far as the nominal type is concerned, we can, on morphological grounds, easily distinguish the categories of *gender, number,* and *case.* All these are intrinsic to nouns, and adjectives, quantifiers, and determiners, as well as pronouns, have sets of forms which allow them to agree in respect of these categories. The personal pronouns are also differentiated according to *person,* though as a grammatical category this is best considered to be a property of the verb.

The verbal group also shares with the nominal group the category of number, since there is a set of person/number affixes for the verb, though number is extrinsic to the verb, being determined by the subject noun phrase. Unique to the verb, however, and intrinsic to it, are the various affixes associated with *tense.* However, tense is a much-abused category, covering a variety of different phenomena, and linguists generally prefer to distinguish it from *aspect*—not one of the traditional categories, but one which seems justified nevertheless. Further intrinsic verbal categories that need some discussion are *mood* (e.g. 'subjunctive') and *voice* (e.g. 'passive').

In the following discussion we shall consider the nature and role of each of these categories, and examine some of the questions and problems that they raise.

Nominal Categories   Nominal categories are those which are intrinsic to the noun: gender, number, and case. In our consideration of declension in Chapter 3 we noted that, although the inflections indicate these three categories, not every combination of each of the three genders, two numbers, and four cases has a unique form. Furthermore, these categories do not have separate affixes: a single affix combines all three. Thus, *gutem* is 'masculine (or neuter) dative singular', *guter* is 'masculine nominative singular', 'feminine genitive (or dative) singular', or 'genitive plural'. The individual categories are thus to a large extent grammatical abstractions, and cannot be isolated in a specific phonological form. It is nevertheless possible to consider each of these separately, and to consider its significance and function in the language.

Gender.   Gender in German is, as we have already noted, a largely arbitrary matter from the semantic point of view: it does not as a rule reflect the sex of what is referred to. There is no sensible semantic reason, therefore, why German windows should be neuter, doors feminine, and gardens masculine. It is also often pointed out that in some cases gender directly contradicts sex, since *Mädchen,* which is clearly reserved for females, is neuter and *Mensch* is masculine, regardless of the sex of the person concerned.

In the case of morphologically derived words, gender is normally determined by the particular affix or derivational process concerned. Suffixes such as *-schaft, -ung, -heit, -(er)ei,* etc. create feminine nouns regardless, in denominal forms, of the gender of the noun stem on which they are based. This is illustrated in 4.16.

(4.16) *der Mann*   *die Mannschaft*
        das Kind   *die Kindheit*
        das Schwein   *die Schweinerei*

Most nominalizing affixes, in fact, determine the gender of the resulting noun, though there are notorious problems with one or two, such as *-nis,* where the gender is less predictable. Similarly, in cases of 'conversion' (where no affixes are used) the gender of the noun is determined, e.g. in neuter nouns formed from verbal infinitives (*das Essen, das Schreiben*) and masculine nouns formed from verb roots (*der Ruf, der Schlag*). In derived nouns, therefore, gender is largely a morphological matter, which accounts for many of the cases of disparity between sex and gender: *Mädchen, Fräulein,* and the like, as well as personal names such as *Gretchen,* are neuter because they have diminutive suffixes.

With underived nouns there are no such determining factors, and the gender is to a large extent arbitrary. Certain general principles are nevertheless identifiable, and rules are found in many comprehensive grammar books; most have many exceptions. Thus, tree-names are feminine: *die Eiche, die Kiefer* ('pine'; *der Kiefer* = 'jaw'); river-names are either feminine or masculine: *die Donau, der Rhein;* and so on. One might speculate as to the historical reasons for such gender assignments, but such speculation is largely fruitless.

Though the grammatical category of gender is clearly distinct from the lexical category of sex, there is nevertheless a tendency to relate them, where other factors do not intervene. Despite the existence of such words as *Mädchen* and *Fräulein,* the gender of nouns referring to humans does tend to reflect their sex, as we see from the examples of 4.17.

(4.17) *der Mann*   *die Frau*
        der Vater   *die Mutter*
        der Sohn   *die Tochter*
        der Onkel   *die Tante*
        der Bruder   *die Schwester*

(There are some exceptions, e.g. *das Weib.*) Furthermore, 'agentive' and some other types of nouns have forms which correspond to sex, as in 4.18.

(4.18)   *der Arbeiter   die Arbeiterin*
          der Lehrer   die Lehrerin
          der Student   die Studentin

In a similar way, nouns referring to animals whose sex is relevant (especially domestic animals) tend to have a gender which reflects the sex, often resulting in pairs such as those of 4.19.

(4.19)   *der Bulle   die Kuh*
          der Hahn   die Henne
          der Eber   die Sau

The noun for the young (and sexually immature) animal is often neuter: *das Kalb, das Lamm,* etc.

There is thus some evidence that grammatical gender, though in principle arbitrary, is not totally independent of sex. This view is reinforced by the fact that, where sex and gender are in conflict—e.g. when a female person is referred to by a neuter noun such as *Mädchen* or *Fräulein*—some grammatical variation may also be found. Consider the examples of 4.20.

(4.20)   (i)   Das junge Mädchen, das nebenan wohnt, ist sehr fleißig.
          (ii) Ein junges Mädchen wohnt nebenan. Sie ist sehr fleißig.

Though words which qualify such a noun—determiners and adjectives, etc.—must agree with it in gender, there is a strong tendency to replace the theoretically required neuter pronouns by the feminine forms, as in sentence 4.20 (ii), where *sie* has replaced *es*. Though either of these could be used, *sie* is the more likely. On the other hand, it would not be usual to replace the relative pronoun *das* of 4.20 (i) by *die;* the grammatical pull of the immediately preceding neuter noun is too strong. With greater distance from the governing noun, the tendency to revert to the lexical category of sex in preference to the grammatical category of gender becomes increasingly strong.

Number.   The semantic significance of number in German—unlike that of gender—is clear: it relates to the distinction between one and more than one. Nevertheless, as we have already seen, such a distinction is not made in all languages, and some languages make other distinctions. Thus, though the singular/plural distinction appears to be natural and well motivated for speakers of German or English, there is nevertheless a sense in which the embodiment of just this number difference in the grammars of these languages is arbitrary. Moreover, even in German and English the category of number is not quite as consistent as one would perhaps think.

The inevitable arbitrariness of classifying all objects as 'singular' or 'plural' for grammatical purposes is reflected in a few cases where German and English disagree on the classification. Cutting-tools with two movable blades are regarded as plural in English—*scissors, sheers, pincers, pliers, tweezers,* etc.—and this is even extended to foreign words such as *secateurs.* But words of this kind are regarded as singular in German: *Schere, Zange,* etc. Garments for the lower half of the body are subject to a similar difference: English words such as *trousers, pants, shorts, knickers,* etc. are plural; the corresponding German words—*Hose,* etc.—are singular. These words do not normally have a singular form in English; we would not usually refer to a *scissor* or a *trouser.*[15] This does not mean that English cannot quantify or count them, but it must be done in another way: we refer to 'two *pairs* of scissors', 'a *pair* of trousers', etc. There is, of course, no sense in which one or other of these languages can be said to be right or wrong in its classification of these words, and it is pointless to ask whether the objects concerned are 'really' singular or plural (it could perhaps be said that trousers are actually singular at the top and plural at the bottom!).

Some objects do not in any case lend themselves to a numerical classification, since they come in uncountable quantities. Words such as *Wasser, Erde, Reis,* etc. refer to objects of this kind. However much we increase the quantity of such objects, they remain for us a single entity, and the nouns concerned remain singular. Nouns of this kind are called MASS-NOUNS, as opposed to COUNT-NOUNS such as *Tasse, Buch,* etc. which can be quantified numerically and which therefore have plural forms. There are plural forms for many mass-nouns, but their use generally involves a different meaning, and not merely an increase in quantity. *Zwei Erden,* for example, would entail a different sense of *Erde,* i.e. 'worlds'. Usage may again differ in English and German; *bread* is rarely found in the plural in English, and would probably mean different kinds of bread, while *Brote* is used in German in the sense of 'loaves', or sometimes 'slices of bread', and the singular *ein Brot* is also found. Mass-nouns can be numerically quantified by the use of an accompanying count-noun: *ein Stück Fleisch, zwei Pfund Reis, drei Liter Wasser,* and so on.[16]

As we have observed, number in German is a grammatical category of noun phrases and verbs, and in the latter case it has to agree with the number of the subject of the sentence. This rule seems to be rather more strictly enforced in German than in English. In the latter we can see a tendency for number

---

[15] A singular form of these nouns is found in compounds (*trouser-leg*), and the clothing trade might well refer to *a new trouser,* but the latter is hardly normal usage.

[16] An unusual case is the English word 'oats', which is a plural mass-noun with no singular.

agreement to break down in certain cases (just as gender agreement occasionally breaks down in German). This happens with nouns which refer to a collective entity or group of people—committees, parties, governments, etc. Thus, while in German we find only 'Die Regierung hat ein neues Gesetz entworfen', English could have either a singular or a plural verb in such cases: 'The government has/have drafted a new law', 'The committee has/have decided ...', etc. We might see such cases as a conflict between lexical and grammatical number: government, committee, etc. are grammatically singular, but since they refer to a collective or group they may be felt to be lexically plural.

Case. A further category that is of importance in German but only marginally so in English (where, apart from the possessive form,[17] it is restricted to pronouns) is *case*. German noun phrases and pronouns must be assignable to one of the four cases *nominative, accusative, genitive,* and *dative,* though there are not distinct forms for all cases in all genders and numbers (the accusative is only distinct from the nominative in the masculine singular, and the feminine singular does not distinguish genitive from dative).

Noun phrases and pronouns have a variety of roles in the sentence, and case may play a part in each instance. A major function of case is to indicate the syntactic function of the phrase, whether it is the subject, or the object, etc. (these functional categories will be considered in detail in the next chapter). Consider the examples of 4.21.

(4.21)   Dieser Mann kennt meinen Freund.
         Diesen Mann kennt mein Freund.

Lexically (i.e. in terms of the lexemes used), these sentences can be said to be identical: the same (lexical) words occur and in the same order. But the cases of the two noun phrases are different, with nominative marking the subject and accusative marking the object. Similarly, the examples of 4.22 show the different functions of dative and accusative; the former indicates the indirect object, the latter the direct object.

(4.22)   Meinem Freund stellte ich meinen Vater vor.
         Meinen Freund stellte ich meinem Vater vor.

---

[17] Although both languages can be said to have a genitive case, its role is more limited in English than in German. In English it is restricted to possessive constructions (*the boy's book,* etc.), while in German we also find it occurring after certain verbs and prepositions as well as in other constructions (see below). It could therefore be argued that since in English it has lost most of its genuinely syntactic functions, it is barely a 'case' at all.

The role of case here is to indicate the syntactic function of the noun phrase, and is thus a grammatical device. It is tempting to interpret this in semantic terms, e.g. to say that the nominative indicates the 'doer' of the action, the accusative the thing 'operated on', and the dative the 'recipient' or 'beneficiary' of the action; but this is really to miss the point (this question will be taken up again in the next chapter). Case serves to indicate the *syntactic* function of the phrase. Like the other grammatical categories already discussed, therefore, it is often semantically arbitrary, in the sense that it reflects not categories of meaning as such but rather those aspects of meaning that happen to be given a grammatical form in the language.

Because case is an indicator of syntactic function, some modern theories of syntax use the term to refer to the functions themselves, regardless of whether they are expressed through the morphological features of the language or not. Even for a language such as English, therefore, which does not (generally) have morphological case, these theories would regard the subject as being in the 'nominative' case, the direct object as being in the 'accusative' case, and so on. This is potentially confusing, and may appear to be a reversion to traditional grammar which, as noted earlier, tended to assume that all languages were (or should be) like Latin, which, like German, marked its syntactic functions morphologically with case. However, this is certainly not the intention here; theories which use the term 'case' in this way—it is here referred to as 'abstract case' as opposed to 'morphological case'—do so in order to incorporate the universal principle that even languages without morphological case have subjects and objects, and that these may have different grammatical properties. Thus, verbs, for example, are said to 'assign' abstract case to their objects, regardless of whether there is an overt morphological marker to indicate this, and the same could be said of prepositions. However, we shall not adopt this approach here.

The case of an object of the verb is not always predictable. Although it is generally in the accusative case, there are some verbs which require a dative object, and a few which even require a genitive object, as in the examples of 4.23.

(4.23) (dative)   Er hilft *seiner Schwester.*
         (genitive)   Er bedarf *unseres Mitleids.*

It has been suggested by some linguists that the dative is essentially a more 'human' case than the accusative, hence beneficiaries and recipients are in the dative, while non-human things which are 'operated on' are in the accusative. They also point to contrasts such as that of 4.24.

(4.24)   (i)   Sie klopfte *ihm* auf den Rücken.

(ii)   Sie klopfte *ihn* auf den Rücken.

The accusative pronoun *ihn* of 4.24 (ii) could be said to indicate a rather less personal, less friendly, gesture than the dative *ihm* of 4.24 (i).[18] It has also been claimed, with rather doubtful justification, that the increasing use of the accusative at the expense of the dative is indicative of the 'depersonalization' of modern society.

Certain noun phrases may have an adverbial function in the sentence (as an ADJUNCT—see Chapter 5). Here too case has a significant role, as in the examples of 4.25.

(4.25)   (i)   *Nächste Woche* fahre ich nach Indien.

(ii)   *Eines Tages* fahre ich nach Indien.

Though most such adjunct noun phrases are in the accusative (indicating a specific time), as in 4.25 (i), indefinite time phrases (as in 4.25 (ii)) are in the genitive.

A third role of case is in noun phrases which are part of a prepositional phrase. Most prepositions are obligatorily followed by a certain case—mostly dative or accusative, but occasionally genitive—but a number may take two different cases, and with a different significance. Examples are given in 4.26.

(4.26)   *Er geht im Haus.*   *'He is walking in the house.'*
       Er geht ins Haus.   *'He is walking into the house.'*

But although an analogous distinction (dative = 'location', accusative = 'motion') is found with other prepositions too, it would be misleading to attach a consistent semantic interpretation to any particular case (*nach*, for example, indicates motion, but it takes the dative).

Verbal Categories   Of the grammatical categories associated with the German verb, number is not intrinsic to it, and it has in any case been dealt with above. It will not be considered further here. The remaining categories are *person, tense, aspect, mood,* and *voice.*

The verbal categories are rather complex. There are a large number of different forms, and although the categories themselves can be identified,

---

[18] The attempt to discern a constant meaning for cases is characteristic of the work of the German linguist Hennig Brinkmann.

their roles are not easy to determine, especially when they occur in combination. Further complexities derive from the relationships between the grammatical categories as such and related lexical categories—not only the meaning of the verb itself, but also the meanings of accompanying words, such as adverbs and modal verbs. The verbal categories thus raise questions, many of which do not admit of simple answers, and it will not always be possible within the confines of this chapter to do more than merely identify the nature of the problem.

Although a general characterization of the meaning of a particular category can often be given, we shall see that such meanings are rarely reflected in a simple way in the grammatical categories of the language. As with the nominal categories, therefore, we shall have to conclude that the verbal categories contain an important element of semantic arbitrariness.

Person. As we have noted, person is not an intrinsic category of the verb, but reflects a choice made elsewhere in the sentence, with which the verb must agree. The person of the verb is derived from the nature of the subject of the sentence. The natural semantic basis for the grammatical category of person is to be found in the roles of participants in the act of speaking: typically, such acts have a speaker, an addressee, and something talked about, giving the three 'persons':

speaker: 1st person
addressee: 2nd person
what is talked about: 3rd person

An illustration is given in 4.27.

(4.27)   Ich werde dir das Buch geben.
          Du wirst das Buch von mir bekommen.
          Das Buch wird auf dem Tisch sein.

In each example of 4.27 there is a speaker (*ich*), a hearer (*du*), and something spoken about (*das Buch*), though not all of these find overt expression in every sentence. As each of these in turn is made the subject of the sentence, the verb form changes to agree with it.

That there should be such persons may seem to be self-evident, since they would appear to be implicit in the very act of communication itself. But this naturally does not mean that they need to be given grammatical expression in particular languages. In fact, though the distinction between different forms of the pronouns seems to be normal in languages, corresponding differences in the verb forms are by no means necessary, and many languages make no such distinctions. In regular verbs, English has only two forms (I/you/we/they *come;* he/she/it *comes*), and then only in the present tense. German has four (occasionally five) forms in the present (ich *komme, fahre;* du *kommst, fährst;* er/sie/es *kommt, fährt;* ihr *kommt, fahrt;* wir/sie/Sie *kommen, fahren*) and four in the past: (ich/er/sie/es *kam;* du *kamst;* ihr *kamt;* wir/sie/Sie *kamen*). Moreover, these different forms include differences of number as well as person, since the two are inseparable. Person as such is not, therefore, very well defined morphologically in German.

But the category of person also contains some interesting problems of its own. Consider the examples of 4.28.

(4.28)   (i)   Wir geben dir das Buch.
         (ii) Wir geben ihm das Buch.

Wir in sentence 4.28 (i) is first person, and thus refers to the speaker, but since it is also plural it must include someone else. The speaker is thus grouping himself or herself with other persons, but not, it must be noted, with the addressee, who is referred to separately in this sentence by the second-person pronoun *dir.* Sentence 4.28 (ii), on the other hand, is ambiguous—though not, perhaps, in an obvious way. Here the other person or persons referred to by the first-person plural pronoun may include the addressee. *Wir* may, in other words, mean *ich und du,* or *ich und er/sie.* The second-person plural pronouns have a similar ambiguity. *Ihr* or *Sie* may mean 'you the addressees and no one else' or 'you the addressee(s) and someone else'. These cases show that 'person' has more possibilities than simply the three persons recognized in the grammar of German (some languages in fact incorporate these additional distinctions into their grammars).

There are also further possibilities. What person, for example, does *man* refer to in a sentence such as 'Man muss essen, um zu leben'? It is sometimes referred to as an 'indefinite pronoun', but its indefiniteness lies in the fact that it refers to all three persons, though grammatically, of course, it is treated as third-person singular. In a similar way, we might consider the impersonal *es* of *es regnet, es gibt,* etc. to refer to no person at all.

What these examples show is that though the grammatical category of person in German has, for the most part, a fairly clear relationship to the participant roles of speakers and hearers, there are points at which these relationships break down. Person, then, like the other categories considered so far, remains a grammatical category, and not a purely semantic one.

There is a further dimension to the use of personal pronouns in German which has no equivalent in English: German not only distinguishes a singular and a plural form of the second-person pronoun (*du* and *ihr*), but also recognizes a third 'polite' pronoun (*Sie*).[19] The use of these forms is a delicate and difficult matter, and one which is also in the process of change. The significance of using *du* or *Sie* as a form of address is very closely bound up with other aspects of social behaviour among German speakers, including the use of names and titles, and is therefore not easy to characterize in a simple way. *Sie* is often thought of as more formal and more polite than *du*, but the implications of their use go further than this.[20]

One effect of using *Sie* and its related forms (*Ihnen, Ihr*, etc.) is to establish a certain distance between speaker and hearer, while the use of *du* and its related forms (*dich, dir, dein*, etc.) implies a closeness. The distance of *Sie* will certainly be appropriate on more formal occasions, and it will also often be polite, but the use of *du* is not necessarily impolite (except in those cases where social convention decrees that *Sie* should be used). But the use of these forms may also have implications for the relative status of speaker and hearer, especially if it is not reciprocal (i.e. if one participant in the conversation uses *du* and the other *Sie*). Non-reciprocal use may occur, for example, where there is a considerable difference of age between the participants. Here the use of *du* and *Sie* becomes an expression of status and power. On the other hand, the reciprocal use of *du*, which is found in many groups—students, fellow workers, etc.—may be an expression of what has been called solidarity.[21]

The status of this distinction as a grammatical category is not completely secure. In the first place its scope is somewhat limited, and there is no comparable distinction for first- or third-person forms. Furthermore, this distinction is certainly not confined to grammatical forms such as these but is also reflected in such clearly lexical matters as the use of titles and names (e.g. *Frau Doktor, Frau Schmidt, Renate, Liebling, Mutti*, etc. which may all refer to the same person). It is probably best to see the purely grammatical aspects of this distinction as belonging to a rather marginal grammatical category, despite their evident social importance.

Tense and Aspect.   The intrinsic verbal category of 'tense' is one of the most important, but also one of the most complex and difficult, and we shall therefore need to examine it more closely than the others. Like number, it

---

[19] The *Sie*-form is historically derived from the third-person plural form. Earlier German also allowed third-person singular forms (*Er, Sie*) to be used in a similar way. This usage may be compared with such English expressions as 'Is your ladyship well?', which similarly uses a third person as a form of address. German *Sie* is, however, no longer to be thought of as third person.

[20] A recent discussion is found in Besch (1996).

[21] The terms 'power' and 'solidarity' were suggested in an influential article by Brown and Gilman (1960).

has a clear basis in a natural conceptual category—here 'time'—but its use in German shows that the relationship between this conceptual base and its manifestation in grammatical form in the language is a variable and at times arbitrary one. Differences in the way different languages deal with time constitute one of the major problems facing the language-learner.

We must bear in mind, of course, that we are not concerned with time as such, but merely with its grammatical expression, and it is therefore important to establish what grammatical devices are available in the language. Some of the many verb forms were illustrated in Chapter 3, though there we were only interested in the structure of words, and were able to discount the complex forms consisting of more than one word. In the present discussion we are concerned with all the forms of the verb.

Omitting subjunctive and passive forms (which will be dealt with under 'mood' and 'voice' below), the verbal structures found are exemplified in 4.29.

(4.29) (i)   simple verb: *macht/machte*
        (ii) auxiliary + past participle: *hat/hatte gemacht*
        (iii) auxiliary + infinitive: *wird machen*
        (iv) auxiliary + past participle
              + infinitive of auxiliary: *wird gemacht haben*

In 4.29 the forms of (i) consist of a single word, a finite main verb. Those of (ii) and (iii) add an auxiliary, with the main verb now appearing as a past participle or an infinitive, while in (iv) the auxiliary is itself formed out of an auxiliary and an infinitive.

These various forms result from the intersection of a number of distinctions. First (expressing these distinctions with the help of traditional terminology), there is the present–past distinction, found in the main verb itself and in the auxiliary (*macht, hat ~ machte, hatte*); second, we can distinguish between the simple verb and the perfect/pluperfect forms (*macht, machte, wird machen ~ hat gemacht, hatte gemacht, wird gemacht haben*); and thirdly, we find the difference between the simple verb or auxiliary verb and the future or future perfect form with *werden* (*macht, hat gemacht ~ wird machen, wird gemacht haben*). Each of these distinctions is of a somewhat different kind and needs to be considered separately.

Clearly, these various distinctions have something to do with time. If we adopt a fairly simple view of the nature of time, we might represent it as a line moving from the past to the future, and passing through the present, 'now', the moment of speaking, as in 4.30.

(4.30)

This simple model provides us with three categories of time: past, present, and future. As far as the first two of these are concerned, we have already noted the existence of a present–past distinction in German. If I write 'Ich sitze an meinem Schreibtisch und schreibe ein Buch über die deutsche Sprache', that is true for the present moment; the sentence 'Ich saß an meinem Schreibtisch und schrieb ein Buch über die deutsche Sprache' would clearly locate those events firmly in the past. Similarly, 'Ich werde an meinem Schreibtisch sitzen und ein Buch über die deutsche Sprache schreiben' evidently refers to the future (though there are reservations to be made here which will be taken up again shortly).

Although, taking 'now' as our point of departure, we can divide time up into past, present, and future, these three categories do not exhaust the possibilities. We can, of course, refer to *any* point in time by using a variety of lexical time-expressions—'am 2. Juli, 1974, um 6 Uhr abends', and so on—but these means are not grammatical and therefore not 'tense'. But even grammatically we are not necessarily restricted to past, present, and future, and many languages make more distinctions than this. Several African languages, for example, distinguish a 'remote past', a 'near past', and a 'today past', according to how close the event is to the present time. Such possibilities are not, however, available in German or English.

Nevertheless, some further differentiation of time is possible in German. We have assumed so far that our reference point is 'now', the moment of speaking, but this is not always the case. Consider the examples of 4.31.

(4.31)   (i)   Ich habe das Buch (gerade) gelesen.
         (ii) Ich hatte das Buch (schon damals) gelesen.
         (iii) Ich werde das Buch (bis morgen) gelesen haben.

The reference point is different in these three examples. In 4.31(i) the event is viewed from the standpoint of the present time, but in 4.31 (ii) it is seen from the perspective of a point in the past (*damals*), and in 4.31 (iii) from a future point in time (*morgen*). The time of speaking remains unaffected by this; it is always the present. What changes is the time from which the event described is viewed. Whereas in the first example only two points are required, therefore, in the latter two cases we need three points: the time of speaking, the reference time, and the time of the event, the last of which is, in these examples, before the reference point.

A graphic representation of the time relations of the sentences of 4.31 requires a more complex model of time than that given in 4.30. A more elaborate model is given in 4.32 (where (i), (ii), and (iii) correspond to (i), (ii), and (iii) of 4.31).

(4.32)

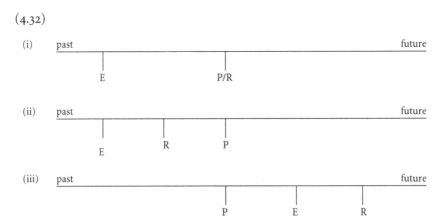

In 4.32 point P represents the present moment, the moment of speaking, which is fixed. Point R is the reference point, which coincides with P in (i), is in the past in (ii), and is in the future in (iii). Point E is the event referred to, which in these examples is always before R, wherever R is located.

In fact, there is some ambiguity in sentence (iii), since although point R follows point P, and point E must precede point R, it is not necessary for point E to follow point P. In other words, to say that an event will have happened in the future (i.e. precedes a future reference point) does not necessarily mean that it has not yet happened (i.e. that it follows the moment of speaking). Thus, although sentence 4.31 (iii) would usually imply that the book has not yet been read, this is not necessarily the case. We could expand this sentence to 'Selbstverständlich werde ich das Buch bis morgen gelesen haben, weil ich es schon gestern gelesen habe!' The model would now need to be as in 4.33.

(4.33)

What is to be noted here is simply that a verb form such as that of 4.31 (iii) locates the event prior to the reference point, but does not specify its location with respect to the moment of speaking.

Verb forms such as those of 4.31(i), in which the reference point is the moment of speaking, are sometimes called *absolute* tenses, since no other point of reference is required. Forms such as those of 4.31 (ii) and 4.31 (iii) are called *relative* tenses, since the time of the event is relative to a reference point other than the present. However, this terminology is not very satisfactory, since the time of the event is in all cases relative to a reference point; it just happens that this reference point in 4.31 (i) coincides with the moment of speaking.

We have so far assumed that German can locate events in the present, past, or future, and therefore implied that it has present, past, and future 'tenses'. The present–past distinction seems clear enough: *ich schreibe* and *ich schrieb*. But consider now the future. German is said to have a 'future tense', namely such forms as *ich werde schreiben, er wird kommen*, and so on, but in practice such forms are rather restricted in use. To refer to a future event the so-called 'present tense' is more commonly used. Compare the sentences of 4.34 (i) with those of 4.34 (ii).

(4.34) (i) Morgen *schreibe* ich einen Brief.
              Er *kommt* nächstes Jahr nach England.
        (ii) Morgen *werde* ich einen Brief *schreiben*.
              Er *wird* nächstes Jahr nach England *kommen*.

All the sentences of 4.34 refer to the future, but those of 4.34 (ii) contain an additional implication, which might be called 'certainty' or 'determination'. Such an implication is not one of time relations, but falls under the heading of 'mood' or 'modality' (see below). As far as reference to pure time is concerned, it is the so-called 'present' forms of 4.34 (i) which are used to convey this. The forms with *werden* of 4.34 (ii) are not, therefore, strictly speaking future-tense forms, and we must conclude that, as a grammatical category, German does not have a 'future tense'.

This also has implications for our interpretation of the 'present tense'. This term too is inappropriate, given that, as in 4.34 (i), it is used to refer to the future. In fact, the present tense has other uses too, illustrated in 4.35.

(4.35) (i) Sie besucht ihre Mutter jeden Tag.
        (ii) Heidelberg liegt am Neckar.

Though the sentences of 4.35 contain the present tense, they in fact do not refer to the present time as such. Sentence (i) refers to a *habitual* action, which began in the past and will continue into the future, while sentence (ii) refers to a *timeless* state, in which past, present, and future are irrelevant.

Given these uses of the 'present tense', it is clear that this is not a very good term to describe it. Since it is opposed only to the 'past tense', an acceptable, though admittedly clumsy, term that is often used is the *non-past* tense; it is defined as not referring to the past.[22]

One might, however, point to the so-called 'future perfect', exemplified by such forms as *ich werde das Buch gelesen haben*. Since, as we have noted, this form can be said to locate an event before a future reference point (cf. 4.32 (iii) and 4.33), this would appear to provide evidence for some grammatical expression of future time. But this case is in fact entirely analogous to the 'simple' future; the expression of these relative time relations is normally achieved in German with a 'present perfect' rather than a 'future perfect' form: *ich habe das Buch bis morgen gelesen* (a usage which, incidentally, has no parallel in English). Despite appearances, this is not the use of a 'past' tense to refer to the future, but simply the extension of a non-past ('present perfect') form to future time reference, as in the case of the simple non-past. (On the significance of the 'perfect', see below.)

We have so far been concerned with the grammatical forms to indicate location in time, whether absolute or relative. But there are other kinds of temporal relationships too. To illustrate some of these we shall, for the moment, concern ourselves with English, since for English speakers this will perhaps make the German situation rather easier to understand. Consider first the sentences of 4.36.

(4.36)   (i)   The delegates voted against the motion.
          (ii) The delegates have voted against the motion.

In both cases the reference point is the moment of speaking, and the events referred to are located prior to this moment, i.e. in the past. But what is the difference in meaning between 4.36 (i) and 4.36 (ii)?

One might be tempted to see the event referred to in (i) as more remote, and further back in the past than that of (ii), but this is not necessarily true. We could easily say 'The delegates voted against the motion five minutes ago', while 'The delegates have voted against the motion' could be true even if the event took place in the more remote past. Nevertheless, the verb form of 4.36

---

[22] We must exclude from this the so-called 'historic present', in which past events are narrated in the non-past tense in order to make them more vivid, e.g. 'Da kommt er zu mir und sagt ...'.

(ii), usually called the *perfect*, does seem to be closer to the present, not in terms of time but in terms of *relevance*. By using the perfect, we imply that the event, whenever it took place, has *current relevance*. This implication is difficult to make precise, though it does seem to fit the various uses of the English perfect quite well. Thus, 4.36 (i) is merely a statement about a past event, while 4.36 (ii) is more a declaration about the present state of affairs, rather like 'The delegates are in a state of having voted against the motion'.

The English perfect cannot be accommodated even in the expanded model of 4.32, which would fail to distinguish it from the 'simple past'. The diagram of 4.37 is an attempt to do justice to the relationships here, where the arrow expresses the relevance of the past event for the reference point, the present time.

(4.37)

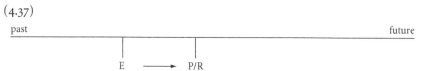

A further problem is raised by other English forms, illustrated in 4.38.

(4.38)　(i)　He wrote an essay on Goethe's *Faust*.
　　　　(ii)　He was writing an essay on Goethe's *Faust*.

Again the reference point in these sentences is the same (the present moment) and the event described takes place before this time, i.e. it is in the past. But the meanings are clearly different. Sentence (i) sees the event as single and complete, while sentence (ii)—the verb form is usually described as the *progressive*—implies continuity or incompleteness. Thus, 'While he was a student, he wrote an essay on Goethe's *Faust*' refers to a single event which took place during the period of his being a student, but 'While he was a student, he was writing an essay on Goethe's *Faust*' suggests either that he continued to write the essay throughout the whole period of his study, or that (amounting perhaps to the same thing) he never finished it.

English progressive forms provide yet another dimension to our model of time relations. The event is here seen not as a single entity, but rather as a continuous activity. Thus, although the model of 4.32 (i) is appropriate for sentence (i) of 4.38, it needs to be modified for sentence (ii), giving 4.39, where the event E is now an extended activity (represented by the box), which is located before the present reference point.

(4.39) (i)

Clearly the time relations of the English perfect and progressive forms are not simply a matter of 'location in time', whether 'absolute' or 'relative'. They involve different dimensions of time, such as 'continuity' or 'relevance'. In order to make clear this distinction, it is usual to differentiate the terminology to describe the grammatical features involved. The term *tense* is traditionally used to describe all the verb forms associated with time, but modern usage reserves it for the grammatical expression of *location* in time (whether 'absolute' or 'relative'), and the term *aspect* is used for other dimensions.[23] In English, therefore, a form such as *was writing* would be described as being in the 'past tense' and in the 'progressive aspect'.

As with other grammatical categories, the meaning involved does not need to be expressed grammatically at all, but may take a lexical form. The temporal implications of words such as *crack* and *crackle,* for example, seem to be different, as do *bite* and *nibble;* in each case there is an implication of duration or repetition in the second word. But this is a lexical, not a grammatical, difference. Such lexical differences of aspect are referred to by the (not entirely appropriate) German term *Aktionsart.*

That tense and aspect are independent dimensions of grammatical time in English is clear from the possibility of combining them. Thus, we may have combinations of past and non-past tense with progressive aspect, as in 4.40.

(4.40)		Non-progressive	Progressive
	Non-past	*he comes*	*he is coming*
	Past	*he came*	*he was coming*

The kind of phenomenon covered by the term 'aspect' is generally a matter of the internal temporal nature of the action of the verb rather than the location of the action in time, i.e. such characteristics as continuity, completion, and the like. The English perfect does not quite fit this description, but since it does not refer to location in time it is also generally included with aspect. Like the progressive aspect, it can combine with non-past and past tense to produce the forms of 4.41.

(4.41)		Non-perfect	Perfect
	Non-past	*he comes*	*he has come*
	Past	*he came*	*he had come*

---

[23] The term 'aspect' is taken from the grammars of Slavonic languages, where this category plays an important role.

The 'past perfect' differs from the 'present perfect' in that the reference point to which the past event has relevance is in the past. This is represented in 4.42, which can be compared with the representation of the 'present perfect' in 4.37.

(4.42)

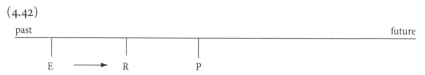

Furthermore, perfect and progressive can combine with each other, as well as with tense, to give the forms of 4.43.

(4.43)

	Non-progressive	Progressive
Non-perfect	*he comes*	*he is coming*
	he came	*he was coming*
Perfect	*he has come*	*he has been coming*
	he had come	*he had been coming*

Using our diagram as before, we could represent the past perfect progressive ('he had been coming') as in 4.44, where the event E is an extended activity in the past which has relevance for a later reference point R in the past.

(4.44)

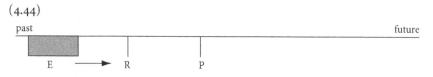

After this digression to examine the forms of English, we can now turn to tense and aspect in German. In one respect, certainly, German is simpler than English: it does not have the progressive aspect. Verb forms such as *er kommt, er kam,* etc. correspond to the English progressive and non-progressive forms, and can be translated as 'he comes' or 'he is coming', 'he came' or 'he was coming', respectively. As we have already seen, a perfect form does exist alongside the non-perfect forms (*er ist gekommen ~ er kam*), but it raises a number of questions which do not apply to the corresponding English forms.

A major consideration with these forms in German is that they are subject to regional and stylistic variations, which tend to obscure other characteristics. Some North German speakers may well have, at least in principle, a system which is quite similar to that of English, with the 'present perfect' form expressing the relevance of the event to a present reference point, and the simple non-perfect past (sometimes called the 'imperfect' or 'preterite') being a pure tense form with no expression of current relevance. For such speakers, the forms of 4.45 would thus be parallel in their major uses to the English forms of 4.41, and the diagrams of 4.37 and 4.42 would be largely applicable to the German forms.

(4.45)   Non-perfect Perfect
          Non-past *er kommt*   *er ist gekommen*
          Past   *er kam*   *er war gekommen*

But spoken South German, as well as Austrian, has a quite different system. The simple (non-perfect) past is not used (except in auxiliary verbs), so that the present perfect form is used on all occasions where Northern usage would have either the present perfect or the simple past. What this means is that the perfect aspect does not exist in Southern German, despite the fact that the 'perfect' *form* does: the 'perfect' does not have a perfect meaning.

But many German speakers, and perhaps the majority in the North, have a system which differs from both of these. A distinction between perfect and simple past may be observed in those cases where the assertion of current relevance is required, e.g. in sentences such as 'Er ist schon gekommen' (not *kam*, since *schon* reinforces the relevance to the present), or 'Er ist müde, weil er den ganzen Tag gearbeitet hat' (not *arbeitete*, because it relates the activity to his present state). But in other cases speakers may use either form without a difference of meaning (e.g. 'Gestern regnete es sehr viel'—'Gestern hat es sehr viel geregnet').[24] The difference here is a matter of style rather than of meaning, though the high prestige of Northern forms means that some speakers may consider the use of the simple past in such circumstances stylistically preferable, especially in writing. But there is considerable variation in usage here.

The situation is a little different with the past perfect ('pluperfect'), e.g. *er war gekommen*. Although apparently parallel to the 'present perfect', it is not in fact entirely analogous. Both the present perfect and the simple past place the event before the reference point (the present), though of course in different ways. Similarly, the past perfect locates the event before a past reference point, but there is here no corresponding simple (non-perfect) tense with a similar role, and so it is difficult to speak of the past perfect as having the same sort of aspectual role as the present perfect. Where, as in Southern German, the aspectual role of the present perfect has in any case

---

[24] It is interesting to note that English does not allow the perfect form where there is a specific time-expression, such as *yesterday*; sentences such as 'It has rained a lot yesterday' are not found. On the other hand, some forms of American English permit a simple past form where current relevance is clearly intended, as in 'He didn't do it yet'.

been lost, the meaning of the past perfect must be considered purely one of (relative) tense: it places an event before a past reference point.

Incidentally, it is interesting to note that in non-standard Southern German and Austrian speech the auxiliary verb of the past perfect, too, is subject to replacement by the perfect, and forms such as *ich habe es vergessen gehabt, ich bin gekommen gewesen* are heard.

From this discussion it will be clear that, although the German system of tense and aspect is ostensibly simpler than that of English, it is rather more variable, particularly as a result of different regional and stylistic usages. There are also some more specific differences between English and German. One such difference is in the verb forms used to describe a state or event which began in the past and continues into the present. Compare the German forms of 4.46 (i) with the English forms of 4.46 (ii).

(4.46)   (i)   Ich arbeite schon zwanzig Jahre hier.
               Er schläft schon seit drei Stunden.
         (ii) I have worked here for twenty years.
               He has been sleeping for three hours.

While English uses the (present) perfect in such cases, German uses the non-past. The situation is made more confusing, however, by the fact that as we have seen, many German speakers use the perfect form in preference to the simple past to refer to past events. The sentences of 4.47 (i), therefore, which superficially resemble those of 4.46 (ii), are in fact equivalent to those of 4.47 (ii).

(4.47)   (i)   Ich habe zwanzig Jahre hier gearbeitet.
               Er hat drei Stunden geschlafen.
         (ii) I worked here for twenty years.
               He slept for three hours.

It may be noticed that German uses the non-past not only for activities which began in the past and have continued up to the moment of speaking, but also to refer to the future. This can in principle lead to ambiguity, as we see from sentences such as those of 4.48.

(4.48)   Ich sitze fünf Minuten draußen.
         Wir fahren zwei Stunden im Zug.

These sentences could have either interpretation, as future ('I shall sit outside for five minutes'; 'We shall travel by train for two hours') or corresponding to the English present perfect ('I have been sitting outside for five minutes'; 'We have been travelling by train for two hours')—though in practice the intended meaning will be clear from the context or from additional words: 'Ich sitze noch fünf Minuten draußen' and 'Wir fahren schon zwei Stunden' are unambiguous. Moreover, this ambiguity can only arise with verbs whose meaning entails duration.

Mood.   If we are able to identify time as the basis of tense and aspect, it is far less easy to establish the area of meaning to which the grammatical category of mood refers. Some linguists include within this category the distinction between the sentence types 'declarative', 'interrogative', and 'imperative' (see Chapter 5). More specifically, however, this term is used to refer to the distinction between 'indicative' and 'subjunctive'. However, not only is this morphological category not easy to assume under one category of meaning, but it is also difficult to separate its functions from that of other, grammatically rather different, features, especially the so-called 'modal' verbs. Finally, as with tense and aspect, there are stylistic and regional factors to be taken into account. In dealing with the category of mood, therefore, we need to be rather flexible.

A convenient starting point for the discussion of mood is the set of verb forms described in the previous chapter as 'subjunctive'. As we saw, there is theoretically a subjunctive form for every indicative form, though in practice the distinction is not always realizable. Furthermore, despite occasional assertions to the contrary, the subjunctive is by no means obsolete in the language, though it is true that some of its forms are fairly rare; the most commonly used, at least in spoken German, are perhaps the subjunctive forms of the past (as opposed to the non-past), and especially those of the auxiliary and modal verbs, for reasons that will become clear below.

But if the forms of the subjunctive are easily described, its uses are not. All grammar books attempt to describe its major uses, and this task will not be undertaken here. Instead, we shall consider some of the questions that the subjunctive raises, in particular whether there is a single meaning or area of meaning common to all its uses, and what such a meaning might be.

One main use of the subjunctive is reported or indirect speech, illustrated in the examples of 4.49.

(4.49)   A. (i) Er sagte, er *tue* es nicht.
            (ii) Er sagte, er *täte* es nicht.
        B. (i) Er sagte, er *habe* es nicht getan.
            (ii) Er sagte, er *hätte* es nicht getan.

The use of the 'present subjunctive' and the 'perfect subjunctive' in sentence (i) of A and B is considered literary. The versions with the 'past subjunctive' and the 'pluperfect subjunctive' given in (ii) in each case are more common in spoken German. The difference between A and B relates primarily to the tense of the original sentence: if the original was 'Ich tue es nicht' then the reported version is likely to be that of A, while B is likely to correspond to the original sentences 'Ich tat es nicht', 'Ich habe es nicht getan', or 'Ich hatte es nicht getan'. With the more common versions of (ii) in each case, it will be clear that is a shift in the tense: the original non-past form becomes past, while the original past becomes pluperfect.

The subjunctive is also found in certain other kinds of clauses, of which those illustrated in 4.50 are merely a selection. (There are many intricacies of usage which are described in detail in grammar books, but we are concerned here with the nature and role of the subjunctive in more general terms.)

(4.50) (i)   Wenn sie es *täte, wäre* es gut.
       (ii)   Sie sah aus, als ob sie krank *wäre*.
       (iii) Es *lebe* die Königin!
       (iv)   Ich *hätte* noch eine Frage.

Example (i) of 4.50 is a 'conditional' sentence, example (ii) an 'as if' construction, sentence (iii) a 'wish', and sentence (iv) a 'tentative statement'.

To some extent the use of the subjunctive in such cases could be seen as a rather arbitrary matter, a question of usage rather than of meaningful choice, but it is nevertheless possible to find a common element in many of these usages. The 'conditional' and 'as if' constructions clearly involve a hypothetical element, something not necessarily true or valid. The same could be said of the 'wish' in sentence (iii): the statement is not yet true, but merely hoped for. Example (iv) expresses a suggested proposition rather than a simple statement; the speaker is attaching conditions to its validity.

There certainly appears to be a common element of meaning here, though it is not easy to find a suitable definition of it. Some linguists speak of such forms as indicating the 'unreality', or 'non-factual' nature, of the action or event. This can be made a little clearer by bringing in the examples of reported speech illustrated in 4.49 above. What characterizes such examples is not necessarily their unreality, but rather that the speaker does not claim responsibility for their validity. The speaker is making the statements, but is at the same time dissociating himself or herself from them. With a little flexibility of interpretation, a similar principle would appear to be valid for the examples of 4.50, too.

The implication behind the use of the subjunctive, then, is that we can express not only some sort of 'content' to our sentences (often called the *proposition*), but can also provide a kind of commentary on it, a simultaneous statement about our relationship, as speakers, to this proposition. This area of meaning, concerned with the status of the proposition from the point of view of the speakers, is known as MODALITY. It is naturally to some extent possible to express modality by lexical means: words or phrases such as *vielleicht* or *es kann sein, dass* ..., and so on, are available for this purpose. But the system of mood does this *grammatically*, without recourse to such lexical means.

We have already noted that the forms of the present subjunctive are rather literary, and those of the past subjunctive are generally preferred. Another possibility is to use forms with the past subjunctive of the verb *werden*, such as those illustrated in 4.51.

(4.51)   Er sagte, er *würde* es nicht tun.
          Er *würde* es getan haben, wenn er das Geld gehabt hätte.
          Wenn sie es tun *würde*, wäre es gut.

Forms of this sort are often described as the 'conditional tenses', and the 'conditional' and 'conditional perfect' are included along with other tenses in the list of verb forms. There are a number of objections to this, however. First, they are clearly not tenses in the more restricted sense used here, since they do not refer to time distinctions as such, whether absolute or relative. Nor do they belong to aspect. They are evidently to do with modality, and thus belong to the mood system. Morphologically, they are parallel to the so-called 'future' forms with *werden*, since they are made up of the past subjunctive of *werden* with the infinitive (or the perfect infinitive) of the main verb. They are, in a sense, the past subjunctive forms of the future and future perfect. These relationships are shown in 4.52.

(4.52)   *Indicative*   *Subjunctive*
          Er wird es tun.   Er werde es tun.
          *Er wurde es tun.   Er würde es tun.
          Er wird es getan haben.   Er werde es getan haben.
          *Er wurde es getan haben. Er würde es getan haben.

As can be seen, the 'past indicative' forms of the 'future' do not exist (not surprisingly, perhaps, since a 'past future' is difficult to envisage), but, as we have seen, a tense shift often takes place in the subjunctive, making a 'past subjunctive future' perfectly possible. Thus the direct speech form 'Er wird es tun' becomes in reported speech 'Er sagte, er würde es tun', and 'Er wird es getan haben' becomes 'Er sagte, er würde es getan haben'.

A complicating factor here is the use of the verb *werden* to indicate the future. This was touched on in the discussion of tense above, where it was suggested that future time is normally indicated by the non-past tense, and that there is therefore no 'future tense' in German. If we examine pairs such as those of 4.53, we note that there are slight differences of meaning here (cf. also 4.34 above).

(4.53) (i)   (ii)
        Ich komme morgen.   Ich werde morgen kommen.
        Es regnet bald.   Es wird bald regnen.
        Er hat es bis morgen gemacht. Er wird es bis morgen gemacht haben.

In general, it would appear that the forms of column (i) indicate simply future (though only in conjunction with a future-time expression; the non-past tense is not specific with regard to present or future). Those of column (ii) seem to indicate a little more than merely future time; they often contain an element of intention, confidence, commitment, and the like (though given the ambiguity of the time reference of the non-past tense it is clear that such an implication may often be required merely to ensure a future interpretation). But such an element of meaning is, it will be noticed, exactly the sort of implication that we have concluded to be conveyed by the grammatical system of mood. The subjunctive enables the speaker to indicate lack of commitment to the proposition of the sentence; here the use of *werden* seems to indicate precisely such a commitment.

There is thus some evidence that the so-called 'future' with *werden* is actually a matter of mood rather than of tense; it refers to modality rather than time. But on the other hand it may be argued that it is in any case difficult to distinguish time from modality when we are referring to the future. If modality is concerned with what the speaker can vouch for or not, then the future, which is always a matter of conjecture, is perhaps inevitably modal as well as temporal.

There are also a number of other verbs which can be said to have modal functions: the so-called *modal verbs,* which are normally taken to include *dürfen, können, mögen, müssen, sollen,* and *wollen,* though occasionally other verbs are added to this list (as we have just seen, a case could be made for including *werden*). These verbs could all be said to contribute a modal element to a sentence, though some of them have non-modal uses too.

Consider the examples of 4.54.

(4.54)   Sie geht.
      Sie kann gehen.
      Sie darf gehen.
      Sie muss gehen.
      Sie soll gehen.
      Sie will gehen.
      Sie mag/möchte gehen.
      Sie wird gehen.

Compared with the first, simple, form, all the others carry a further implication: the chief implication of *kann* is physical possibility, of *darf* permission, of *muss* necessity, of *soll* obligation, and of *will* volition, while *mag* may, among other things, imply possibility. To accommodate these various implications, the concept of modality must clearly be extended beyond what we have considered so far.

In fact, modal implications in languages tend to fall into two main types. The modality associated with the German subjunctive is concerned with the validity of the proposition from the point of view of the speaker's knowledge. Also of this type are some uses of *werden, können,* and *mögen,* and one use of *sollen,* where it means 'to be said to'. Implications of this kind are known as EPISTEMIC modality. But *müssen, dürfen,* and *sollen* (in another of its uses) do not convey this meaning; they are concerned with obligation, permission, and necessity, while *wollen* is concerned with volition. Here, the implication is to do with the speaker's *will* rather than the speaker's knowledge. This is known as DEONTIC modality.

Although the implications of epistemic and deontic modality may seem to be rather different, they do have certain things in common. They both constitute an addition to the propositional content of the sentence—a kind of subjective element superimposed on the objective proposition. Furthermore, some forms can have either an epistemic or a deontic interpretation. Consider the examples of 4.55.

(4.55)   (i)   Der Chef *soll* im Büro sein.
     (ii)   Der Student *muss* dieses Buch lesen.
    (iii)   Der Student *muss* dieses Buch gelesen haben.

Sentence (i) is ambiguous: it may be epistemic ('The boss is said to be in the office') or deontic ('The boss ought to be in the office'). In sentence (ii) *muss* is deontic, expressing a necessary action, while in (iii) it is again ambiguous, since it can be epistemic, reflecting the speaker's supposition ('I suppose the student has read this book'), or deontic ('The student must have read this book by tomorrow or else!'). There is evidently a relationship of some kind between the two types of implication which allows this double usage.

The expression of modality by means of the subjunctive forms is, of course, a grammatical device, and we may regard the modal verbs as grammatical too, though the distinction between grammatical and lexical means is a little hard to draw here, since it is not completely clear what is or is not a modal verb, especially since some verbs have both modal and non-modal uses. On the other hand, the case for including the so-called 'modal particles' within a grammatical system of mood is less strong, even though the implications that they carry may well be close to those of modal verbs. Consider the examples of 4.56.

(4.56) (i) Er ist *wohl* gestern gekommen.

(ii) Er ist *ja* gestern gekommen.

(iii) Er ist *doch* gestern gekommen.

In each case the basic proposition ('Er ist gestern gekommen') is accompanied by a particle which qualifies its validity in some way. *Wohl* in (i) indicates that the speaker assumes it to be true; *ja* in (ii) confirms its truth; while *doch* in (iii) asserts its truth in the face of the addressee's assumption or assertion to the contrary. Such implications are clearly those of epistemic modality. But since these particles cannot really be said to form a coherent grammatical system, they are probably best not considered as part of the grammar of mood.

Voice. The category of voice covers those forms of the verb that are called 'active' and 'passive'. These forms are for the most part easily identified: the passive is constructed with the auxiliary verb *werden* (or *sein*: see below) and the past participle of the main verb. The use of these forms involves the whole sentence, however, the active and passive having a regular structural relationship to one another, as we see from the examples of 4.57.

(4.57) *Active*
         Petra hat das Buch gelesen.
         Ihr Mann trug die blaue Hose.

         Passive
         Das Buch ist von Petra gelesen worden.
         Die blaue Hose wurde von ihrem Mann getragen.

It can be seen that the direct object of the active sentence appears as the subject of the corresponding passive sentence, while the subject of the active sentence appears as the 'agent'—a noun phrase preceded by *von* or *durch*. This is illustrated in 4.58.

(4.58)   Noun-Phrase$_1$ + Active-Verb   ~   Noun-Phrase$_2$ + Passive Verb
            +Noun-Phrase$_2$ +*von* Noun-Phrase$_1$

The difficulty arises not with the forms themselves, however, but with the significance of their use. There is a sense in which the pairs of sentences of 4.57 are the same; the sentences have the same elements in them (though in a different order), and the meaning appears to be virtually identical. What, then, is the difference between them?

Various explanations of the difference between the active and the passive are current. One is based on the relationship between the subject of the sentence and the verb: in the active sentence the subject 'acts', but in the passive sentence the subject merely receives the action 'passively'—hence the terminology. Another way of explaining this is to invoke the 'direction' of the action of the verb: in the active sentence the action passes *away from* the subject (towards the object), but in the passive sentence it passes *towards* the subject.

Neither of these explanations is really sustainable, however, as the examples of 4.59 show.

(4.59)   Er bekommt ein Fahrrad zum Geburtstag.
            Er erhält 2000 Mark im Monat.

In these sentences the subject can hardly be described as 'acting'; nor could one consider the action of the verb to be 'passing away' from it. These attempts to explain the nature of the active/passive distinction are thus not very helpful.

In order to come a little closer to the nature of this distinction it is useful to establish first of all the observable differences between active and passive sentences, apart from the form of the verb itself. There are three such differences: first, the word order of the sentences is usually different; second, a different noun phrase appears as the subject; and third, the passive sentence has an agent. Each of these three differences may give a clue to the role of these two voices.

It is important to note, as in the case of mood, that the differences here do not lie in the propositional content of the sentence, but in the way in which this content is presented or viewed. One aspect of this is the degree of importance or 'weight' which is attached to the various parts of the sentence in a particular context, and which to some extent depends on what has gone before. The word order of the sentence can reflect the different weight of its parts, and thus the different word order found in active and passive sentences can be seen as a means of achieving this different weighting (for further discussion of 'weight', see Chapter 7).

As the sentences of 4.60 show, however, word order is in principle independent of voice.

(4.60) (i)   Meine Tante hat dieses Buch geschrieben.
         (ii) Dieses Buch ist von meiner Tante geschrieben worden.
         (iii) Dieses Buch hat meine Tante geschrieben.

Sentence (i) of 4.60 is active and sentence (ii) passive, and this results in a different order of the sentence elements, and hence a different weight being accorded to them. But it is clearly unnecessary to use the passive merely to obtain this order, as sentence (iii), though active, has a similar order to sentence (ii). We must thus look elsewhere for the significance of the voice distinction.

A related, and more plausible, interpretation has to do with the role of the subject in the sentence. In a continuous piece of speech or written language the sentences are linked together by various means, a common tendency being to take up something mentioned in one sentence as the subject of the next. Thus, in the short text given in 4.61, each sentence takes up an element of the previous sentence in this way.

(4.61) Morgen besuche ich meinen Bruder in Hamburg. Er wohnt in einem alten Haus in der Stadtmitte. Die Wohnung ist klein, aber sehr schön.

The choice of subject (in the grammatical sense) for the sentence is thus important: it reflects the development of the argument or conversation. Since active and passive express the same proposition with a different subject, they allow the sentence to be constructed appropriately for such an organization of the argument. An example of this use of the passive is given in 4.62. In 4.62(i), *Buch*, the object in the first sentence, is taken up as the subject of the second, allowing the use of the passive, though the active version is still possible, as in 4.62(ii). German does, however, tend to avoid the passive, and the most natural version would again probably be that of 4.62(iii), where *Buch* (or rather the pronoun replacing it) is put first but the sentence is still active.

(4.62) (i)   Kennst du dieses Buch? Es wurde von meinem Sohn geschrieben.

       (ii) Kennst du dieses Buch? Mein Sohn hat es geschrieben.

       (iii) Kennst du dieses Buch? Das hat mein Sohn geschrieben.

This explanation for the use of the different voices seems reasonable, but there is also another factor: the agent. As we saw, the agent of a passive sentence corresponds to the subject of an active sentence. But there is a difference: whereas active sentences must have a subject, passive ones need not have an agent. In fact, in most passive sentences the agent is not expressed at all. This means that the passive sentences of 4.63 do not have an active equivalent.

(4.63)   Das Haus wird renoviert.
         Ihr Antrag wird nicht angenommen.
         Er wurde leicht verletzt.

The passive is chosen in these cases precisely because it allows the omission of the agent, which may, as in these examples, be unknown or irrelevant.

Normally the passive construction can be used only with transitive verbs (those which may have a direct object), since it is this object which forms the subject of the passive sentence. But the desire to avoid specifying the subject of an active sentence may also extend to intransitive verbs, which cannot have a direct object. In this case German may use a 'dummy' subject *es*, as in the examples of 4.64.

(4.64)   Es wird getanzt.
         Es wurde gesprochen.

There are other means available for avoiding precise specification of the subject or agent, such as the use of the indefinite pronoun *man* ('Man renoviert das Haus', 'Man hat getanzt').

German is usually said to have two passives: the 'Vorgangspassiv' and the 'Zustandspassiv', the former using forms of the verb *werden*, the latter forms of *sein*. This gives contrasts such as those of 4.65.

(4.65)   Die Vorhänge wurden mit Staub bedeckt.
         Die Vorhänge waren mit Staub bedeckt.

The second sentence indicates a state ('Zustand') rather than an action ('Vorgang'), and it can often be said to express the state *resulting* from an action.

There is thus some relationship between this kind of sentence and one containing the perfect aspect (in those forms of German which have it), which can be said to indicate the current relevance of a past action. This gives the pair of 4.66.

(4.66) Die Vorhänge waren mit Staub bedeckt.
Die Vorhänge waren mit Staub bedeckt worden.

Since, however, the 'Zustandspassiv' expresses a state rather than an action, it would be possible to regard such forms not as complex verb forms at all, but simply as the combination of *sein* with an adjective, the participles here being used adjectivally.

FURTHER READING

Word Classes (General)

Schachter (1985).

German Word Classes

Bergenholtz and Schaeder (1977); Eichler and Bünting (1996: ch. 3); Eisenberg (1999); Heidolph, Flämig, and Motsch (1981: ch. 3); Kufner (1962: ch. 4); Meibauer et al. (2002: 129–33); Wöllstein-Leisten, Heilmann, Stepan, and Vikner (1997: 20–6).

Grammatical Categories (General)

Blake (1994); Comrie (1976, 1985); Corbett (1991, 2000); Lyons (1968: ch. 7, 1977: vol. ii, ch. 17); Palmer (1994, 2001); Weinrich (2001).

Grammatical Categories of German

Brinker (1982); Eisenberg (1999: ch. 4); Gelhaus and Latzel (1982); Gerstenkorn (1976); Helbig (1973); Helbig and Buscha (2001: ch. 2); Hentschel and Weydt (2003); Herbst, Heath, and Dederding (1980: chs. 11–14); Jäger (1982); Markus (1977); Schipporeit (1971); Wunderlich (1973).

EXERCISES AND DISCUSSION QUESTIONS

1. Why are there problems in establishing a definitive set of word classes for German? How can these problems be resolved, if at all?
2. Take a paragraph of written German and attempt to assign each word to a word class.
3. Establish, as far as possible, different subclasses of adverbs in German.

4. Can gender be said to have any meaningful role in modern German?

5. What grounds can we find for regarding the masculine as the unmarked gender in German? Does this suggest that German is biased in favour of the male sex?

6. Find as many verbs as you can that take (i) the dative and (ii) the genitive in German.

7. Find out under what circumstances Germans use *du* and *Sie*, e.g. in talking to someone older or younger, to people in authority, neighbours, friends, etc. In the light of this, discuss the role of this distinction in German.

8. Compare the tense/aspect systems of German and English, and of any other language you know.

9. To what extent is the use of the subjunctive mood in German a matter of speaker choice, and to what extent a matter of rule?

10. Analyse all the verb forms you can find in a paragraph of written German, identifying the categories involved.

5

Syntax

Introduction

The study of grammatical structure is conventionally, and conveniently, divided into two parts, morphology and syntax; the former, which we considered in detail in Chapter 3, dealing with the structure of words, the latter, to which the present chapter is devoted, dealing with the structure of sentences. Morphology and syntax have many features in common: they are both concerned with grammatical entities and with the principles that underlie their combinations. But words and sentences are rather different kinds of units; words are not only very much shorter and simpler than the majority of sentences; they are also much more stable and fixed in their structure, offering fewer possibilities for innovation and improvisation. The more complex and much freer structure of sentences makes syntax a rather different kind of subject from morphology, requiring a different type and wider range of descriptive concepts and categories. Syntacticians make much of the fact that the vast majority of the sentences that we produce and understand are new and have never been uttered before, and yet we are able to produce and understand them without difficulty. Clearly, then, as speakers and hearers of our language we are making use of some sort of knowledge that goes beyond the mere memorising of structures, and we could therefore see the study of syntax as an investigation of this knowledge.

Advocates of this approach go one step further, however, and suggest that much of this knowledge is not specific to any particular language but applies to all languages, and to language in general, and is probably innate—part of our human inheritance, along with having ten fingers and ten toes, among other universal human characteristics. If this is so, then all languages must have a great deal in common. But since all languages are also different from one another, inheritance cannot account for *all* of language. Just which characteristics of languages are general and universal and which are specific to individual languages, and how general and specific features relate to one another, are matters of debate.

As far as our present discussion of German syntax is concerned, we are less interested here in such debates than in the basic task of establishing the characteristics of German sentence structure. Nevertheless, questions of universals and the nature of the syntactic knowledge of speakers of German will inevitably surface from time to time. As elsewhere in this book, we shall use any such theoretical considerations in order to elucidate aspects of German rather than using German as a means of elucidating the theory.

The sentence, the central concept of syntax, poses the same sorts of problems of definition as the word (cf. Chapter 3). Popularly, it is sometimes defined as a 'single idea' or a 'complete thought', but such definitions are inaccurate and unsatisfactory. The sentence, like the word, is a *grammatical* unit and hence is best defined in grammatical terms. If the word is conveniently thought of as the *smallest* independently viable grammatical entity, then the sentence can be defined as the *largest* such unit.

Such a definition is, like that of 'word' given in Chapter 3, not without its difficulties, and indeed is not altogether unambiguous. What it means is simply that the sentence is the largest unit whose structure can be legitimately described in grammatical terms. Larger units, consisting of more than one sentence, can certainly be found—the paragraph in written language, for example—but the relationship of the component sentences of a paragraph to one another is not really a grammatical one; it is primarily a question of meaning. There are, of course, relationships between the sentences in a text or stretch of speech, which contribute to welding such sentences into a meaningful whole and link it to its context (these will be discussed in Chapter 7), but these are not essentially matters of grammar. The relationships of the component parts of a sentence, on the other hand, are primarily of a grammatical kind.

As we concluded in the case of the word, however, it is inadvisable to dwell too long on problems of definition. Our aim in this chapter is not to define the sentence as such, but rather to examine its characteristics in German. The remainder of this chapter will be devoted to such an examination.

Syntactic Structure

One obvious characteristic of German sentences is that they are made up of words, but that in itself tells us little. Clearly the sentence is not just a sequence of words; these words are not isolated and independent, but are connected to one another in a variety of ways. Our first task, therefore, is to examine the nature of these connections.

Constituent Structure

One aspect of the words of the sentence is that they can be grouped together into larger entities. This can be illustrated with the following sentence:

Die Arbeiter rauchen türkische Zigaretten.

It is clear that the relationship between, say, *die* and *Arbeiter* is much closer than that between *rauchen* and *türkische*; the first two obviously belong together in a way in which the latter do not. Similarly, *türkische* goes together with *Zigaretten*. We can thus establish *word groups* within the sentence. But we can also take this a little further: *rauchen* seems to belong rather more closely with *türkische Zigaretten* than with *die Arbeiter*, so that the group *türkische Zigaretten* itself forms part of a still larger group.

The structure of sentences is thus hierarchical: sentences consist of parts which themselves consist of parts, and so on. The clearest way of indicating these groupings is with the help of a TREE DIAGRAM (though syntactic 'trees' are generally drawn upside down, with their roots in the air and their branches on the ground), as in 5.1.

(5.1)

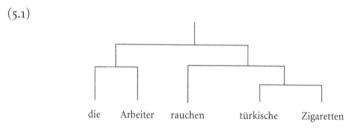

die   Arbeiter   rauchen   türkische   Zigaretten

In syntactic analysis parts of any unit are called its CONSTITUENTS: *die Arbeiter*, for instance, is a constituent of the sentence as a whole, while *türkische Zigaretten* is a constituent of *rauchen türkische Zigaretten*, and *türkische* is a constituent of *türkische Zigaretten*. In a tree diagram such as 5.1, each 'branch' forms a constituent. Thus, *Arbeiter rauchen* or *rauchen türkische* are not constituents of this sentence or of any of its parts, as these groups of words do not coincide with any branches of the tree.

There is a sense in which each word is, ultimately, a constituent part of the sentence, but in practice we are more interested in adjacent levels, i.e. with what is *directly* a part of what. Such parts are called the IMMEDIATE CONSTITUENTS of the unit concerned. For example, *die Arbeiter* and *rauchen türkische Zigaretten* are immediate constituents of the sentence as a whole; *rauchen* and *türkische Zigaretten* are immediate constituents of *rauchen türkische Zigaretten*, while *die* and *Arbeiter*, and *türkische* and *Zigaretten*, are immediate constituents of *die Arbeiter* and *türkische Zigaretten* respectively.

The significance of immediate constituents is largely a matter of procedure; in analysing a sentence it is often convenient to proceed one step at a time, starting with the sentence as a whole and progressively dividing it up into smaller and smaller units, finding the immediate constituents at each stage.[1]

One of the tests that can be used to determine what the immediate constituents of a sentence are is SUBSTITUTION. In the above sentence the phrase *türkische Zigaretten* could be replaced by a variety of other phrases—*französische Zigarren; die Zigaretten, die ihnen der Fabrikant spendiert hat,* and so on—and also by single words, such as *Haschisch* or *Gauloises.* Since all these items can take the place of *türkische Zigaretten,* they can be regarded as structurally equivalent to this phrase; and since some of the items that are structurally equivalent are single words, *türkische Zigaretten* must constitute a single unit, and therefore a constituent of a larger unit. By contrast, although we might find other words to replace *rauchen türkische,* such as *kaufen französische, haben gern englische,* and the like, no single, structurally equivalent word could replace this phrase, which thus cannot be a constituent in the same way that *türkische Zigaretten* is. Another test is TRANSPOSITION: *türkische Zigaretten* can be moved to different places in the sentence, to give e.g. 'Türkische Zigaretten rauchen die Arbeiter' or 'Rauchen die Arbeiter türkische Zigaretten?', but this cannot be done with *rauchen türkische:* '*Rauchen türkische die Arbeiter Zigaretten' is impossible. Any German sentence, then, can be analysed using procedures of this kind, and a tree diagram can be given which reflects its CONSTITUENT STRUCTURE.

One interesting use of such trees is in explaining the ambiguity of certain sentences or parts of sentences. The phrase *schöne Blumen und Bäume,* for example, may be analysed in two different ways, reflecting two different meanings, as in 5.2.

(5.2)

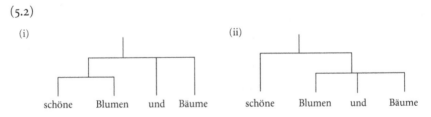

| (i) | | | | (ii) | | | |
| schöne | Blumen | und | Bäume | schöne | Blumen | und | Bäume |

In 5.2 (i) *schöne* refers to *Blumen* alone, in 5.2 (ii) to both *Blumen* and *Bäume.*
The analysis of constituent structure is not always so straightforward, however. One minor problem is illustrated in the sentences of 5.3.

---

[1] Immediate-constituent analysis was developed in America in the 1940s and 1950s by Leonard Bloomfield and his followers, whose main concern was with analytical procedures in linguistics.

(5.3) *Er kam gestern*   ~   *Er ist gestern gekommen*

      Er kommt morgen   ~   *Er wird morgen kommen*

The first sentence of each pair presents no difficulty. Each consists of two parts, *er* and the remainder, the latter again having two constituents. But the second example of each pair is less easy to describe. We are tempted to say that *ist gekommen* and *wird kommen* are single units, since they are exactly parallel to *kam* and *kommt* respectively. But since the two words of these forms are separated by another word how can they be a single constituent? A simple solution is to allow 'discontinuous constituents'; with a little ingenuity they can be represented graphically, as in 5.4.

(5.4)

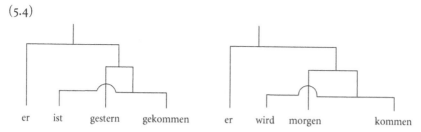

More serious difficulties arise in some cases. Consider the sentence 'Sie liest oft Romane'. There are several possible analyses of this sentence, three of which are given in 5.5.

(5.5)

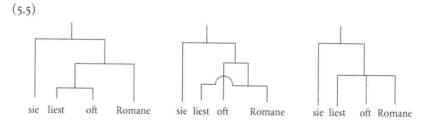

Should we group *liest* with *oft* as in (i), with *Romane* as in (ii), or regard all three as independent of one another, as in (iii)? Opinions differ on these matters, and the solution we adopt may reflect other assumptions we make. For example, we might insist—rather unreasonably—that there can be only two constituents at any level, in which case version (iii) would be excluded. The solution may also vary from case to case. In the sentence 'Er sagt es oft' we may wish to regard *sagt* and *oft* as a single item in view of the parallel with 'Er wiederholt es'; in 'Er schreibt oft Gedichte', on the other hand, the same arguments lead us to regard *schreibt Gedichte* as a single entity, because of the parallel with 'Er dichtet oft'.

Despite these difficulties, constituent-structure analysis is a valuable tool in the syntactic description of sentences. It remains, however, rather rudimentary; it tells us about the groupings of units in the sentence, but does not tell us, for example, about the kinds of units that are involved, nor about their roles in the sentence. It is therefore necessary to supplement a tree diagram with other information.

Phrase Types

Since the end points of the tree diagram are words, these units can at least be identified (see the discussion of word classes in Chapter 4). But what kinds of units are involved at the higher levels? *Zigaretten* may be a noun, but what is *türkische Zigaretten?* Generally speaking, such groupings are known as PHRASES, but different kinds of phrases can be recognized. The most useful way of classifying them is in terms of their major constituent, which is known as the HEAD of the phrase (see also the discussion of heads in Chapter 3). Phrases with a noun as their head are thus noun phrases, those with a verb as their head are verb phrases, and so on.

How is the head of a unit determined? In the case of a phrase such as *türkische Zigaretten* it is perhaps clear that the noun, rather than the adjective, is the head, since we could say that *türkische* describes *Zigaretten* rather than the other way round; similarly, in *die Arbeiter* it is natural to see *die* as a minor addition to *Arbeiter* rather than the reverse. An objective test to support such intuitive judgements is DELETION: all the other parts of a unit except for the head can usually be omitted—in suitable circumstances—without affecting the syntactic role of this unit. Thus, wherever we can have *die Arbeiter* we can also have *Arbeiter,* and wherever we can have *türkische Zigaretten* we can also have *Zigaretten* alone. Typically, then, the head is syntactically equivalent to the whole phrase, in the sense that it occupies the same position in the structure of the sentence as the phrase as a whole. In the same way, we can say that *rauchen* is the head of *rauchen türkische Zigaretten,* since 'Die Arbeiter rauchen' has the same basic structure as 'Die Arbeiter rauchen türkische Zigaretten'.

Using the heads of the various constituents to determine the categories, we may thus expand the tree of 5.1 to 5.6. The following abbreviations are used: S = sentence, NP = noun phrase, VP = verb phrase, Det = determiner, N = noun, V = verb, A = adjective.

The heads of the phrases *die Arbeiter* and *türkische Zigaretten* are the nouns *Arbeiter* and *Zigaretten* respectively, so these are noun phrases. The head of *rauchen türkische Zigaretten* is the verb *rauchen;* this is therefore described here as a verb phrase.

(5.6)

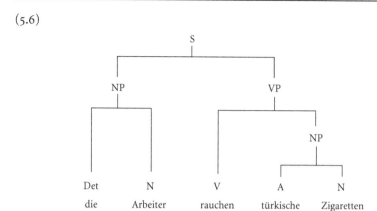

As a further illustration, 5.7 contains an adjective phrase (AP) and an adverb phrase (AdvP), with an adjective and an adverb (Adv) respectively as their heads (Deg = degree-word).

(5.7)

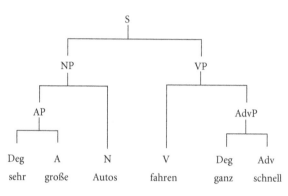

There are a number of further problems, however, as the head is not always as easily identifiable as this. In a prepositional phrase (PP), such as *in Berlin, mit ihm,* etc., neither part can be omitted while retaining syntactic equivalence: the noun or pronoun cannot be omitted at all, and omitting the preposition changes it from a prepositional phrase to a noun phrase. The preposition is usually regarded as the 'head' of such a phrase, but clearly it is not the head in quite the same sense that a noun is the head of a noun phrase.[2]

Another difficulty arises with complex verbs. Verbs may consist of more than a single word, e.g. *haben geraucht, werden fahren,* and so on. To be

---

[2] Constructions with a head which is syntactically equivalent to the whole, e.g. Determiner + Noun, are called ENDOCENTRIC; those in which the parts are of a different type from the whole, e.g. Preposition + Noun, are called EXOCENTRIC.

consistent, we could call such phrases 'verb phrases', since they have a verb (the auxiliary) as their head. But we have already recognized phrases such as *rauchen türkische Zigaretten* and *fahren ganz schnell* as verb phrases, since they, too, have a verb as their head. This means that a phrase such as *haben türkische Zigaretten geraucht* would appear to have two levels of verb phrases, each with its own head, as in 5.8. The head of VP$_1$ is the VP$_2$, i.e. the verb phrase *haben … geraucht*, while the head of the latter is the auxiliary verb (Aux) *haben*.

(5.8)

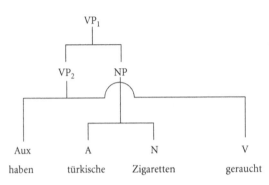

If we wish to avoid this confusing analysis there are various ways around it. We could simply rename the higher phrase (VP$_1$ of 5.8) the 'predicate phrase' (PredP), restricting the term 'verb phrase' to the lower level (VP$_2$ of 5.8), though this of course undermines our convention of naming the phrase after its head. The whole sentence would now have the structure given in 5.9.

(5.9)

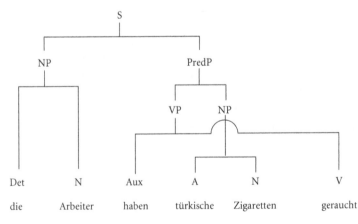

In some approaches, however, the problem is avoided altogether by regarding the auxiliary not as part of the same phrase as the main verb but as a separate constituent of the sentence (AUX). The structure now assumes the form of 5.10.

(5.10)

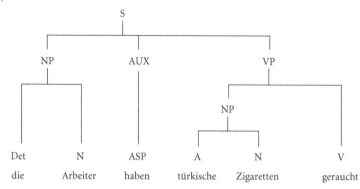

Note that we have now renamed the auxiliary verb ASP (aspect), leaving the label V for the main verb of the sentence. Since this analysis separates the two parts of what is felt to be a single constituent (*haben geraucht*), however, it is not acceptable to all linguists. For the moment we shall adopt the solution of 5.9, though we shall have more to say about this analysis later.

In trees such as 5.6–5.10, sentences are shown to consist typically of phrases, while phrases consist of words. We also see that some phrases contain others—a verb phrase may contain a noun phrase and a noun phrase may contain an adjective phrase, and so on. But consider the examples of 5.11.

(5.11) (i)   ein Mann, der sehr berühmt ist
        (ii) er sagte, er sei krank.
        (iii) ich schreibe, wenn ich Zeit habe.

In 5.11(i) we have a noun phrase, with *Mann* as its head. The expression *der sehr berühmt ist* has a role rather like that of an adjective phrase (cf. *ein sehr berühmter Mann*), except that it follows the noun, but its own structure is that of a sentence (cf. *er ist sehr berühmt*). The second part of 5.11(ii) (*er sei krank*) has the role of a noun phrase (cf. *er sagte die Wahrheit*), and the second part of 5.11(iii) (*wenn ich Zeit habe*) has the role of an adverb phrase (cf. *ich schreibe sehr bald*), but both of these also have a structure comparable with that of a sentence, since they contain a noun phrase and a predicate phrase ('er sei krank', 'ich habe Zeit').

A distinction is traditionally made here between SENTENCE and CLAUSE. A clause is usually considered to be a grammatical unit containing a single verb (i.e. a single predicate phrase), so that 5.11(ii) and (iii), which contain two such phrases, each consist of two clauses. A sentence, on the other hand, is an *independent* grammatical unit, which may contain one or more clauses. Both our original example ('Die Arbeiter rauchen türkische Zigaretten') and 5.11(ii) and (iii) are therefore sentences. Where there is more than one clause in a sentence, the clauses may simply be joined together, as in 'Mein Vater ist vor zehn Jahren gestorben, aber meine Mutter lebt noch', in which case they are traditionally called CO-ORDINATE, but where, as in 5.11(ii) and (iii), the second clause has the role of a phrase within the first clause the included clause is called a SUBORDINATE or DEPENDENT clause. A clause which is not included inside another one is called a MAIN clause. Where a sentence consists of only a single clause, this will therefore be a main clause.

It is important to recall, however, that in a sentence like 'Er sagte, er sei krank' the structure of the subordinate clause (*er sei krank*) is analogous to that of a simple sentence with a noun phrase and a predicate phrase. Subordinate clauses may have characteristics which distinguish them as dependent, e.g. their word order or verb form, but in their basic constituent structure they do not differ from simple sentences with a single predicate phrase. The structure of this sentence could thus with some justification be represented as in 5.12, where the subordinate clause is a sentence (S) within the predicate phrase of the main sentence (Pro = Pronoun).

(5.12)

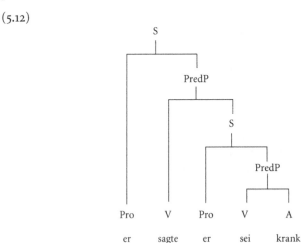

What this makes clear is that our tree diagrams must make provision not only for smaller units inside larger ones, but also for larger units inside smaller ones. Sentence structure is thus RECURSIVE: as we proceed with our immediate constituent analysis from the sentence as a whole (S) through phrases to words, the same categories, including S itself, may recur. This in turn means that we can never exhaust the possibilities for different structures. If a sentence may include a phrase, but a phrase can include a sentence, then there can never be a 'most complex German sentence'. It is always possible (in theory, though of course hardly in practice) to increase the complexity indefinitely by expanding a phrase to include a sentence, which itself consists of phrases, and so on.

The trees we have just been considering are clearly more informative than those given earlier, since they provide labels for the points where the branches join or diverge (the NODES). However, they also contain some inconsistencies. As we have seen, in the majority of cases the head is the constant part of the phrase while the other elements are 'optional' in the sense that they can be omitted without affecting the syntactic role of the unit. The phrase can therefore be seen as a kind of expansion of the head—a head with extras. Consider the noun phrases of 5.13.

(5.13) (i)   Maria bewundert Blumen.
        (ii) Maria bewundert schöne Blumen.
        (iii) Maria bewundert sehr schöne Blumen.

In 5.13(ii) and 5.13(iii) the final noun phrases can be regarded as expansions of the head noun *Blumen*. Example 5.13(i) does not have such an expansion, but since the noun *Blumen* has the same syntactic role in this case as the expanded phrases of the other examples, it is more consistent to regard it, too, as a phrase: a minimal noun phrase consisting of only a single word. The same applies to the initial noun *Maria*, which can, by a similar argument, also be regarded as a minimal noun phrase. Since *sehr schöne* in 5.13(iii) can be seen as an expansion of *schöne*, as in 5.13(ii), the latter can again be regarded as a minimal adjective phrase. The verb *bewundert* could likewise be expanded to *hat bewundert*, and hence this is a minimal verb phrase. More consistent analyses of the sentences of 5.13(i) and 5.13(ii) would therefore be those of 5.14, with additional labels introduced for nodes above A, N, and V, even where there are no branches. This means that these trees are now more general, each covering a range of possible sentences.

But consider now the phrase *diese schönen roten Blumen*. The tree diagram given in 5.15 is widely accepted by linguists for structures of this kind, and it can be justified by applying the procedures mentioned above: both *roten Blumen* and *schönen roten Blumen* can be replaced by single items, e.g. *Blüten, Rosen,* etc.

(5.14)

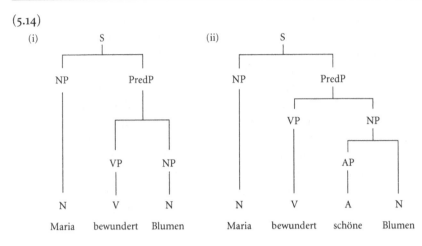

(5.15)

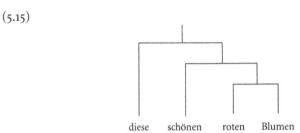

We can give labels to the words (Det, A, and N), and to the phrase as a whole (NP), but what labels do we give to the intermediate nodes? In each case the head is clearly the noun, hence each phrase is a noun phrase, and the fully labelled tree would need to be that given in 5.16.

(5.16)

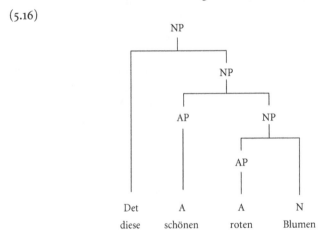

Whereas previously we found that noun phrases could contain adjective phrases, and predicate phrases could contain noun phrases, etc., here we observe that noun phrases contain more noun phrases. Furthermore, by adding more and more adjectives before the noun we could in principle have an indefinite number of noun phrases in such a tree. We encountered a similar situation above with regard to the phrase with a verb as its head, and solved the problem by calling the higher node 'predicate phrase', and the lower node 'verb phrase'. But this solution will not work here; the structure is recursive, and we cannot simply devise new names for each node indefinitely.

One approach to describing these structures is to use the idea that the phrase is an expansion of its head. In 5.16 *roten Blumen* is an expansion of *Blumen*, and may itself be expanded to *schönen roten Blumen*, and so on. Let us represent this by saying that the category N (noun) may be expanded to N′, which may be expanded to N″, and this to N‴, etc. (which are pronounced 'N-bar', 'N-double-bar', and 'N-treble-bar'). Hence, *roten Blumen* is N′, while *diese schönen roten Blumen* would be N‴. This would give the structure of 5.17.

(5.17)

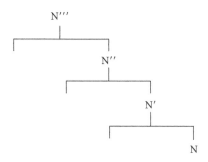

However, we may note that the recursion here is in fact restricted to the phrases containing 'true' adjectives such as *schön* and *rot*; we cannot have more than one determiner such as the demonstrative adjective *diese* ('*die diese roten Blumen*') nor more than one noun ('*diese schönen roten Blumen Bäume*'). A more satisfactory representation of this structure would therefore be to recognize only three levels: N (the noun itself), N′ (the recursive part with the 'true' adjectives), and N″ (the phrase as a whole, including the determiner). For convenience we can still use the label NP, but restrict it to the last of these, equivalent to N″. Where there is no 'true' adjective, N′ could be omitted, though many linguists assume that it should be present even if there is no branching, but where there is more than one such adjective it will appear more than once. The structure of 5.17 can now be rewritten as 5.18, where the dotted line and N′ in brackets are the optional recursive part.

(5.18)

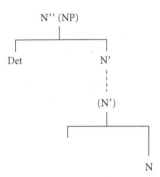

Similar principles can be applied to other phrase types, though recursion is less common here, and for the most part we only need two levels. Thus, if *schönen* is A (adjective), then *sehr schönen* is A″ or AP. However, categories such as A can also have intermediate nodes (A′) if we extend this approach to cover further elements within the phrase, including those that come after the head. Consider the expression *Sie ist sehr stolz auf ihren Sohn.* Here, the head is *stolz* and the whole expression *sehr stolz auf ihren Sohn* is therefore an adjective phrase (AP). It could further be argued that *stolz auf ihren Sohn* is also an adjective phrase, again with *stolz* as its head, and it can therefore be represented as A′. The structure of the whole phrase can thus be represented as in 5.19.

(5.19)

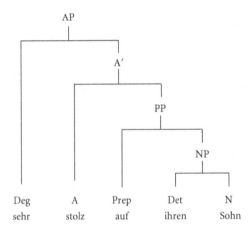

In terms of this approach, then, 5.16 can be rewritten as 5.20, with each adjective phrase consisting of A′ as well as A.

(5.20)

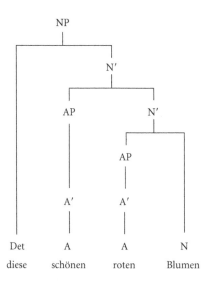

We can easily extend the same principles to other types of phrases, of which a selection is given in 5.21.

(5.21)

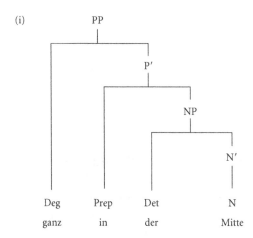

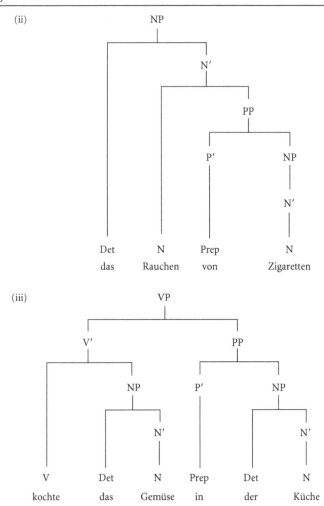

(ii)
NP — N' — PP — P' / NP — N'

Det: das / N: Rauchen / Prep: von / N: Zigaretten

(iii)
VP — V' — NP — N' / PP — P' / NP — N'

V: kochte / Det: das / N: Gemüse / Prep: in / Det: der / N: Küche

(Note that in order to simplify matters the predicate phrase has been renamed VP.)

It is evident that in this approach the structure of the phrases has become rather complex, and the reader may feel that the analysis has got rather out of hand, with an implausible number of intermediate nodes and labels. However, there are some interesting implications of the approach which are worth pursuing a little further. First, we observe that a similar kind of structure is now proposed for *all* types of phrases, so that the structure of these trees can be generalized to that of 5.22, where X stands for any class of word, Spec = 'Specifier', and Comp = 'Complement'—the labels for the constituents which combine with the head at the XP and X' levels, respectively. For obvious

reasons, this approach to phrase structure has become known as X′ (or
X-BAR) syntax.[3]

(5.22)

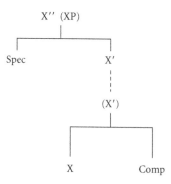

The claim of this approach, then, is that all kinds of phrase have the same
structure, and that the principles according to which phrases are constructed
are part of the grammatical knowledge of speakers of German, and, indeed, if
this structure is universally valid, of speakers of all languages. We must note,
however, that the tree of 5.22 should be understood as representing a *structure*
and does not imply a particular *order* of the constituents. We have already
seen that constituents may occur either before or after the head, but this does
not affect the structural relationships between them: *rote Rosen* can be said to
have the same basic structure as *stolz auf ihren Sohn* in the sense that it
contains an X (*Rosen, stolz*) with a complement (*rote, auf ihren Sohn*). The
internal structure of this complement is different in each case, but its structural role in the phrase is analogous.

So far, we have applied the scheme of 5.22 only to parts of sentences, such as
the verb phrase (VP), the noun phrase (NP), and the adjective phrase (AP).
Can we apply it to the sentence as a whole? As we have seen, the sentence
consists not only of a verb phrase, but also of a noun phrase (NP), as in 5.6, so
that the structure to be described has the form of 5.23.

(5.23)

 [3] X′ syntax was first proposed by Chomsky (1970), and developed by Jackendoff (1977) and others.

Whichever constituent we take to be the head here (the verb phrase seems more plausible than the noun phrase, but it is not certain), we face the difficulty that we cannot really add more 'bars' to either of them. Furthermore, clauses such as the following suggest a still more complex structure:

weil es regnet, (können wir nicht wegfahren).
wenn er morgen kommt, (gehen wir in die Stadt).
(er sagte,) dass er nicht kommen könnte.
(wir wissen nicht,) ob sie das Buch schon gelesen hat.

Here the subordinate clauses are introduced by a conjunction—also called a COMPLEMENTIZER—so that the structure is evidently that of 5.24. However, this structure only conforms in part to that of 5.22; the complementizer can be treated as the 'specifier', but can we regard the sentence proper as 'SP'? And where is S'?

(5.24)

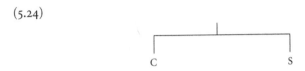

Some linguists do indeed attempt to carry through the scheme of 5.22 to the sentence as a whole, but it requires a very much more abstract kind of analysis than that which we have adopted hitherto. As we saw earlier, an alternative analysis of the sentence, given in 5.10, above, recognizes three constituents: NP—Aux—VP, where Aux includes the auxiliary verb. In some versions of X' theory, the Aux constituent is regarded as containing not only the Auxiliary itself, but all the features of the finite verb, such as tense, person, and number, and is labelled INFL (inflection). Thus, the example of 5.21(iii), which consists of a verb phrase, could be regarded as part of a larger sentence constituent—let us again for the moment call it the predicate phrase—which also includes INFL (Aux), and the latter will contain the category PAST, since the verb *kochte* is past (the verb itself now just consists of the bare lexeme KOCH, without the past inflection). This is illustrated in 5.25.

A solution to the problem of the analysis of the whole sentence—for example, *die Köchin kochte das Gemüse in der Küche*—now becomes available. Abbreviating INFL to I, we can regard the predicate phrase as I' and the sentence (S) as IP, as in 5.26. Note that this solution requires us to regard INFL as the head of the whole sentence.

(5.25)

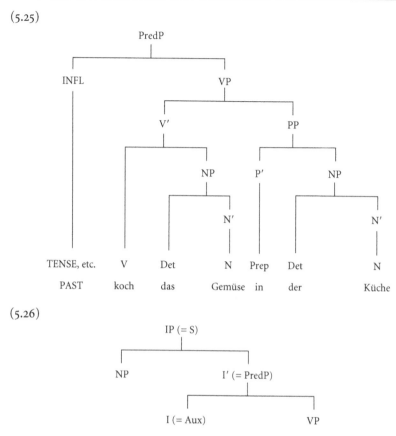

(5.26)

But we are still left with sentences which are preceded by a conjunction or complementizer, such as *während die Köchin das Gemüse in der Küche kochte* (*ging er in den Garten*). A similar structure can be provided for this, too, given as 5.27, where the complementizer (C) is combined with IP to produce C', and an additional category, CP, with its own specifier, is added to dominate the whole structure.

We have now travelled a very long way from our initial concern with the constituent structure of the sentence, and some readers—along with many linguists—may certainly feel that we have gone too far. In our attempt to apply the same structural principles to *all* sentence constituents and to the sentence as a whole, we have been obliged to recognize a highly complex hierarchical structure with several apparently unnecessary branches and labels. In fact, this approach, with abstract elements such as INFL, cannot actually be accommodated within the descriptive framework that we have adopted so far, and requires a different model, which we shall consider below.

(5.27)

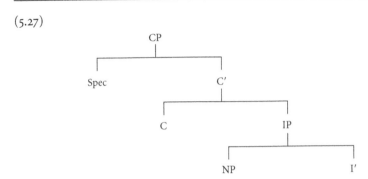

Nevertheless, this general approach may have a number of advantages. By assuming a common structure for all phrase types we are able to relate different syntactic structures to one another. We saw in our discussion of morphology in Chapter 3 that derivation allows lexemes to appear in a number of different syntactic guises while preserving their relationships to one another. In 3.41, repeated here as 5.28, it was suggested that the relationships between the basic lexemes—HAUS, TOTAL, and ZERSTÖR—remain the same in spite of the different morphological forms they assume and the different syntactic functions they fulfil in each sentence.

(5.28) (i)   man hat das Haus total zerstört
        (ii)   die totale Zerstörung des Hauses
        (iii) das total zerstörte Haus

When we examine these expressions in the light of X′ syntax we note that (i) and (ii) have rather similar basic structures, although the labels have changed. 5.29(i) gives the tree for the relevant part of 5.28(i), while 5.29(ii) corresponds to 5.28(ii). In each case *das Haus* appears as the complement of *zerstör-*, while *total* appears at a higher level than the phrase containing these two. 5.28(iii) does not conform to the same pattern, as the head has changed from the verb to its complement (*Haus*).

A number of general conclusions can be drawn from this discussion of constituent structure. The basic principle underlying this kind of analysis—the assumption that sentences have a hierarchical organization, with parts which themselves consist of parts—seems valid enough, and the corresponding tree diagrams, which represent this organization in graphic form, are without doubt a useful tool in clarifying the syntactic relationships involved. On the other hand, the discussion will have made it clear that the theory, when applied to specific cases, is not without its limitations. Syntactic structure is evidently extremely complex, and any theory or descriptive model will

(5.29)

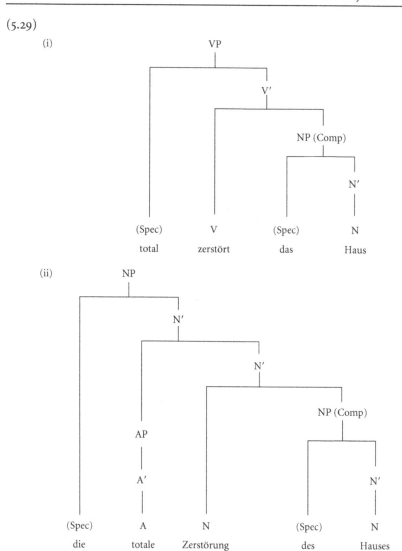

itself need to be similarly complex. The theory of constituent structure and its more elaborate development X′ syntax go some way towards accounting for this complexity, without, however, being able to encompass it all.

Dependency

In our examination of syntactic structure so far we have encountered two main kinds of relationships between the various parts of the sentence. Firstly, there is the 'part – whole' relationship: certain units can be said to consist of others, and units can be grouped together into larger entities. Immediate-constituent analysis deals primarily with this aspect of sentence structure, providing criteria for dividing the sentence into parts, and these parts into smaller parts, and so on. But we have also found another kind of relationship: that between the head and the other constituents of a unit. This is not a matter of grouping or division of units, but rather of the relationship between units of a similar kind. We have seen that the head is the constant part of a unit, while the other parts are in some sense variable and optional. This sort of relationship is not explicitly dealt with in immediate-constituent analysis, but must be considered when we attempt to label the various nodes of the tree. X-bar theory incorporates it to some extent, since X and X′ are explicitly recognized as the heads of their constituents, but it is possible to take it somewhat further than this.

The relationship between the head and the other parts of a unit is, as we have noted, based primarily on occurrence: the head can occur without the other parts but the other parts cannot occur without the head. The other parts can thus be regarded as subordinate to, or *dependent upon,* the head. In our first example, 5.1, *türkische* is dependent on *Zigaretten,* rather than the other way round, because *Zigaretten* can occur alone in this place in the sentence, while *türkische* cannot. Similarly, *türkische Zigaretten* is dependent on *rauchen,* since the latter, but not the former, can occur by itself in this position in the sentence.

We can therefore recognize the relationship of DEPENDENCY as a further dimension to syntactic structure, complementing that of constituency.[4] The two go together, in the sense that there are constituent parts of units and these parts are dependent on one another in different ways and to different extents. In some ways, too, these two notions compete with one another: we may represent the structure of a sentence *either* in terms of constituency *or* in terms of dependency.

Dependency may be displayed in a similar manner to constituency, with a tree diagram, though the branches and nodes will have a different significance. The tree of 5.1, for example, may be replaced by a 'dependency tree', as in 5.30.

(5.30)

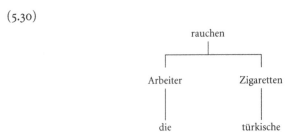

[4] The concept of dependency in syntax was first explored systematically by the French linguist Lucien Tesnière in his book *Éléments de syntaxe structurale* (1959).

This tree must not, of course, be interpreted as indicating groupings into larger units; *rauchen* clearly does not consist of *Arbeiter* and *Zigaretten*. It will also be noticed that the tree, at least in the form given here, makes no attempt to preserve the actual order of the various words (though a representation could be devised, as in the case of discontinuous constituents, which would keep the items in their proper order), but places dependent items under those on which they depend. It may be further observed that *Arbeiter* is shown as being dependent on the verb *rauchen*; this calls for some explanation, and will be discussed shortly.

Dependency trees can often be constructed fairly easily from constituency trees, provided that the heads of the constituents are known. This is true in the case of noun and adjective phrases, for example, so that the phrase *sehr schöne Blumen*, which has the constituency tree of 5.31(i), will have the dependency tree of 5.31(ii), since *Blumen* is the head of the whole phrase and *schöne* the head of *sehr schöne*.

(5.31)

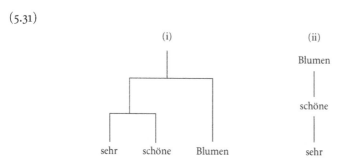

The tree given in 5.30 shows both noun phrases dependent on the verb in a parallel fashion. This is slightly at odds with the structures discussed above, where the initial noun phrase (the subject—see below) has a rather special status: whereas other noun phrases (objects, etc.) are ultimately part of the verb phrase, and therefore clearly dependent on the verb, the subject is independent of it. Nevertheless, it is possible to regard the subject noun phrase as dependent on the verb on other grounds, for example because it is equivalent to other dependent noun phrases in certain kinds of sentences. The noun phrases of 'Die Hauptstadt Englands ist London' are virtually interchangeable: 'London ist die Hauptstadt Englands', which suggests that they are both of equal syntactic status, and that it would be inappropriate to regard the second noun phrase as dependent on the verb, but not the first.

A tree such as 5.30 has lines connecting the different words, and implies that the dependency relationships are between individual words. This is not really true, however.[5] It is whole phrases, rather than individual words, that are dependent on the head. In the phrase *rauchen türkische Zigaretten*, for example, it is *türkische Zigaretten*, and not just *Zigaretten*, that is dependent on *rauchen*, though within this phrase *türkische* depends on *Zigaretten*. Dependency relationships are thus not completely separate from constituency relationships; dependencies exist between constituents.

We have seen that in a dependency analysis of a sentence the central and most significant element is taken to be the verb, so that all other parts of the sentence are ultimately dependent on it. The items that are immediately dependent on the verb (in 5.30 the noun phrases *die Arbeiter* and *türkische Zigaretten*) can be of a variety of kinds, with different types of relationship to the verb. Consider, for example, the sentence 'Mein Bruder verkauft alte Möbel in Frankfurt'. A dependency tree for this sentence is given in 5.32.

(5.32)

There are three elements in this sentence which are dependent on the verb. In terms of their contribution to the meaning of this sentence, the two noun phrases *mein Bruder* and *alte Möbel* could be said to have a rather more direct relationship to the verb than the prepositional phrase *in Frankfurt*; they are participants in the 'action' of the verb, while *in Frankfurt* merely provides the setting for the action. The French terms 'actants' and 'circonstants' are sometimes used for these two types; in German they are generally known as 'Ergänzungen' and 'Angaben'. We shall call them 'participant elements' and 'circumstantial elements', respectively.

These dependent elements also differ in another respect: whether they are obligatory or optional. Participant elements are often obligatory; we could not say, for example, '*Verkauft alte Möbel in Frankfurt' or '*Mein Bruder verkauft in Frankfurt'. Circumstantial elements like *in Frankfurt* are optional: 'Mein Bruder verkauft alte Möbel' is perfectly satisfactory. However, we also find optional participants—such as *Briefe* in 'Mein Bruder schreibt Briefe'—and not all prepositional phrases can be omitted. In the sentence 'Er wohnt in

---

[5] This was in fact the view of Tesnière (see n. 4), though it now seems inappropriate.

Frankfurt' *in Frankfurt* is obligatory, as '*Er wohnt' is unacceptable. This means that the categories 'participant' and 'circumstantial' cannot be defined in terms of obligatory and optional occurrence, nor, indeed, in terms of phrase type. Generally speaking, the term 'circumstantial element' ('circonstant', 'Angabe') is reserved for optional elements such as prepositional or adverbial phrases, while obligatory prepositional phrases are regarded as 'participant elements' ('actants', 'Ergänzungen'). But these categories are defined by the function of the phrase in the sentence, and not by whether or not it can be omitted. (For discussion of these functions, see the next section.)

The number and kind of the dependent elements will vary from verb to verb; *verkaufen* and *wohnen* have different possibilities here. It is therefore possible to classify verbs according to which dependent elements they can, or must, have. A parallel with the combinatory possibilities of chemical elements has been invoked here, using the concept of VALENCY. In chemistry, different elements are said to have different valencies, requiring different numbers of atoms from other elements in the formation of compounds. Hydrogen has a valency of 1 and oxygen a valency of 2; hence two atoms of hydrogen are required to combine with one of oxygen to form water (H_2O). Although linguistics is a far cry from chemistry, we may see something similar in the possibilities for combining the verb with its dependent elements. Since circumstantial elements tend to be fairly free in their possibilities for combination, the classification of verbs has generally been undertaken on the basis of the number and type of participant elements that they may have.

Verbs such as *kommen, lachen,* etc. (the traditional 'intransitive' verbs) have only one participant: 'Der Bürgermeister kommt/lacht/springt'; they are thus said to have a valency of 1 (they are 'monovalent'). Verbs with a valency of 2 ('divalent' verbs) include *machen, nehmen, brauchen* (traditional 'transitive' verbs): 'Der Bürgermeister macht (nimmt/braucht) es' but not '*Der Bürgermeister macht (nimmt/braucht)'. Verbs may also have three participants, and a valency of 3 ('trivalent' verbs), e.g. *geben, sagen*: 'Der Bürgermeister gibt seiner Frau den Schlüssel/sagt seiner Frau die Wahrheit'.

In work on the valency of German verbs, the principle has also been extended to embrace types of dependent elements other than noun phrases, though here it becomes difficult to give a purely numerical valency. Though *wohnen*, for example, requires a prepositional phrase or an adverbial phrase, *leben* does not: *er lebt* is acceptable in the sense of 'he is alive'. Many verbs have still further possibilities. For example, *hoffen* may be followed by a clause with *dass* ('Ich hoffe, dass ich ihn sehe') or by an infinitive with *zu* ('Ich hoffe, ihn zu sehen'), while *sagen* may have the former ('Ich sage, dass ich ihn sehe') but not the latter ('*Ich sage, ihn zu sehen*'). These two verbs thus have different valencies. Valency has also been extended to other word classes, especially adjectives. In English we may say 'He is tired *of waiting*' and 'She is proud *of her son*', but in German although we can say 'Er ist *des Wartens* müde' we must say 'Sie ist stolz *auf ihren Sohn*' and not '*Sie ist *ihres Sohns* stolz*'.

Dependency, and its derivative notion valency, are thus useful concepts in the description of sentence structure. But, like constituency, this approach is not without its problems. One difficulty that we have already encountered is in determining the head of units where no part can be easily omitted. In 5.30 we had to use other criteria to decide that the initial noun phrase is dependent on the verb, but the same problem also occurs elsewhere. In a prepositional phrase, for example, such as *in Frankfurt* in 5.32, it is not clear in what sense the preposition is the head, since neither the preposition nor the noun phrase can be omitted without changing the role of the phrase. A dependency tree such as 5.33, though generally accepted for a phrase such as *auf der Straße*, is thus to some extent arbitrary.

(5.33)

In fact, though dependency is generally assumed to be a matter of occurrence and co-occurrence (the head, but not its dependents, can occur alone), there is some problem in applying this criterion. This is clear from the distinction between obligatory and optional elements. The idea of an obligatory dependent element seems to contradict the very basis of dependency, if we assume that a dependent item is in principle dependent because it can be omitted. It thus appears that there is more to dependency than can be covered by occurrence and omissibility.

The question can indeed be raised whether, and to what extent, dependency and valency are properly matters of syntax. Certain of the characteristics of dependent elements that we have just discussed are evidently more a matter of meaning than of sentence structure. For example, the terminological distinction between participant and circumstantial elements rests on the idea that some elements in the sentence are more directly involved in the action of the verb than others—they 'participate' in this action while others merely form the 'circumstances' in which this action takes place. Yet the relationship between active sentences and their corresponding passives, as in the examples of 5.34, shows that syntactic roles may vary while participant roles remain the same.

(5.34)　(i)　Mein Bruder hat das Buch verkauft.
　　　　(ii)　Das Buch ist von meinem Bruder verkauft worden.

In both of these sentences the same action is described, with the same participants, but *Bruder,* as part of a prepositional phrase, is not as close to the verb, syntactically speaking, in 5.34(ii) as in the noun phrase of 5.34(i).

Another example of a disparity between syntactic and semantic roles is found in 'impersonal' verbs, such as *es regnet, es friert,* etc. The *es* of *es regnet* has virtually no semantic content, and could hardly be called a participant in the action of the verb. For this reason such verbs have been described as 'avalent'—having a valency of 0. But one could argue that the pronoun here has the same syntactic relationship to the verb as *er* has in, for example, *er liest.* From this point of view German does not have 'avalent' verbs, in the sense of verbs which (syntactically) have no dependent noun phrase or pronoun.

There is some doubt, therefore, whether the theory of dependency and valency is based on syntactic or semantic relationships. Though syntax is certainly involved to some degree, some of the concepts concerned seem to be matters of meaning rather than grammar. A distinction can be made, therefore, between 'syntactic' and 'semantic' dependencies. We could say, for instance, that *regnen* has a semantic valency of 0, since it has no participant element associated with it; syntactically, however, it requires a noun phrase (here a pronoun), and could thus be said to have a syntactic valency of 1.[6]

Syntactic Functions

We have so far been concerned with the relationships between words, word groups, and sentences as a matter of syntactic structure, i.e. from the point of view of the combinations and configurations of units within the sentence. As a result of these combinations, the various elements of the sentence come to

---

[6] The theory of dependency and valency has been taken very much further than it has been possible to present here, especially in its application to German. It is also of interest as one of the few current theories of syntax which have developed outside the English-speaking world, and which have been applied primarily to a language other than English.

take on different roles or functions. In the sentence 'Der Lehrer gibt dem Schüler den Apfel', for example, we can identify three noun phrases, and each of these can be said to have a different function within the sentence: *der Lehrer* is called the SUBJECT, *den Apfel* the DIRECT OBJECT, and *dem Schüler* the INDIRECT OBJECT. These differences are also reflected in the morphological features of the phrases: *der Lehrer* is in the nominative case, *den Apfel* in the accusative, and *dem Schüler* in the dative.

What do labels such as 'subject' or 'object' mean? Popularly, these categories are often thought of as referring to the relationship of the noun or noun phrase to the action of the verb: the subject is the 'doer' of the action, the direct object is the 'patient', which 'undergoes' the action of the verb, while the indirect object is the 'recipient' or 'beneficiary' of the action, and so on. In many cases, such as the sentence 'Der Lehrer gibt dem Schüler den Apfel', this interpretation seems appropriate enough, but it is easy to demonstrate its inadequacy. In a passive sentence such as 'Der Apfel wird dem Schüler gegeben', the subject (*der Apfel*) is hardly the doer of the action, but rather the item that undergoes it; and in 'Der Schüler bekommt den Apfel vom Lehrer' the subject is the recipient. As so often before, then, we see that grammatical categories are not adequately covered by semantic definitions, but require an explanation in grammatical terms. The categories here are functions of the noun phrases involved, but they are syntactic and not semantic functions.

How, then, can we define a syntactic function? If we consider the sentences just mentioned, we find that the one thing that all the 'subjects' have in common is not their role as the 'doer of the action' but simply their place in the structure of the sentence. Thus, in our grammatical tradition, the sentence is said to have two parts, 'subject' and 'predicate' (the former being conventionally regarded as 'what the sentence is about', the latter 'what is said about the subject'). Expressed in terms of constituency, and therefore in syntactic rather than in semantic terms, this means that the sentence has two immediate constituents, a noun phrase and what we have termed a verb phrase or a predicate phrase. The subject can thus be regarded simply as that noun phrase which, together with a verb phrase, forms a sentence. This definition is independent of the role of the noun phrase as 'doer', etc. of the action, since it covers the subject of a passive sentence such as 'Der Apfel wird dem Schüler gegeben', as well as that of a sentence such as 'Der Schüler bekommt den Apfel', where the subject is the recipient of the action. It also covers the subject of 'avalent' verbs such as *regnen*, where definition as the 'doer of the action' is clearly totally inappropriate, but where the *es* of 'es regnet' has exactly the same place in the syntactic structure as *Der Lehrer* in the above sentence.

The predicate (or verb phrase) itself can, as we have noted, be further divided; it contains a verb and, optionally, various other elements. The grammatical tradition does not provide us with a functional name for the verb as such, but this lack has been remedied in some grammatical descriptions with the term PREDICATOR. A noun phrase which combines with the predicator to form the predicate is (in many cases, at least) the 'object'. We are able, therefore, using the basic grammatical relations of constituent structure, to distinguish the categories 'subject', 'predicator', and 'object'. The structure of the sentence 'Mein Vater trinkt Schnaps' allows us to identify these categories in a straightforward way, as in 5.35, where the functional categories are simply a reflection of a constituency tree such as that of 5.5, and do not require us to resort to misleading and inaccurate definitions such as 'the doer of the action', etc.

(5.35)

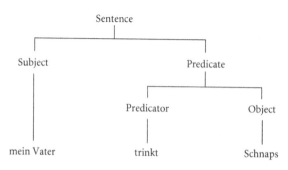

Although this approach works in the majority of cases, in some cases further criteria are necessary. The two noun phrases *dem Schüler* and *den Apfel* in the sentence 'Der Lehrer gibt dem Schüler den Apfel' appear to occupy the same place in the structure of the sentence, since they combine with the predicator to form the predicate. Although they can, of course, be distinguished morphologically as dative versus accusative, differences in their syntactic roles are not necessarily evident from the tree.

That these different objects have different syntactic characteristics, and therefore different syntactic functions, can be demonstrated in another way, however: by converting the sentence into one in which these roles assume different forms. For example, in an equivalent passive sentence the phrase *den Apfel* becomes the subject, while the subject takes the form of a prepositional phrase with *von*: 'Der Apfel wird dem Schüler vom Lehrer gegeben'. But this cannot be done with *dem Schüler*: '*Der Schüler wird den Apfel vom Lehrer gegeben' is unacceptable. The roles of these two noun phrases in this sentence must therefore be different. (It may be noted that this test would not work for

English, where we can say not only 'The apple was given the pupil by the teacher', but also 'The pupil was given the apple by the teacher'.)

It is important to note that these categories refer to the different roles that the various phrases may have in the sentence, rather than to the nature or structure of the phrases themselves. This can be illustrated by the traditional category of COMPLEMENT. In the sentence 'Der Lehrer ist ein sehr netter Mann', the phrase *ein sehr netter Mann* is regarded as the 'complement' rather than the object and its case is nominative rather than accusative. Unlike the direct object, it cannot be made the subject of a passive sentence: '*Ein sehr netter Mann wird vom Lehrer gewesen' is impossible. But the complement is not necessarily a noun phrase: 'Der Lehrer ist sehr nett' can be said to have the same functional elements, but here the complement is an adjective phrase.

The situation is similar with the category ADJUNCT. This covers those elements of sentence structure which are not subjects, objects, or complements and whose relationship to the 'action' of the verb is less direct (the 'circumstantial elements' of dependency theory). Typically, such elements are adverbs or adverb phrases, as in 'Er fährt *schnell*', and in fact another name for this category is 'adverbial'. However, adjuncts do not need to be adverbs, but may be, for example, prepositional phrases ('Er fährt *im März*') or even noun phrases ('Er fährt *jeden Tag*').

In fact, it is not only phrases as such that may have functions of this sort. We have already observed that sentences (clauses) may appear as parts of other sentences, and in these cases they take the place of other constituents and take over their functions. In the sentence 'Der Präsident kann sagen, was ihm gefällt', the clause *was ihm gefällt* has the function of a direct object (compare 'Der Präsident kann die Wahrheit sagen'); in 'Was ihm gefällt, ist ein großes Bier' it is the subject, while in 'Das ist gerade, was ihm gefällt' it is the complement.

Other sentence elements besides whole sentences and predicate phrases can be said to have functional parts. Within a noun phrase such as *die zwei großen Häuser*, for example, we might regard the elements before the head noun as fulfilling the role of, say, 'qualifier'. Again, such functions may also be fulfilled by whole sentences (clauses): in *die zwei Häuser, die mein Bruder gekauft hat* the relative clause qualifies the noun in the same way that *groß* does.

But the description of grammatical functions is not entirely without its problems. One difficulty, as with dependency grammar, is in determining what is actually syntactic and what belongs to other areas of linguistic description. Sometimes the categories seem to be morphological rather than syntactic; in German, although most 'objects' are in the accusative case, there are a number of verbs which are followed by the dative ('ich helfe *ihm*'), and a very small number which take the genitive ('wir haben *deiner* gedacht'). Though most grammars of German treat all these as different ('accusative object', 'dative object', and 'genitive object'), it is not clear whether these differences have any real syntactic consequences (though neither dative nor genitive objects, unlike accusative objects, can be made the subjects of corresponding passive sentences). Similarly, some distinctions may well be semantic rather than syntactic. A distinction is sometimes made, for example, between an 'affected object' and an 'effected object', according to whether the element concerned is operated on by the action of the verb ('er zerriss *mein Kleid*'), or is only brought into being by the action of the verb ('er schreibt *einen Brief*'). From the syntactic point of view such a distinction is again rather doubtful.

A related problem is that in the differentiation of functions it is difficult to know where to stop. Although we can recognize major functional categories such as 'subject', 'object', 'complement', and 'adjunct', each of these covers a range of different roles. A distinction may be made, for instance, between a 'subject complement', in which the complement relates to the subject (e.g. 'er wurde *glücklich*'), and an 'object complement', in which it relates to the object (e.g. 'sie machte ihn *glücklich*'). Such problems make it difficult to agree on a fixed and definitive set of functional categories.

The situation here is not helped by the fact that there are different approaches to the notion of 'grammatical function'. In philosophical discussions of logic, the role of the noun phrases in sentences such as 'Mein Vater trinkt Schnaps' are usually seen in terms of their relationship to the verb (as, indeed, they are in the dependency approach discussed earlier); they are ARGUMENTS of the verb, and this can be expressed by a formula such as *trinkt (mein Vater, Schnaps)*, where the items in brackets are arguments to the verb *trinkt*. The subject noun phrase (*mein Vater*) can be distinguished from the object (*Schnaps*) as the EXTERNAL argument as opposed to the INTERNAL argument.

Another approach sees these functions in terms of THEMATIC ROLES. The idea behind this is that elements in the sentence have certain functions which are to some extent independent of their purely syntactic roles. We saw earlier that a sentence such as 'Der Lehrer gibt dem Schüler den Apfel' could appear in different versions: 'Der Apfel wird dem Schüler vom Lehrer gegeben', 'Der Schüler bekommt den Apfel vom Lehrer', and so on. We used these examples to show that the subject of the sentence is not necessarily the 'doer of the action', but it is also evident that the roles of the noun phrase containing the nouns *Lehrer*, *Apfel*, and *Schüler* are in a certain sense the same throughout: it is the *Lehrer* who is doing the giving, the *Apfel* which is undergoing the action, and the *Schüler* who is the recipient. Clearly, these are not syntactic functions in the sense in which this term has so far been used here, since the grammatical subject of the sentence is different in all three versions, but there is no doubt that they are functions of some sort.

The term that has been used for these functions in recent linguistic discussions is 'thematic roles'. The sort of roles that have been recognized here include the following:

Agent—the entity which carries out the action of the predicate
Patient/Theme—the entity which undergoes the action of the predicate
Experiencer—the entity which experiences the state expressed by the predicate
Beneficiary—the entity which benefits from the action of the predicate
Goal—the entity towards which the action of the predicate is directed
Source—the entity from which something is moved by the action of the predicate
Location—the entity which is the place where the action of the predicate takes place

Among the difficulties with such 'functions' is the problem of whether they are syntactic in any meaningful sense or merely semantic, and also the problem of deciding exactly how many such functions there should be. Once we move away from syntactically definable relationships it becomes difficult to decide what the possible thematic roles are.

Syntactic Models

In our discussion so far we have identified a number of different dimensions in terms of which the syntactic structure of a language may be described: units can be recognized, relationships of constituency and dependency can be established between them, and they can be assigned to functional categories such as 'subject' and 'object'.

Account must be taken of all these dimensions in the description of the syntax of a language. But how is this to be achieved? Several different descriptive frameworks, or 'models', have been proposed which attempt to do this, and the characteristics of these models have been explored in some detail, but it cannot be said that there is a consensus of views among linguists as to which is to be preferred. Further, syntactic theory is in a state of constant development, and this is naturally reflected in the kinds of models that linguists use. In the present discussion, of course, we cannot do more than outline some of the more significant aspects of a number of the approaches adopted.

Sentence Plans

Perhaps the most straightforward approach to the description of sentence structure is to identify typical sentence patterns or SENTENCE PLANS ('Satzbaupläne'). Here we assume that the sentences of a language fall into a limited number of types, each consisting of an arrangement of basic constituents. For example, we may take sentences such as those of 5.36(a) and describe their structures in terms of the phrase types (noun phrase, etc.) which they contain, as in 5.36(b). But more often they are represented in terms of functional categories such as 'subject', 'predicator', and 'object' as in 5.36(c), providing us simultaneously with a description of structure and functions.

(5.36) (a) (i)   Mein Vater schläft.
           (ii) Der Student schreibt einen Aufsatz.
           (iii) Mein Freund gibt seiner Mutter zwei Euro.
       (b) (i)   NP V
           (ii) NP_1 V NP_2
           (ii) NP_1 V NP_2 NP_3
       (c) (i)   S P
           (ii) S P O
           (iii) S P O_1O_2

This form of description, which is quite traditional, is very useful for the description of basic structures, but it nevertheless has some weaknesses. One obvious point is that the phrases do not necessarily follow one another in such a simple way as this; not infrequently they overlap, e.g. in the sentence 'Mein Freund hat seiner Mutter zwei Euro gegeben', where the discontinuous phrase *hat... gegeben* is interrupted by two other phrases. In principle, sentence plans are not intended to carry any particular implication as to the ordering of the items concerned, but it would nevertheless be possible to accommodate this dimension, and to describe this sentence with a representation such as

S P- O_1 O_2 -P

though this naturally makes the plan less readable.

But the basic problem with this form of representation of sentence structure is that it is purely *linear*, and thus cannot deal adequately with the *hierarchical* nature of the structure which we have explored earlier. This is clear from recursive structures. As we have already noted, phrases can be expanded by the addition of subordinate clauses. The phrase *zwei Euro* in sentence 5.36(iii), for example, might be expanded to 'die zwei Euro, die er auf der Straße gefunden hat', and this might be further expanded to 'die zwei Euro, die er auf der Straße, die an der Kirche vorbeigeht, gefunden hat', and so on. Such expanded phrases have the same functions as the simple phrases, and thus in principle still belong to the same category, but they also contain functional categories of their own. The sentence 'Mein Freund gibt seiner Mutter die zwei Euro, die er auf der Straße, die an der Kirche vorbeigeht, gefunden hat' could simply be described as

S P O_1 O_2

which is satisfactory as a representation of the sentence as a whole, but included within the second object is the clause 'die er auf der Straße, die an der Kirche vorbeigeht, gefunden hat', which has the structure

O S A P

(where A = 'adjunct'). Within the adjunct ('auf der Straße, die an der Kirche vorbeigeht') we in turn find the clause 'die an der Kirche vorbeigeht', whose structure is

S A P

A plan to accommodate all these expansions would clearly be rather complex, and to list all the categories in sequence:

S P O O O S A S A P P

would be merely confusing. The solution is to include labelled brackets which are, in fact, entirely equivalent to the hierarchical tree diagrams that we used earlier.

S P $O_1[_{O_2}$ S$[_A$ S A P$]_A$ P$]_{O_2}$

'Sentence plans' can thus be used to display various aspects of the structure of sentences, using a range of different categories. Many grammars attempt to list all, or at least the major, sentence plans that occur in the language. It becomes apparent when we attempt to do this, however, that although the categories—whether phrase types or functional types—belong to a relatively limited set, the number of possible combinations of these categories is very large. One solution here is to combine a number of different structures together into one plan by the use of brackets to enclose optional constituents. For example, the sentences of 5.36 could be generalized into a single pattern:

S P $(O_1)(O_2)$

But the recursiveness of syntactic structures means that even such formulae cannot describe all the possibilities. The number of adjuncts (prepositional phrases, adverbial phrases, etc.), for example, is in principle unlimited, and each noun phrase may, as we have noted, be expanded indefinitely by the addition of relative clauses which themselves may be expanded in a similar way. The sentence-plan model may be useful for many purposes, but it clearly has its limitations.

Generative Grammar

A different approach to this problem has been adopted under the name of *generative grammar.*[7] The aim of this approach is to enumerate and describe (in technical parlance, to 'generate') *all* the possible sentences of the language. Since this cannot be achieved by listing all the patterns (which are in theory infinite in number), a different mechanism is required. The descriptive device used is the REWRITING RULE, and a grammar of the language consists of a set of such rules. (It should be noted that a 'rule' in this sense is a descriptive device expressing the generalization about the structure of sentences; it is not to be understood as indicating what should or should not be said, like some of the normative rules of prescriptive grammarians.)

In their original and simplest form these rules define categories such as phrases in terms of their constituents. Consider the set of rules given in 5.37.

(5.37) (i)   S   → NP   VP
        (ii) VP → V   (NP)
        (iii) NP → (Det) (AP) N
        (iv) AP → (Deg) A

Rule (i) defines the category S (sentence) by 'rewriting' it as a noun phrase and a verb phrase, while rule (ii) defines a verb phrase in terms of a verb and an optional noun phrase. A noun phrase is defined by rule (iii) as consisting of an obligatory noun preceded by an optional determiner and adjective phrase, while an adjective phrase is in turn defined as consisting of an optional degree word and an obligatory adjective.

This set of rules—they are, of course, for illustration only, since the actual rules required for German are much more complex—describes a range of

---

[7] The theory of generative grammar is associated primarily with the American linguist Noam Chomsky. It was first put forward in the late 1950s (see his *Syntactic Structures*, 1957), rapidly became the dominant theory in America, and has been extremely influential elsewhere. Current approaches within this framework, of which the most popular is the theory of Government and Binding, differ substantially from earlier versions.

occurring sentence patterns. The rules are general, in the sense that they describe *all* the possibilities; an individual sentence may require only a subset of the rules. Taken together, rules (i) and (ii) give us the two structures, and the corresponding sentence patterns, of 5.38.

(5.38)

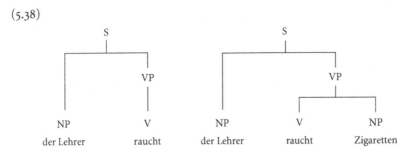

Rule (iii) describes four different structures for the noun phrase, exemplified in 5.39.

(5.39)

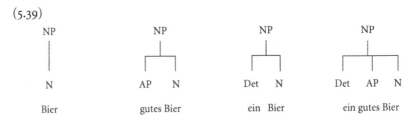

Similarly, rule (iv) allows for two different structures for the adjective phrase, as in 5.40.

(5.40)

If we combine all these possibilities, then we see that this set of four rules describes a fairly large number of possible sentence patterns (thirty-six, in fact). Naturally, the rules given here would need to be greatly amplified in order to cater for other possible structures—as they stand they do not allow for prepositional or adverbial phrases, or for more than two noun phrases in the sentence, for example—but it is clear that even a modest expansion of the rules will accommodate a very large number of sentence patterns indeed.

However, although the number of sentences that can be 'generated' by these rules is very large, it is still *finite*, and if we patiently work through the rules we can eventually list all the possible structures described. By a simple extension, however, we can also incorporate the recursive property of sentence structures. Consider the case of relative clauses, by which, as we have noted, noun phrases can be indefinitely expanded. To include such clauses in the set of possible structures generated by the rules of 5.37, we need merely to revise rule (iii) to read

(iii') NP $\rightarrow$ (Det) (AP) N (S)

with the category S reappearing in the structure of the noun phrase. If we now allow our set of rules to be repeated indefinitely, then the structures that they generate become infinite.

Earlier in this chapter we discussed the principles of X-bar syntax, which provides a systematic way of incorporating recursion within phrase types. Using these principles, it would naturally be possible to generalize rules of the kind presented here. It will be recalled that, according to these principles, all phrases have an identical structure. This structure, which was given in 5.21, above, could be generated by the set of rules of 5.29, where Y is a category different from X, but subject to the same rules, and rule (ii) is optional and recursive.

(5.41) (i)   XP $\rightarrow$ (Spec) X′
      (ii) X′ $\rightarrow$ X′ YP
      (iii) X′ $\rightarrow$ X (Comp)

Such a set of rules is actually a generalization of a number of different rules, since X (and Y) here stand for any category. It is therefore known as a RULE SCHEMA. The X would need to be replaced by specific categories in the actual description of sentences. However, further consideration of this particular approach would take us too far into theoretical matters, and we shall not discuss these issues further here.

A simple set of rules, such as the ones given in 5.37, generates in effect a set of constituency trees, since it defines each category in terms of its component parts. Rules of this kind are called PHRASE-STRUCTURE RULES. In the development of generative grammar, however, other types of rules have been devised, which considerably increase the possibilities for describing the structure of sentences. An important kind of rule, used by many early generative grammarians, is the TRANSFORMATION, and generative grammars which incorporate such rules are known as TRANSFORMATIONAL GENERATIVE GRAMMARS. Although such rules are no longer widely accepted in syntactic theory, the principles underlying them are still employed in much current theoretical work, under the heading of MOVEMENT RULES, and we shall therefore briefly consider these principles and their significance.

In order to appreciate the significance of movement rules let us consider the examples of 5.42.

(5.42)   (i)   Wer schenkte der Studentin die Blumen?
         (ii) Was schenkte der Professor der Studentin?
         (iii) Wem schenkte der Professor die Blumen?

There is clearly a sense in which all these sentences have the same structure; the elements of which they are composed, and the grammatical relationships of these elements to one another, are the same in each case: each sentence has a subject, a direct object, and an indirect object. In terms of these functional categories, the three versions of 5.42 differ in the order of the noun phrases, as described in 5.43.

(5.43)   (i)   S   V   IndO   DirO
         (ii) DirO   V   S   IndO
         (iii) IndO   V   S   DirO

In each case, the first place in the sentence is occupied by an interrogative word, which has a different function in each case.

A simple and rather traditional way of describing these sentences assumes a single basic structure for this sentence:

S   V   IndO   DirO

This structure is valid for all the sentences of 5.42, though of course the order of the constituents only applies to 5.42(i). To describe the individual sentences, we now need two rules, which can be expressed informally as follows:

1. The interrogative word moves to the first position
2. If the interrogative word is not the subject, the subject moves to the position immediately after the verb

How can we express these rules in explicit formal terms? In current generative grammar, the X-bar framework is widely used, so that the basic structure underlying 5.42(iii) will be that of 5.44, with CP and IP at the top of the tree. It will be noted that the direct- and indirect-object noun phrases are both considered to be complements of V′, but at different levels, the direct object being 'closer' to the verb. The order of the constituents is therefore not the same as in the actual sentence. The structure of the three noun phrases is of no concern to us here, and they have therefore not been further analysed.

(5.44)

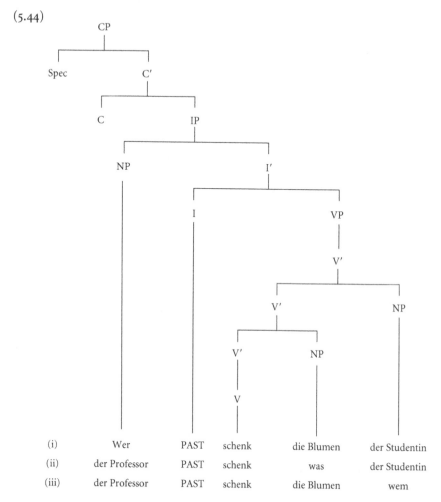

(i)	Wer	PAST	schenk	die Blumen	der Studentin
(ii)	der Professor	PAST	schenk	was	der Studentin
(iii)	der Professor	PAST	schenk	die Blumen	wem

Was in sentence (ii) and *wem* in sentence (iii) are not where we want them, so in accordance with the first of our rules we need to move them to the beginning of the sentence. Now we see the significance of the empty 'Spec' at the top of our tree: in this model it is assumed that the interrogative word is moved under this 'node'. Another rule is required to invert the subject and verb in sentences (ii) and (iii), and a further rule to put the direct and indirect objects in the correct order in sentence (i).

It will be clear that movement rules such as these have a very different function from the phrase-structure rules of 5.37. Whereas the latter define a structure, these rules move constituents around within a structure. Notice, however, that, given the structure of 5.44, the rule which moves the interrogative word does not actually change the structure but merely changes the position of the words in the structure.

Another case where movement rules would appear to be needed is in the placing of the verb in German sentences. The sets of phrase-structure rules given so far, and also the movement rules discussed above, all produce structures in which the verbal element is in second position. This is not always correct, however, since the verb regularly occupies final position in most kinds of subordinate clause. Perhaps the obvious solution within this model would be to have movement rules which move the verb from its 'normal' position to the end in subordinate clauses.

It has been argued, however, that a more satisfactory solution would be to assume that the basic position of the verb in German is, in fact, at the end. One argument in favour of this is that with complex verb forms (those with an auxiliary), the main verb appears at the end even in main clauses: 'Er hat das Buch *gelesen.*' According to this view, therefore, the verb is moved from the end of the sentence in all cases.

What will be clear from this discussion is that this model assumes two different 'levels' for the syntactic structure of sentences: a 'deeper' and more abstract level (earlier called 'Deep Structure' but now simply 'D-structure') and the observable structure itself (earlier called the 'Surface Structure' and now the 'S-structure'), together with a set of rules for relating the two. We must, however, beware of taking this model literally as a description of speakers' behaviour; these levels and rules are *descriptive devices*, and do not imply that speakers actually take D-structures and convert them into S-structures. They are, in effect, a means of relating the structures of different sentences to one another.

The generative approach to syntactic structure has been taken a great deal further than it is possible to indicate here, and it continues to be highly influential. However, since our aim is not the pursuit of theory as such but merely the examination of possible models for the description of German, we shall not consider it further here. Readers who wish to find out more can be referred to the works given under Further Reading.[8]

---

[8] There are a number of other models for the description of syntactic structure that are currently in use. One such is the Lexical Functional Grammar, another Head-Driven Phrase-Structure Grammar. We shall not consider such models here.

The German Sentence

Having discussed some of the general principles involved in the study of syntax, we are now in a position to examine some of the details of German sentence structure more closely. No attempt will be made, of course, to provide a comprehensive description of German syntax, such as is often attempted in reference grammars of the language; the aim here is merely to identify the major characteristics of German sentence structure, and to see how these characteristics can be described from a linguistic point of view.

Sentence Types

Sentences are of a variety of different kinds, and in investigating their structure we shall need to refer to these different types. Consider first the examples of 5.45.

(5.45)　(i)　Er schreibt einen Brief.
　　　　(ii)　Schreibt er einen Brief?
　　　　(iii) Schreib einen Brief!

These sentences differ from one another in a number of respects. In (i) and (ii) there is a subject noun phrase (the pronoun *er*), while in (iii) there is none. Sentence (i) has the subject in initial position and the verb in second place; in (ii) their positions are reversed. These sentences also differ in their typical uses: while (i) could be said to be making a statement, (ii) asks a question, and (iii) issues a command. We could therefore describe sentences of these types as 'statements', 'questions', and 'commands', respectively.

　But consider now the sentences of 5.46.

(5.46)　(i)　Er schreibt einen Brief?
　　　　(ii)　Du sollst einen Brief schreiben.
　　　　(iii) Willst du endlich einen Brief schreiben!

Sentences (i) and (ii) of 5.46 have the same form as sentence (i) of 5.45, with a subject pronoun preceding the verb, but it could be argued that neither is a 'statement' in the normal sense: (i) asks a question (the question mark at the end would probably be reflected, in the spoken form, in a different intonation), while (ii) has the effect of a command. Sentence (iii) is likewise a form of command, though it resembles sentence (ii) of 5.45 in having the verb preceding the subject pronoun.

　The point to be made here is that terms such as 'statement', 'question', and 'command' are not always appropriate to differentiate the *structure* of different types of sentence. They refer to the *use* or *function* of the sentence rather than to characteristics of its structure. Sentences with the same structure may be put to different uses, and, conversely, sentences with a different kind of structure may be put to similar uses. We must be careful, therefore, to make clear what we mean by 'sentence type'. On the one hand we have functional categories such as 'statement', 'question', and 'command', but, since these do not completely coincide with different types of structure, we need further categories for the structures themselves. Sentences with the characteristics of 5.45(i) are called DECLARATIVE, those with the structure of 5.45(ii) INTER-ROGATIVE, and those with the structure of 5.45(iii) IMPERATIVE. But these terms refer to structural types rather than functions; a declarative, for ex-ample, might be used not only as a statement (as in 5.45(i)), but also as a question (as in 5.46(i)) or a command (as in 5.46(ii)). A further advantage of making this distinction is that whereas the types of sentence use are extremely varied (we might distinguish a whole range of categories—not only the three given here but also such categories as 'demand', 'answer', 'request', 'confirma-tion', 'exclamation', and so on), the types of sentence structure are more limited, and much easier to enumerate.

We can usefully make a number of other distinctions. Firstly, we may distin-guish between complete and incomplete sentences. The sentences given in 5.45 and 5.46 are all grammatically complete. But consider the examples of 5.47.

(5.47)   Drei Pfund, bitte.
          Schrecklich!
          Aber wann?

Such phrases are not complete in the sense that the sentences of 5.45 and 5.46 are, since they do not contain a verbal element (as we have seen, a verbal element is central to the sentence; without it, a sentence could be seen merely as a string of one or more phrases). This does not mean, of course, that they are incorrect; they are perfectly acceptable in appropriate contexts, such as those of 5.48.

(5.48)   'Wieviel möchten Sie?' 'Drei Pfund, bitte.'
          'Wie finden Sie meinen Aufsatz?' 'Schrecklich!'
          'Der Regen wird aufhören.' 'Aber wann?'

Examples such as those of 5.47 create problems for grammarians, who are reluctant to consider these as genuine sentences on account of their structure but must acknowledge that they are perfectly normal answers to questions such as those of 5.48. One escape is to draw a distinction between *sentences* and *utterances,* where the former refers to an 'ideal', complete, grammatical structure and the latter to an actual, and not necessarily complete, manifestation of the former.[9] What speakers actually produce, in other words, is an utterance, and behind every such utterance is a sentence, seen as a rather abstract set of grammatical forms and relationships. In the process of 'uttering' a sentence, various modifications may occur, such as, in the present case, the omission of parts of the structure. The examples of 5.47, therefore, can be seen as *elliptical,* i.e. they are structures from which something has been omitted. If we put these examples into the contexts of 5.48, we can see them as corresponding to the sentences of 5.49.

(5.49)   Ich möchte drei Pfund, bitte.
          Ich finde ihn schrecklich.
          Aber wann wird er aufhören?

Such an approach is actually quite traditional (in traditional grammar one might say that the omitted items are 'understood'). The sentence–utterance relationship can also be expressed in a straightforward way in generative grammar, since rules can be employed to 'delete' the unwanted items from a complete 'deep' or D-structure. But there are difficulties here, since it is not possible in all cases to say exactly what has been omitted. Our utterance 'Drei Pfund, bitte', for example, might also be derived from 'Geben Sie mir drei Pfund, bitte', 'Ich nehme drei Pfund, bitte', and so on. It can be seen that the choice of a sentence from which items have been omitted may be rather arbitrary.

Unlike the distinction between complete and incomplete structures, the difference between *main* and *subordinate* clauses is uncontroversial. This too is significant for a discussion of sentence types, since the characteristic structures of each of these are regularly different, as we have already noted. In 5.50, example (i) contains two main clauses and example (ii) a main clause and a subordinate one, and the structure of the second clause is different in each case.

(5.50)   (i) Er sagte: 'Morgen kommen die Delegierten.'
          (ii) Er sagte, dass die Delegierten morgen kommen.

Another relevant distinction is that between *finite* and *non-finite* clauses. Consider the examples given in 5.51.

(5.51)   (i) Er hofft, dass er die Ausstellung besuchen kann.
               Er bedauert, dass er die Einladung verloren hat.

---

[9] We shall consider the significance of utterances further in Ch. 7.

(ii) Er hofft, die Ausstellung besuchen zu können.
Er bedauert, die Einladung verloren zu haben.

Although all the sentences of 5.51 contain two verbal elements, in those of (i) the second verb is finite—i.e. it has the inflections of person, number, and tense/aspect—while in those of (ii) it is non-finite, being merely an infinitive with *zu*. This distinction has repercussions elsewhere: the finite clauses have a subject pronoun (*er*), while the non-finite ones do not. If the presence of an inflected verb is regarded as indispensable for a complete sentence or clause, then non-finite clauses clearly do not qualify as complete. Again it is possible to regard such clauses as truncated versions of finite sentences, in effect deriving the examples of (ii) from those of (i).

Sentence Structure

Many basic characteristics of the structure of German sentences have already been considered in our discussion of syntactic principles. Whatever the sentence type involved, the main sentence constituents that are usually identified are those given in 5.52.

(5.52)   predicator (P)
subject (S)
object (O)
complement (C)
adjunct (A)

Behind these labels, of course, lie a variety of different categories. While the predicator is always a verb, the other constituents may vary. Subjects and objects are usually noun phrases, complements either noun or adjective phrases, and adjuncts generally adverb phrases or prepositional phrases, but this does not exhaust the possibilities. For our present purposes, however, we are not concerned with the type of phrase involved, merely with the functional category.

All 'complete' sentences have a predicator, and all, with the exception of some imperative sentences, also have a subject. Thus, the simplest structure for declarative and interrogative sentences is

S + P

(we are not, for the present, concerned with the order in which these occur; in interrogative sentences this order is generally reversed). Examples of this structure, with a variety of phrase and clause types as the subject, are given in 5.53.

(5.53)   Der Student liest.
        Er kommt.
        Dass er kommt, stimmt.
        Wer will, soll kommen.
        Wer spricht?
        Kommt er?

In imperative sentences a subject is required in the polite form (*kommen Sie!*), but not in the informal forms (*komm!, kommt!*).

This basic structure can be expanded by the addition of an *object,* giving the structure

S + P + O

It is necessary, however, to distinguish a variety of types of object, differing primarily in their case. The most common is the accusative object (O_a), but a number of verbs take a dative object (O_d), and a few even a genitive object (O_g) (these are rare, and generally rather formal in style). These types are illustrated in 5.54.

(5.54)   Er schreibt *einen Brief.* (O_a)
        Der Lehrer hilft *dem Schüler.* (O_d)
        Wir gedenken *der Gefallenen.* (O_g)

The distinctions here are purely grammatical, in the sense that the type of object is determined by the verb and not by considerations of meaning. Compare further the pairs of sentences given in 5.55.

(5.55)   (i)   Ich helfe *ihm.*
           Ich unterstütze *ihn.*
      (ii) Ich gratuliere *ihm.*
           Ich beglückwünsche *ihn.*
     (iii) Ich bedarf *seines Rates.*
           Ich brauche *seinen Rat.*

The sentences of each pair have related meanings, but the case of the object is different. It is thus largely arbitrary which case is required with each verb. Nevertheless, dative objects tend to be characteristically 'personal', i.e. they involve animate beings.[10] A further reflection of this is found in so-called

---

[10] But see Ch. 4 n. 18.

'impersonal' verbs, where animate beings are affected by some outside agency. The outside agency takes the form of the non-specific *es*, the animate being takes that of a dative object, as in 5.56.

(5.56)   Es gelingt ihm.
          Es schadet ihm.
          Es reicht ihm.

There are also a number of impersonal verbs which take an accusative object (*es hungert mich, es friert mich*), and these may also dispense with the *es* (*mich hungert, mich friert*), giving subjectless sentences. Such a construction is rare, however, and stylistically very restricted.

A further category that it is convenient to recognize is the prepositional object (O_p). As its name suggests, this consists of a prepositional phrase. Examples are given in 5.57.

(5.57)   Ich zweifle *an seiner Ehrlichkeit.*
          Er besteht *auf seinen Rechten.*
          Sie hängt *von ihrer Mutter* ab.
          Er denkt *an seine Geliebte.*
          Wir flehen *um Gnade.*

Again, the preposition is required by the particular verb. There is a difficulty here, however, in distinguishing such objects from adjuncts, which may have a similar form (see below). The sentences of 5.58, for example, appear to have the same structure, but the prepositional phrase of 5.58(i) is arguably an adjunct, and that of 5.58(ii) a prepositional object. (This distinction was encountered earlier in our discussion of dependency grammar, where a prepositional phrase could be either a 'participant' or a 'circumstantial' element.)

(5.58)   (i)   Er steht auf der Straße.
          (ii) Er besteht auf seinen Rechten.

Syntactic tests can be applied in a number of cases to distinguish these. The basic principle is that prepositional objects are more closely bound to the predicator; certain verbs can be said to 'require' specific prepositions after them, so that the resulting prepositional phrases are more like objects. For example, *denken* requires *an* ('Ich denke an meine Familie') and *hoffen* requires *auf* ('Wir hoffen auf ein Wunder'). This is reflected in the corresponding questions, which incorporate this preposition into the question-word ('Woran denken Sie?', 'Worauf hoffen Sie?'), as does the 'anaphoric' form[11] of the prepositional phrase, with a pronominal element replacing the noun phrase ('Ich denke daran', 'Wir hoffen darauf'). In adjuncts, however, the preposition is not dependent on the verb, and is not incorporated into the question-word or anaphoric prepositional phrase; the question corresponding to 'Ich fahre am Mittwoch' is not 'Woran fahren Sie?', but rather 'Wann fahren Sie?', nor would one say 'Ich fahre daran' as the anaphoric form. The question 'Worauf warten Sie?' could be appropriately answered by 'Auf den Zug' but not (except as a joke) by 'Auf dem Bahnsteig'.

Objects (whether accusative, dative, genitive, or prepositional) may also be REFLEXIVE, providing further complications. Not all occurrences of reflexive pronouns (*sich*, etc.) with verbs are actually cases of genuine reflexive verbs. Such a pronoun is used where the object is merely the same as the subject, as in the examples of 5.59, where other objects could replace it.

(5.59) Er wäscht sich.   (cf. Er wäscht seine Hose.)
        Sie hat sich verletzt.   (cf. Sie hat den Hund verletzt.)
        Ich musste mich verstecken.   (cf. Ich musste das Geld verstecken.)

But in genuine reflexive verbs the reflexive pronoun cannot be replaced by another object, as in 5.60.

(5.60) Er erholt sich.   (*Er erholt seinen Freund.)
        Er nähert sich.   (*Er nähert seinen Wagen.)
        Er bedankt sich.   (*Er bedankt seine Schwester.)

While the 'pseudo-reflexives' of 5.59 conform to the S—P—O structure, a case could be made for treating the genuine reflexives of 5.60 as simply S—P, the reflexive pronoun being regarded as part of the verb.

The S—P—O structure can be extended by the addition of a further object, giving

$$S + P + O_1 + O_2$$

Examples of such double objects are given in 5.61.

(5.61) Der Professor lehrt *sie Geschichte*. $(S—P—O_a—O_a)$
        Meine Mutter gab *mir zwei Euro*. $(S—P—O_d—O_a)$
        Der Polizist verdächtigte *ihn des Verbrechens*. $(S—P—O_a—O_g)$

[11] The term ANAPHORIC refers to those words which refer back to items mentioned earlier. Items which refer forwards are called CATAPHORIC. For further discussion see Ch. 7.

> Sie verständigte *mich über den Beschluss.*   (S—P—O$_a$—O$_p$)
> Ich gratulierte *ihr zum großen Erfolg.*   (S—P—O$_d$—O$_p$)
> Er sprach *mit mir über die Probleme.*   (S—P—O$_p$—O$_p$)

Again, one or other of these multiple objects may be a reflexive pronoun, as in the examples of 5.62.

(5.62) Er bedient *sich* dieser Gelegenheit.
        Sie gibt *sich* Mühe.
        Wir beschäftigen *uns* mit den Vorbereitungen.

(The first two of these are genuine reflexives, the third is a 'pseudo-reflexive'.)
    Instead of an object we may have a complement, which may be a noun phrase or an adjective phrase. The structure here is

S + P + C

Examples are given in 5.63.

(5.63) Meine Frau ist *Lehrerin.*
        Das ist *eine Katastrophe.*
        Das Gebäude war *riesig.*
        Das Wetter wurde *sehr schön.*

In this construction a noun-phrase complement is, unlike the objects, in the nominative case. A complement may also occur together with an object, as in 5.64.

(5.64) Der Richter nannte ihn *einen Verbrecher.*
        Sie machte ihn *glücklich.*

Despite the apparent similarity between the first example of 5.64 and the double-object construction of 5.61, these two can be considered different. Compare the sentences of 5.65.

(5.65) (i) Sie lehrte mich *Geduld.*
        (ii) Sie nannte mich *einen Dieb.*

The differences can be observed when we attempt to put these sentences into the passive, as we see from 5.66.

(5.66) (i) *Ich wurde (von ihr) Geduld gelehrt.
             Mich wurde (von ihr) Geduld gelehrt.

(ii) Ich wurde (von ihr) ein Dieb genannt.
      *Mich wurde (von ihr) ein Dieb genannt.

The final major category in terms of which we can describe the structure of German sentences is the *adjunct*. Adjuncts can be added to any kind of sentence, and in virtually unlimited numbers. We thus find structures such as those of 5.67.

(5.67) S + P + A
        S + P + A + A
        S + P + O + A
        S + P + O + A + A
        S + P + C + A
        S + P + C + A + A
        S + P + O + O + A
        S + P + O + O + A + A
        etc.

Furthermore, adjuncts may take a variety of forms, most commonly adverb phrases and prepositional phrases, but also noun phrases. Some examples are given in 5.68.

(5.68) Meine Frau kauft neue Möbel *in der Stadt*
        Vorgestern schrieb ich ihr einen langen Brief.
        Er hat *dieses Jahr* sehr viel Geld verdient.
        Eines Tages werde ich reich sein.
        Gegen drei Uhr kam sie *ohne Geld* zurück.

We have not so far considered the status of subordinate clauses within sentences, other than those which appear as subjects (cf. 5.53). In fact, such clauses may have a variety of roles, as object, complement, or adjunct; they may also have a number of different forms, e.g. finite or non-finite, with several varieties of each. Consider the examples of 5.69.

(5.69) Ich weiß nicht, *wer er ist.*
        Ich hoffe, *ihn zu sehen.*
        Ich fragte, *ob er kommt.*
        Ich gab zu, *dass ich es nicht wollte.*
        Ich sagte, *ich hätte ihn nicht gesehen.*

All the examples of 5.69 can be regarded as objects (the second clause could in all cases be replaced by *es*, with suitable adjustments to the word order). It is also possible to distinguish different kinds of such objects, though the differences are not always immediately evident. The examples of 5.70 illustrate a number of these possibilities.

(5.70)   (i)   Er wusste, dass sie Geburtstag hatte.
         (ii) Er freute sich, dass sie Geburtstag hatte.
         (iii) Er erinnerte sich, dass sie Geburtstag hatte.

Sentence (i) is similar to the examples of 5.69, and its subordinate clause could be replaced by *es*: it could thus be regarded as an accusative object. But no such replacement could occur in the other two examples. The anaphoric form in (ii) would be 'Er freute sich darüber' (or 'darauf or 'daran'). The subordinate clause here is thus equivalent to a prepositional object. The same is true of sentence (iii) ('Er erinnerte sich daran'), though here there is also the possibility of a genitive object: 'Er erinnerte sich dessen'. In fact it is often possible in these cases to insert the appropriate pronoun (it is here 'cataphoric'—referring forwards—rather than 'anaphoric'—referring backwards) in the main clause as well, giving the versions of 5.71.

(5.71)   Er wusste es, dass sie Geburtstag hatte.
         Er freute sich darüber, dass sie Geburtstag hatte.
         Er erinnerte sich daran, dass sie Geburtstag hatte.
         Er erinnerte sich dessen, dass sie Geburtstag hatte.

Subordinate clauses are frequent as adjuncts. Some typical examples are given in 5.72.

(5.72)   Als ich um die Ecke kam, sah ich das alte Haus.
         Ich gehe ins Theater, wenn ich Zeit habe.
         Ich musste es selber machen, weil der Chef nicht dort war.
         Obwohl er schon alt ist, ist er noch gesund.

We have, of course, considered only the major functional categories and merely the most important kinds of combinations that occur in German sentences. The intention has been not to give an exhaustive treatment, but simply to show the way in which these basic structures may be described. The reader will find more elaborate, and more comprehensive, treatments in many of the works listed as Further Reading.

'Word Order'

The sentence patterns discussed above have been expressed solely in terms of the presence of specific functional categories, without regard to the order in which these categories occur. Indeed, it is important that such structures should be seen as in principle independent of the linear order of their component parts. The sentences of 5.73, therefore, can be said, despite their obvious differences, to have the same basic structure: $S + P + O_1 + O_2 + A$.

(5.73)   Sie hat ihm zum Geburtstag ein Buch geschenkt.
         Hat sie ihm zum Geburtstag ein Buch geschenkt?
         (Ich weiß, dass) sie ihm zum Geburtstag ein Buch geschenkt hat.

However, the order of elements (usually called 'word order', but in fact primarily a matter of the order of whole sentence constituents) is also significant, and it constitutes the main syntactic difference between the various sentence types discussed above. We must distinguish, however, between different orders of elements which reflect different sentence types and those which reflect other factors. For example, the first sentence of 5.73 may appear in a variety of forms, illustrated in 5.74, yet all these are still of the same declarative type.

(5.74)   Zum Geburtstag hat sie ihm ein Buch geschenkt.
         Ihm hat sie zum Geburtstag ein Buch geschenkt.
         Ein Buch hat sie ihm zum Geburtstag geschenkt.
         Geschenkt hat sie ihm zum Geburtstag ein Buch.

Differences such as those exemplified in 5.73 are required by the different types of sentences, and could thus be said to be instances of SYN-TACTIC ORDERING. Differences such as those of 5.74 depend on the particular context in which the utterance occurs, or even on speech style; this could thus be called PRAGMATIC ORDERING. The factors involved here will be considered further in Chapter 7.

As far as syntactic ordering is concerned, we have noted that the predicator (verb) has generally been accorded a central position in German sentence structure, especially in dependency theory, where it is seen as the element on which all the other elements depend. The *position* of the predicator is also crucial, as this is the clearest indicator of the type of sentence involved.

A major feature of declarative sentences is that the predicator occupies second place. This usually applies whatever 'pragmatic' word order is selected; all the sentences of 5.74, for example, have the predicator second, whatever element occupies the first position. By contrast, interrogative sentences of the type illustrated in 5.75 have the predicator in first position.

(5.75)   *Lesen* Sie gern Romane?
          Kennst du meine Mutter?
          Gab er ihr meinen Brief?

A distinction must be made here, however, between interrogative sentences such as those of 5.75 and those containing a question-word, illustrated in 5.42 above. In the latter case the predicator occupies second place, as in declarative sentences. In English grammatical usage interrogative sentences containing a question-word are often called '*wh*-interrogatives', since most English question-words (though not all—e.g. *how*) begin with *wh*; we might therefore call the equivalent German sentences '*w*-interrogatives'. Interrogatives of the types illustrated in 5.75 are sometimes called 'yes/no interrogatives', since they require either *yes* or *no* (or their equivalents) as an answer. One could not legitimately answer *ja* or *nein* to a question such as 'Wo wohnen Sie?'. Less picturesquely, they could be called 'non-*w*-interrogatives'.

Imperative sentences, with or without a subject, have the same initial position for the verb as non-*w* interrogatives, giving rise to potential ambiguity. A sentence such as 'Lesen Sie Romane' can be ambiguous as to interrogative or imperative, though in written German the punctuation may come to our aid ('Lesen Sie Romane?' ~ 'Lesen Sie Romane!'), and in spoken German the intonation. Where a subject is not present in the imperative, there is of course no ambiguity ('Lest ihr Romane?' ~ 'Lest Romane!').

These two positions for the predicator—first and second in the sentence—characterize main clauses. A third position—final—is typical of the majority of subordinate clauses, as in the examples of 5.76.[12]

(5.76)   Ich weiß, dass er keine Kinder *hat*.
         Er kommt nicht, weil seine Frau krank *ist*.
         Die Leute, die solche Bücher *kaufen*, haben keinen Geschmack.

Not all subordinate clauses have a final predicator, however, as we see from examples such as those of 5.77.

(5.77)   *Schreibt* er, so muss ich darauf antworten.
          Er sagte, er *käme* nicht.

---

[12] Some German grammarians use the terms 'Kernform', 'Stirnform', and 'Spannform' to refer to structures with the verb in second, first, and final positions respectively.

One case where a main clause in a declarative sentence appears to have the predicator in first position is where a subordinate clause precedes. Some examples are given in 5.78.

(5.78)   Wenn die Sonne scheint, *gehen* wir gern spazieren.
Obwohl er krank war, *ging* er ins Theater.
Weil der Zug verspätet war, *kam* ich erst um neun Uhr an.

However, the predicator is not actually initial in these cases, since the first position is occupied by the subordinate clause. The first part of the structure is therefore

A + P ...

with the predicator in the regular second position.

The position of the predicator, then, is crucial for the syntactic organization of German sentences. However, not all of the predicator will necessarily occupy the characteristic position—first, second, or final. Where the predicator is a phrase consisting of more than one word, only the finite part (the item which carries the inflections for person, number, and tense) occurs in this position, the remainder being relegated to the end. In complex verb forms it is the auxiliary verbs which are finite; hence, as the verb forms become more complex, more and more of the predicator will find itself in final position, as illustrated in 5.79.[13]

(5.79)   Es *wurde* gestern *gemacht.*
Es *konnte* gestern *gemacht werden.*
Es *hat* gestern *gemacht werden können.*
Wurde es gestern *gemacht?*
Konnte es gestern *gemacht werden?*
Hat es gestern *gemacht werden können?*

As each verbal component is amplified by the addition of an auxiliary, its non-finite portion is assigned to the end, following any other components that may be there. Where the normal position of the predicator is the final position, the same principle applies, except that the finite component is itself relegated to the end, usually as the last word of all, as in 5.80. (Exceptions are found in complex verbal expressions with verbs such as *lassen* and *sehen*, e.g.

---

[13] It will be recalled that this is the main motivation for the assumption made in some current theories, that the 'underlying' position of the verb in German is at the end of the sentence.

'Ich habe den Brief gefunden, den ich gestern *habe fallen lassen*', or with modal verbs, e.g. 'Er hat das Auto genommen, obwohl er es nicht *hätte tun sollen*'.)

(5.80)   Ich weiß, dass es gestern *gemacht wurde*.
Ich weiß, dass es gestern *gemacht werden konnte*.

It can be seen that in complex verb forms such as those of 5.79 the predicator is split into two, with other components of the sentence between the two parts. This structure, highly typical of German sentences, is referred to as the FRAME or BRACKET construction ('Satzrahmen', 'Satzklammer'). It is found not only with complex verb forms involving auxiliary + participle, or auxiliary + infinitive (both of which are illustrated in 5.80), but also with 'separable' verbs, where the verbal particle is treated as an independent non-finite form (see 5.81(i)). Where the particle and the verb on which it depends are *both* relegated to the end, either because the verb is non-finite (5.81(ii)) or because the finite verb is in final position (5.81(iii)), they are joined up again.

(5.81)   (i)   Er *nimmt* es *weg*.
         (ii)   Er *hat* es *weggenommen*.
         (iii) Ich weiß, dass er es *wegnimmt*.

The frame construction is also found with certain other complex elements, including some with predicator + object and predicator + complement, where the object or complement is so closely dependent on the verb as to be virtually part of it, as in 5.82.

(5.82)   Ich *fahre* jeden Tag *Auto*.
         Er *leistet* ihr ständig *Gesellschaft*.
         Wir *nehmen* es *übel*.

Since the position of the predicator in the sentence is so important, the other elements of sentence structure—subject, objects, adjuncts, etc.—tend to have to accommodate themselves to it, and fit into whatever positions remain. Where the predicator is in second position, the regular position for the subject is either immediately before or immediately after it, so that if any element besides the subject occupies the first position (e.g. an object or adjunct, or, in *w*-interrogatives, a question-word), then the subject will usually be in third position, as in the examples of 5.83.

(5.83)   Gestern ist *mein Bruder* ins Krankenhaus eingeliefert worden.
         Diese Frage kann *ich* leider nicht beantworten.
         Warum hat *die Regierung* diese Maßnahme eingeführt?

The positions of other elements in the sentence are less easy to determine, since they are susceptible to a certain amount of pragmatic variation. Other things being equal, accusative objects are likely to precede genitive and prepositional objects, but follow dative objects, as in 5.84.

(5.84)   Ich verdächtige den Bürgermeister dieses Verbrechens.
          Ich beauftragte meinen Freund mit dieser Aufgabe.
          Ich gab meiner Mutter die Einkaufstasche.

But a further factor here is whether the elements concerned are nominal or pronominal, i.e. whether they are or contain a noun or a pronoun. Where there is a dative object and an accusative one, one of which is pronominal and the other nominal, the pronominal one comes first. Thus, if pronouns are substituted in the final sentence of 5.84, we get the sentences of 5.85.

(5.85)   Ich gab ihr die Einkaufstasche.
          Ich gab sie meiner Mutter.

This principle can to some extent override some of the others discussed above. The principle that the subject comes immediately after the predicator in sentences such as those of 5.83 may fail to apply if the subject is nominal and the object pronominal, as in the examples of 5.86(i), though the 'standard' order is certainly possible here, as in 5.86(ii).

(5.86)   (i)   Gestern hat es *mein Bruder* gefunden.
                Für diese Aufgabe hat ihn *der Chef* ausgesucht.
          (ii) Gestern hat *mein Bruder* es gefunden.
                Für diese Aufgabe hat *der Chef* ihn ausgesucht.

The position of adjuncts is still more variable, and difficult to cover by a general rule. Apart from the initial position in the sentence, adjuncts may occur either before or after other elements, such as objects or complements. The sentences of 5.87(i) and 5.87(ii) illustrate both these possibilities.

(5.87)   (i)   Mein Vater kaufte *vor zwei Wochen* ein neues Auto.
                Ich habe *im Urlaub* diesen Roman gelesen.
          (ii) Du kannst diese Arbeit *zu Hause* machen.
                Sie hat ihre Uhr *auf der Straße* verloren.

One factor which determines this ordering is the closeness of the dependence of the adjunct on the verb. It could be argued, for example, that *zu Hause machen* in 5.87(ii) constitutes a single semantic entity, whereas *vor zwei*

Wochen kaufen does not. Thus, the predicator + adjunct structure of the sentences of 5.87(ii) resembles the predicator + object structure given in 5.82, where, as we saw, the relationship between the elements is so close that they constitute a single syntactic unit, and hence form a 'frame' in the same way that auxiliary + main verb, or verb + separable particle, do.

There is no doubt some truth in this, but it is also the case that the ordering of objects and adjuncts in the sentences of 5.87 is not fixed; it is possible to reverse these elements, as in the examples of 5.88.

(5.88)   Mein Vater kaufte ein neues Auto *vor zwei Wochen*
          Ich habe diesen Roman *im Urlaub* gelesen.
          Du kannst *zu Hause* diese Arbeit machen.
          Sie hat *auf der Straße* ihre Uhr verloren.

Some of these sentences may perhaps be felt to be less usual than those of 5.87, but they are nevertheless possible. It is, in fact, likely that in some of these cases the most natural solution would be to place an adjunct or object at the beginning of the sentence ('Vor zwei Wochen kaufte mein Vater ein neues Auto', 'diese Arbeit kannst du zu Hause machen'), in which case the ordering question does not arise.

Foreign learners are familiar with a general formula for cases when more than one adjunct occurs in the sentence: TMP, i.e. 'time' before 'manner' and 'manner' before 'place'. This rule can be illustrated with the sentences of 5.89.

(5.89)   Wir gehen um acht Uhr ins Theater.   (T + P)
          Er kam voller Begeisterung aus China zurück.   (M + P)
          Sie fährt morgen verzweifelt nach Hause.   (T + M + P)

But this is only a rough guide, and instances where the rule is broken are common, e.g. in the sentences of 5.90.

(5.90)   Man kann in Deutschland sehr gut leben.   (P + M)
          Gäste können in diesem Hotel zu jeder Zeit essen.   (P + T)

To some extent we can invoke the same principle that the last item belongs closely with the verb in such cases: *sehr gut leben* is in some sense a single entity. But this seems less appropriate for *zu jeder Zeit essen*. It should also be noted that a string of adjuncts, such as in the third example of 5.89, is not particularly common; in such cases one of them is likely to be placed at the beginning of the sentence: 'Morgen fährt sie verzweifelt nach Hause'.

It is clear, then, that attempts to explain the intricacies of German word order in terms of syntactic rules are only partly successful, particularly with more peripheral elements of the sentence, such as adjuncts. We shall therefore take up the issue of the ordering of constituents again within a different context (see Chapter 7).

Conclusion

The present discussion of syntax has inevitably been rather limited, the purpose being to consider some of the general principles involved in syntactic analysis rather than to give an exhaustive description of German syntax. Many areas of German have not been considered at all, and no attempt has been made to apply the full range of available theoretical concepts and models to the phenomena. This is not meant to imply that other approaches are not worthwhile or valid, but is simply a reflection of the limited scope of the present book. A satisfactory account of the intricacies of German syntax, and of the theoretical frameworks which can be applied to it, would need several volumes in itself—if indeed it were feasible at all. The reader who wishes to take this discussion further is referred to the suggestions for Further Reading.

FURTHER READING

Syntax (General)

Matthews (1981); Palmer (1991); Tallerman (1998); Van Valin (2001).

German Syntax

Descriptions of the 'facts' of German syntax will be found in any grammar. This list contains works which deal with German syntax from a more theoretical perspective.

Bünting and Bergenholtz (1995); Drosdowski et al. (1995); Dürscheid (2000); Eichler and Bunting (1996); Eisenberg (1999); Eisenberg et al. (1998); Engel (2004); Flämig (1998); Heidolph, Flämig, and Motsch (1981); Helbig (1999); Helbig and Buscha (2001); Hentschel and Weydt (2003); Meibauer et al. (2002: 121–61); Wöllstein-Leisten, Heilmann, Stepan, and Vikner (1997).

Contrastive

Kufner (1962).

Dependency and Valency

Tarvainen (1981); Weber (1992); Eichinger and Eroms (1995); Heringer (1996); Agel (2000).

Generative (General)

Carnie (2002); Freidin (1992); Haegeman (1994); Napoli (1993).

Generative (German)

Boase-Beyer and Lodge (2003: ch. 2); Haegeman (1994: ch. 11); Grewendorf (1991); Toman (1985); Vikner (1995).

EXERCISES AND DISCUSSION QUESTIONS

1. Draw tree diagrams for the following sentences (i) without using labels and (ii) using labels for the constituents, but restricting the categories to S, NP, VP, Det, AP, A, N, AdvP, Adv, Pro, PP, Prep. What difficulties do you encounter in drawing these trees?

   (i) 'Ein sehr großer Vogel sitzt auf dem hohen Baum'
   (ii) 'Ich fahre ziemlich oft in die Schweiz'
   (iii) 'Meine Mutter gibt mir jeden Tag mein Taschengeld'
   (iv) 'Ich kenne den Mann, der dieses Haus gekauft hat'

2. Explain the principles of X-bar syntax. What is the motivation for using this model to describe the structure of phrases in German, and what are its strengths and weaknesses?

3. Draw dependency trees for the sentences of question (1).

4. Identify the functions of the major constituents of the sentences of question (1) (i.e. as subject, direct object, adjunct, etc.).

5. What advantages might there be in using a rule-based generative grammar rather than sentence plans for describing the structure of German sentences?

6. What principles govern the placing of the finite verb in German sentences?

7. Can we draw a clear distinction between syntactic ordering and pragmatic ordering of elements in a German sentence?

6

Lexical Semantics

Introduction

We have so far been concerned primarily with the 'formal' aspects of language: with the various units, categories, structures, rules, etc. in terms of which German may be described. Though we have by no means ignored the meanings of these (some attention was given to the meanings of grammatical categories in Chapter 4, for example), meaning has mostly been kept in the background, in an attempt to focus attention on the forms themselves. The balance will to some extent be redressed in this chapter, where we turn our attention more explicitly to matters of meaning.

The study of meaning in language is called SEMANTICS, though we must be careful with this word, as it is used in several different ways. Semantics is not an easy area of language to delimit or to describe systematically, and until recent years it was rather neglected by linguists. This is partly because of its inherent difficulty, but primarily because some linguists have felt that semantics does not really belong to their subject, since meaning is what language conveys or communicates rather than part of language itself. In addition, the study of meaning is inevitably bound up with 'thoughts', 'perceptions', and 'concepts', which, as unobservable entities, are considered not to be amenable to objective scientific study. Nevertheless, since the communication of meaning is the object and purpose of language, it is evident that linguistics ought to have something to say about it, and more attention has been paid to semantics by linguists in recent years.

Linguists are not the only people with a professional interest in meaning. Philosophers too have found that many of the problems that they face are bound up with the meaning of expressions, and they have devoted considerable attention to this topic. In particular, they have been concerned with the nature of meaning itself, with the relationship between meanings and the expressions which can be said to have these meanings, and with problems of truth and falsehood that arise from these concerns. Linguists have, on the whole, been rather less ambitious, and have contented themselves with exploring *what* expressions can be said to mean rather than with *how* they can be said to mean.

Within the confines of this short chapter we cannot enter into a discussion of the various philosophical problems surrounding meaning, important though they are. We shall also limit our scope still further, focusing only on certain aspects of linguistic meaning at the expense of others. It is clear, for example, that meaning is a property of most linguistic units (other than purely phonetic or phonological ones):[1] sentences, phrases, syntactic constructions, etc. all have meaning. Some of these meanings have already been considered in earlier chapters, and we shall not explore them further here. Instead, we shall limit our field of view primarily to the narrower and more traditional topic of the meaning of *words*, an area which is known as *lexical semantics*.

In considering word meanings we must recall some of the theoretical and practical problems surrounding the 'word' which were discussed in Chapter 3. Not only is 'word' a difficult concept to define, but the term itself is used in several different ways, to cover what we have distinguished as *word form*—an individual phonological and morphological form, such as *liebt, lieben*, etc.— and the *lexeme*—the entity which covers all such word forms belonging to the same inflectional set (the lexeme LIEBEN includes the word forms *liebt, lieben*, etc.). In talking about the meaning of words we are generally considering the meaning of lexemes; the meanings of the various inflections that are found with the word forms of a given lexeme are not generally taken to be aspects of the meaning of the words themselves.

The use of the term 'word' has in earlier chapters been primarily a grammatical one, and the identification of words has been justified mainly in terms of their morphological and syntactic properties: words have a certain morphological shape, and are used in certain ways in the sentence. When we consider the word as a semantic unit (i.e. as a lexeme) further problems arise, since the grammatical 'word' does not necessarily correspond in a simple way to a unit of meaning. This point is easily demonstrated with words such as articles, prepositions, etc. which might be said to have little or no 'meaning' of their own. Thus, a prepositional phrase such as *auf dem Tisch* can be said to consist of three grammatical words, but it does not necessarily follow that there are therefore three 'meanings' here. Similarly, the so-called 'separable' verbs in German—*aufnehmen, hinfahren*, etc.—appear in two different

---

[1] This depends, however, on what we understand by 'meaning'. If we interpret this term in a wide sense, equivalent to 'linguistic function', then it is clear that phonological units also have meaning. But this usage is rather misleading and best avoided.

syntactic shapes, as one word and as two, yet the meaning of such verbs is not altered by this.

A slightly different problem is presented by compound lexemes, such as *Schreibtisch, Regenmantel,* etc. Syntactically speaking, such words are single items, but it may be open to dispute how many meanings are present in such cases. On the other hand, some expressions which appear to consist of more than one lexeme are more appropriately analysed as a single unit of meaning, as in the examples of 6.1.

(6.1)   Ich habe ein Hühnchen mit ihm zu rupfen.
         Sie zieht ihn durch den Kakao.
         Er führt sie an der Nase herum.

These are of course idioms, and their meaning is not to be taken at face value. The expressions *ein Hühnchen rupfen, durch den Kakao ziehen,* and *an der Nase herumführen* would, taken literally, contain more than one lexeme; here this makes little sense, and they are probably best considered as single units of meaning.

From these considerations it will be clear that, although it greatly simplifies the task of describing meaning to restrict the discussion to the word, this in itself raises some problems. We cannot assume that words are actually semantic units, even though the existence of dictionaries, which list words and give their meanings, would imply that this is so. The lexeme, as a unit of lexical meaning, does not always correspond to the word in a grammatical sense.

Apart from the problems of identifying the units of meaning, there are considerable difficulties in describing the meanings themselves. A simple view of the meanings of lexemes is that they *refer* to something. Although it is true, of course, that speakers *are* able to refer to objects, etc. by means of lexemes, this view of meaning as REFERENCE is, as we shall see shortly, much too narrow. As in other areas of language, it is important to see language as a *system,* and, as we have seen elsewhere, the character of the entities within such a system is largely determined by the *relationships* that exist between them. Although lexical meaning is not as highly structured as some other areas of language, such relationships between semantic entities do exist, and they provide a different way of looking at meaning from merely establishing their reference. This aspect of the meaning of lexemes is often called SENSE rather than reference, and lexemes are said to have various kinds of SENSE RELATIONS to one another.[2]

---

[2] It should be noted that this use of the term 'sense' does not quite correspond to its use by philosophers.

Reference

As we have noted, an important semantic characteristic of lexemes is that they refer to something. But what is it that they refer to? A simple, and probably the most natural, view is that they refer to objects, actions, states, etc. in the world in which we live. Thus, there are such things as cats, trees, and cars, and German has the lexemes *Katze, Baum,* and *Auto* to refer to them. Unfortunately, this view, at least if taken literally, can easily be shown to be false, since it is perfectly easy for lexemes to refer to things that do not exist. If lexemes refer to objects, then such lexemes should be impossible or at least meaningless. The objective reality of the objects referred to by *Hexe* or *Riese,* for example, is at best doubtful, yet this clearly does not render these lexemes meaningless. On a more mundane level, it is perfectly possible for an unmarried man to speak of *meine Frau,* or for someone without children to use the expression *mein Sohn.* This again does not make such expressions meaningless, even if their use may be inappropriate.[3]

But if lexemes do not necessarily refer to objects, etc. what *do* they refer to? A plausible alternative is to replace 'object' by 'concept': lexemes do not refer to the world in itself but rather to how we perceive it or conceive of it; they refer to the world of the mind or the senses, not the physical world of objective reality. Thus, though witches may not exist objectively, the concept *witch* does, and hence it is perfectly legitimate for lexemes to refer to it. The concept of *meine Frau* is perfectly plausible for any man, even if he does not have one, and there is thus no problem with having an expression to refer to it.

The 'concept' approach is clearly an advance on the 'object' approach. It also solves a further problem, that different lexemes can refer to the same object but not mean the same thing. A famous example that is always cited in this context is the difference between *morning star* and *evening star*; objectively, the entity referred to is the same (not, in fact, a star, but the planet Venus), but the expressions clearly do not mean the same thing. Coming down to earth once more, we must acknowledge that there is a difference between the meanings of *Frau, Dame,* and *Weib,* though in terms of the particular 'object' referred to we could argue that they mean the same thing. In such cases the distinction between object and concept saves us from the dilemma: the concepts are different, even if the objective reality behind them is not.

But 'concepts', though certainly better than 'objects', are not altogether satisfactory either, as it is difficult to say what we actually mean by a concept,

---

[3] An expression such as *meine Frau* is not necessarily inappropriate for an unmarried man, who may, for example, say 'Wenn ich heirate, wird meine Frau sehr reich sein müssen'.

even if we could actually identify the concepts referred to by the lexemes. Furthermore, though concepts might often be identifiable for nouns to refer to, it is far less easy to think of appropriate concepts for other kinds of words, such as adverbs or adjectives. But in any case, when we attempt to find concepts for our lexemes, we are usually merely trying to conceptualize the meanings of lexemes rather than to identify the concepts themselves. It is thus not clear that 'concepts' can be identified other than as 'meanings', which of course makes the notion of reference completely vacuous: if lexemes refer to concepts, and concepts are meanings, then lexemes simply refer to their meanings. We have not advanced very far.

Given difficulties such as these, which relate to the nature of 'meaning' itself, it is easy to see why the study of meaning has been neglected by linguists and abandoned to philosophers. The kind of problem posed by the nature of reference would seem to lie outside the description of language itself, and beyond the scope of the linguist's enquiry. Nevertheless, we can go a little further, and consider some of the more linguistic questions involved here.

One important consideration for the linguistic analysis of meaning is that lexemes do not exist in isolation from the sentences in which they occur. In analysing the meaning of lexemes, therefore, we must be prepared to look beyond the lexemes themselves, to the contexts (both linguistic and non-linguistic) in which they are uttered. One problem here is that the meaning of a lexeme may vary from one context to another. Consider the examples of 6.2.

(6.2)   (i)   Er setzte sich auf die *Bank.*
              Er ging in die *Bank,* um Geld zu holen.
        (ii) Der Turm leuchtet im *Schein* der Sonne.
              Du musst diesen *Schein* in Münzen umwechseln.

The examples of 6.2(i) both contain the lexeme *Bank,* and those of 6.2(ii) the lexeme *Schein,* but the meaning in each case is very different. What, then, are the meanings of the words *Bank* and *Schein?* Is it possible to identify *the* meaning in each case?

A sensible response to these questions is to distinguish two different lexemes for each word, identical in form but different in meaning. Dictionaries would almost certainly distinguish these different words, e.g. as $Bank_1$ and $Bank_2$, and $Schein_1$ and $Schein_2$. Since these meanings are so different, it makes little sense to regard the word forms as part of the same lexeme. (Note that the historical facts have little or nothing to contribute here; historically, the two lexemes *Bank* have a common source, but that does not prevent us from treating them as different words in modern German.)

But not all cases of contextually determined meaning are quite as clear-cut as this. Consider the examples of 6.3.

(6.3)   Shakespeare war ein *großer* Dramatiker.
         Ich trinke ein *großes* Bier.

Groß has a different significance in the two examples of 6.3, and we could proceed as with *Bank* above, recognizing two lexemes: *groß₁* and *groß₂*. But it is at least arguable that in this case the two interpretations are not as distinct as in the case of *Bank*; they appear to have something in common, and should not be regarded as totally separate meanings. Consider further the examples of 6.4.

(6.4)   (i)   Das Haus steht auf einem festen *Grund.*
         (ii)   Im *Grund* des Tals fließt ein kleiner Bach.
         (iii)   Er hat sein Glas bis auf den *Grund* geleert.
         (iv)   Wir wollen diesem Problem auf den *Grund* gehen.
         (v)   Das Bild hat gelbe Blumen auf einem blauen *Grund.*
         (vi)   Er hat keinen *Grund,* auf mich böse zu sein.

Again the interpretation is slightly different in each case, progressing, one might say, from the purely physical meaning of 'ground' to the more abstract meaning of 'reason'. But how many different meanings should we recognize here? Is *Grund* in the sense of 'bottom' the same meaning in (ii) and (iii), and is this the same as the meaning 'base' in (v)?

Of course, the fact that we might use different English words to translate these various uses of the German *Grund* is not a satisfactory criterion for deciding that these are different meanings, since there is no necessity for the same distinction to be made in different languages. There are numerous examples where English and German differ in this respect. English distinguishes, for example, a *street* from a *road,* and *jam* from *marmalade,* while German has a single lexeme in each case—*Straße* and *Marmelade*—to cover these areas of meaning; English distinguishes a *board* from a *shelf,* German does not: both are *Brett.* Conversely, German distinguishes *Stuhl* from *Sessel,* both of which would be simply a *chair* in English; and where English uses the single lexeme *mouth,* German distinguishes *Mund* (of a person), *Maul* (of an animal), and *Mündung* (of a river). One must beware of assuming that, where German has only one lexeme for two or more in English, the German word must have more than one meaning.

This discussion suggests that we should distinguish cases where one word form corresponds to two (or more) lexemes with different meanings, as in 6.2, from cases where a single lexeme merely has different shades of meaning in different contexts but basically a single meaning. Thus, we might differentiate between cases of genuine *ambiguity* on the one hand and cases of *generality* (sometimes called *vagueness*) on the other. The word *Bank* is clearly ambiguous—there is no general meaning which would cover both interpretations; while the meaning of *Grund* in at least some of the cases of 6.4 could be covered by a single general meaning. But how does one distinguish between the two? One suggested test is that of ambiguity: is the word form ambiguous when contextual clues are removed? In 6.2 the words at issue were illustrated in contexts which make their different meanings clear, but in a sentence such as 'Wo ist die Bank?' the immediate linguistic context is of no help, and the sentence is ambiguous (though of course in actual use the wider linguistic or non-linguistic context would be likely to rule out one interpretation or the other). If the meaning is the same then there should be no ambiguity; we would not wish to say that German *Straße* is ambiguous because it can mean either 'street' or 'road': 'Wo ist die Straße?' does not have two meanings. But the test of ambiguity is not easy to apply, since there may be ambiguities between shades of the 'same' meaning as well as between separate meanings. The meaning of *Grund* when applied to *Tal*, for example, seems close to its meaning when applied to *Glas*, but the question 'Siehst du den Grund?' could still be ambiguous if both *Tal* and *Glas* were present.

Though difficult to draw, the distinction between different meanings of the same lexeme and different lexemes is sufficiently useful for us to introduce some terms to refer to the different types. In the case of *Bank* or *Schein* we might say that there are separate lexemes which happen to sound alike. This is called HOMONYMY: the words are HOMONYMS. But a case such as (at least some of the meanings of) *Grund*, where we could consider that there is a single lexeme with a range of related meanings, is called POLYSEMY ('multiple meaning'). Homonymy, with its potential for ambiguity, may be regarded as an inconvenience for a language (though often exploited for puns by those who are so minded), whereas polysemy, which allows lexemes to take on different shades of meaning in different contexts, is perfectly normal, indeed even essential. As words are used in a variety of contexts, it is necessary for their meanings to be able to be extended to fit new situations, which to some extent redefine the meaning of the word itself. Polysemy is thus a reflection of the essential creativity of speakers in their use of lexemes.

This creativity is at its most striking in cases of *metaphor*, where words are employed in contexts which are in some sense inappropriate. Some examples are given in 6.5.

(6.5)   Sie hat eine sehr *scharfe* Intelligenz.
        Ich *brenne* vor Ungeduld.
        Er ist ein richtiger *Affe*.

The lexemes *scharf, brennen,* and *Affe* are not, of course, intended in their 'real' meanings here, though these real meanings have a part to play in the interpretation of the metaphors. But this is not a case of ambiguity either; the lexeme *Affe* does not have a completely different meaning here from its usual one. The word and its meaning are simply being extended to a different context for expressive and stylistic purposes. Nor is metaphor an exclusively literary device; it is quite common in the normal usage of language, and is a manifestation of the general capacity of language to respond to the needs of communication and expression.

But this range and flexibility in the use of lexemes creates some difficulties for the description of lexical structure, since the 'real' meanings of words are often hard to establish. For dictionary-makers, of course, this is more than a theoretical problem, as the range of meanings must somehow be represented in the dictionary. In general, homonyms tend to be given separate entries in dictionaries, as noted above (*Bank*₁, *Bank*₂, etc.), while cases of polysemy are reflected in a list of meanings for a single entry (*Grund*₁: ground; base; bottom).

By way of exemplification let us consider the meanings of a number of lexemes to see if we can establish what they refer to. (Since we are here appealing to the more subtle aspects of our knowledge of the language, it is probably better to begin with English words before proceeding to a German case.) One way to determine such a meaning is to take a set of related words, so that, in order to delimit their meanings from one another, we are forced to decide exactly which features of their meaning are crucial and which are not.

English has several lexemes to refer to drinking vessels, e.g. *cup, mug, glass,* and *beaker.* In what ways do their meanings differ? *Glass* presumably differs from the others in that it specifically requires the object to be made of a particular material, but it is possible to have a glass cup; why is it not a glass? Unlike a cup, a glass does not have a handle, but then neither does a beaker. A mug is probably felt to be larger than a cup, and in addition it does not usually have a saucer; but is a small mug with a saucer the same as a cup? Is a mug without a handle a beaker?

The reader will doubtless have his or her own answers to some of these questions, but will soon discover from asking others that his or her perceptions about the meanings of the words are not necessarily exactly shared by other speakers of the language. It will also be found that it is not at all easy to decide what criteria are appropriate for delimiting the meaning of a particular word, and that there are marginal cases where a decision is hardly possible at all.

As a further illustration consider the German words for 'seats'. Though the main word that is available here is *Stuhl*, there are several others, notably *Sessel*, *Hocker*, and *Schemel*. (Other possibilities are *Sofa*, *Couch*, and *Bank*, but they differ in that they accommodate more than one sitter.) Of course, these lexemes may be further differentiated if they are turned into compounds: *Lehnstuhl*, *Liegestuhl*. The characteristic feature of both *Hocker* and *Schemel* is that they do not have a back (cf. English *stool*), and of these two *Schemel* is more likely than *Hocker* to be used for the feet. As for *Stuhl* and *Sessel*, the latter is generally softer and more comfortable than the former, and usually has arms. (There is, incidentally, some regional variation here; in Austria *Sessel* is the usual word for a 'chair', corresponding to Standard German *Stuhl*, while the equivalent of Standard German *Sessel* is *Fauteuil*.) But it is interesting to note that the boundary between *Stuhl* and *Sessel* is not very clear. One linguist[4] investigated the use of these words by a variety of speakers, as applied to different styles of seats, and found considerable variation, and even inconsistency. Very few types of seats were consistently designated one or the other by all the speakers, though in many cases the term *Stuhl* was preferred by a majority, and in other cases the term *Sessel*. In general, the more upholstered a chair was, especially if it also had arms, the more likely it was to be called *Sessel*. Straighter, harder, and more upright chairs without arms were more likely to be called *Stuhl*, but there was no clear dividing line between the two.

These attempts to clarify what lexemes refer to could be repeated for many other areas of the vocabulary of English and German, and the results would be the same: though certain major characteristics of the meanings of the lexemes may be reasonably clear, the boundaries between the meanings are frequently imprecise. Our goal of precisely delimiting the meanings of lexemes seems unattainable. In the light of this we could perhaps regard the meaning of a lexeme not as covering a particular piece of the conceptual world but rather as consisting of a fairly well-defined central 'core' of meaning surrounded by a less well-defined periphery. Hence, the boundaries between the lexemes may be fuzzy and imprecise. Alternatively, we could perhaps think of a lexeme as having a 'typical' meaning, which may be applied and adapted in a somewhat ill-fitting way to the conceptual categories of our world. But however we

---

[4] Helmut Gipper (1959), 'Sessel oder Stuhl? Ein Beitrag zur Bestimmung von Wortinhalten im Bereich der Sachkultur' (see References).

choose to view the meanings of lexemes, we cannot escape the conclusion that 'reference' involves more than merely identifying the object or concept to which the word refers.

Sense and Sense Relations

Our discussion of reference will have made it clear that the meanings of lexemes cannot be seen in isolation. On the one hand, words occur in contexts, and it is only through the context that the specific meaning, or shade of meaning, can be determined. On the other hand, lexemes relate to one another in their meanings, and we must take whole sets of lexemes into account in attempting to establish the meaning of any one lexeme.

This dependence of meanings upon contexts and upon one another is hardly surprising. As we have seen before, in phonology, morphology, and syntax language does not just contain isolated elements, but *systems*, consisting of mutually interacting elements, etc. and we should not expect this to be any different for semantics. Here, as elsewhere, the relations among the various items are as important as, if not more important than, the nature of the items themselves. This relational aspect of meaning is of course in conformity with structuralist linguistic theory, as discussed in Chapter 1, and an approach to meaning in these terms is often called *structural semantics*.

But we can go somewhat further in the exploration of lexical relationships than we have done so far. One difficulty with comparing the reference of different lexemes is that generalization is virtually impossible: each lexeme appears to have a virtually unique reference. In order to make general statements about meaning we must look not at the specific reference of lexemes, but rather at the kinds of relationships that exist between the meanings. These general kinds of relationships are usually called *sense relations*. Sense relations can be of several different kinds, and no attempt will be made here to cover all the possibilities. In what follows, however, we shall consider the major types that have been recognized by linguists.

Synonymy

One of the traditional categories of meaning-relation is SYNONYMY, or 'sameness of meaning'; lexemes with the same meaning are said to be SYNONYMS. We could argue, for example, that the pairs of lexemes given in 6.6 fall into this category.

(6.6)   *Orange — Apfelsine*
        automatisch — selbsttätig

gratulieren — beglückwünschen
Telefon — Fernsprecher

Various tests are used to determine which two lexemes are or are not synonymous. In particular, the lexemes can be placed in sentences where sameness or difference of meaning determines whether or not the sentences are acceptable. To test whether *Orange* and *Apfelsine* are synonyms we might, for example, construct sentences such as those of 6.7.

(6.7) (i)   ?Das ist eine Orange und es ist eine Apfelsine.
    (ii)   ?Das ist eine Apfelsine und es ist eine Orange.
    (iii) *Das ist eine Orange, aber es ist eine Apfelsine.
    (iv)   *Das ist eine Apfelsine, aber es ist eine Orange.
    (v)   *Das ist eine Orange, aber keine Apfelsine.
    (vi)   *Das ist eine Apfelsine, aber keine Orange.

Of these sentences, the only ones that make any sense are (i) and (ii), and even here the statements are odd because they are tautologous, i.e. they state what has already been stated. But compare these sentences with those of 6.8, where the lexemes have no such relationship.

(6.8)   Er ist Pianist und er ist Engländer.
    Er ist Engländer und er ist Pianist.
    Er ist Pianist, aber er ist Engländer.
    Er ist Engländer, aber er ist Pianist.
    Er ist Pianist, aber kein Engländer.
    Er ist Engländer, aber kein Pianist.

Given certain assumptions and contexts (for example, if the person concerned is entering for music competitions, some of which are open only to English musicians, and others open only to pianists, etc.), these sentences could all be acceptable.

If we use such sentences to test the relationship between *Frau* and *Dame*, which might also be potential candidates for synonymy, the pattern of acceptability is different again, as in 6.9.

(6.9) (i)   Sie ist eine Frau und sie ist eine Dame.
    (ii)   ?Sie ist eine Dame und sie ist eine Frau.
    (iii) *Sie ist eine Frau, aber sie ist eine Dame.
    (iv)   *Sie ist eine Dame, aber sie ist eine Frau.

(v)   Sie ist eine Frau, aber keine Dame.

(vi) *Sie ist eine Dame, aber keine Frau.

The fact that sentences such as (i) and (v) are perfectly acceptable shows that these lexemes cannot be exact synonyms, though the doubtfulness of (ii), which is tautologous, and the impossibility, or at least improbability, of the others, makes it clear that there are close relationships between the meanings of these lexemes.

Tests such as these show that we can identify lexemes such as *Orange* and *Apfelsine*, but not *Engländer* and *Pianist*, or *Frau* and *Dame*, as synonyms; but we must nevertheless be careful about the nature of this claim, since it is actually extremely doubtful whether even such 'synonymous' pairs are really identical in their meanings. Consider, for example, the lexemes *sterben*, *entschlafen*, and *krepieren*. One cannot distinguish the meanings of these using tests for synonymy of the kind described; a sentence such as '*Er ist entschlafen, aber er ist nicht gestorben' is unacceptable. The point is that such lexemes have the 'same' meaning only if we restrict 'meaning' to 'reference'; they do not mean the same thing if 'meaning' is taken to embrace the stylistic effect of the word. These three lexemes belong to different stylistic levels in the language, and are therefore not interchangeable. We would not expect to hear an official announcement that 'Der Bundespräsident ist in der Nacht krepiert', nor indeed to be told that 'Der Hund ist überfahren worden und ist entschlafen'.

A distinction can be drawn, therefore, between different kinds of meaning. On the one hand there is meaning in the sense of 'what the word refers to', and there is meaning in the sense of 'how the word is used', specifically the stylistic level, the positive or negative implications of the lexemes, and so on. Terminologically, these different kinds of meanings are sometimes distinguished as DENOTATION and CONNOTATION respectively. Thus, the lexemes *sterben*, *entschlafen*, and *krepieren* have the same denotation; they differ in their connotations.

A common source of 'synonyms' in German is the 'Fremdwort', and the pairs of lexemes given in 6.6 involve native and foreign words. But the lexemes of such pairs are seldom without different connotations. Where there is a perfectly acceptable native lexeme, the foreign equivalent may sound learned or pretentious; where the foreign lexeme has become the norm, the native lexeme may sound pedantic. There is also a regional dimension to this question, since 'synonyms' may be forms from different parts of the German-speaking area. Pairs such as *Sessel* — *Fauteuil*, *Kamin* — *Rauchfang*, *Kühlschrank* — *Eiskasten*, *Marille* — *Aprikose*, etc. are of this type. Given this stylistic and regional variety in the use of 'synonyms', it is clear that the specific connotation of a lexeme (as opposed to its denotation) may vary considerably according to the speaker and hearer's own background and status, including social class, regional origin, level of education, and even political or religious convictions. Apart from differences of connotation, lexemes may differ in the degree to which they are or are not synonymous. As we saw above, *Frau* and *Dame* are not synonyms, since it is possible to say 'Sie ist eine Frau, aber keine Dame', but their meanings are obviously very close. We could certainly call them 'near synonyms'. But true or 'absolute' synonyms appear to be rare; where different lexemes exist with apparently the same meaning, they will usually be found on closer examination to have some difference of connotation.

Hyponymy

If we take our examples of *Frau* and *Dame* once more, which we have already found not to be synonymous, we can identify another relationship, that of INCLUSION or, more technically, HYPONYMY. That we can say 'Sie ist eine Frau, aber keine Dame', but not '*Sie ist eine Dame, aber keine Frau', follows from the fact that the meaning of *Dame* is *included* within the meaning of *Frau,* in the sense that the latter has a wider meaning than the former: every *Dame* is a *Frau,* though not every *Frau* is a *Dame,* since *Dame* is a type of *Frau* and not the reverse. The included lexeme is called a HYPONYM of the lexeme which includes it (the SUPERORDINATE): *Dame* is a hyponym of *Frau.*[5]

Many other examples of this relationship can be found. *Hund, Katze,* and *Elefant* are hyponyms of *Tier; rot, blau,* and *gelb* are hyponyms of *farbig; ermorden, hinrichten, erschießen,* and *schlachten* are hyponyms of *töten.* Their status can be tested with sentences such as those used for *Frau* and *Dame;* the formula 'X, aber nicht Y' will be valid as long as X is the superordinate and Y the hyponym, but will be invalid if they are reversed. We thus obtain sentences such as those of 6.10.

(6.10) Das ist ein Tier, aber keine Katze.
  *Das ist eine Katze, aber kein Tier.
  Die Fahne ist farbig, aber nicht gelb.
  *Die Fahne ist gelb, aber nicht farbig.

---

[5] To state that one meaning is 'included' in another may perhaps be misleading, since it might suggest that the included meaning is automatically *implied* by the 'including' one, e.g. that *Dame* includes the meaning of *Frau* since it implies it. This is the reverse of the intended use here, however, where an included meaning is merely *part* of the including one.

Der Polizist hat ihn getötet, aber nicht erschossen.
*Der Polizist hat ihn erschossen, aber nicht getötet.

Lexemes that are hyponyms of some superordinate lexeme may themselves be superordinate with regard to other lexemes, so that there are several levels of hyponymy. Consider the sets of lexemes given in 6.11.

(6.11)   *Tier — Hund — Dogge*
          Pflanze — Blume — Narzisse
          Mensch — Kind — Mädchen

Dogge is a hyponym of *Hund,* which is in turn a hyponym of *Tier.* Furthermore, since there may be more than one hyponym at any level (so-called CO-HYPONYMS), we obtain a branching 'tree' of meanings, as in 6.12.

(6.12)

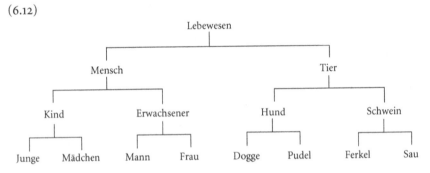

Hyponymy thus reflects a hierarchical principle in lexical structure: meanings can be progressively differentiated to whatever level is appropriate. One common means of obtaining such differentiation is through the morphological process of compounding. Taking the lexeme *Tisch,* for example, we may produce sets of hyponyms such as *Schreibtisch, Esstisch, Arbeitstisch,* etc. while *Tasche* gives us *Aktentasche, Einkaufstasche, Hosentasche,* etc.

As the examples of 6.12 show, hyponyms of a particular superordinate can be established using a variety of different characteristics. For example, *Junge* and *Mädchen* and *Mann* and *Frau,* respectively, are differentiated according to sex; *Ferkel* and *Sau,* on the other hand, according to both sex and maturity (*Ferkel* does not distinguish sex but *Sau* is always female), while *Dogge* and *Pudel* are different varieties or breeds. Thus, no consistent criterion has been employed throughout this particular table. In fact, although it is sometimes possible to find parallels between different parts of the lexical system, this is somewhat exceptional. Consider, for example, the lexemes of 6.13.

(6.13)

The pattern of relationship is the same for each set of lexemes. But it is not always possible to extend this to other parts of the farmyard vocabulary—at least not without resorting to specialized technical vocabulary—as 6.14 shows.

(6.14)

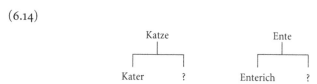

Here there is no specific lexeme for 'female cat' or 'female duck' which is distinct from the superordinate term *Katze* and *Ente*, respectively.[6]

Similarly, if we examine 6.12 once more we shall see that there are both imbalances and gaps in the lexical system. Though *Mensch* and *Tier* are both co-hyponyms of *Lebewesen*, only the former has a distinction between 'immature' and 'mature' (*Kind* and *Erwachsener*). A comparable distinction is found only for *hyponyms* of *Tier* (e.g. *Rind* has *Kalb* and *Schwein* has *Ferkel* as a hyponym), but there are no lexemes meaning 'immature animal' or 'adult animal' as such, apart perhaps from the rather general term *Junges* which is applicable to some animals.

Such imbalances are not peculiar to nouns. Consider the set of lexemes given in 6.15.

(6.15)

Though there is a superordinate verb for various kinds of movement, there is no such term for various ways of being stationary. It is clear, then, that there is little consistency in the hierarchical arrangement of meanings in different parts of the vocabulary.

---

[6] It is, of course, possible to distinguish between the male and female of any animal using terms such as *Männchen* and *Weibchen*, but these are very general terms, and they are not hyponyms of *Katze* or *Ente*.

A further important point is that the same superordinate may have different sets of hyponyms, as illustrated in 6.16.

(6.16)

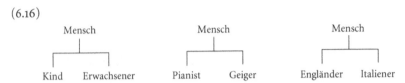

As we saw above (6.8), such co-hyponyms as *Pianist* and *Engländer* are not synonyms, but neither are they in a relationship of hyponymy.

Compatibility and Incompatibility

A further dimension in the relationship between lexical items involves COM-PATIBILITY and INCOMPATIBILITY. Both of these are normally only significant when we are concerned with co-hyponyms with a common superordinate. The former is found where the meanings are not the same, nor is one included in the other, but it is possible for both to be true simultaneously. We have already observed such a case in 6.8 with *Pianist* and *Engländer*; the meanings are essentially independent of each other, but they may overlap since they are not in conflict.

Incompatibility is of more interest; it arises when the meanings are in conflict since they are mutually exclusive. But there are different kinds of incompatibility between two co-hyponyms of a common superordinate. Consider the examples of 6.17.

(6.17)

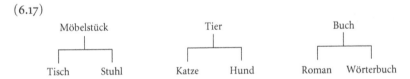

Here the hyponyms are simply mutually exclusive alternatives from a list of possibilities, with no specific relationship between them other than that they share the same superordinate. But this does not apply to the pairs of 6.13, where there is a clear and systematic relationship between the co-hyponyms, the area of meaning covered by the superordinate being divided into two mutually exclusive meanings.

The relationship between the incompatible co-hyponyms is particularly evident in the case of oppositeness of meaning. The pairs of 6.13 could perhaps be regarded as 'opposites' in a loose sense, but it is easier to apply the term to lexemes such as those exemplified in 6.18.

(6.18)   *wahr ~ falsch*
       lang ~ kurz
       heiß ~ kalt
       schön ~ hässlich

Though the members of each pair are opposite in meaning, the relationships are not always exactly the same. With *wahr* and *falsch*, if one is invalid then the other must be valid: *nicht wahr* implies *falsch*, and *nicht falsch* implies *wahr*; it is not possible for any assertion to be neither one nor the other. These words are, furthermore, not GRADABLE, i.e. they cannot usually have variable quantities. One would not normally speak, for example, of a statement as *sehr wahr* or *nicht sehr falsch*, and their comparative forms (*wahrer, falscher*) are odd. The situation is different, however, with *lang* and *kurz*: *nicht lang* does not necessarily imply *kurz*, and *nicht kurz* does not necessarily imply *lang*; something can be *weder lang noch kurz*. These words are also gradable, since we may readily have *sehr lang, kürzer*, etc. The same is true of *heiß* and *kalt*, and *schön* and *hässlich*. Pairs of this latter type are known as ANTONYMS. The term is sometimes taken to include pairs such as *wahr* and *falsch* too, but these are also classed as COMPLEMENTARIES.

But even the pairs of 'true' antonyms are not all identical in their relationships, as we see from the examples of 6.19.

(6.19)   (i)   Es ist lang, aber kürzer als meines.
           Es ist kurz, aber länger als meines.
     (ii) *Es ist schön, aber hässlicher als meines.
           Es ist hässlich, aber schöner als meines.
     (iii) *Es ist heiß, aber kälter als meines.
           *Es ist kalt, aber heißer als meines.

While *kürzer* and *länger* are perfectly appropriate for things that are *lang* and *kurz*, respectively, nothing can be *kälter* if it is *heiß*, nor *heißer* if it is *kalt*. But while *hässlicher* cannot apply to something that is *schön*, it is perfectly possible for something which is *hässlich* to be *schöner* than something else.

It is evident, then, that 'oppositeness' covers a variety of different kinds of relationship. The type to which a particular pair of lexemes belongs is also not necessarily the same in all languages. It has been claimed, for example, that the German pair *gut ~ schlecht* is not quite parallel to the English pair *good ~ bad*: the English pair is like *schön ~ hässlich*, while the German pair is like *lang ~*

kurz. Thus, it is claimed, the English sentence of 6.20 is not acceptable, but the equivalent German sentence is.[7]

(6.20)   *It is good, but worse than mine.
          Es ist gut, aber schlechter als meines.

Semantic Fields

The sense relationships discussed here—mainly synonymy, hyponymy, and antonymy—are merely the most easily identifiable ones, and it is possible to go further and identify still more kinds. But those discussed here do illustrate the general point that the meaning of a lexeme cannot be seen in isolation: it must be viewed in the light of the meanings of other lexemes to which it may be, in a variety of ways, related. Some German linguists have drawn further conclusions from these relationships, by developing the theory of the SEMAN-TIC FIELD. It represents a characteristic attempt to apply the principles of structural linguistics to the vocabulary of the language, drawing on parallels with other, and less intractable, areas of linguistic structure, notably phon-ology and morphology.

One difference between lexical structure and, say, phonology, is that whereas the latter forms a closed system, with a strictly limited set of items, such as phonemes, the former is an open system, where the number of items is in principle unlimited (one can easily add a new lexeme to the language, but only rarely a new phoneme). This means that the structuralist principle, according to which each item in a system defines all the others, is less easy to apply to the lexical system than to the phonological system. The theory of the semantic field, however, allows us to deal with lexical structure more easily, by assuming that the vocabulary may be broken down into a number of areas ('fields') of more limited scope, and within which the mutual relation-ships between the lexemes are comparable to those of phonological units, in that each item can be seen to limit and define the others.

This approach originated with the German linguist Jost Trier, who applied it to the historical study of the German vocabulary, one of his important conclusions being that changes in the vocabulary do not merely affect indi-vidual lexemes but involve the reorganization of the whole field.[8] But some linguists have taken this further, seeing in the concept of the 'word-field', and

---

[7] D. A. Cruse (1986: 219); see Further Reading.
[8] See Further Reading. Trier was concerned specifically with how changes in the vocabulary reflected cultural and social changes in medieval Germany.

the mutual relations between the lexemes within it, a reflection of how speakers of a particular language view the world, the structure of the field being the result of the speakers' 'wording of the world' ('Worten der Welt').[9]

Since such a 'wording of the world' is the product of a particular culture, we could expect it to be different in different cultures. We would also expect the differences to be more obvious in areas of human belief, perception, understanding, etc. where these cultural factors have more scope than in the area of the natural, objective world. Not surprisingly, therefore, Trier's original work in this area was on the semantic field of 'knowledge'. But the principles have also been applied more widely, to other areas of human activity.

As an illustration, let us consider the German verbs concerned with the causation or organization of various kinds of events.[10] There are various German verbs which can be regarded as covering the semantic field of 'occurrence': *geschehen, sich ereignen, sich abspielen, stattfinden, erfolgen*, etc. These differ in their applicability to different events: natural events (volcanic eruptions, earthquakes, etc.) *ereignen sich*, but those requiring human agency (meetings, lectures, parties, etc.) *finden statt*. A related semantic field is concerned with causing things to happen in this latter sense: verbs such as *abhalten, veranstalten, halten, unternehmen, vornehmen, durchführen*.

Let us now consider the differences in the meanings of these last lexemes. Some typical frames into which they can be inserted are given in 6.21 (see n. 10).

(6.21)　eine Versammlung wird *abgehalten*
　　　　　ein Vortrag wird *gehalten*
　　　　　eine Ausstellung wird *veranstaltet*
　　　　　eine Reise wird *unternommen*
　　　　　eine Eröffnung wird *vorgenommen*
　　　　　ein Prozess wird *durchgeführt*

Typically, *abhalten* is used for meetings, courses, examinations, etc. which have a fixed time and plan; *veranstalten* is used for festivals, concerts, etc. involving a certain amount of organization; *halten* applies to official events, such as ceremonies; *unternehmen* is used for journeys, trips, etc. where the participants are intimately involved with the activity; *vornehmen* is more impersonal, used for events from which the participants maintain a certain

---

[9] This approach is especially associated with Leo Weisgerber's *Vom Weltbild der deutschen Sprache*. (See References.)

[10] This example is taken from Leo Weisgerber, 'Zur innersprachlichen Umgrenzung der Wortfelder'. (See References.)

objective aloofness; *durchführen* lays stress on the goal of the activity. In this way we can say that this particular field is divided up among the participant lexemes, each defining the scope of the others.

Thus far there is perhaps little to take issue with, but further, rather more controversial, claims have also been made. It has been asserted, for example, that the meanings within a particular field exactly cover it, with no gaps or overlaps, the boundaries between the meanings being clear-cut. But, as we have seen, such gaps and overlaps are by no means impossible; the boundaries of meaning are often fuzzy. These claims about the structure of the fields therefore seem to be too strong.

There is, furthermore, a problem with the identification of the fields themselves. If the principle of a limited set of mutually defining meanings is valid, then we would expect such a set to be easily identifiable. But the area of meaning which constitutes the field is not always easily delimitable. A glance at a thesaurus[11] will show that areas of meaning are not particularly well defined, but merge into one another.

Although the concept of the semantic field seems an attractive one, therefore, allowing us to isolate parts of the vocabulary and analyse them in terms of the mutual relationships of their component parts, it creates some fundamental theoretical problems. The objection is not that it views meaning as derived from relationships between lexemes, but rather that the notion of the 'field' itself is suspect—partly because fields are not readily separable from one another, and partly because the relationships found between lexemes are often more elaborate than is presumed by this theory.

In terms of our previous discussion, we could perhaps say that a semantic field is a set of lexemes sharing a common superordinate (though, as we have seen, there may be a gap where the superordinate would be). But we have seen not only that there may be a hierarchy of hyponymy but also that lexemes may have several sets of overlapping hyponyms. This means that a simple model of the vocabulary as consisting of a number of separate, non-overlapping fields, each structured into a set of non-overlapping meanings, is unrealistic.

Componential Analysis

A major difficulty that will have become evident in our attempts to describe the complexities of lexical structure is that meanings do not merely exist as a set of neatly delimitable entities, perhaps in the way that we might view a

---

[11] A dictionary in which words are arranged under meanings. The best-known one for English is that of Roget; for German there is, for example, that of Dornseiff (see References).

system of phonemes, cases, tenses, etc. These meanings are related to one another in various ways, and the relationships are not of a simple kind. We might think, therefore, that attempts to draw parallels with, say, phonology, with its limited set of distinctive units, are inappropriate. However, it will be recalled from our consideration of phonological matters in Chapter 2 that it is not necessarily satisfactory to see phonology in these simple terms either, since phonemes too have a variety of different relationships to one another. We can therefore attempt to take our phonological parallel still further.

One significant characteristic of the relationships between phonemes is that they involve a *cross-classification* rather than merely a *subclassification*. In other words, although we might divide phonemes into types (e.g. consonants and vowels) and then proceed to divide the types into subtypes (e.g. stops, fricatives, nasals, or front and back vowels), and these into still smaller groups (e.g. voiced stops, voiceless stops, voiced fricatives, voiceless fricatives, etc.), such a classification is not entirely satisfactory, since generalizations about the characteristics of these phonemes, and rules which describe the various processes that they undergo, will frequently need to cut across these categories. Some characteristics are shared by stops, others by voiced consonants, some by close vowels, others by rounded vowels, and so on.

For the description of such intersecting properties it has been found useful to regard the phonological units (phonemes) as consisting of a number of distinctive features, as discussed in Chapter 2. Each phoneme thus constitutes a specific combination of these features: in terms of one established set of such features, /b/ is [+anterior, −coronal, −continuant, +voice], and so on.

A parallel situation can be recognized in semantics. Using the principle of hyponymy it is possible to relate the meanings of lexemes to one another in the form of a branching tree, as in 6.12, but this does not quite encompass the relationships between the various meanings, since it ignores the nature of the relationships between the various branches. In 6.12 the relationship between the hyponyms of *Kind* and *Erwachsener* is parallel (and the same relationship is found between the pairs of hyponyms given in 6.13), but the relationship between the hyponyms of *Hund* and *Schwein* is of a different kind. A branching tree is thus not the best way of accommodating these relationships. An obvious solution is to devise a descriptive technique which is parallel to that used in distinctive-feature theory in phonology: to regard the meanings of lexemes as composed of a number of simultaneous characteristics. Such characteristics are known as SEMANTIC COMPONENTS, and the analysis of meanings in these terms is COMPONENTIAL ANALYSIS.

As in phonological analysis, we are concerned with characteristics which determine whether the items concerned are the same or different, and hence we can express these components as features with the values + or −. For example, we may say that *Baum, Katze,* and *Mensch* differ from *Stein* in being [+living]; *Katze* and *Mensch* are [+animate], while *Baum* is [-animate]; *Mensch* is [+human], while *Katze* is [−human]. We thus obtain a matrix of meaning components as in 6.22.

(6.22)	[living]	[animate]	[human]
Stein	−	−	−
Baum	+	←	−
Katze	+	+	−
Mensch	+	+	+

Similarly, 6.23 gives a matrix for a number of other lexemes.

(6.23)	[human]	[bovine]	[adult]	[male][12]
Mann	+	−	+	+
Frau	+	−	+	−
Kind	+	−	−	
Junge	+	−	−	+
Mädchen	+	−	−	−
Bulle	−	+	+	+
Kuh	−	+	+	−
Kalb	−	+	−	

In these terms therefore, the meaning of *Mädchen* can be represented as [+living, +animate, +human, −adult, −male].

As with phonological features, such concepts as 'redundancy' and 'neutralization' can be employed. *Stein* is [−animate] and [−human], but these features are redundant, so do not need to be specified: anything which is [−living] *must* be [−animate] and anything which is [−animate] *must* be [−human].[13] Similarly, the feature [−bovine] does not need to be specified for *Mädchen*, since it is implicit in [+human]. *Junge ~ Mädchen* and *Bulle ~ Kuh* are [+male] ~ [−male] respectively, but this feature is neutralized for *Kind* and *Kalb* (and is left blank for these lexemes in the matrix of 6.23).

These examples suggest that a semantic description of the lexical units of German using components of this kind can provide a representation of the

---

[12] This feature could, of course, with equal justification be [female] (in which case the values would be reversed), though there is some evidence that German, like many other languages, treats male forms as 'unmarked', e.g. with agentive nouns such as *Lehrer ~ Lehrer + in.* See also Ch. 4, n. 14.

[13] This is not strictly true, as presumably a corpse is still [+human] even though it is no longer [+living]. The features for these meanings should evidently be a little more elaborate than those given here.

meanings of lexemes which is comparable to a distinctive-feature representation of phonemes. But matters are unfortunately not quite as simple as this. In the first place, semantic properties of words are not as easy to identify and isolate as phonetic properties of phonemes, as we have seen in our discussion of *cup*, etc. in English and of *Stuhl* and *Sessel* in German. More importantly, it is not quite as convincing to see the meanings of words as combinations of semantic features as it is to see phonemes as combinations of phonological features.

To exemplify some of the problems involved here, let us examine the components required to specify the semantic field of 'kinship' in German, i.e. the field containing lexemes referring to family relationships. This field has a clear structure, involving a number of different dimensions; each person has a *Vater* and a *Mutter*, a *Großvater* and a *Großmutter*, an *Urgroßvater* and an *Urgroßmutter*, and so on, and may have a *Sohn* and a *Tochter*, an *Enkel* and an *Enkelin*, an *Urenkel* and an *Urenkelin*, and so on. There are also collateral relationships such as *Bruder* and *Schwester*, *Onkel* and *Tante*, *Neffe* and *Nichte*, as well as relationships by marriage: *Schwager*, *Schwägerin*, *Schwiegervater*, *Schwiegermutter*, *Schwiegersohn*, and *Schwiegertochter*.

Apart from the feature [± male] (or [± female]), which runs through the whole system, we need features to deal with these other dimensions. But features such as [± child] and [± parent] are not enough, since we must specify whose child or parent the individual is. Similarly, the components [+related by marriage] (which is the meaning of *Schwieger-*) and [+sibling] can only be interpreted in relation to other components. The combination [+sibling, +child, +male, +related by marriage], for example, could have different interpretations according to the order in which the features are taken. It could be my nephew's wife (my sibling's male child's spouse), or perhaps the brother or sister of my daughter-in-law (my male child's spouse's sibling).

Further problems are caused by the different kinds of antonyms (opposites) discussed earlier, since, as we saw, the relationship between the lexemes of the various pairs may not be quite the same. The pair *tot* ~ *lebendig* can be covered by a single feature [± living], since the one implies the other, but *lang* ~ *kurz* demands two features, [± long], [± short], since it is possible for something to be [−long] and [−short] simultaneously. But the real problems are created by the comparatives, since although *heißer* implies [+hot], *länger* does not imply [+long]. It is difficult to see how all these various characteristics of the meaning of the lexemes can be covered by a set of semantic components.

It would also appear that an approach through components works better for some aspects of the vocabulary than for others. Certain aspects of meaning, such as living ~ non-living and human ~ non-human, seem to be quite important for a substantial part of the vocabulary, and may in fact also be accorded some grammatical status (in English, for example, living things are referred to by different pronouns from non-living ones). In all languages there are restrictions on possible combinations of lexemes involving such features: a sentence such as '*Das Buch trinkt Bier*', for example, is semantically unacceptable, except in some metaphorical sense. Other characteristics of meanings are more localized than these, however: the component of meaning which differentiates *Stuhl* from *Sessel*, for example, is unlikely to recur in any other part of the vocabulary. A distinction has been made by some linguists, therefore, between these two kinds of components, the former being called CLASSEMES, the latter SEMEMES. Whether it is actually possible to draw this distinction consistently is rather doubtful, but if it is, then we may note that it is those areas of the vocabulary where classemes are involved that are more readily analysable in terms of components; the areas which involve sememes are more difficult since the definition of sememes is, as we have seen, often difficult to make precise. Indeed, in some parts of the vocabulary the use of components does not seem to be very helpful. The lexeme *Elefant*, for example, though it may be distinguished by classemes such as [+animate, −human], will still need a sememe such as [+elephantine] to characterize it adequately, and it is not clear how such a meaning is a component at all, and not simply the meaning of the lexeme.

One final difficulty that may be mentioned is the *universality* of semantic components. The distinctive features used in phonology are sufficiently restricted to be regarded as universal in the sense that we may assume a limited number of phonetic characteristics of phonemes that are available to languages, and which ultimately derive from the physiology and acoustics of speaking. We have tacitly assumed this to be the case for semantic components, too, by using English labels (e.g. [± long]) to describe the meanings of German words. But even if a considerable number of meanings are common to the vocabularies of languages, especially those used by societies with a similar cultural tradition, the differences between languages in this respect are still considerable. Again, general features of the 'classeme' type are likely to be more widely used than the more specific 'sememes'. Universality seems less plausible in semantics, therefore, than in phonology.

Conclusion

From our discussion of lexical semantics in this chapter it will be evident that the investigation of lexical structure is a complex and difficult matter, and the misgivings of linguists that their methods can be extended into this field may appear to have some justification. Nevertheless, it is also clear that the vocabulary of German, as of other languages, is not without structure; there is ample evidence for systematic relationships between lexemes, in particular sense relations such as those discussed in this chapter. What is less demonstrable, however, is that such systematic relations are sufficient to account for the whole of lexical meaning. Indeed, attempts to embrace lexical structure within such general frameworks as the theory of the 'semantic field', or 'componential analysis', seem to founder upon the complexities involved and on the imbalances, irregularities, and idiosyncrasies which characterize this part of the structure of language.

FURTHER READING

General

Cruse (1986); Hurford and Heasley (1983); Kempson (1977); Lyons (1977, 1995); Palmer (1981).

German

Blanke (1973); Boase-Beier and Lodge (2003: ch. 6); Geckeler (1982); Herbst, Heath, and Dederding (1979: ch. 8); Leisi (1975); Löbner (2003); Lutzeier (1985); Philipp (1998); Schaff and Klaus (1997); Schwarz and Chur (2001); Wunderlich (1998).

Semantic Fields

Hoberg (1970); Lutzeier (1993); Schmidt (1973); Trier (1931).

EXERCISES AND DISCUSSION QUESTIONS

1. Attempt to find criteria to distinguish the meanings of the words in the following set: *Buch, Zeitschrift, Zeitung, Broschüre, Prospekt, Akte, Heft.*
2. Determine whether the following pairs of words are cases of *homonymy* or *polysemy*: *Boden* (1 = floor, 2 = ground, 3 = soil); *Brett* (1 = board, 2 = shelf); *Hut* (1 = hat, 2 = protection); *schwer* (1 = heavy, 2 = difficult); *Gang* (1 = passageway, 2 = walk, gait). What criteria can one use to decide and how reliable are they?
3. Draw a tree to establish the *hyponyms, co-hyponyms,* and *superordinates* in the following set of words: *Kleid, Hose, Unterhose, Kleidungsstück, Schuh, Stiefel, Schuhwerk, Sandale, Pantoffel, Strumpf.*

4. Explain what is meant by a *semantic field*. Using the words given in question 3 as an example, discuss the usefulness and limitations of this concept in the description of the field of *Kleidung* in German.

5. Attempt to devise a set of semantic components to cover the meanings of the following German words: *Mann, Frau, Kind, Tier, Katze, Hund, Baum, Pflanze, Kohle, Stahl*. Do you consider that it would be possible to devise a set of components to cover the whole of German vocabulary? Give reasons for your answer.

7

German in Use

Introduction

The theme of this book is, as the title asserts, the *structure* of German. Our analysis of the language so far has therefore focused on this structure: the various units—phonemes, morphemes, words, etc.—and the way in which they fit together to form larger entities, the largest of which is the sentence. In our discussion of the complexities of this structure, we have explicitly excluded the way in which the language is actually *used* by speakers of the language, an area of linguistic study that, as we observed in Chapter 1, goes by the name of *pragmatics*.

However, we cannot disregard the use of German entirely, even if this were desirable, since sentences do not exist by themselves, but only as part of the communicative activity in which the speaker/writer and hearer/reader are engaged. What is more, many aspects of this communicative activity are relevant even for the description of the individual sentences since, as we shall see, they are reflected in the structure and organization of the sentence itself. We must therefore turn our attention to the sentence from a different perspective: not primarily as a grammatical unit, whose structure can be described in terms of the categories and methods outlined in Chapter 5, but rather as an UTTERANCE, a unit in the process of communication. In some respects, too, we must go beyond the sentence/utterance to larger pieces of language, such as 'dialogues', 'conversations', 'texts', etc. all of which can be grouped together as 'discourse'.[1]

Pragmatics is a very broad subject, potentially involving all aspects of language use, including the relationship between the utterance, the speaker (writer), the hearer (reader), and the situation in which the utterance is used. Since our concern is primarily with the structure of sentences and utterances, we shall not consider all of these areas, but rather concentrate on those aspects

---

[1] The scope of these different terms is somewhat variable, and writers on the subject define them differently. We shall not attempt definitions here.

of pragmatics that are concerned with the way in which features of the contexts where utterances are used impinge upon the structure and interpretation of the utterances themselves. However, it is not necessarily easy to isolate such factors, in part because more may be communicated than is actually said; much may be 'understood' rather than expressed, and the distinction between the features of the utterance and those of the context may be difficult to draw.

In any case, we must clearly broaden our perspective and our framework beyond the purely grammatical aspects of sentences that we have considered in Chapter 5. Although utterances, as part of communication, cannot necessarily be described in purely grammatical terms, it is evident that their features are not random or arbitrary; they are systematic, and still part of the structure of the language. However the nature of this structure, and the organization of utterances, inevitably involve rather different concepts and categories from those used hitherto, and it is naturally a moot point where linguistic analysis stops and other disciplines, such as sociology, philosophy, psychology, or literary study, take over.

In the remainder of this chapter we shall consider a number of topics that are concerned with utterances as part of communication: the structure of utterances, the role of utterances in context, the nature of the act of speaking itself, and the structure of conversation.

The Structure of Utterances

In Chapter 5 we examined the ways in which the structure of the sentence can be described in terms of constituents, their relationships, and their functions. There are, however, other dimensions that must be taken into account when we consider the sentence as an *utterance*, some of which have been touched on in previous chapters.

'Pragmatic Ordering'

In Chapter 5 the ordering of sentence constituents in the German sentence was considered. While the order of some of the constituents of the sentence—notably the verb—is relatively fixed ('syntactic ordering'), in other cases we observed there is some variability, and, though there may be a 'preferred' or 'normal' order, there are different possibilities. This was called 'pragmatic ordering', since the ordering in these cases is not determined strictly by syntactic rules but by the role they play in the act of communication: for example, the particular emphasis required, what has been said before, and so on. We must now consider some of the factors involved here.

One of these factors relates to the relative importance or 'weight' of the sentence constituents in the context in question. This notion of 'weight' is difficult to make precise, but it is clear that the speaker may wish to give more emphasis to one constituent than another, depending on what has gone before, what is assumed, etc. The general principle that appears to be at work in many cases is that 'weightier' elements are placed after less 'weighty' ones, which often means that the weightiest item in the utterance will be placed as near as possible to the end. Consider one of the examples used in Chapter 5, and repeated here as 7.1.

(7.1) (i) Mein Vater kaufte vor zwei Wochen ein neues Auto.
       (ii) Mein Vater kaufte ein neues Auto vor zwei Wochen.

Though sentence (i) of 7.1 may be regarded as the more 'correct' version (though a version with 'vor zwei Wochen' at the beginning of the sentence might be more natural), sentence (ii) could also be used where the phrase *vor zwei Wochen* is particularly emphasized, or is more significant than *ein neues Auto*. Thus, in the dialogue of 7.2 the question already mentions *Auto*, which is therefore of less importance for the answer, and the main communicative point of this answer lies in *vor zwei Wochen*.

(7.2) A: Hat dein Vater je ein neues Auto gekauft?
       B: Mein Vater hat ein neues Auto vor zwei Wochen gekauft.
          (or: Ein neues Auto hat mein Vater vor zwei Wochen gekauft.)[2]

This principle means that the weightiest position in the sentence is at the end, and the main point of the utterance will tend to be found there, though this excludes any verbal element which occurs in final position for purely syntactic reasons (such as *gekauft* in 7.2); such elements may be communicatively quite weak.

In cases such as 7.2(B) the basic principles of syntactic ordering allow scope for pragmatic variation. In some cases, however, pragmatic ordering goes further, and can apparently override the syntactic principles themselves. One example of this is with the 'frame' construction. As we noted in Chapter 5, complex predicators are regularly split into two parts, with the non-finite part occurring at the end ('ich *habe* das Buch *gelesen*', 'das Haus *ist* auf dem Land *gebaut worden*'), forming the 'frame' construction ('Satzrahmen' or

---

[2] A further method of adding emphasis to an element in the sentence is to give it the main 'sentence stress'. This will be discussed below; for the moment we are considering only differences of word order.

'Satzklammer'). This 'rule' is not always observed, however, and sentences such as those given in 7.3 are quite common.

(7.3)   Ich habe Glück gehabt in meinen Prüfungen.
         Der Student musste nach Hause fahren wegen seiner Mutter.

This type of construction, in which the frame is brought prematurely to an end, leaving an element or elements outside it, is called 'Ausrahmung' or 'Ausklammerung'. The motivation for this is again to be found in pragmatic considerations. Since the sentence is not just a syntactic unit, but is also a communicative entity (an 'utterance'), the frame, which encloses and combines the elements of the sentence into a syntactic whole, also integrates them into a communicative whole. Putting elements outside the frame, as in the examples of 7.3, therefore has the effect of giving them a degree of communicative, as well as syntactic, independence; it effectively breaks the sentence into two communicative units. As we shall see, this is also often reflected in other characteristics of the utterance, in particular intonation (see Chapter 2), since it is common for the utterance to be broken into two intonation units in such cases as well. (We shall consider this role of intonation further below.)

Cases such as this, where syntactic rules are apparently broken for communicative purposes, raise some very general questions. If rules can be broken, in what sense are they rules? One could argue, of course, that such cases are exceptional, and therefore do not affect the validity of the rules. This is generally the attitude which dominates language-teaching; learners would probably have sentences such as those of 7.3 marked wrong if they included them in their translations or essays. On the other hand, one could argue that such sentences are in fact perfectly regular if we are prepared to take into account factors other than the purely syntactic. From this point of view no rule is broken here, since our original rule, which prescribes the frame in all cases, is wrongly stated.

A more general point relates to the concept of 'normal' word order in German sentences. Many grammar books describe German syntax in terms of such a normal order, adding a further section on 'abnormal' or 'emphatic' ordering. Normal order would involve, for example, having the subject in first position in declarative sentences, any other element in this position being treated as exceptional or emphatic. While it is certainly true that such an order is frequent, it must nevertheless be pointed out that it is 'normal' only under specific circumstances, which usually means when the sentence is uttered in isolation and out of context—a rather abnormal use of language.

It is possible to go further than this in exploring the pragmatic role of ordering in syntactic structure. Not only may the constituents of the sentence be ordered differently in order to achieve particular 'weighting', but the choice of structure for the sentence as a whole may be determined by such considerations. Consider the examples of 7.4.

(7.4) (i)   Hans hat rote Rosen an seine Frau geschickt.
     (ii) Rote Rosen wurden von Hans an seine Frau geschickt.
     (iii) Es war Hans, der rote Rosen an seine Frau geschickt hat.
     (iv) Es waren rote Rosen, die Hans an seine Frau geschickt hat.
     (v)   Es war seine Frau, an die Hans rote Rosen geschickt hat.

There is a sense in which all these sentences mean the same: the basic action described (that Hans sent his wife red roses) is constant throughout, but the structure of the sentence varies, not simply in the *order* in which the elements are presented but also in the *manner* in which they are presented. If sentence (i) is regarded as the 'normal' way of presenting the information, sentence (ii) (the passive) changes the construction so that the direct object of (i) is now the subject, reversing the priorities, as it were, while sentences (iii), (iv), and (v) use a different structure, in which an item is first isolated and the remainder of the sentence expands on it with a further clause. Though the differences in pragmatic effect may be difficult to define, it is certainly clear that, pragmatically speaking, these sentences do *not* mean the same thing, but give different weight, and a different communicative perspective, to the basic action described.

Thematic Structure

Utterances are generally 'about' something, otherwise there would usually be no point in uttering them.[3] It has been suggested that, alongside the normal syntactic division of a sentence into subject and predicate, there is a communicative division into what the utterance is 'about' on the one hand, and what is said about it on the other. Terms that are current for these categories are TOPIC and COMMENT, or alternatively THEME and RHEME. However, there are different ways of defining these terms; some regard topic and theme as synonymous, others distinguish them. Here we are not interested in definitions as such, but rather in what lies behind the categories themselves.

If the topic/theme is what the utterance is 'about', what does this mean, and how do we identify it? First, we must distinguish between what a 'text', 'discourse', etc. is about and what a particular utterance is about. This book,

---

[3] This assertion must be qualified somewhat, since certain types of utterance—so called 'phatic' utterances, such as greetings—are not intended to be 'about' anything, but merely serve to 'lubricate' the conversation, as it were.

for example, is about the structure of German; this section is about thematic structure; but this is not what is at issue here. The question of 'aboutness' (this term is, in fact, used to identify this particular problem) is a more local one, relating specifically to the organization of an utterance, sentence, or clause. Thus, the sentence 'Mein Vater hat einen grauen Bart' could reasonably be said to be about 'mein Vater'.

Because of the ambiguity of the term 'topic', it may be preferable to refer instead to the *theme* of the utterance. However, again there are ambiguities here. In addition to the definition of the theme as 'what the sentence/ utterance is about', it has also been described as the 'starting point' or the 'centre of attention' of the sentence. Consider the examples of 7.5.

(7.5)   (i)   Meine Mutter—ist 85 Jahre alt.
         (ii)   Diesen Mann—kenne ich seit zwanzig Jahren.
         (iii) Morgen—fährt er nach Berlin.

In these examples we can identify an element—separated from the rest of the utterance by a dash—which can be said to be 'what the utterance is about'. Sentence (i) of 7.5 is about *meine Mutter,* sentence (ii) about *diesen Mann,* and sentence (iii) about what will happen *morgen*. It will be noted that it is only on the first example that the division corresponds to the subject–predicate division discussed in Chapter 5, making it clear that what we are concerned with here is a separate dimension of structure.

These examples also justify the claim that the theme is the 'starting point' of the sentence, since in each case the speaker first identifies what is being talked about and then says something about it. For some, then, the theme is always the first element in the utterance. German has considerable scope for varying what is placed in this position—more than in English—and we can argue that the choice is motivated by what is taken to be the theme in individual cases.

Communication is a *dynamic* process: each utterance is made in the context of what has gone before. An utterance will therefore frequently take up as its theme something from a previous utterance and develop it. This is illustrated in the text given in 7.6.

(7.6)   Die moderne Prosa beginnt mit Proust, aber seinem ersten Buch war das noch nicht anzumerken. *Es* erschien Mitte Juni 1896 und enthielt eine Reihe von Prosastücken. *Die meisten davon* waren bereits in kurzlebigen Zeitschriften seiner Freunde veröffentlicht.

In the second and third sentences of this text an element (here italicized) is taken from the preceding sentence and developed: *es* in the second sentence develops *Buch* from the first, while *die meisten davon* in the third takes up *Prosastücke* from the second. This principle of THEMATIC PROGRESSION ensures the continuity of the text, which develops in an orderly fashion. In each case the theme is placed at the beginning of the sentence, where it links up with the previous sentence. The text of 7.6 also illustrates the clear difference between 'discourse theme' and 'sentence/utterance theme'; the former is constant, applying to the text as a whole, while the latter varies from sentence to sentence.

The concept of the theme as the 'starting point' is not always so applicable, however. Consider the sentences of 7.7.

(7.7)   (i)   Jetzt fahren wir los.
        (ii)   Da kommt er schon.
        (iii) Es regnet wieder.

Though we might just accept that in 7.7 sentence (i) is in some sense about what is happening *jetzt,* it is difficult to argue that sentence (ii) is about *da,* and still less easy to believe that sentence (iii) is about *es.* It is evident, therefore, that if the theme is the first element in the sentence then it cannot be what the sentence is 'about'. And if the theme is not the first element, then how do we identify it?

One way of identifying the theme in the sentence/utterance is to use the phrase 'as for X' (or, in German, 'Was X betrifft, …'). Thus, the sentences of 7.5 could all be rephrased in this way to give those of 7.8.

(7.8)   (i)   Was meine Mutter betrifft—sie ist 85 Jahre alt.
        (ii)   Was diesen Mann betrifft—den kenne ich seit zwanzig Jahren.
        (iii) Was morgen betrifft—da fährt er nach Berlin.

An interesting effect of applying this test is that the theme that we identify may not even be in the sentence at all. The third example of 7.8 could equally well be rephrased as 'Was den Plan betrifft—morgen fährt er nach Berlin.' This is a case which might justify a distinction between 'theme' and 'topic': if *der Plan* is the theme, then *morgen* could be regarded as the topic of the utterance. But there is naturally a problem in identifying an element of the utterance which is not actually present in its structure.

A final way in which the theme can be defined is as the 'centre of attention' of the utterance. The idea is that this is the item that the speaker 'is thinking of'—it is also called the 'psychological subject'.[4] The difficulty here is that we cannot know what the speaker is thinking of and there are no criteria for identifying the theme in this sense, other than the other criteria that we have mentioned: what the sentence is about and what comes first.

In spite of all these difficulties of definition and of identification, the idea that utterances are 'about' something, that an utterance is a part of a dynamic act of communication, and that this is reflected in the way the utterance is structured, seems valid enough, and justifies our recognition of categories such as 'theme' or 'topic'. As we shall see, there are also other ways in which this dimension can be described.

Information Structure

An utterance can be said to convey information (in a fairly wide sense of this term) to the hearer, but the hearer is not completely ignorant of everything that is relevant for interpreting what is said. He or she knows, for example, that I am talking, that I am sitting here, that it is Wednesday, that he has just asked me to pass the salt, that he is my father, and so on. Thus, some aspects of the situation are known in advance, and though my utterance may provide something new, it will also reflect this prior knowledge. If I say 'Where is it?', for example, the identity of 'it' must have been established beforehand if the utterance is to have any meaning at all.

The 'same' sentence may also have different communicative significance according to what is, and what is not, known, and in particular what is provided by the context. Take, for example, the sentence 'Herr Müller fährt morgen nach Hamburg'. We might imagine a range of circumstances when this sentence might be uttered, as a response to a variety of previous utterances, or to none at all. The speaker may have been asked 'Wer fährt morgen nach Hamburg?', 'Wann fährt Herr Müller nach Hamburg?', 'Wohin fährt Herr Müller morgen?', or, more generally, 'Was geschieht morgen?', 'Was ist der Plan?', and so on. Each of these questions provides information which is then assumed to be known, and it is clear, therefore, that what is new in the reply 'Herr Müller fährt morgen nach Hamburg' will vary from case to case. This sentence may also be unsolicited, uttered as the speaker enters the room, for example, in which case much of it will be new (though not everything: unless we know who Herr Müller is and have heard of Hamburg, the sentence will not make much sense to us).

---

[4] A distinction is sometimes made between the 'grammatical subject', the 'logical subject', and the 'psychological subject'. The first is a purely syntactic matter; the second refers to the 'doer of the action'; and the last to the 'theme' in the sense discussed here.

We can therefore distinguish between two kinds of information in the utterance: what is NEW and what is GIVEN, that is, what is being communicated as opposed to what is assumed to be already known by the listener. The difference between these does not merely affect how we interpret the utterance, but may also be reflected in its structure. Parts of a sentence may often be omitted, but this happens, of course, only if they are already given. The answer to 'Wohin fährt Herr Müller morgen?' may well be simply 'Nach Hamburg', omitting all the given information contained in the question. But not everything that is given can or needs to be omitted. We might equally well reply 'Er fährt nach Hamburg', replacing the noun phrase *Herr Müller* by the pronoun *er*, which refers back to it.

This principle is also relevant for the notion of thematic structure discussed above. As we have seen, in many cases the 'theme' can refer back to a previous sentence. In fact, it is quite common for the initial position to be occupied by a given element, and rare for it to be new. Consider the dialogues of 7.9.

(7.9) (i) A: Was hat sie ihm zum Geburtstag geschenkt?
           B: Zum Geburtstag hat sie ihm ein Buch geschenkt.
    (ii) A: Wird sie ihm zu Weihnachten ein Buch schenken?
           B: Nein. Ein Buch hat sie ihm zum Geburtstag geschenkt.

In each case speaker B takes up a given element from speaker A's question and puts it in initial position, as the 'theme' of the answer. But it is clear that speaker B is not required to do this; the answers to speaker A's enquiries in 7.9 (i) and (ii) could also be those given in 7.10 (i) and (ii), respectively (though B would not usually repeat the given elements).

(7.10) (i) A: Was hat sie ihm zum Geburtstag geschenkt?
        B: Sie hat ihm zum Geburtstag ein Buch geschenkt.
     (ii) A: Wird sie ihm zu Weihnachten ein Buch schenken?
         B: Nein. Sie hat ihm zum Geburtstag ein Buch geschenkt.

However, the reader will have found that, in order to convey the appropriate meaning for these sentences, so that the dialogues make sense, they have to be spoken in a particular way. This is achieved by means of intonation (cf. Chapter 2): the position of the nucleus of the intonation pattern (also called the 'sentence stress') can be moved around, with consequences for the interpretation of the sentence. If the utterances of 7.10 (i) and (ii) are to be appropriate, then the nucleus must coincide with *Buch* and *Geburtstag*, respectively.

The general principle here is that the intonational nucleus will fall on the main communicative point of the sentence, which will always be a 'new' element. This element is sometimes labelled the FOCUS of the utterance. Thus, taking the same example as before, we can adjust its communicative effect as in 7.11, in which the focus, the sentence element on which the nucleus occurs, is printed in capitals.

(7.11) (i)   Sie hat ihm zum Geburtstag ein Buch GESCHENKT.

(ii) Sie hat ihm zum Geburtstag ein BUCH geschenkt.

(iii) Sie hat ihm zum GEBURTSTAG ein Buch geschenkt.

(iv) Sie hat IHM zum Geburtstag ein Buch geschenkt.

(v)   SIE hat ihm zum Geburtstag ein Buch geschenkt.

Though the item which bears the nucleus is always new, other items may or may not be. But the nucleus is generally on the *last* new item, so that anything *after* the nucleus must normally be given. (We must say 'generally' and 'normally' here because there is an important exception in German: the final verb in subordinate clauses or in 'frame' constructions or such as the one given here. This may follow the nucleus even if it is new. In this respect English differs from German, since it does not have these constructions.)[5] Thus, in sentence (iii) of 7.11, *zum Geburtstag* must be new and *ein Buch* must be given, since it follows the nucleus. This would therefore be an appropriate response to a question which provides the latter and not the former (e.g. 'Wann hat sie ihm ein Buch geschenkt?'), but not to a question in which the reverse is true ('Was hat sie ihm zum Geburtstag geschenkt?'). In sentence (v), where the nucleus is on *sie*, all the rest of the utterance must be given. Dialogue (i) in 7.12, repeated from dialogue (ii) of 7.10, is therefore perfectly acceptable, since speaker A's question provides *ein Buch* but not *zum Geburtstag*, while dialogue (ii) of 7.12, where the question provides *zum Geburtstag* but not *ein Buch,* is deviant. Here we would feel that communication has broken down.

(7.12) (i)   A: Wird sie ihm zu Weihnachten ein Buch schenken?
        B: Nein. Sie hat ihm zum GEBURTSTAG ein Buch geschenkt.

(ii) A: Hat sie ihm zum Geburtstag eine Platte geschenkt?
        B: *Nein. Sie hat ihm zum GEBURTSTAG ein Buch geschenkt.

---

[5] There are some kinds of utterance in both languages in which the nucleus regularly does not fall on the last item, such as 'The HOUSE is on fire', 'Mein AUTO ist kaputt'. These are difficult to explain, and have been much discussed.

Thus, the order of elements and intonation collaborate so as to give the sentence the appropriate information structure and communicative effect.

Example 7.11(ii), in which the nucleus falls on the last item in the utterance apart from the final verb of the frame, allows everything else in the utterance to be new. It could therefore be the response to a very general question in which none of the elements of this utterance are mentioned (apart, that is, from the persons denoted by *sie* and *ihm*, who must have been mentioned before), for example 'Was ist geschehen?'. In this case one can speak of 'broad focus'. The other examples of 7.11 (including the first, in which the nucleus falls exceptionally on the final verb) are said to have 'narrow focus', since they could be responses to questions in which individual items are singled out.

Intonation has a further role in the communication of 'information' apart from the location of the nucleus. As we saw in Chapter 2, intonation can be described in terms of an *intonation unit* of which the nucleus is the most prominent part. How an utterance is divided up into intonation units is variable, and this variation is not random, but relates to the information structure of the utterance. Consider the examples of 7.13, where the sign || indicates the boundaries of the intonation units and the nucleus of the intonation pattern is printed in capitals.

(7.13)   (i) || Er fährt morgen nach HAUSE ||

       (ii) || Er fährt MORGEN || nach HAUSE ||

In sentence (i) of 7.13 the utterance consists of a single intonation unit with a single nucleus; sentence (ii) is divided into two intonation units, each of which has a nucleus. With appropriate intonation patterns (for example, a falling pitch on each nucleus), the effect is of a single piece of 'information' in (i) and two pieces of 'information' in (ii). The intonation unit could therefore be said also to constitute an INFORMATION UNIT.

Cohesion

In our discussion of 'pragmatic ordering', and in particular in the case of 'Ausrahmung', where elements of the sentence are placed outside the sentence 'frame', we saw that the sentence has a certain unity as a piece of information: the sentence structure has a unifying role, and items placed outside it will therefore be perceived as constituting a separate piece of information. But the whole discourse or text itself, which may consist of a number of sentences, also has a unity, and there are features of the structure and organization of the component sentences which serve to bind them together into a coherent whole. This binding is called COHESION, and the features themselves are called COHESIVE TIES.[6]

By way of exemplification, let us examine the brief text given in 7.14.

(7.14)   Professor Bienenkopp fliegt heute nach New York. Er wird dort eine Vorlesung über die Schmetterlinge Südostasiens halten. Seine Frau, die sich auch für diese Insekten interessiert, fährt aber nicht mit; sie findet solche Reisen zu anstrengend. Voriges Jahr sprach er über die roten Schmetterlinge, diesmal spricht er über die blauen.

Apart from the thematic progression, which was discussed above, the sentences of this text are linked together by a number of cohesive ties, of a variety of types. One of the most obvious devices of this kind is cross-reference: words may refer back to parts of other sentences, thus linking the sentences together. For instance, the words *er* and *seine* refer back to *Professor Bienenkopp*, and *sie* to *seine Frau*. This reference may be achieved by personal pronouns or possessive adjectives, but also by other words such as *diese, solche,* and *dort.* Such reference is generally backwards, when it is called ANAPHORIC, but it is also possible for it to be forwards, when it is called CATAPHORIC, as in the example given in 7.15.

(7.15) Dies war sein einziger Wunsch: er wollte seine Heimat wieder sehen.

Here *dies* refers forwards to the second sentence.

Anaphora and cataphora are a kind of linguistic 'pointing', referring to another item *within the text itself*. In fact, the same devices may also refer *outside* the text, to something in the physical environment. The difference is admittedly not always very significant; if I say 'Das ist gut', the *das* may be referring either to something non-verbal (e.g. the food I am eating), or to something that has just been said. The same linguistic device (the demonstrative pronoun) is being used, but only in the latter case could one regard its use as 'cohesive'. Reference outside the text is neither anaphoric nor cataphoric; it is EXOPHORIC.

There are other cohesive ties to be found within the text of 7.14. Consider the phrase *diese Insekten. Diese* is a cross-referencing device, referring back to the previous sentence, but *Insekten* is a new word used to replace *Schmetterlinge.* This substitution of one word for another is another common cohesive device. Very often a more general word replaces a more specific one, a 'superordinate' term is chosen to replace a 'hyponym' (cf. the discussion of

---

[6] The most comprehensive description of cohesive ties (applied to English) is found in the work of M. A. K. Halliday and R. Hasan (see Further Reading).

hyponymy in Chapter 6). At its most extreme, this substitution may involve the use of a very general term such as *Ding* or *Sache* for nouns, or *tun* or *machen* for verbs, as in the examples of 7.16.

(7.16)   (i)   Er hat eine Stereoanlage gebaut. Solche Dinge/Sachen haben ihn immer interessiert.
(ii)   Er ist nach Spanien gefahren. Das tut/macht er jedes Jahr.

Another cohesive tie is found in the last sentence of 7.14, or rather it is *not* found, as it consists in the omission of an item. The phrase *die blauen* can be interpreted as *die blauen Schmetterlinge*, where the noun has been omitted and must be 'understood'. The reader or listener must therefore supply the missing item from the previous text. This device is known as ELLIPSIS. Ellipsis can go far beyond the omission of a single word; most of a sentence may be omitted, as in 7.17.

(7.17)   (i)   Er interessiert sich für Schmetterlinge. Seine Frau auch.
(ii)   Wird er Geld dafür ausgeben? Gar nicht!

The second sentence in each case can be regarded as elliptical, standing for 'Für Schmetterlinge interessiert sich seine Frau auch' and 'Geld wird er dafür gar nicht ausgeben', respectively.

There are some differences in the way in which these cohesive devices are used in English and German. In some cases where English uses the noun-substitute *one*, German prefers ellipsis, as in the examples of 7.18.

(7.18)   der schwarze (Mantel)   the black one
das zweite (Auto)   the second one
dieses (Haus)   this one
ihr neuer (Freund)   her new one

The sentences of a text may also be linked together by more obvious means, with explicit words or phrases suggesting how they fit together. This is known as CONJUNCTION, including, but extending beyond, the use of 'conjunctions' in the traditional sense. Thus, it is not only words such as *und, aber, denn,* and the like which have this linking function, but also adverbs and adverbial phrases such as *trotzdem, andererseits, nichtsdestoweniger,* etc.

More subtle are the relationships between the lexical words of the text (lexical cohesion). Words relating to a particular area of meaning (e.g. a 'semantic field'—cf. Chapter 6) tend to occur together; words like *Bach,*

Baum, Vogel, Wald might well be encountered in the same text; they are said to COLLOCATE with one another. Hence, the use of words from the same field tends to reinforce the impression of unity within the text, while use of words which do not belong to the same field will have the opposite effect, producing an impression of discontinuity or inconsistency.

Utterances in Context

We have seen that the structure of utterance may be directly influenced by its role in the act of communication. It is also the case that the interpretation of the *same* utterance may vary according to features of the context in which it is used. We shall examine a number of such features here: deixis, presupposition, and implicature.

Deixis

Consider the examples of 7.19.

(7.19)   Morgen gehe ich spazieren.
          Sie müssen hier bleiben.
          Der Mann drüben hat grüne Haare.
          Das Endspiel findet am Mittwoch statt.

These sentences are not interpretable out of the context in which they are uttered, since they contain expressions whose meaning is variable: *morgen, hier, drüben,* and *Mittwoch.* The precise times and places to which these words refer is determined only in conjunction with the time and place in which the sentence is uttered. If I utter them on the Alte Brücke in Heidelberg on Monday, 17 May 2004, then *morgen* refers to Tuesday, 18 May, *hier* may mean 'auf der Alten Brücke', or 'in Heidelberg', etc. *drüben* may refer to the other side of the bridge, and *Mittwoch* to Wednesday, 19 May. But if I am standing at the top of the Fernsehturm in Stuttgart on Thursday, 13 February 2003, then the meaning of all these expressions changes drastically.

Such words as these are therefore variable in meaning, allowing them to be used by all speakers in all situations. They are in some ways the verbal equivalent of pointing (in fact, words such as *drüben* may well be accompanied by actual pointing, to make clear their precise meaning). This phenomenon is known as DEIXIS, and words such as these are called DEICTIC expressions.

Deixis falls into a number of categories, relating primarily to *person, place,* and *time.* For the most part, utterances are likely to be focused on the speaker as the first person, the speaker's location as the place, and the time of speaking as the time. Together these form what has been called the DEICTIC CENTRE of the utterance. Thus, when anyone says 'Morgen gehe ich spazieren', *ich* is the speaker and *morgen* refers to the day after the day on which the utterance is made. If someone says 'Sie müssen hier bleiben', *Sie* is clearly the addressee, while *hier* indicates the location where the speaker is situated. A distinction can also be made between deixis which points to *another part of the text*, and deixis which points *outside the text*. This distinction has already been considered in our discussion of cohesion, where we identified anaphoric and cataphoric reference of pronouns on the one hand, and exophoric reference on the other (see above). The *das* of the sentence 'Das ist gut' would be anaphoric if it referred to what has been said previously, but exophoric if it was accompanied by pointing to an object.

Person deixis is largely a matter of personal pronouns, with the familiar three persons discussed in Chapter 4. This can, however, be extended to include the relationship between the participants (such as the *Sie/Du* relationship in German, but also including titles, terms of address, etc.). This has been called *social deixis*. Place deixis is a matter of place adverbs such as *hier*, *dort*, etc. but also the demonstrative pronouns *dieser* and *jener*, all of which depend on the context for their interpretation. Time deixis is perhaps the most complex, since, as we saw in Chapter 4, it involves the location in time of an event with respect to the time of speaking (tense), but also the nature of the temporal relationship (aspect). A sentence such as 'Er hatte das Buch nicht gelesen' therefore requires a complex set of temporal circumstances for its interpretation.

There are other cases of deixis which are less easy to categorize. If we hear an expression such as 'So schön war es auch nicht', or 'Das war eine solche Frechheit!', the words *so* and *solch* indicate that the quality is being measured against some sort of standard, but it is not clear if this should be regarded as a form of deixis. Overall, however, it is evident that deixis is an essential aspect of the interpretation of German utterances.

Presupposition

Another pervasive way in which the context of an utterance determines its interpretation is through PRESUPPOSITIONS—the prior assumptions on which the utterance is based, and without which it would hardly be possible to converse. Consider, for example, the sentences of 7.20.

(7.20) (i)   Es war Goethe, der das gesagt hat.
        (ii) Ich habe nicht gewusst, dass Werner gestorben ist.
        (iii) Es ist meinem Bruder nicht gelungen, die Stelle zu bekommen.

The satisfactory interpretation of these sentences depends on our accepting the assumptions on which they are based and which they presuppose. Sentence (i), for example, presupposes that there was a person called Goethe and that something has been said; sentence (ii) that there was a person called Werner and that he has died; sentence (iii) that a job was available, that I have a brother, and that my brother tried to get the job. These assumptions must be shared by speaker and hearer if effective communication is to take place. If any of these presuppositions is invalid, then communication will be unsuccessful.

It would of course be possible for someone who does not have a brother to utter sentence (iii) without technically lying—'Es ist meinem Bruder nicht gelungen... weil ich keinen Bruder habe'—but, though true, this would generally be considered to be flouting the rules of conversation. More serious violations of conversational etiquette involving presuppositions are frequent in political discussions, where opponents may not share the same presuppositions. A claim such as 'Die Regierung hat diese notwendigen und wünschenswerten Maßnahmen eingeführt' might be attacked by opponents on the grounds that the measures were neither necessary nor desirable, though they are presupposed by the claim. Similarly, the difficulty with answering the English question 'Have you stopped beating your wife?' stems from the fact that it presupposes that you have beaten her, and by answering merely 'yes' or 'no' you are unable to deny this presupposition, but actually endorse it.

Implicature

Closely related to such presuppositions are features of the meaning of an utterance which are *implied* but not stated. Consider the examples of 7.21.

(7.21) (i)   Ich habe drei Schwestern.

      (ii) A: Kann ich *Krieg und Frieden* haben?
           B: Der Bücherschrank ist im Wohnzimmer.

Although sentence (i) of 7.21 does not explicitly say so, we are entitled to *infer* from it that the speaker has only three sisters, and not more. In (ii) B's reply implies that A can have the book, even though it does not actually state this. Such implied features are called IMPLICATURES.

As with presuppositions, implicatures can be abused, in the sense that things can be implied that are not merely not stated, but are actually untrue. In the sentences of 7.21, for example, if the speaker of (i) has four sisters, or if speaker B in (ii) has no intention of giving speaker A the book, they are failing to conform to the normal rules of conversation, even though they cannot actually be accused of lying.

The Cooperative Principle

Presuppositions and implicatures rely on the principle that more is meant than is actually said: presuppositions assume certain things that are not said, while implicature allow inferences from what is said. In neither case is the information explicitly given. As we have seen, both can lead to misunderstandings where the conventions are not observed.

The success of any conversation thus depends on the speaker and hearer knowing, and observing, the implicit 'rules'. An attempt was made by the philosopher Grice to make these 'rules' more explicit by devising a set of 'maxims of conversation' (also called 'conversational implicatures', though they are not the same as the implicatures just discussed). Essentially, they amount to the principle that speakers cooperate with one another in ensuring efficient use of language, e.g. by not lying and by avoiding ambiguity. These maxims are therefore subsumed under the general heading of the COOPERATIVE PRINCIPLE. Grice lists four sets of maxims: the maxims of QUANTITY, the maxims of QUALITY, the maxim of RELATION, and the maxims of MANNER. These are not the only maxims that might be involved, but together they account for most of the principles of cooperation between participants in a conversation that make the conversation 'work'. These maxims can be explained as follows:

Maxims of Quantity

1. Make your contribution as informative as required for the current purposes of the exchange.
2. Do not make your contribution more informative than is required.

Maxims of Quality

1. Do not say what you believe to be false.
2. Do not say that for which you lack adequate evidence.

Maxim of Relation
Be relevant.

Maxims of Manner

1. Avoid obscurity.
2. Avoid ambiguity.
3. Be brief.
4. Be orderly.

The idea behind these principles is not that speakers always observe them (if they did, then conversations would always be successful, and misunderstandings would not arise), but rather that they represent a set of assumptions in terms of which participants conduct their conversations. Consider, for example, the brief conversations of 7.22.

(7.22)   (i)   A. Kommst du mit in die Stadt?
                  B. Es hat angefangen zu regnen.

          (ii)   A. Haben Sie Kinder?
                  B. Ja, drei.

On the face of it, conversation (i) appears to be incoherent, since B's answer seems to ignore A's question, and thus to violate the maxim of relation. However, A will *assume* that B is observing this maxim and therefore conclude that B's utterance *is* relevant to the question; B is therefore probably asserting that he will not go into town *because* it has begun to rain. Similarly, B's answer in conversation (ii) could theoretically be true even if he has more than three children (though it would violate the maxim of quantity), but A will naturally assume that the maxim is observed, and conclude that B has *only* three children.

In some case the maxims are deliberately flouted, though not necessarily with the intention of misleading. In the dialogue of 7.23, speaker B is clearly deliberately being *irrelevant*, but since speaker A will immediately understand that this is a conscious and ironic ploy intended to avoid answering the question; the rules of conversation have, in a sense, been complied with, despite the flouting of the maxim of relevance.

(7.23)   A. Hast du deine Prüfungen bestanden?

          B. Schönes Wetter heute, nicht wahr?

Thus, as long as we understand the status and limitations of the Cooperative Principle, as a framework in terms of which speakers may interpret what is said, and not as a set of rules which speakers must always observe, these maxims enable us to understand how conversation can be made to succeed.

Speech Acts

From the point of view of language use, speech is not just an abstract structure but an activity; each utterance constitutes an *act* carried out by an individual speaker under specific circumstances, and for a particular purpose. The principle that utterances are acts has been especially emphasized by some philosophers and, following them, by some linguists, in the form of

SPEECH-ACT THEORY.[7] We may, of course, easily regard each utterance as consituting a statement on the part of the speaker, but in this approach it is argued that utterances are used to perform a variety of acts of different kinds, not merely the act of stating. In syntactic theory, as discussed in Chapter 5, it is usual to recognize a number of different sentence types which have different roles ('statement', 'question', 'command') and which depend on the use of different sentence structures ('declarative', 'interrogative', 'imperative'). But this can be taken somewhat further, since the kinds of acts performed by speakers are not restricted to these three. Speakers may, for example, make promises, threats, demands, etc. or may warn, inform, undertake to do something, and so on. This conception of a speech act therefore goes well beyond these traditional sentence types, and is also not dependent on the limited kinds of sentence structures used.

In some cases speakers may make the act that they are engaged in explicit, by the use of a particular kind of verb, as in the examples of 7.24.

(7.24)   Ich verspreche, morgen zu kommen.

Ich taufe dieses Schiff auf den Namen 'Seewolf'.

Ich wette fünf Euro, dass du es nicht machen kannst.

In such cases as these, saying the sentence constitutes an action in itself, sometimes a legally binding one, provided, of course, that the person who says it does so with the appropriate authority and in the right spirit. Verbs such as *versprechen, taufen, wetten,* and the like are called PERFORMATIVE verbs, since by using them the speaker is 'performing' an act.

A distinction is sometimes drawn between such performative utterances and those which are CONSTATIVE, i.e. those where the speaker is merely making a statement. Constative equivalents of the sentences of 7.24 might be, for example, those of 7.25.

(7.25)   Ich komme morgen.
Dieses Schiff heißt 'Seewolf'.
Ich glaube nicht, dass du es machen kannst.

But this distinction is not very satisfactory, since one could argue that the sentences of 7.25 also constitute 'speech acts' and contain an implicit performative element, such as 'Ich behaupte, dass...'. In fact, it can be argued

---

[7] The theory originated with Austin (1962), and has been developed by others, especially Searle (1969)—see Further Reading.

that *all* utterances contain some sort of performative element, whether explicit, as in 7.24, or merely implicit.

We have already seen that a sentence/utterance may have different kinds of 'content': the linguistic content in the narrow sense, including the words and grammatical constructions used, and other kinds of content relating to the role of the sentence/utterance in its communicative context, such as thematic structure and information structure. The idea that all utterances contain a performative element adds another dimension: its role as a speech act. It is therefore said to constitute not simply a LOCUTIONARY act—providing the basic grammatical and lexical content—but also an ILLOCUTIONARY act. But we do not need to stop here; since utterances are usually part of an interactive process, we can consider the effect of the utterance—for example, it may convince, persuade, or dissuade, etc. This has been called the PERLOCUTION-ARY force of the utterance.

Of course, in order for certain kinds of speech act to be successful, such as naming a ship, performing a wedding ceremony, sentencing a convicted person, etc. it is not enough merely to perform the speech act involved. Certain conditions—known as FELICITY CONDITIONS—must be met: the speaker must be qualified to perform the act, it must be done under the right circumstances, at the right time, etc. A speech act which does not meet these conditions is regarded as INFELICITOUS; it does not constitute a valid act.

Although the theory of speech acts goes some way towards identifying what is involved in seeing utterances as acts rather than merely as pieces of linguistic structure, it does nevertheless raise some problems. In the first place, the nature of the speech act concerned may be obscured by the form of the sentence itself. Consider the sentences of 7.26.

(7.26)   (i)   Schreib ihm einen Brief.
         (ii) Warum schreibst du ihm keinen Brief?
         (iii) Du sollst ihm einen Brief schreiben.

Syntactically speaking, each of these sentences has a different form: (i) is an imperative, (ii) an interrogative, and (iii) a declarative sentence. The type of sentence is normally an indication of the kind of speech act involved, but here this is not the case: the illocutionary force of all these three can be regarded as the same (they amount to a command). In (ii) and (iii), therefore, we must distinguish between the apparent speech act and the actual speech act of the utterance. Here we have what is called an INDIRECT SPEECH ACT.

A further difficulty is that of classifying the speech acts themselves. Is there a fixed set of possibilities? Unfortunately, different writers on the subject have not agreed on what such a set should be, as it depends partly on the degree of generalization required. One suggestion,[8] for example, is that there are basically five kinds of speech act: *representative* (e.g. asserting), *directive* (e.g. asking a question), *commissive* (e.g. promising), *expressive* (e.g. congratulating), and *declarations* (e.g. baptizing); but it will be evident that any such classification is bound to be to some extent arbitrary, as the range of possibilities is so large. It seems unlikely that there is a limited list of possible speech acts. Furthermore, a single utterance may constitute more than one of these simultaneously. For example, the utterance 'Weißt du, dass du den Preis gewonnen hast?' can be both a directive act (a question) and an expressive act (a congratulation). It is therefore often difficult to assign utterances to specific speech acts without some arbitrariness. Although the theory rightly draws attention to the role of utterances in conversations, the difficulty of identifying the speech acts involved and of producing a definitive set of acts, limits its value in investigating German in use.

The Structure of Conversation

We noted above that the sentence is the largest grammatical unit, and that the relationships between sentences cannot really be described in grammatical terms. But this does not mean that larger units—texts, conversations, etc.— are arbitrary collections of sentences; clearly they are not. They have a structure, even if this structure is not strictly a grammatical one. Furthermore, the limits of what is 'grammatical' are not very clearly defined, so that some of the structural features of texts and conversations have some resemblance to the grammatical features of sentences, as we shall see.

A relatively simple approach to the structure of conversation is to recognize a set of progressively more inclusive units, comparable, perhaps, to the 'morpheme', 'word', 'phrase', and 'sentence' of syntactic analysis. We might see each individual ACT of the speaker as contributing to his or her MOVE, which is in turn part of an EXCHANGE within the whole TRANSACTION. A typical exchange, for example, might be said to involve a series of moves, such as a question–answer pair with a follow-up, as in 7.27.

(7.27)   A: Wo ist das Brotmesser?
         B: In der dritten Lade.
         A: Danke.

---

[8] Made by Searle (1976)—see Further Reading.

However, a more elaborate and more influential approach to investigating the structure of conversation has been undertaken particularly by a number of sociologists known as 'ethnomethodologists', who concentrate on detailed analysis of individual face-to-face encounters without trying to formulate a theory *a priori*. Their approach is known as CONVERSATION ANALYSIS.[9] Since this is primarily a method within sociology, and is not restricted to the purely linguistic aspects of conversation, we shall not need to explore all its characteristics, but will confine ourselves to illustrating the nature of the approach.

A starting point for the investigation of conversation structure may be found in a simple dialogue such as that given in 7.28.

(7.28)   A: Wo ist das Postamt, bitte?
          B: Da drüben in der Berliner Straße.

This is a fundamental, if obvious, kind of structure in which an utterance by one speaker is followed by a response by the other. Such a simple combination has been called an ADJACENCY PAIR, and it is the basic building block of conversation. We may link this with our earlier discussion of speech acts, since each part of such a pair has a particular, and complementary, illocutionary force—here a question and an answer. Other kinds of pairs might involve reciprocal greetings, a summons and a response, and so on, as illustrated in 7.29.

(7.29)   (i)   A: Guten Tag, Herr Müller.
                 B: Guten Tag, Frau Schmidt.

          (ii)   A: Mutti!
                 B: Ja, Gerhardt?

But many conversations may be a little more elaborate, as in the exchange of 7.30.

(7.30)   A: Haben Sie *Krieg und Frieden*?
          B: Von Tolstoi?
          A: Ja.
          B: Leider nicht.

Between the question and the answer there is here interposed a further question and answer (called an INSERTION SEQUENCE). We can easily imagine further elaborations, such as the sequence of 7.31.

---

[9] Two major scholars in this area are Sacks and Schegloff—see Further Reading.

(7.31) A: Haben Sie *Krieg und Frieden*?
       B. Von wem ist das?
       A: Wissen Sie das nicht?
       B: Sie meinen den Roman von Tolstoi?
       A: Natürlich.
       B: Haben Sie es im Schaufenster nicht gesehen?
       A: Sollte es dort sein?
       B: Ja.
       A: Nein.
       B: Dann haben wir es nicht.

Such conversations are by no means atypical. They reveal a quite complex overall structure, though we may argue that the component parts largely remain pairs of questions and answers. The participants in such conversations typically take turns to speak rather than both trying to speak at once. There are inevitably overlaps, when one speaker interrupts the other, but the speakers appear to collaborate in not talking at the same time. Speakers evidently perceive the importance of *organizing* the conversation.

Different kinds of organization are found in different kinds of conversation. Telephone conversations, for example, where the participants cannot see each other, are likely to begin with some form of 'identification sequence', in which both parties identify themselves. This might take the form of a general greeting ('Hallo'), or a name ('Hans Schmidt', 'Hotel Berlin'), followed by the caller's identification of him- or herself, after which the purpose of the call may be announced and a response given. At the end of the conversation there will be a 'termination sequence' ('Auf Wiederhören', 'Auf Wiederhören' or 'Tschüss', 'Tschüss', etc.).

An important principle of conversation is TURN-TAKING. Perhaps suprisingly, participants generally appear to be able to organize their conversations in such a way that turn-taking occurs smoothly, usually with no breaks and with minimal overlap. There are often points ('transition relevance places') in the conversation, for example when one participant asks a question of another, or when a speaker completes a particular point, which are appropriate for a change of turn. Again, the form of organization may vary according to the type of conversation; in doctor–patient interviews, for example, the rules will clearly be different from those which operate for a chat between friends.

Things do not always proceed smoothly in a conversation, however. Sometimes mistakes are made and the speaker may correct him- or herself, or be corrected by another participant, as in 7.32(i) and (ii), respectively.

(7.32)   (i) Mein Bruder ist nach Südafrika gefahren—Ach nein,
              Entschuldigung, nach Australien.
         (ii) A. Mein Bruder ist nach Südafrika gefahren.
              B. Sie meinen Australien.
              A. Ach ja, Entschuldigung.

These are known as 'repair sequences', either *self-initiated* (7.32(i)) or *other-repair* (7.32(ii)).

It can be seen that Conversation Analysis offers detailed analysis and classification of many aspects of conversation that other approaches may easily overlook. Starting from actual conversational data, it painstakingly examines the details of the interaction itself and thus builds up a picture of its structure. Such an analysis forces linguists to look more carefully at the linguistic features of utterances by means of which successful interaction is achieved.

Conclusion

The various aspects of German that we have considered here make it clear that the structure of the language cannot be seen in complete isolation from the use to which the language is put. This use impinges on the structure of the language at numerous points and in numerous ways. We have seen, furthermore, that it is possible to find some regularity here, even if the organization of discourse cannot be systematized as rigorously as the structures of phonology, morphology, or syntax.

Of course, the existence of structures beyond the sentence does not render the analysis and description of the sentence itself and its parts unnecessary, nor does it make the inevitable idealization of such an analysis illegitimate. What it does show, however, is that the structure of German is complex and many-sided, and that we are still a long way from being able to describe it comprehensively.

FURTHER READING

General

Brown and Yule (1983); Jaszczolt (2002); Leech (1983); Levinson (1983); Lyons (1977: vol. 2); Meibauer et al. (2002: ch. 6); Meibauer (2001); Yule (1996b).

Word Order, Theme, and Information Structure

Eroms (1986); Fox (1982); Kirkwood (1969); Lambrecht (1994); Pheby (1975); Tomlin et al. (1997).

Cohesion

Halliday and Hasan (1976).

Speech Acts

Austin (1962); Hindelang (2000); Mey (1993); Psathas (1995); Sacks (1992); Sacks, Schegloff, and Jefferson (1974); Schiffrin (1994); Searle (1969, 1976); Thomas (1995).

Conversation

Mey (1993); Schiffrin (1994); Thomas (1995); Wooffitt and Hutchby (1998).

EXERCISES AND DISCUSSION QUESTIONS

1. Linguists are generally more interested in 'sentences'—grammatically complete pieces of language—than 'utterances'—instances of actual speech. Explain why you think this is so and argue for or against this position.

2. Examine a piece of written German and establish which sentence constituent (subject, object, adjunct, etc.) occurs in initial position in each sentence. See if you can establish the reason for the writer's choice of initial element in the light of the context in which the sentence occurs.

3. The term 'theme' has been used to designate 'what the sentence is about'. In the light of your findings in question 2, how far do you consider that it is possible to determine what a particular sentence is 'about'?

4. The following German sentence could be pronounced with the intonational nucleus on different words, giving a different 'focus' in each case. Try to determine the difference this makes to the meaning of the utterance, and identify the circumstances in which each version would be appropriate: 'Karls Schwester ist gestern nicht gekommen'.

5. Take a paragraph of written German and identify as many 'cohesive' devices as you can which link the sentences together into a 'text'.

6. Examine the following sentences, and identify as many presuppositions as possible that are necessary in order to interpret them appropriately:

   (i) Eduards Frau bedauert, dass sie die Einladung zum Konzert nicht annehmen kann.

   (ii) Ihre Reise nach Indien musste sie wegen der Geburt ihres zweiten Kindes absagen.

   (iii) Sogar der Professor hat den Vortrag seines Freundes über die australischen Krokodile nicht verstehen können.

7. Classify the following utterances in terms of the class of 'speech act' that you think is involved (representative, directive, commissive, expressive, or declaration):

(i) Ich wette, dass du es nicht machen kannst.

(ii) Bitte, sagen Sie mir, wie ich am besten zum Fernsehturm komme.

(iii) Die Hitze ist im Sommer unerträglich.

(iv) Ich bestehe darauf, dass Sie diese Beleidigung sofort zurücknehmen.

(v) Entschuldigen Sie bitte, ich wollte Sie gar nicht beleidigen.

(vi) Ich erkläre Wolfgang Schmidt zum Sieger dieses Wettbewerbs.

References

Abercrombie, D. (1968), *Elements of General Phonetics*. Edinburgh: Edinburgh University Press.

Agel, V. (2000), *Valenztheorie*. Tübingen: Narr.

Anderson, S. R. (1985), *Phonology in the Twentieth Century*. Chicago: University of Chicago Press.

Archangeli, D. and D. T. Langendoen (1997), *Optimality Theory. An Overview*. Oxford: Blackwell.

Austin, J. L. (1962), *How to Do Things with Words*. Oxford: Clarendon Press.

Ball, M. J. and J. Rahilly (1999), *Phonetics: The Science of Speech*. London: Hodder Arnold.

Barbour, S. and P. Stevenson (1990), *Variation in German: a Critical Approach to German Sociolinguistics*. Cambridge: Cambridge University Press.

Bauer, L. (2003), *Introducing Linguistic Morphology*, 2nd edn. Edinburgh: Edinburgh University Press.

Beedham, C. (1995), *German Linguistics. An Introduction*. München: Iudicium.

Bergenholtz, H. and B. Schaeder (1977), *Die Wortarten des Deutschen. Versuch einer syntaktisch orientierten Klassifikation*. Stuttgart: Klett.

Bergmann, R., P. Pauly, and M. Schlaefer (2001), *Einführung in die deutsche Sprachwissenschaft*, 3rd edn. Heidelberg: Winter.

Besch, W. (1996), *Duzen, Siezen, Titulieren*. Göttingen: Vandenhoeck & Ruprecht.

Blake, B. J. (1994), *Case*. Cambridge: Cambridge University Press.

Blanke, G. H. (1973), *Einführung in die semantische Analyse* (München: Hueber).

Bloomfield, L. (1933/1935), *Language*. New York: Holt, Rinehart and Winston; London: Allen and Unwin.

Boase-Beier, J. and K. Lodge (2003), *The German Language. A Linguistic Introduction*. Oxford: Blackwell.

Brinker, K. (1982), *Das Passiv im heutigen Deutsch: Form und Funktion*. München: Hueber.

Brown, G. and G. Yule (1983), *Discourse Analysis*. Cambridge: Cambridge University Press.

Brown, R. and A. Gilman (1960), 'The pronouns of power and solidarity', in T. A. Sebeok (ed.), *Style in Language*. Cambridge, Mass.: MIT Press, 253–76.

Bünting, K.-D. (1996), *Einführung in die Linguistik*, 15th edn. Frankfurt: Athenäum.

—— and H. Bergenholtz (1995), *Einführung in die Syntax*. Kronberg/Ts.: Athenäum.

Carnie, A. (2002), *Syntax. A Generative Introduction*. Oxford: Blackwell.

Carstairs-McCarthy, A. (1992), *Current Morphology*. London: Routledge.

Chomsky, N. (1957), *Syntactic Structures*. The Hague: Mouton.

—— (1970), 'Remarks on Nominalisation', in R. A. Jacobs and P. S. Rosenbaum (eds.), *Readings in English Transformational Grammar*. Waltham, Mass.: Ginn, 184–221.

—— (1981), *Lectures on Government and Binding*. Dordrecht: Foris.

—— and M. Halle (1968), *The Sound Pattern of English*. New York: Harper and Row.

Clark, J. and C. Yallop (1995), *An Introduction to Phonetics and Phonology*, 2nd edn. Oxford: Blackwell.

Clyne, M. (1984), *Language and Society in the German-speaking Countries*. Cambridge: Cambridge University Press.

—— (1995), *The German Language in a Changing Europe*. Cambridge: Cambridge University Press.

Comrie, B. (1976), *Aspect*. Cambridge: Cambridge University Press.

—— (1985), *Tense*. Cambridge: Cambridge University Press.

Corbett, G. (1991), *Gender*. Cambridge: Cambridge University Press.

—— (2000), *Number*. Cambridge: Cambridge University Press.

Cruse, D. A. (1986), *Lexical Semantics*. Cambridge: Cambridge University Press.

Crystal, D. (1997), *The Cambridge Encyclopedia of Language*. Cambridge: Cambridge University Press.

Davenport, M. and S. J. Hannahs (1998), *Introducing Phonetics and Phonology*. London: Arnold.

De Boor, H., H. Moser, and C. Winkler (eds.) (2000), *Siebs: Deutsche Aussprache*. Berlin: de Gruyter.

Donalies, E. (2002), *Wortbildung im Deutschen*. Tübingen: Narr.

Dornseiff, F. (1970), *Der deutsche Wortschatz nach Sachgruppen*, 7th edn. Berlin: de Gruyter.

Drosdowski, G., et al. (1995), *Duden Grammatik der deutschen Gegenwartssprache*. Mannheim: Bibliographisches Institut/Duden.

Durrell, M. (1979), 'Some Problems in the Morphological Structure of the German Noun Phrase', *Transactions of the Philological Society*, 55–89.

Dürscheid, C. (2000), *Syntax. Grundlagen und Theorien*. Wiesbaden: Westdeutscher Verlag.

Eichinger, L. M. (2000), *Deutsche Wortbildung: eine Einführung*. Tübingen: Narr.

—— and H.-W. Eroms (eds.) (1995), *Dependenz und Valenz*. Hamburg: Buske.

Eichler, W., and K.-O. Bunting (1996), *Deutsche Grammatik*, 6th edn. Weinheim: Beltz Athenäum.

Eisenberg, P. (1999), *Grundriss der deutschen Grammatik*. Stuttgart/Weimar: Metzler.

—— H. Gellhaus, H. Henne, H. Sitta, and H. Wellmann (1998), *Duden Grammatik der deutschen Gegenwartssprache*. Mannheim: Bibliographisches Institut.

Engel, U. (2004), *Deutsche Grammatik*, 4th edn. München: Iudicium.

Erben, J. (2000), *Einführung in die deutsche Wortbildungslehre*, 4th edn. Berlin: Schmidt.

Eroms, H.-W. (1986), *Funktionale Satzperspektive*. Tübingen: Niemeyer.

Féry, C. (1993), *German Intonational Patterns*. Tübingen: Niemeyer.

Flämig, W. (1998), *Grammatik des Deutschen*. Berlin: Akademie.

Fleischer, W. and I. Barz (1995), *Wortbildung der deutschen Gegenwartssprache*, 2nd edn. Tübingen: Niemeyer.

Fox, A. (1982), 'Remarks on intonation and "Ausrahmung" in German'. *Journal of Linguistics*. 18: 89–106.

—— (1984), *German Intonation: an Outline*. Oxford: Clarendon Press.

Freidin, R. (1992), *Foundations of Generative Syntax*. Cambridge, Mass.: MIT Press.

Fromkin, V., R. Rodman, and N. M. Hyams (2003), *An Introduction to Language*, 7th edn. Boston, Mass.: Heinle.

Geckeler, H. (1982), *Strukturelle Semantik und Wortfeldtheorie*, 3rd edn. München: Fink.

Gelhaus, H. and S. Latzel (1982), *Studien zum Tempusgebrauch im Deutschen*, 2nd edn. Tübingen: Narr.

Gerstenkorn, A. (1976), *Das 'Modal'-System im heutigen Deutsch*. München: Fink.

Giegerich, H. J. (1985), *Metrical Phonology and Phonological Structure: German and English*. Cambridge: Cambridge University Press.

Gipper, H. (1959), 'Sessel oder Stuhl? Ein Beitrag zur Bestimmung von Wortinhalten im Bereich der Sachkultur', in H. Gipper (ed.), *Sprache, Schlüssel der Welt: Festschrift für Leo Weisgerber*. Düsseldorf: Schwann, 271–92; also in L. Schmidt (ed.), *Wortfeldforschung* (see below), 371–98.

Grewendorf, G. (1991), *Aspekte der deutschen Syntax: eine Rektions-Bindungs-Analyse*, 2nd edn. Tübingen: Stauffenburg.

Gussenhoven, C. and H. Jakobs (1998), *Understanding Phonology*. London: Arnold.

Haegeman, L. (1994), *Introduction to Government and Binding Theory*, 2nd edn. Oxford: Blackwell.

Hall, C. (1992), *Modern German Pronunciation*. Manchester: Manchester University Press.

Halliday, M. A. K., and R. Hasan (1976), *Cohesion in English*. London: Longman.

Hammer, A. E. (1971), *German Grammar and Usage*. London: Edward Arnold.

Hawkins, P. (1984), *Introducing Phonology*. London: Hutchinson.

Heidolph, K.-E., W. Flämig, and W. Motsch (1981), *Grundzüge einer deutschen Grammatik*. Berlin: Akademie.

Helbig, G. (1973), *Die Funktionen der substantivischen Kasus in der deutschen Gegenwartssprache*. München: Hueber.

—— (1999), *Deutsche Grammatik. Grundfragen und Abriss*, 4th edn. München: Iudicium.

—— and J. Buscha (2001), *Deutsche Grammatik*. Berlin/München: Langenscheidt.

Hentschel, E. and H. Weydt (2003), *Handbuch der deutschen Grammatik*. Berlin: de Gruyter.

Henzen, W. (1983), *Deutsche Wortbildung*. Tübingen: Niemeyer.

Herbst T., D. Heath, and H.-M. Dederding (1980), *Grimm's Grandchildren. Current Topics in German Linguistics*. London: Longman.

Heringer, H.-J. (1996), *Deutsche Syntax Dependentiell.* Tübingen: Stauffenburg.

Hindelang, G. (2000), *Einführung in die Sprechakttheorie.* Tübingen: Niemeyer.

Hoberg, R. (1970), *Die Lehre vom sprachlichen Feld.* Düsseldorf: Schwann.

Hurford, J. R. and B. Heasley (1983), *Semantics: A Coursebook.* Cambridge: Cambridge University Press.

Jackendoff, R. (1977), *X' Syntax: A Study of Phrase Structure.* Cambridge, Mass.: MIT Press.

Jäger, S. (1982), *Der Konjunktiv in der deutschen Sprache der Gegenwart.* München: Hueber.

Jaszczolt, K. M. (2002), *Semantics and Pragmatics. Meaning in Language and Discourse.* London: Longman.

Johnson, S. (1998), *Exploring the German Language.* London: Arnold.

Katamba, F. (1989), *An Introduction to Phonology.* London: Longman.

—— (1993), *Morphology.* London: Macmillan.

Keller, R. E. (1961), *German Dialects: Phonology and Morphology.* Manchester: Manchester University Press.

Kempson, R. (1977), *Semantic Theory.* Cambridge: Cambridge University Press.

Kirkwood, H. W. (1969), 'Aspects of Word Order and its Communicative Function in English and German'. *Journal of Linguistics,* 5: 85–107.

Kohler, K. J. (1995), *Einführung in die Phonetik des Deutschen.* 2nd edn. Berlin: Erich Schmidt.

König, W. (1998), *dtv-Atlas Deutsche Sprache.* München: dtv.

Kufner, H. L. (1962), *The Grammatical Structures of English and German.* Chicago: University of Chicago Press.

Ladefoged, P. (2001), *A Course in Phonetics,* 4th edn. Orlando: Harcourt, Brace.

Lambrecht, K. (1994), *Information Structure and Sentence Form.* Cambridge: Cambridge University Press.

Lass, R. (1984), *Phonology: An Introduction to Basic Concepts.* Cambridge: Cambridge University Press.

Laver, J. (1994), *Principles of Phonetics.* Cambridge: Cambridge University Press.

Leech, G. (1983), *Principles of Pragmatics.* London: Longman.

Leisi, E. (1975), *Der Wortinhalt,* 5th edn. Heidelberg: Quelle & Meyer.

Levinson, S. C. (1983), *Pragmatics.* Cambridge: Cambridge University Press.

Löbner, S. (2003), *Semantik.* Berlin: de Gruyter.

Löffler, H. (2003), *Dialektologie. Eine Einführung.* Tübingen: Narr.

Lühr, R. (2000), *Neuhochdeutsch.* 6th edn. München: Fink.

Lutzeier, P. R. (1985), *Linguistische Semantik.* Stuttgart: Metzler.

—— (1993), *Studien zur Wortfeldtheorie.* Tübingen: Niemeyer.

Lyons, J. (1968), *Introduction to Theoretical Linguistics.* Cambridge: Cambridge University Press.

—— (1977), *Semantics,* 2 vols. Cambridge: Cambridge University Press.

—— (1995), *Linguistic Semantics. An Introduction.* Cambridge: Cambridge University Press.

MacCarthy, P. (1975), *The Pronunciation of German*. London: Oxford University Press.

Markus, M. (1977), *Tempus und Aspekt: Zur Funktion von Präsens, Präteritum und Perfekt im Englischen und Deutschen*. München: Fink.

Matthews, P. H. (1981), *Syntax*. Cambridge: Cambridge University Press.

—— (1991), *Morphology*, 2nd edn. Cambridge: Cambridge University Press.

Meibauer, J. (2001), *Pragmatik*. Tübingen: Stauffenburg.

—— et al. (2002), *Einführung in die germanistische Linguistik*. Stuttgart: Metzler.

Mey, J. L. (1993), *Pragmatics, An Introduction*. Oxford: Blackwell.

Motsch, W. (1999), *Deutsche Wortbildung in Grundzügen*. Berlin: de Gruyter.

Moulton, W. G. (1962), *The Sounds of English and German*. Chicago: University of Chicago Press.

Napoli, D. J. (1993), *Syntax. Theory and Problems*. New York/Oxford: Oxford University Press.

Naumann, B. (2000), *Einführung in die Wortbildungslehre des Deutschen*, 3rd edn. Tübingen: Niemeyer.

Olsen, S. (1990), *Wortbildung im Deutschen: Eine Einführung in die Theorie der Wortstruktur*. Stuttgart: Kröner.

Palmer, F. R. (1981), *Semantics*, 2nd edn. Cambridge: Cambridge University Press.

—— (1991), *Grammar*. Harmondsworth: Penguin.

—— (1994), *Grammatical Roles and Relations*. Cambridge: Cambridge University Press.

—— (2001), *Mood and Modality*, 2nd edn. Cambridge: Cambridge University Press.

Paul, H. (1975), *Prinzipien der Sprachgeschichte*, 9th edn. first pub. 1880. Tübingen: Niemeyer.

Pheby, J. (1975), *Intonation und Grammatik im Deutschen*. Berlin: Akademie.

Philipp, M. (1974), *Phonologie des Deutschen*. Stuttgart: Kohlhammer.

Philipp, M. (ed.) (1998), *Semantik des Deutschen*. Berlin: Weidler.

Psathas, G. (1995), *Conversation Analysis. The Study of Talk-in-Interaction*. Thousand Oaks, Calif.: Sage.

Robins, R. H. (1997), *A Short History of Linguistics*, 4th edn. London: Longman.

Roca, I. and W. Johnson (1999), *A Course in Phonology*. Oxford: Blackwell.

Russ, C. V. J. (ed.) (1990), *The Dialects of Modern German*. London: Routledge.

Russ, C. V. J. (1994), *The German Language Today: a Linguistic Introduction*. London: Routledge.

Sacks, H. (1992), *Lectures on Conversation*. Oxford: Blackwell.

—— E. A. Schegloff, and G. Jefferson (1974), 'A simplest systematics for the organization of turn-taking in conversation'. *Language*, 50: 696–735.

Saussure, F. de (1995), *Course in General Linguistics*. London: Duckworth.

Schachter, P. (1985), 'Parts-of-speech systems', in T. Shopen (ed.), *Language Typology and syntactic description I: Clause structure*. Cambridge: Cambridge University Press, 3–61.

Schaff, A. and G. Klaus (1997), *Einführung in die Semantik*. Hamburg: Rowohlt.

Schiffrin, D. (1994), *Approaches to Discourse*. Oxford: Blackwell.

Schipporeit, L. (1971), *Tense and Time Phrases in Modern German.* München: Hueber.

Schmidt, L. (ed.) (1973), *Wortfeldforschung: Zur Geschichte und Theorie des sprachlichen Feldes.* Darmstadt: Wissenschaftliche Buchgesellschaft.

Schwarz, M. and J. Chur (2001), *Semantik.* Tübingen: Narr.

Searle, J. R. (1969), *Speech Acts.* Cambridge: Cambridge University Press.

—— (1976), 'The classification of illocutionary acts'. *Language in Society*, 5: 1–24.

Seibicke, W. (1972), *Wie sagt man anderswo? Landschaftliche Unterschiede im deutschen Sprachgebrauch.* Mannheim: Duden/Bibliographisches Institut.

Seuren, A. M. (1998), *Western Linguistics. An Historical Introduction.* Oxford: Blackwell.

Spencer, A. (1991), *Morphological Theory.* Oxford: Blackwell.

—— (1996), *Phonology.* Oxford: Blackwell.

Stevenson, P. (ed.) (1995), *The German Language and the Real World.* Oxford: Clarendon Press.

Stevenson, P. (1997), *The German Speaking World. A Practical Introduction to Sociolinguistic Issues.* London: Routledge.

Tallerman, M. (1998), *Understanding Syntax.* London: Arnold.

Tarvainen, K. (1981), *Einführung in die Dependenzgrammatik.* Tübingen: Niemeyer.

Tesnière, L. (1959), *Éléments de syntaxe structurale.* Paris: Klinksieck.

Thomas, J. (1995), *Meaning in Interaction. An Introduction to Pragmatics.* London: Longman.

Toman, J. (ed.) (1985), *Studies in German Grammar.* Dordrecht: Foris.

Tomlin, R. S., L. Forrest, M. M. Pu, and M. H. Kim (1997), 'Discourse semantics', in T. A. van Dijk (ed.), *Discourse Studies: a multidisciplinary introduction. vol. 1: Discourse as Structure and Process.* London: Sage, 63–111.

Trier, J. (1931), *Der deutsche Wortschatz im Sinnbezirk des Verstandes.* Heidelberg: Winter.

Van Valin, R. D. (2001), *An Introduction to Syntax.* Cambridge: Cambridge University Press.

Vikner, S. (1995), *Verb Movement and Expletive Subjects in the Germanic Languages.* Oxford: Oxford University Press.

Wängler, H.-H. (1983), *Grundriss einer Phonetik des Deutschen*, 4th edn. Marburg: Elwert.

Weber, H. J. (1992), *Dependenzgrammatik.* Tübingen: Narr.

Weinrich, H. (2001), *Tempus: Besprochene und erzählte Welt.* München: C. H. Beck.

Weisgerber, L. (1950), *Vom Weltbild der deutschen Sprache.* Düsseldorf: Schwann.

—— (1951–2), 'Zur innersprachlichen Umgrenzung der Wortfelder'. *Wirkendes Wort*, 2: 138–43; also in L. Schmidt (ed.), *Wortfeldforschung* (see above), 278–87.

Werner, O. (1972), *Phonemik des Deutschen.* Stuttgart: Metzler.

Wiese, R. (1996), *The Phonology of German.* Oxford: Clarendon Press.

Wöllstein-Leisten, A., A. Heilmann, P. Stepan, and S. Vikner (1997), *Deutsche Satzstruktur.* Tübingen: Stauffenburg.

Wooffitt, R. and I. Hutchby (1998), *Conversation Analysis: Principles, Practices and Applications*. Cambridge: Polity Press.

Wunderlich, D. (1973), *Tempus und Zeitreferenz im Deutschen*, 2nd edn. München: Hueber.

—— (1998), *Arbeitsbuch Semantik*, 2nd edn. Berlin: Hain.

Yule, G. (1996a), *The Study of Language*. Cambridge: Cambridge University Press.

—— (1996b), *Pragmatics*. Oxford: Oxford University Press.

Index